WITHDRAWN
UTSA Libraries

RENEWALS: 691-4574
DATE DUE

DEC 17

Anti-Semitism in France

Studies in Social Discontinuity

General Editor   Charles Tilly, The New School for Social Research

Studies in Social Discontinuity began in 1972 under the imprint of Academic Press. In its first 15 years, 53 titles were published in the series, including important volumes in the areas of historical sociology, political economy, and social history.

Revived in 1989 by Basil Blackwell, the series will continue to include volumes emphasizing social changes and non-Western historical experience as well as translations of major works.

Published:

The Perilous Frontier
Nomadic Empires and China
Thomas J. Barfield

Regents and Rebels
The Revolutionary World of an Eighteenth-Century Dutch City
Wayne Ph. te Brake

Nascent Proletarians
Class Formation in Post-Revolutionary France
Michael P. Hanagan

Coercion, Capital, and European States,
AD 900–1990
Charles Tilly

Social Evolutionism
A Critical History
Stephen K. Sanderson

Coffee, Contention, and Change
in the Making of Modern Brazil
Mauricio A. Font

Anti-Semitism in France
A Political History from Léon Blum to the Present
Pierre Birnbaum

In preparation:

The European Experience of Declining Fertility
1850–1970
Edited by John R. Gillis, Louise A. Tilly, and David Levine

Anti-Semitism in France

A Political History from Léon Blum to the Present

PIERRE BIRNBAUM

Translated by
Miriam Kochan

BLACKWELL
Oxford UK & Cambridge USA

Copyright © Librairie Arthème Fayard 1988

English translation © Basil Blackwell Ltd 1992

First published as *Un mythe politique: La 'République juive'* in 1988 by Librairie Arthème Fayard

First published in English in 1992

Blackwell Publishers
108 Cowley Road
Oxford OX4 1JF, UK

Three Cambridge Center
Cambridge, Massachusetts 02142, USA

All rights reserved. Except for the quotation of short passages for the purposes of criticism and review, no part of this publication may be reproduced, stored in a retrieval system, or transmitted, in any form or by any means, electronic, mechanical, photocopying, recording or otherwise, without the prior permission of the publisher.

Except in the United States of America, this book is sold subject to the condition that it shall not, by way of trade or otherwise, be lent, re-sold, hired out, or otherwise circulated without the publisher's prior consent in any form of binding or cover other than that in which it is published and without a similar condition including this condition being imposed on the subsequent purchaser.

A CIP catalogue record for this book is available from the British Library.

Library of Congress Cataloging-in-Publication Data

Birnbaum, Pierre.
  [Mythe politique, la 'République juive.' English]
  Anti-semitism in France: a political history from Léon Blum to the present
  Pierre Birnbaum.
    p. cm. – (Studies in social discontinuity)
  Translation of: Un mythe politique. la 'République juive.'
  Includes bibliographical references and index.
  ISBN 1-55786-047-5
  1. Anti-Semitism – France – History. 2. Jewish statesmen – France.
  3. Jews – France – Politics and government. 4. France – Politics and government – 1789– 5. France – Ethnic relations. I. Title.
  II. Series: Studies in social discontinuity (Basil Blackwell Publisher)
DS146.F8B5713 1992
305.892'4044 – dc20   91-31806
                                                                                        CIP

Typeset in 10 on $11\frac{1}{2}$ pt Ehrhardt by TecSet
Printed in Great Britain by TJ Press (Padstow) Ltd, Padstow, Cornwall
This book is printed on acid-free paper.

Contents

Editor's Preface ix
Acknowledgements xii

Introduction: Assessing Anti-Semitism in France 1
A Non-Existent Anti-Semitism? 2
A Simplifying Debate: Anti-Semitism and Fascism 3
Hannah Arendt's Flawed Hunch 6
To Each its Own: Anti-Semitism on Both Sides of the Atlantic 8
Self-Hatred: From Disraeli to Rathenau 13
Political Anti-Semitism versus the Republican State: The French Paradigm 15

PART I THE FATE OF FRANCO-JUDAISM

Introduction: From Court Jews to State Jews 29
1 **Between State, Republic and Socialism** 34
 A Long Way from Marx? 34
 Resort to the Strong State 36

2 **Israelite, Jew or Zionist?** 42
 Born a Jew 42
 Judaism, Socialism and Republic 47
 Fighting Anti-Semitism 50
 Zionism and Israel 52

3 **The Jews of France *vis-à-vis* the Blum and Mendès France Governments** 62
 The Communal Institutions 62
 The Case of the Nationalist Jews: The Example of Maître Edmond Bloch and Some Others 68

The Case of the Left-wing Jews: The Example of Bernard Lecache
and Some Others — 75

PART II DRUMONT'S LEGACY: JEWISH MONEY, PERVERSION AND NOMADISM

Introduction: Neither Right nor Left? — 85
4 The Wandering Jew — 99
'Karfunkelstein' and 'Mendès Palestine' — 102
Oriental Origins — 103

5 The Land and the Dead — 109
The Blood Question: From Ritual Murder to the Jewish Wars — 111
Is a Jew Worth a Breton? — 113
The *Massilia* Affair — 118
Riom and Clermont-Ferrand — 119

6 Wine, Water and Milk — 129
From Narbonne to Louviers: Landless Jews — 129
To Drink or not to Drink: The Mythology of Wine — 133
Local Anti-Semitism — 136

7 Hermaphroditism and Sexual Perversion — 147
Joan of Arc, Marianne and Judith — 147
Jews, Women and Madness — 148
Dandies and Bohemians — 153
'Don Juan of the Synagogue' — 157
Homosexuals — 162
'Semitic Swordsmanship' — 165

8 The Antichrist — 178
Catholicism and Anti-Semitism in the 1930s — 179
Mauriac and Mounier: Ambiguous Philo-Semitism — 182
The New Alsace-Lorraine Question — 187
The 'Black International' versus Pierre Mendès France — 190

9 Bloated Capitalist and Little Revolutionary — 199
From the Right Wing — 201
From the Left Wing — 206
Anti-Semitic Rumblings in the SFIO — 213
What were the Radicals Thinking? — 217

PART III POLITICAL ANTI-SEMITISM: 'THE JEWISH REPUBLIC'

Introduction: Out of the State! Anti-Semitism and Anti-Protestantism 227
10 A State within the State? 232
   State Anti-Semitism and the End of the Republic 234
   From Xavier Vallat to Darquier de Pellepoix: Political Anti-Semitism
      Enters the Republic 242
   From Pierre Boutang to Pierre Poujade 247
   Louviers and Grenoble 250

11 Society Betrayed 261
   Secularism or Quasi-Civil War 261
   France Faces War: Jewish War-mongering 267

12 The Empire Abandoned 278
   From the Crémieux Decree to the Blum–Violette Plan 278
   From Peace in Indo-China to War in Algeria 286

Conclusion 296

Postscript 300

Index 306

For Judith

Editor's Preface

THIS SERIES

Studies in Social Discontinuity present historically grounded analyses of important social transformations, ruptures, conflicts, and contradictions. Although we of Blackwell Publishers interpret that mission broadly, leave room for many points of view, and absolve authors of any responsibility for propaganda on behalf of our intellectual programme, the series as a whole demonstrates the relevance of well-crafted historical work for the understanding of contemporary social structures and processes. Books in the series pursue one or more of four varieties of historical analysis: (1) using evidence from past times and places systematically to identify regularities in processes and structures that transcend those particular times and places; (2) reconstructing critical episodes in the past for the light they shed on important eras, peoples, or social phenomena; (3) tracing the origins or previous phases of significant social processes that continue into our own time; (4) examining the ways that social action at a given point in time lays down residues that limit the possibilities of subsequent social action.

The fourth theme is at once the least familiar and the most general. Social analysts have trouble seeing that history matters precisely because social interaction takes place in well-defined times and places, and occurs within constraints offered by those times and places, producing social relations and artifacts that are themselves located in space–time and whose existence and distribution constrain subsequent social interaction. The construction of a city in a given place and time affects urban growth in adjacent areas and subsequent times. Where and when industrialization occurs affects how it occurs. Initial visions of victory announce a war's likely outcomes. A person's successive migrations have cumulative effects on his or her subsequent mobility through such simple matters as the presence or absence of information about new opportunities in different places and the presence or absence of social ties to

x *Editor's Preface*

possible destinations. A population's previous experience with wars, Baby Booms, and migrations haunts it in the form of bulging or empty cohorts and unequal numbers of the sexes. All these are profoundly historical matters, even when they occur in the present; time and place are of their essence. They form the essential subject-matter of **Studies in Social Discontinuity**.

Edward Shorter, Stanley Holwitz, and I plotted the **Studies in Social Discontinuity** in 1970–1; the first book, William Christian's *Person and God in a Spanish Valley*, appeared in 1972. Over the years, Academic Press published more than 50 titles in the series. But during the early 1980s publication slowed, then ceased. In 1988, happily, Basil Blackwell agreed to revive the Studies under my editorship. The original French version of Pierre Birnbaum's *Un mythe politique: la 'République juive'* appeared that same year, and soon attracted my attention. After the usual delays for negotiation, translation, and editing, I am delighted to make the book available to anglophones.

THIS BOOK

Pierre Birnbaum confronts a paradox: on the one hand, the French state itself was exceptionally open to Jews; on the other, anti-Semitism became a staple of French politics in the nineteenth and twentieth centuries. He relates it to the strong state/weak state distinction he has made famous in his political sociology. Does anti-Semitism only gain political strength when the state itself adopts it, or when a weak state fails to counter discrimination? No, he says. Countering Hannah Arendt, Birnbaum argues that 'It is the strength of the state and not its decline which causes political anti-Semitism to appear.' Strong states insist on homogeneity, while weak states tolerate diversity. Birnbaum contrasts the politically murderous anti-Semitism of strong-state France with the politically ineffectual social discrimination of a weak-state Great Britain or United States.

French Jews adopted what Birnbaum calls Franco-Judaism – a fairly secular and civic adaptation to living in a world of Christian resonance that made Jewish identity and practice private matters – only to confront the persecution of Dreyfus, the vilification of Léon Blum, the organized and lethal anti-Semitism of Vichy, the postwar attacks on Pierre Mendès France. Precisely because Jews were able to get relatively equal treatment from the French state, he indicates, every anti-state movement aligned itself with anti-Semitism, and some took it up with a vengeance. In this he sees direct parallels between France and Germany.

Birnbaum documents France's political anti-Semitism in painful detail. The images and allegations horrify, their shock value gaining from our tendency to suppress such excruciating memories. He displays images of the Wandering

Jew, of the sexual pervert, of the Antichrist, of the scheming capitalist. He documents the repeated uses of these images in France's major political battles. Eventually we begin to see that political anti-Semitism is more than an occasional deviation from a main line of universalistic politics. In a time of renewed chauvinism in France and elsewhere, it is sobering to see that the great hatreds are more than passing follies. Pierre Birnbaum's analysis indicates that the extinction of anti-Semitism as a political force will take more than benign education, sermons on toleration, and the experience of living together. If he is right, it will take deep political change.

CHARLES TILLY

Acknowledgements

First of all I should like to thank the Vidal Sassoon International Center for the Study of Antisemitism, at the Hebrew University, Jerusalem, whose generous assistance made a long study visit to the University at Jerusalem possible. Its director, Professor Yehuda Bauer, gave me a most friendly welcome. As for the research itself, my access to the sources was greatly eased by Mme Bonnazi, who is responsible for the contemporary section of the Archives Nationales; M. Georges Weil and Mme Yvonne Levine, who direct the very rich library and archives of the Alliance Israélite Universelle; Mme Halperyn and M. Jacobsen, who know all the treasures in the Centre de Documentation Juive Contemporaine; Mme Marie-Claude Mendès France, thanks to whom I was able to consult the still-unpublished archives of the Fonds Pierre Mendès France at the Bibliothèque de l'Alliance Israélite Universelle, as well as those in her own keeping; Mme Françoise Chapron, who is responsible for the Bibliothèque de l'Institut Pierre Mendès France and herself an expert on Pierre Mendès France as a political personality in the Eure; Mme Simone Gros, who worked closely with Pierre Mendès France and agreed to pass on several unpublished documents to me; Mme Janine Bourdin, responsible for the Fonds Léon Blum at the Fondation Nationale des Sciences Politiques; M. Philippe Landeau, responsible for the Archives du Consistoire de Paris; and M. Yves Deloye, thanks to whom I was able to examine certain documents in the Archives de la France d'Outre-Mer in Aix-en-Provence. I was able to consult at length the very many interviews conducted by the Institut d'Histoire du Temps Présent on the life and work of Pierre Mendès France. Messrs Michel Abitbol, Richard Cohen and Simon Epstein of the Hebrew University of Jerusalem were kind enough to give me some general guidance in my work. Research for this book was also conducted in the Archives de la Préfecture de Police de Paris, in the various departments of the Bibliothèque Nationale in Paris, and in several libraries in New York and the United States, the University of Indiana in particular.

Introduction
Assessing Anti-Semitism in France

In 1899, five years after the Dreyfus Affair had erupted, when the whole of France appeared to be ablaze, a Breton peasant considered with astonishment the excitement that the arrival of a train was causing among the bystanders. It was Dreyfus, he was told, being escorted to his trial at Rennes. 'Dreyfus, who's he?' he asked.[1] And yet as early as November 1897 a policeman maintained that 'This affair is taking on enormous proportions . . . Nobody talks about anything else.'[2] During the first two months of 1898, sixty-nine anti-Semitic riots took place in France, involving 4,000 people at Angers and Marseille, 3,000 at Nantes, 2,000 at Rouen. Mobs destroyed shops; synagogues were attacked and people injured.[3] Memory and awareness of such events were therefore variable, so to gauge the actual extent of anti-Semitism in the early days of the Republic is no easy matter.

The same applies to the inter-war period when Léon Blum led the Popular Front government. In Brittany again, this time in 1938, 700 people, primarily peasants, attended a meeting of the Rassemblement de l'Alliance Nationale de L'Ouest: as they were only interested in having a jolly get-together, anti-Semitic allusions to Blum by different speakers evoked no response at all.[4] Yet reports by informers state that anti-Semitic rallies were common throughout France in this period of violence. As in the Dreyfus Affair, they were provoked by an unbridled press.

To take another example: on 16 January 1956, at the Vélodrome d'Hiver, Léon Dupont, leader of peasant action within the Poujade movement, attacked 'the Mendès and others who do not even dare stand with their baptismal names', arousing frenetic applause from a stamping crowd of over 20,000,[5] even though this was a time when, contrary to earlier periods, anti-Semitism was in no way central to the prevailing ideological disputes. In short, what place has anti-Semitism really held in the Republic from the end of the nineteenth century to the present?

2　Anti-Semitism in France

A NON-EXISTENT ANTI-SEMITISM?

According to Eugen Weber, the very late unification of the national territory explains the extreme weakness of the symbol of France, the Hexagon. Far from emerging as a vital element in the collective consciousness in the first part of the twentieth century, it never in fact became a generally accepted factor.[6] This absence of unification in national political life, says Weber, makes it possible to understand why, outside of ideologies and at the level of everyday life, 'to most French during most of the nineteenth century and to many French in the twentieth century, it [anti-Semitism] was a minor question, or no question at all ... they had other fish to fry.'[7] Did anti-Semitism in France – from Toussenel to Drumont, Léon Daudet, Maurras, Pierre Gaxotte, Henri Béraud, Henry Coston or Pierre Poujade, from *La Libre Parole* to *La Croix, Gringoire, Candide, Je suis partout, Rivarol* or *Fraternité française* – remain purely ideological, devoid of all concrete meaning for the vast majority of citizens? It did, of course, mobilize intellectuals on all sides, but was the nation itself largely indifferent? Did anti-Semitism, like fascism, belong solely to the history of ideas in this particular context?

Like fascism, it appeared untraceable in France, so much so that neither historians nor sociologists proved able to give an account of this imaginary fact that belonged solely to the realm of ideas.[8] This seems to have been the attitude of historians of contemporary French society, who, in France at least, appear to have turned away deliberately from the study of a social fact which they probably considered non-existent. Apart from a few pioneering works relating primarily to the end of the nineteenth century,[9] the majority of important books on anti-Semitism in contemporary France have been written by anglophone historians.[10] The classic works on the Third and Fourth Republics are almost silent on the subject or at most make one or two allusions to it. There seems to be the feeling that, excepting the Vichy episode, as soon as the ideological realm is left, to consider the area of local or national political life, there is barely anything to be found but windmills. Just as historians of contemporary France have usually glossed over the existence of a revolutionary Right attracted to extremist ideologies, so they have only very rarely turned their attention to the reality of anti-Semitism.

But since the end of the nineteenth century, anti-Semitism has not only constituted an ideological constant. That it has been present to a varying degree and assumed a variety of forms does not alter the fact that it is also a social practice that reveals itself in political activity and frequently in collective action (riots, street demonstrations, electoral meetings, marches, and the like). Of course, anti-Semitism as a political fact did not always appear in the same form, and its visibility as well as its intensity could vary, from the Dreyfus Affair to the more recent period of decolonization following the Mendès France experiment, by way of the years of the Cartel of the Left, the Popular Front, Munich and the

Vichy era. From the Dreyfus Affair to the Poujade movement, its political geography – as a social fact and not only as an ideological or literary practice – continually changed. Sometimes it affected a particular rural or urban area, sometimes one right- or left-wing political group. Latent or actual, on the scale of a shout or a whisper, of graffiti or leaflet, political programme or newspaper article, caricature or song, street theatre or cabaret, anonymous denunciation or deliberately provocative march, the anti-Semitic attitude really does constitute a social fact in France. Its memory is carefully preserved in police archives as well as in prefects' reports, libraries and specialist archives.

A SIMPLIFYING DEBATE: ANTI-SEMITISM AND FASCISM

All too often this vast body of very extensive, very varied material has for some reason been left in the obscurity of shelves, boxes and microfiches, and French historians have rarely taken any notice of it. For the most part, the debate has been limited to the Vichy period: an exceptional and atypical moment in contemporary history when an authoritarian regime, subject to Hitler's domination, was established. Going back in time, historians have worked on the inter-war leagues in the same spirit. They have carefully analysed the biographies of the men who later became the spokesmen of French-style fascism, and yet almost never have they specifically examined their anti-Semitic attitude. Now, as George Mosse has rightly emphasized, 'racism and antisemitism did not always form the essential elements of fascism'.[11] That is why the debate on French-style fascism as myth or reality, which historians have engaged in for the last few years, is largely one-sided as regards anti-Semitism. Though this, as we have said, is a distinct social fact in its own right, they only take it into account very marginally. In France, historians of the multifarious right-wing parties are in fact silent on this point.[12] If they come to the conclusion – as they increasingly do nowadays – that French-style fascism is an 'insignificant' phenomenon, its 'intrinsic weakness'[13] being primarily explicable by its extensive fragmentation and immense heterogeneity, then the anti-Semitism inherent in this ideological trend must inevitably be insignificant. And at various periods when the Republic felt threatened by the radical Right and its allies, those Breton peasants whom we have already met, as well as those in the various provinces, because of their indifference would only react with common-sense arguments to quarrels between ideas which did not really concern them, any more than any other Frenchmen. 'Remote from all reality... the ideological war of the thirties', for example, was 'a sham more than anything else... a war of words'.[14] This in its turn would make the anti-Semitic hatred which we set out to examine more specifically here, both in this context and in the 1950s, no more than a parody, a feeble echo of the real confrontations in the outside world.

4 Anti-Semitism in France

Zeev Sternhell, who himself emphasizes that fascism in France 'never went past the stage of theory',[15] looked for the foundations of fascist ideology in a synthesis which, he says, occurred at the end of the nineteenth century between a radical Right and a socialist-inclined Left, both determined to break up liberal democracy. For him, 'the generation of 1930 more or less adopted and extended the attitudes of the men of 1890 . . . because fascism in France took its sources, and its men, from both Left and Right, very often much more from the Left than from the Right.'[16] Does this interpretation of fascist ideology as a quasi-constant in the history of French society, winning the vote of both extremes, enable us to approach the specific phenomenon of anti-Semitism more readily? Can it also be perceived as a sham or understood as the common denominator of various types of extremism? Again according to Zeev Sternhell, 'from the end of the [Dreyfus] Affair until the Great War, anti-Semitism was a weapon used exclusively for the forces attacking the republican consensus. Until 1914, anti-Semitism survived on the left only in the ranks of the non-conformist wing of Socialism, the wing that refused to play the game of liberal and bourgeois democracy'.[17] As a result, some people regarded fascist ideology as almost unchanging from one period to the next, but anti-Semitism as changing profoundly. Before 1914 it was common to both extremes of the political chess board; thereafter in the inter-war period it was primarily present on the extreme Right. Note from the outset that such a hypothesis specifically implies an element of risk in approaching the phenomenon of anti-Semitism in French society solely by examining the origin of fascism, since from one period to the next and *a fortiori* during the Fourth Republic, they cannot be reduced one to the other. In addition, even if fascism was not transformed into a real collective movement capable of seizing power, it still remained an ideology which often had very real and concrete consequences. Anti-Semitism in fact constituted an empirical reality, quite apart from the speeches, observable from the end of the nineteenth century up to the most recent period, to a far greater extent than most historians of French society admit.

Anti-Semitism, as a social fact and not as pure ideology, is in no sense limited to the extremes. Although it cannot be seen as a constant feature in a purely imaginary generalized French ideology[18] – and even though its strongest expression is to be found very far back on the extreme Right – none the less in the twentieth century it is also present to varying degrees both in the ranks of the great left-wing parties (not only among the non-conformists) and in pressure groups and organs which seek their inspiration from the Catholic side, as was the case at the end of the nineteenth century.

Does this mean that the 'Franco-French wars' are to be seen as an endless series of Dreyfus Affairs with strong correspondences existing between them?[19] Unlike fascism, must analysis of contemporary anti-Semitism be approached as an almost constant system built up of a collection of unchanging features? The Jews would figure in this system as the perfect scapegoats, responsible for the decadence of French society, the decline of its morals, the degenerate state of its traditions. This interpretation of an almost timeless anti-Semitism in the recent history of French society would imply that every time 'order is absent or jeopardised by the scapegoat, it is re-established or established through the mediation of the factor that first disturbed it'.[20] For the perceived omnipotence of the scapegoat to be destroyed in successive periods an extreme liberating violence must necessarily be deployed, to re-establish the destroyed unity of the nation. The Jews are incessantly likened to devils and are often identified with the maleficent and oppressive power wielded by the rich and powerful.[21] They are foreigners to the French people, pariahs[22] to borrow Max Weber's word, which Hannah Arendt also uses. As such, they appear as marginals,[23] perverts threatening the values and traditions inherent in the French soul, either because their differences and specific behaviour make them appear essentially other, or, on the contrary, because their complete assimilation to the common norms causes them to appear even more formidable because they become invisible. By coming 'out of the ghetto',[24] as Jacob Katz shows, 'the Jew was conceived of as a former pariah who had moved from the margin of society to its very centre'.[25] Thus they create phantasms of both fear and rejection which are all the more disturbing because the actors have become invisible.

Unlike the traditional types of anti-Semitism of a religious or racial nature, the 'political anti-Semitism' specific to the period of emancipation transformed the Jews into perfect political scapegoats. For James Parkes,[26] the political anti-Semitism in Germany, Austro-Hungary and France, from the Dreyfus Affair to Pétain, which particularly interests us here, consisted of an identification of the Jews with liberal industrial and secular society. This new paradigm then became unalterable within the modern Western world, despite the diversity of the specific crises which gave free rein to this atmosphere of fear. This emotion was all the more irrational because it now concerned citizens who had become identical with everyone else in every way – in the public domain at least. Everywhere, from one Western society to the next, 'the entrance of the Jews into society'[27] would therefore result in their profound metamorphosis, yet without the loss of the demoniacal nature that had been attributed to them since the Middle Ages.[28]

This paradigmatic interpretation of contemporary anti-Semitism, valid for all democratic capitalist societies, encounters many difficulties. Comparative historical sociology, which stresses the essential features distinguishing societies from each other in the Western world, can help to solve them. The fact is that, though these societies are entirely capitalist, liberal and secular, they are so to varying degrees, and it is important to remember these dissimilarities. The variables which structure the specific context of the emancipation of the Jews in every society in the Western world and which consequently throw new light on the manifold forms of anti-Semitism, cover a wide range of phenomena: whether capitalism came late or early; the role of the aristocracy and the bourgeoisie within the wider framework of the market, and the confrontation between the different social groups; the nature and tactics of the working class;

the strength or weakness of the peasantry; the dominant Catholic or Protestant cultural code; the extent of de-Christianization; the method of foundation or institutionalization of secularism in its various aspects; political democracy; the extension of the right to vote; legitimate political representation of the diverse particularist groups, including those based on the ethnic or national differences; the significance of citizenship; and lastly and most importantly, the role of the state. Anti-Semitism is certainly not an identical phenomenon on both sides of the Atlantic, the consequence of watering down and hiding an identity – an illusory rejection. On the contrary, like any social phenomenon it is embedded in specific historical contexts which must be considered if one is to achieve a better understanding of its particular significance.

In our time, comparative political sociology has shown how important it is to differentiate carefully between each type of state, the result of a long history of its own within Western society.[29] In this sense, strong states can be contrasted with weak states. Strong states exercise a firm hold over society through the creation of a powerful administrative bureaucracy. This bureaucracy recruits its members on merit, is open to all on an egalitarian basis, and strives to demonstrate its independence of all social, religious or ethnic particularisms. In weak states, on the other hand, political democracy blossoms rapidly, facilitating the representation of a multiplicity of interest groups – including religious and ethnic groups – the state relying on only a limited bureaucratic apparatus. In the first model, the secularization of state space as well as of citizenship is evidence of the almost unique character of identification with the state. In the second, on the other hand, private space is infinitely more extensive, and this permits each citizen to have various religious or ethnic allegiances. Amongst the large states in contemporary Western society, France is a good example of the first category; Great Britain or better still, the United States, of the second.

Making the type of state a variable, which is essential to an understanding of the collective behaviour characteristic of society itself, seeking to pursue the specific logic of one particular type of state, which the actors and the social groups confront at every turn, is to attempt to see collective behaviour such as strikes or even nationalist action in a different light.[30] To focus on the state also implies taking a new look at the unfolding of anti-Semitic mobilization and its significance. This perspective has remained absent for too long from traditional thought which is almost always based on religious factors, the racial issue or even economic modernization.

HANNAH ARENDT'S FLAWED HUNCH

Hannah Arendt was perhaps the only person to have some intuition of this phenomenon when she stated that 'modern anti-Semitism must be reset in the more general framework of the development of the nation-state'.[31] In her opinion, the Jews fostered the economic activity of the state, which granted them privileges in return. In this sense the Jews were loyal allies of the state, and the court Jews, in particular, symbolized this privileged relationship. Using France as a more specific example, Hannah Arendt reckoned that at the time of the Dreyfus Affair, 'from the state's point of view, the Jews were the most reliable element of the state at that time because they did not really form part of it'.[32] Taking a more general view, she writes that in France as elsewhere – Germany, for instance – with the definitive rise of imperialism at the turn of the century 'the Western Jewish community disintegrated at the same time as the nation-state in the last few decades before the First World War'.[33] In France more specifically, at the time of the Dreyfus Affair, 'the decline of the state machine led to the disintegration of Jewish society, which had been linked to it for so long'.[34]

Hannah Arendt's hunch remains formidable because she makes the state a vital variable in the appearance of contemporary anti-Semitism. None the less, she is to a large extent inaccurate. By adopting – strangely – the analyses of a Drumont which, as far as the role of the Jews is concerned, are akin in some respects to those of a Marx, Arendt postulates a purely economic interpretation of the Jews' place in the state. This is only partly valid in the case of Germany and very inadequate and questionable in the case of France. Here, a strong and largely meritocratic state was in fact open to Jews on universalist and egalitarian bases. As they were neither 'pariahs' nor 'parvenus' of necessity, French Jews at the end of the nineteenth century were primarily loyal citizens of a strong, emancipating and republican state. Many of them were 'state Jews' and not court Jews.[35] On the same lines and without regard to comparative state sociology, Arendt offers a purely economic interpretation of anti-Semitism as a consequence of the growth of imperialism which caused the decline of the nation-state.[36] This thesis takes no account of the strengthening of the republican state at that time and greatly overestimates the disintegration of the French Jewish community which is said to have resulted from it. The state remains in place, as does the synthesis of Franco-Judaism which rests precisely on liberating political emancipation and access to republican citizenship. However, this does not prevent the maintenance of structures of particularist affiliation. We shall return to this essential point later. In addition and most importantly, Arendt in her turn adheres to a simplified and economic vision of the origin of anti-Semitism inherent in the various right- or left-wing popular movements which raged in the nineteenth century. We have already referred to the reasoning behind this, superbly analysed by Robert Byrnes,[37] when we examined the connections which united, or separated, fascism and anti-Semitism. Arendt does not realize that Drumont still belonged to classical nineteenth-century anti-Semitism and that in France, on the contrary, the new anti-Semitism would be born as a reaction within society to the definitive strengthening of the republican state. It is the strength of the state and not its decline which causes political anti-Semitism to appear.

TO EACH ITS OWN: ANTI-SEMITISM ON BOTH SIDES OF THE ATLANTIC

A brief summary of the characteristics of the specific anti-Semitism apparent in the Anglo-Saxon world and which is in direct contrast to the French variety, is sufficient to show that a general theory of modern anti-Semitism valid for all Western countries misses the main point. Take the United States for example: here we have a weak state where multiple forms of self-organization of collective life have always been thick on the ground as a result of the very early establishment of a political democracy with essentially pluralist foundations. Here, the associative life, characteristic of the Jews, has never been a problem because it is similar to the associative life of all the other communities. Better still, it is just as legitimate. The Jews, along with all the other cultural, ethnic or religious communities, benefited as early as the eighteenth century from an emancipation which in no way involved the disappearance of their own particularist allegiances. Integrating their activities into the wider framework of the general associative life, or even into the normal tactics common to all pressure groups, the Jews never aroused a collective anti-Semitic movement. That is why, in the United States, according to John Higham, 'antisemitism never appeared as a subject of crucial importance. No essential event, no profound crisis, no social movement of any extent, no famous individual is linked in any degree to antisemitism.'[38]

In this land of 'ethnic democracy' and religious pluralism, only one death specifically attributed to anti-Semitism is recorded throughout the whole of American history. The individual concerned was Leo Frank who died in Georgia in 1913.[39] We mention him to emphasize that anti-Semitism led to no form of collective mobilization whatsoever. It has always remained a form of social discrimination at the level of everyday life. Furthermore, in that Protestant society, close in many ways to Old Testament culture, religion-based anti-Semitism has usually been absent:[40] it was rather the Catholics who were ostracized. The only visible form of anti-Semitism in fact bears witness to the Jews' complete integration into American values, valuing economic success, the individualism of the market, social mobility and, lastly, the laws of liberal capitalism – which says it all in that Protestant society. There where the state was weak and where capitalism blossomed rapidly, it was quite logical that the Jews should in fact integrate through society and not through a state of limited legitimacy which was itself decentralized and fragmented. In this sense, rapidly expanding capitalism at the turn of the century favoured the individual social mobility of all those who were ready to penetrate its mysteries. American Jews, like many others, plunged in legitimately. Very widely represented in the world of lawyers, the liberal professions and certain limited sections of the industrial world, the Jews reached the Protestant establishment. Here too they aroused certain forms of rejection and exclusion with an anti-Semitic basis – from the most exclusive clubs, for example.[41] In general, only hostile economic stereotypes of Jews were published. As early as the nineteenth century, Shylock inspired a large number of anti-Semitic caricatures, pride of place being given to the Rothschild family.[42] However, even this traditional form of anti-Semitism, which was temporarily exacerbated during the hey-day of the agriculturally based popularist movements,[43] remained mild. American disciples of Drumont found very few followers.[44] During the inter-war period, at the height of the crusade for pure, hard Americanization, the anti-Semitic campaign led by Henry Ford through the *Dearborn Independent* met with no great response,[45] even though from 1920 it was supported by the wide distribution of the *Protocols of the Elders of Zion*.[46]

In the United States the Jews have primarily sought social integration compatible with the maintenance of their particularism, which practically everyone regards as a legitimate aim. Anti-Semitism, which is in any case very limited, thereby assumed an almost exclusively economic form; it never became political. From this point of view, as Denis Wrong notes, the Jews cannot serve as scapegoats because they are barely present in the expanding bureaucratic structures of the federal state.[47] In such a pluralist context, where the state was weak the Jews, therefore, never became scapegoats capable of provoking violent collective reaction.

Great Britain is another country where the state is weak and where democracy, born early, favours the expression and representation of every social or cultural particularism. Colin Holmes emphasizes this when he writes that since the mid-nineteenth century, 'antisemitism was never a vehicle for political success in British society and those who drew from European experience and attempted to inject it into British political life were to be frustrated and disappointed by the results'.[48] Here too, as in the United States, the Jews benefited from rapid emancipation compatible with the maintenance of highly structured forms of particularist representative organizations.[49] Here also, in the framework of this predominantly Protestant country, favourable to liberalism and capitalism, their integration was achieved via society rather than the state.

Anti-Semitism in Great Britain first appeared basically in a religious form. In this society, where religious conflict between Catholics and Protestants was even more intense than in the United States, the Jews were for a long time accused of being responsible for ritual murders. After they had gained political emancipation, however, they were soon able to challenge the obligation to swear allegiance to the Christian religion. After they had been completely integrated – from the second half of the nineteenth century – this aspect of anti-Semitism diminished very considerably. As in the United States, the Jews turned at the turn of the century mainly to the liberal professions and to the business world at the height of its expansion to achieve social integration. For the same reason, in Britain in more recent times, anti-Semitism was expressed essentially through the stereotypes simultaneously found in France in Drumont's writings. Joseph Bannister, for example, published *England under the*

Jews in 1901, denouncing their economic domination and linking up with a left-wing stream of anti-Semitism which, as in France, thought in terms of a cosmopolitan world conspiracy. In the same period, Henry Hyndman, leader of the Social-Democratic Federation, followed a similar line of thought after his conversion to Marxism.[50]

As in France or Germany, on both the Left and the Right, at the turn of the century the ineluctable consequences of their maleficent influence were described in terms such as 'parasites', 'vermin' and even 'infection'. In the same way as on the Continent, the *Protocols of the Elders of Zion* was widely disseminated, and England, like France, saw the formation of organizations such as the British Brothers' League (1901) and, later, the Britons (1919), or later still the Imperial Fascist League (1928), and the British Union of Fascists (BUF) (1932) which mobilized tens of thousands of individuals, especially in the inter-war period. At just one meeting in 1934 the BUF drew more than 20,000 people.

Despite transitory success, however, 'anti-Semitism failed to become a relevant political force in England' because of 'its lack of historical tradition' there – unlike the Continent.[51] Despite everything, the anti-Semitic mobilization of the inter-war period, facilitated by the rise of Hitlerism with which it established direct connections, amounted to no more than a flash in the pan in this country, built on pluralism and the recognition of ethnic and religious minorities. It was rapidly extinguished by the unambiguous and unfaltering actions of the authorities in upholding democratic laws. Contrary to the very violent forms that anti-Semitic action could take in France, Germany or Austria, hatred of the Jews in Great Britain, as in the United States, did not result in large-scale deaths or violence. Nor did it appear as an instrument, however ineffective, for seizing political power, since none of these movements ever won a single seat in an election. Consequently, anti-Semitism always remained peripheral in England, unlike France or Germany.[52]

Here again, Great Britain, a fundamentally Protestant country based on consensus, seems closer to the United States. In both societies anti-Semitism emerged mainly from values and attitudes of social exclusion: the closing of the most prestigious clubs; the limited nature of exogamy within the Protestant establishment. For a long time there was restricted entry to the great universities and public schools where the socialization of the elite occurred and through which access to the political and administrative elite was gained on the basis of mutual acquaintance within a fairly homogeneous social milieu. Disraeli is an illuminating example. He was outside Victorian society and could only succeed politically because he was baptized. And even if he provocatively acknowledged that he was a Jew, even if he explicitly favoured Jewish emancipation, he did so because he desired the ultimate conversion of the Jews to Christianity. This, in his eyes, was the best outcome for biblical Judaism.[53] A rootless Jew, if ever there was one, Disraeli became spokesman for a triumphant Jewish 'race' giving Christianity to the world. Only this ambiguity, evidence of a profound personal malaise, secured him both political integration and access to power itself. Later, at the end of the nineteenth century, and in the twentieth, other Jews joined the political elite without converting. They were few in number at this level of power in a state which never claimed to dominate society nor, when all is said and done, to represent it; this handful of Jews however aroused real political anti-Semitism, but it had no real future because it had no real target. For this reason it was surely ridiculous to write vengefully on the door of 10 Downing Street, 'None but Hebrews may apply'.[54] In Great Britain, as in the United States, political anti-Semitism had no great prospects.

Within the contemporary Western world, Germany seems to be an entirely different case. This was another country where the majority of the population had long been Protestant. A strong state had been created, supported by a gigantic bureaucratic machine set up by the absolutist system. Both Hegel and Max Weber have described it as the very image of the bureaucratic spirit seeking the sole foundation of its legitimacy in rationality. None the less, even in the nineteenth century this state was largely controlled by a military-type landed aristocracy which was so powerful that it succeeded in curbing the expansion both of the bourgeoisie and of democracy itself.[55] In this aristocratic and deeply Christian state, devoid of all pluralist tradition, anti-Semitic violence was a commonplace for centuries. The fact that the rationalism of the Enlightenment remained fragile and faced the powerful, organically based, Romantic tradition, made it all the easier to reject *Judentum* as a general category from the German *Volk*.

In this eminently reactionary framework, the term anti-Semitism was born from the pen of William Marr. In 1879, a few years before Drumont's *La France juive* (1886), Marr published *Der Sieg des Judenthums über das Germanenthum* (The Victory of Judaism over Germanism). Writing from a viewpoint only similar on certain points to that of Marx (whose writings he knew and whom he had even met), Marr proposed 'general mobilization' against the Jews. As in France at almost the same period, this 'new Luther' created an Antisemitic League, offered his assistance to his rival Stoecker's anti-Jewish movement, and unceasingly denounced the non-Christian, 'state within the state' of Eastern origin which he claimed the Jews had formed in Germany and which must be abolished.[56]

The end of the nineteenth century saw the blossoming, as in France, of a broad anti-Semitic movement, given intellectual legitimacy by the great historian Treitschke. A large number of anti-Semitic leagues were created, particularly in student circles, to fight the Jews who were frequently identified with capitalism and with the modernity which threatened the German soul.[57] Rejected by the ruling political and administrative circles, despite final emancipation granted in 1869, held in check by an army bound to Christian values which denied Jews access to the higher ranks,[58] and to a very large extent effectively excluded from the state itself until the birth of the Weimar Republic,[59] the German Jews were left with few options. They had the choice of converting in large numbers[60] or of trying to rise socially outside the state structure and via society in the business world, banking, the liberal or the intellectual professions. Thenceforth, as the Jews strove for wider social integration, they were seen as the embodiment of all the evils of foreign and cosmopolitan capitalism. From Marx to Liebknecht and Kautsky, it was the strategy of German social democracy not to belittle the revolutionary potential which it perceived taking shape via the popular anti-Semitic movement.[61] As in France at the same period, there was an open unacknowledged union, or at least an amalgam, of right- and left-wing anti-Semitism, and here too it gave rise to genuinely violent and destructive collective movements.

Shared for such diverse reasons by so many social groups, anti-Semitism thrust into the innermost recesses of German ideology, of the German nation's vision of the world, and even more, its cultural code.[62] The Jews incarnated all the dangers, all the perversions endangering German identity. It was Germany which saw the birth in the sixteenth century of the myth of the wandering Jew, Ahasuerus, who bears witness to the eternal guilt of the Jewish people, condemned to wander forever for refusing to help Christ. He is the very symbol of the stranger, of someone passing through, who has no roots, no soil. The Jew has come from the darkness; throughout German history he acquired a diabolic dimension which, in the land of Siegfried, further emphasized the failings which first caused him to wander. Romantic nationalism and later Nazism were inspired by this anti-Christian and anti-capitalist myth, expiation finding its logical and ultimate end in collective murder.[63]

Infiltrating Christian countries from the Orient and far-off Asia, the Jews brought with them all the vices, all the diseases of these distant lands. At the end of the century, the *Ostjude* – the Eastern Jew – symbolized the Outsider, the uprooted.[64] The Jews had come from nowhere; they remained foreigners, even if they had donned the modern dress of emancipated citizens. This may have made their oddness disappear – superficially, at least – but it still persisted despite their formal assimilation. In Germany, during the rapid process of industrialization at the turn of the century, the Jews appeared both as greedy capitalists and as cosmopolitans condemned to remain marginals, come from who knows where, despite their assimilation and their oft-proclaimed love for the *Vaterland*, the home land.[65] In a strange way, a bizarre synthesis occurred at this time between the supposed vices of capitalism and those of the Orient. The Jews appeared as stateless persons with an unhealthy sexuality – feminine and homosexual at one and the same time – perverting the Aryan race. George Mosse identifies it with remarkable success, when he states that nationalism and sexuality here combined on a basis of racism.[66] It will be examined later in greater depth in this book, using France as our example.

SELF-HATRED: FROM DISRAELI TO RATHENAU

The Jews in modern Germany therefore failed to achieve social emancipation. It was the only form of emancipation really open to them, the only one to which they devoted all their efforts, going as far as imitation, self-hatred, conversion. Access to this aristocratic and Christian state, as we have said, remained closed to them. In this respect the situation was fairly similar to the one the Jews faced in Anglo-Saxon societies, where they only reached the establishment on a very limited scale, even if their own legitimacy was unassailable. On closer inspection, the strongly pluralistic Anglo-Saxon societies, rather than the Anglo-Saxon establishment, may have assured the Jewish minority of equal rights. In Germany, on the contrary, it was the state which opened its doors, slowly and belatedly, to Jews with certificates of higher education. They became, though in very small numbers, high officials, or sometimes, under the Weimar Republic, deputies and ministers. The example of Walter Rathenau comes to mind. He was a famous figure in the political world, Minister for Foreign Affairs, but he was also a Jew filled with self-hatred: 'Look at yourselves in the mirror!', he said to his co-religionists. 'Nothing, unfortunately can be done about the fact that all of you look frighteningly alike and that your individual vices, therefore, are attributed to all of you. Neither will it console you that in the first place your east Mediterranean appearance is not very well appreciated by the northern tribes.'[67] This illustrates the extent of the self-hatred that could be felt by Jews who were amongst the leaders of social democracy.[68] It is expressed in the accounts of Otto Weininger, a Viennese Jew, who converted like so many others at that time in Vienna and Berlin. In his book *Geschlecht und Charakter* (Sex and Character) (1903), which had considerable influence on the German-speaking intellectual and political world, the pure, hard Prussian model prevails over the Viennese myth entirely dominated by decadence and sexuality. For Weininger, 'the state represents the totality of ends ... that Kantian reason which is nothing other than the mind is as foreign to the Jew as to the woman. Humanity once again has the choice between Jewishness and Christianity, between business and culture, between woman and man, between nothingness and the divinity.'[69] In Germany, as well as in Austria-Hungary, a very large number of Jewish intellectuals were ineluctably drawn into self-hatred. In this specific context, where modernity and emancipation existed but where the Jews found their paths blocked at every turn, both in the state and in society, not only Weininger, but also Kraus, Nordau and many others saw self-denigration as the way out.[70]

This phenomenon was crucially important in Berlin, Vienna and Budapest, in countries were contradictory tendencies co-existed. It always remained very limited in other Western countries. There, Judaism fitted acceptably into a general pluralistic framework, as in the Anglo-Saxon world or in a country such as France, where the Jews had long identified themselves with a genuinely emancipating citizenship.[71] In fact, a rather surprising comparison can still be drawn between Rathenau and Disraeli on this one count: they were both rare examples of Jews who gained high office while totally denying – by conflicting arguments – their own Jewishness. Despite everything, Disraeli remained an important, albeit eccentric, figure in British political history and did not give rise to any collective anti-Semitic movement. Rathenau, on the other hand, and the other Jews who occupied vital positions in the Weimar Republic, provoked a real anti-Semitic political mobilization in society, which culminated in Rathenau's assassination and, later, in Nazism. An immense gulf is thus revealed between the aristocratic and mainly Christian state and the new-born republic which made it possible for a few Jews to gain access to certain powerful positions. As Peter Gay notes, the Jews in the Weimar Republic at last moved from being 'outsiders' to become 'insiders' who appeared to threaten German society with complete 'Judaisation'.[72] The state, with fragile institutions and of dubious strength, would be swept away once the imaginary 'Jewish republic' had been overturned by the violent mobilization of movements preaching a specific anti-Semitism. The establishment of Hitlerian totalitarianism thus represented the overthrow, in the name of political anti-Semitism, both of the republic and of the state itself, perceived ideologically, and probably erroneously, as strong and alien to the identity of the nation and the German race.[73]

Thus political anti-Semitism only appeared in Germany from the time of the Weimar Republic in reaction to the recent and low-key entry of the Jews into the sphere of politico-administrative power. Almost entirely unknown in the United States or Great Britain where, as we have said, Jewish integration up to the present has taken place through society, the appearance of political anti-Semitism (on which this book will concentrate) was not in this case a consequence of the cultural and religious code or of capitalist modernization. It was really the outcome of a particular *modus operandi* of a state which was sufficiently institutionalized to employ the criteria of egalitarian and meritocratic recruitment.

There is no doubt that the conjunction of a strong state with an egalitarian and secular republic increases the probability of an upsurge of collective political anti-Semitism. This has been seen in the example of the Weimar Republic which was formed alongside the old bureaucratized Prussian state. When the Jews of the Western world left the ghetto, they were consequently implanted into different state systems which either did or did not favour their political integration and the reaction to this sometimes caused the birth of an essentially new form of anti-Semitism. It is very instructive to compare France and Germany in this respect. Whatever the differences in relationships between social classes, in the rhythm of industrialization or the expansion of capitalism, it is rather the time when nation and state were built – purely political variables – that sheds light on similarities and, particularly, on differences. The national unification of France – and, even more, of Great Britain – took place several centuries before Germany. Like Italy, Germany is situated on the centre line of Europe, as drawn by Stein Rokkan,[74] which runs from Hamburg to Venice, passing through Berne and Milan. In the nineteenth century, the period of the rise of nationalism, Germany was always striving to build both a united state and a true national identity. What is more, in France the unification of the nation was the work of a centralized and egalitarian state, a task which the Prussian state, in spite of its strength, was unable to carry through. Thus it was through the romantic idea of the return of the *Volk* and the supposedly pure Aryan race that the nation was, very belatedly, built in Germany. In this society – homogenized in this way on a quasi-ethnic basis, opposed to rationality and secularism – the Jews appeared as fundamentally alien elements who exploited to their own advantage an abstract republic which was *a fortiori* foreign to German-ness. All in all, after the defeat of 1918, a state with inadequate strength and legitimacy could not control anti-Semitic political mobilization against this 'Jewish republic'.

POLITICAL ANTI-SEMITISM VERSUS THE REPUBLICAN STATE: THE FRENCH PARADIGM

By way of contrast, the historical sociology of states demonstrates the very precocious character of the state in France. From the absolutist regime to the Revolution and the Second Empire, the state was constantly strengthening its bureaucratic apparatus. Its army of officials acted within the framework of public law. They were recruited on meritocratic criteria and socialized in schools and universities controlled by the state. State space increased, reducing national or linguistic particularisms, which it destroyed sometimes by force, sometimes simply through educational socialization. And the citizenship that it established implied direct allegiance to the state by every citizen, which was incompatible with any form of particularist identity. This state was strongly interventionist from all points of view and intolerant of social and political diversity because it claimed to embody national legitimacy in itself. The strength of the state therefore seemed to entail a relatively weak democracy which rested on the acceptance of pluralism.

For a long time, the weakness of the state in Great Britain and the United States was justified by the strength of their democracy. The state in Germany could only claim power as long as democracy itself remained eminently fragile and barely legitimate. In France the unchallengeable strength of the state found it hard to tolerate the construction of a pluralist political democracy.[75] What is more, the state in France found its definitive form in the republican ideal which finally prevailed under the Third Republic. For Claude Nicolet, 'it is still almost impossible to expound separately the ideas of State, Nation, Regime, People, Government in the French vocabulary. The State, taken in a very similar sense to the word Republic, really describes the "res publica", the "public thing", which concerns all members of a society at the same time'.[76] And from the French Revolution to the Third Republic, it was on the base of secularism, of the separation of Church and state, that the unity of the state and the Republic was built up through educational socialization. This is the way in which France is quite different from most other western countries; certainly, from those just briefly described: 'Secularism remains the most original feature of French political history, but also its most challenged contradictory feature'.[77] It was this secularism which finally achieved complete osmosis between the equalizing state and the liberating Republic. It even made possible the emancipation and integration into the state of citizens, whatever their particularisms, inevitably driving these particularisms into the realm of private life. Step by step, through many confrontations, the republican state was built up: from the French Revolution to the Third Republic, from the proclamation of emancipatory citizenship to the 'absolute Republic' established by Gambetta. He was truly 'the Moses of the land of the Republic', who was destined 'to point the way but not to establish a Republic. Its Joshua was Jules Ferry, certainly more a legist than a prophet'.[78]

Historians themselves have acquired the habit of using the Old Testament metaphorically to bring out the messianic dimension of the Third Republic in which, via a series of crises, the separation of Church and state, longed for since the French Revolution, was definitively instituted in the wake of the rationalist Enlightenment. From 1793 to the laws of 1903–5, universalist citizenship finally triumphed, rejecting tradition in the name of omnipotent reason. Its brilliance was propagated by the spontaneous teachings of those 'black hussars' of the Republic, the teachers from the *écoles normales*.[79] Service to the Republic was the mission of the bureaucracy of this strong state which set out to impose its own norms of emancipation, opposed to all forms of particularism. It was truly the state which triumphed through republican ideology, for after centuries of effort it found that it was finally able to overcome resistance from all the localisms, and from all the organic structures that perpetuated community traditions. Typically, from an early feudal period, every local, political and religious power had exercised total autonomy, and this had always limited its efforts to unify the nation.

Tocqueville writes that 'under the *ancien régime* as in our time, there was not a city, country town, village, or even the smallest hamlet in France, hospital, factory, convent or college which could have an independent will in its specific affairs, or administer at its will its own possessions. Then, as today, the administration thus kept all Frenchmen under its supervision.'[80] Actually, it was primarily from the time of the Third Republic that particularisms no longer seemed capable of resisting republican claims to state control. Deliberately turning its back on its traditional mission as the Church's elder daughter, republican France was obliged to undertake a substantial replacement of the old politico-administrative elites which had remained loyal to more Christian and often more conservative world views. The 'Republic of comrades' opened its arms to a new professionalized political body which recruited its members from lawyers, journalists or teachers favourably disposed to secularism.[81] In this context of radical change, the Third Republic extended and carried through the universalist philosophy of the French Revolution which seemed like a new 'flight from Egypt', a 'modern Passover' to emancipated Jews.[82] For them, despite the deep-seated repercussions of the Dreyfus Affair, 'the golden age of symbiosis' had at last set in,[83] the age of the most perfect adherence to the abstract and universalist virtues of the Republic.

France consequently seems to be the best available model of real integration of Jews into a state. Very early on they enjoyed complete political emancipation in that they obtained absolute citizenship and saw the whole politico-administrative area of the state open to them. However, apart from a few episodes, the history of contemporary France after this period appears to a large extent to have been 'half a century's slide to the Right'.[84] After many vicissitudes, this drift to the Right led to the Vichy regime which had no hesitation in instantly abolishing both the republican form of the State and, more specifically, its corollary, the emancipation of the Jews and their integration in this vigorously institutionalized State. Against a background of world economic crisis and international confrontation, this drift took place in a period of tumultuous social and political tension. Street fights broke out between supporters of conflicting ideologies who often donned uniforms which indicated where they stood. There was governmental instability and profound intellectual disarray. This was as propitious to every type of non-conformity[85] as to the intensification of the Franco-French wars, during which the Republican framework, once thought established, became itself an essential issue. From the Cartel of the Left to the Popular Front, from Munich to Vichy, French and immigrant Jews suddenly found themselves caught up in turbulence which concerned more than just themselves, but in which, almost always without their volition, they became a crucial factor. Looked at from the point of view of the specific fate of the Jews, Vichy actually took place well before Vichy.[86] The most virulent anti-Semitism was allowed free play right through the inter-war period. In Paris as well as in the remotest provinces, it inspired physical violence, innumerable books, lampoons and pamphlets, and the most solemn threatening proclamations, aimed not only at the Republic itself but particularly at the Jews through the Republican form of the state.

From the France of the Popular Front, led by Léon Blum, to the France of the decolonization that was undertaken under the aegis of Pierre Mendès France, there was immense anti-Semitic mobilization which specifically attacked the 'Jewish republic'. This social movement, which went far beyond a simple ideological debate, shows features identical to the movement born under the Weimar Republic. In the one as in the other, the specific target was the presence of Jews within the state and the party system.

The main hypothesis that this book wishes to explore now becomes more explicit. *What, in short, is the degree of correlation between the integration of Jews in the state or, at least, in certain crucial sectors of the political system, and the appearance of a new form of anti-Semitism?* Of course, this latter can sometimes be transmitted through the traditional myths of religious, racial or economic anti-Semitism, but it nevertheless exhibits an entirely new character due to the presence for the first time in modern history of Jews at the summit of states. What we want to do in this book is to assess this new political anti-Semitism, carefully differentiated in this way from its predecessors, and bring out its characteristic features. We shall do this by interpreting it as a reaction to the quasi-completion of a universalist, republican and secular state, open to all on a purely meritocratic basis. Such a state, particularly if it were France, could only welcome the Jews into its bosom in a purely functional way, on the same grounds as other categories of individual who only retain their particularist dimension in their private lives. This political anti-Semitism also operated in Weimar Germany against Jews who held a certain degree of political power, who were often ashamed of their own origins and converted or openly denied their Judaism in favour of other ideals, such as socialism, which had a more universalist appeal. Its significance was quite different in a secular country like France. Here, a well-established republican state allowed them to remain loyal to their past, while assigning to them a purely universalist type of activity based on the possession of a specific field of competence within the politico-administrative apparatus.

The aim of this book is therefore clear: in a country where the strong state is seen in the republican mould, to show the connection between the Jews' integration into a state, conducted on the universalist model of equal citizenship for all, and the outbreak of a genuinely political anti-Semitism that rejects both the republican state and the Jews whose integration it made possible. Such a case is extremely unusual in the modern period; there is the exceptional example in ancient Egypt, where Joseph governed Pharaoh's land. The French example is almost unique.[87] Furthermore, it recurred on several occasions. After the successive governments led by Léon Blum both during the inter-war period and immediately after the war, René Mayer and also, and most particularly, Pierre Mendès France took over the leadership of the state. None of them rejected their adherence to the Jewish world. Moreover, this was true of a pleiad of Jews who headed ministries vital to the functioning of the state, such as the Ministry of the Interior or the Ministry of Justice, from the Third to the Fifth Republics. From Abraham Schrameck to Jules Moch, from Georges Mandel to Robert Badinter, ministers of Jewish, more than of any other, origin have personified the maintenance of law and order in the state. Whether they belonged to right- or left-wing parties, they did this by assuming important responsibilities in the government of the Republic, that is to say, by scrupulously fulfilling their mission as public servants for the benefit of all.

France is thus one of the very rare nations in which public space was strictly defined by a body of roles and rights which incessantly and increasingly institutionalized it up to the present period. This runs counter to the sweeping interpretation of relationships between public and private space, formulated by Hannah Arendt, for example, or Jürgen Habermas.[88] According to this theory, in the market society the increasing privatization of public space marks the ineluctable decline of state order and of citizenship in all capitalist societies. However, the strengthening of the state in France since the turn of the century, under the auspices of the republican regime, set the scene for the accession of Jews to situations of power, on a purely functional basis.

The Jews of the French republic consequently appear as state Jews now, and not, as they sometimes did at an earlier period in both Germany and France, as court Jews whose specific influence was primarily based on the possession of economic resources. The new anti-Semitism which is the subject of this study broke out against those state Jews with essentially meritocratic resources and with secure citizenship. It can also be interpreted – and this is an essential factor – as the rejection of a state perceived as alien to national traditions by broad sections of society who were still trying to escape from triumphalist secularism. Throughout the history of French society, particularly since the emergence from feudalism, the state was always forced to strengthen its own machinery in the face of solid resistance to its centralizing activities from various peripheral groups. At the turn of the century, and even today, numerous groups are still trying to elude its hold, by claiming Catholic identity, for example, which is hardly compatible with secular republican ideology. They are often followers of a conservatism fundamentally hostile to capitalist modernization, urbanization and progress in general. They have always coloured their world view with a large dose of traditional anti-Semitism of the religious or economic type. This was particularly apparent at the time of the Dreyfus Affair and in Drumont's later writings and the diatribes of *La Croix*. As I shall attempt to show, this traditional anti-Semitism underwent a fundamental change which historians of Catholicism have indubitably underestimated.

At the turn of the century, the start of the period that this book aims to cover, traditional Catholic anti-Semitism changed, thereby strengthening the new political anti-Semitism, hostile to the republican state and to the Jews who had become its loyal servants on a universalist basis. But, contrary to many illusions entertained by official republican ideology, the French nation – despite deChristianization or the decline of religious practice – remained wide open to Christian values.

In reality, the Republic has hardly been born and its legitimacy remains uncertain. It masks France's deep allegiance to the history of Christianity, which only today is being uncovered. In the very long term, France is not republican, it is Christian. France is 'the garden of Christ' but also the 'garden of the Virgin', the promised land and the holy land of the new covenant with God. Well before the era of republican ideology, which considered itself the creator of national unity, Clovis – archetype of the Most Christian King, like Saint Louis, Philip the Fair or Charles V – prescribed the 'birth of the nation France' as that of a community which found in Catholicism the basis of its identity.[89] For a long time, the myth of the origin of the nation was bound up with Catholicism and, as people realize increasingly today, the republican idea appears as a late and eminently fragile political formula in a country where the collective consciousness has always been fashioned by the belief in a privileged relationship with Christ, at the level of everyday life, and of holidays, traditions and even more of the sacred nature of the king. The memory of France, its most significant cultural heritage, is inscribed in religious–political representations and places of belief, such as the monasteries and cathedrals scattered throughout the land.[90] Even more importantly, the state itself, now perceived as universalist so naturally does it appear to be cast in the republican mould, was in fact for a long time charged with Christian symbolism.[91]

When we look today at the period of republican synthesis, in order to examine the innovative nature of political anti-Semitism, we must have a sharper awareness of the actual substructures of national identity. It is as though only a detour via the 'long term' can put the birth of the Republic into perspective and make its contradictions more apparent.[92] Until not so very long ago in 'the very Christian kingdom . . . where neither Jew nor pagan lived', the king's blue blood formed the nation into a 'racial community', in a religious context where anti-Semitism and xenophobia were a corollary of the purity of the faith.[93] In those days at least, things were clear: the Jews were consigned to their ghettos; even their clothing was marked. They were frequently expelled and had to pay dearly to return. They were persecuted and attacked both in their persons and their possessions, heavily and arbitrarily taxed, accused of ritual murder. They were targets of incessant violence and often sent into exile.[94] This complete exclusion from the national body disappeared with the advent of the Republic. This indicates just how closely the fate of the Jews in France was connected with the fate of the republican regime. It thereby touches on the essential point: the enemies of the Republic would be equally the enemies of the Jews, whom only the Republic had been able to transform into citizens. On leaving the ghetto the French Jews entered the Republic: their fate was therefore definitively linked to that of the republican state, sharing its emancipating ideal which assured them of both freedom and citizenship. They were 'insiders' espousing the structures of a strong state, and their fate in France henceforth seemed to be more bound up with the nature of their integration into the state than with their social integration. Loud in their praise of the state, they would share its fate, and the end of the republican state would coincide with their own tragedy. Perfect political scapegoats[95] for all who hated their guts, their expulsion from the state symbolized for their enemies the end of the reviled republican synthesis. With the outbreak of the most extreme anti-Semitism that Léon Blum's presence as leader of the Popular Front movement aroused, Charles Maurras, the fiercest enemy of the Republic, took care to warn the Jews: from now on 'one thing is dead: it is the spirit of demi-tolerance accorded the Jewish State since the war. I say: the Jewish State . . . A formidable *à bas les juifs* smoulders in every breast and will pour forth from every heart.'[96] From Léon Blum to Pierre Mendès France, the new political anti-Semitism could now enjoy free rein in seeking to sweep away the republican state.

Introduction 21

NOTES

1 See Guy Chapman, *The Dreyfus Trials* (B. T. Batsford, London, 1972), p. 219; and Michael Burns, 'Qui ça, Dreyfus? The Affair in rural France', *Historical Reflections*, 5 Jan. 1978.
2 Quoted by Stephen Wilson, *Ideology and Experience: Antisemitism in France at the time of the Dreyfus Affair* (Associated University Press, London, 1982), p. 12.
3 Ibid., ch. 3.
4 See the *Bulletin du Comité de Vigilance*, Bibliothèque de l'Alliance Israélite Universelle (BAIU), 21 July 1938, no. 7.
5 See *Bulletin d'information interne du CRIF*, BAIU, 13 February 1956.
6 Eugen Weber, 'L'hexagone', in Pierre Nora (ed.), *Les Lieux de Mémoire* (Gallimard, Paris, 1986), vol. 2, p. 110.
7 Eugen Weber, 'Reflections on the Jews in France', in Frances Malino and Bernard Wasserstein (eds), *The Jews in Modern France* (Brandeis University Press, London, 1985), pp. 8 and 16.
8 See the debate which broke out around Zeev Sternhell's book, *Ni droite ni gauche: l'idéologie fasciste en France* (Le Seuil, Paris, 1983; reprinted, revised and enlarged, Complexe, Brussels, 1987); and especially Michel Winock, 'Fascisme à la française ou fascisme introuvable?', *Le Débat*, May 1983; Shlomo Sand, 'L'idéologie fasciste en France', *Ésprit*, Aug.–Sept. 1984; Jacques Julliard, 'Sur un fascisme imaginaire', *Annales*, July–Aug. 1984; Zeev Sternhell, 'Sur le fascisme et sa variante française', *Le Débat*, Nov. 1984; Antonio Costa Pinto, 'Fascist ideology revisited: Zeev Sternhell and his critics', *European Historical Quarterly*, no. 4, Oct. 1986. One can also consult the older work by Philippe Machefer, *Ligues et fascismes en France (1919–1939)* (PUF, Paris, 1974); and also J. Plumyène and R. Lasierra, *Les fascismes français, 1923–1963* (Le Seuil, Paris, 1963). Very recent is P. Milza, *Fascisme français: passé et présent* (Flammarion, Paris, 1987).
9 See, for example, Jeanne Verdès-Leroux, *Scandales financiers et antisémitisme catholique: Le krach de l'Union nationale* (Le Centurion, Paris, 1969); and Pierre Pierrard, *Juifs et catholiques français* (Fayard, Paris, 1970).
10 See Robert Byrnes, *Anti-Semitism in Modern France* (Rutgers University Press, New Brunswick, N.J., 1950); Wilson, *Ideology and Experience*; Paul Kingston, *Antisemitism in France during the 1930s: Organisations, personalities and propaganda* (University of Hull Press, Hull, 1983); Michael Marrus and Robert Paxton, *Vichy France and the Jews* (Basic Books, New York, 1981); Frederick Busi, *The Pope of Antisemitism: The career and legacy of Edouard Drumont* (University Press of America, NewYork, 1986).
11 George Mosse, *Masses and Man: Nationalist and fascist perceptions of reality* (Howard Fertig, New York, 1980), p. 189.
12 See, for example, the classic work by René Rémond, *La Droite en France, de la Première Restauration à la 5ᵉ République* (Aubier, Paris, 1963).
13 Philippe Burin, *La Dérive fasciste: Doriot, Déat, Bergery, 1933–1945* (Le Seuil, Paris, 1986), pp. 25–6.
14 Serge Berstein, 'L'affrontement simulé des années 1930', *Vingtième Siècle*, no. 5 (Jan.–March 1985), pp. 52–3.
15 Sternhell, *Ni droite ni gauche*, Le Seuil edition, p. 293.
16 Ibid., pp. 28–9.
17 Zeev Sternhell, 'The roots of popular anti-Semitism in the Third Republic', in Malino and Wasserstein, *Jews in Modern France*, p. 121.
18 See Bernard-Henri Lévy, *L'Idéologie française*, (Grasset, Paris, 1981).
19 Michel Winock, 'Les Affaires Dreyfus', *Vingtième Siècle*, no. 5 (Jan.–March 1985), p. 20; Simon

Epstein, *L'Antisémitisme français aujourd'hui et demain* (Belfond, Paris, 1984), sees a permanent quality in the structure and manifestation of anti-Semitism in France, independent of the manifold changes in society.
20 René Girard, *Le Bouc Émissaire* (Le Livre de Poche, Paris, 1986), p. 66.
21 Pierre Birnbaum, *Le Peuple et les gros: Histoire d'un mythe* (Grasset, Paris, 1979).
22 Hannah Arendt, *The Jew as Pariah* (Grove Press, New York, 1978).
23 Everett Stonequist, 'The marginal character of the Jew' (1942), in I. Graeber and S. Britt (eds), *Jews in a Gentile World* (Greenwood Press, Westport, Conn., 1979).
24 Jacob Katz, *Out of the Ghetto: The social background of Jewish emancipation, 1770–1870* (Harvard University Press, Cambridge, Mass., 1973).
25 Jacob Katz, *From Prejudice to Destruction: Antisemitism, 1700–1933* (Harvard University Press, Cambridge, Mass., 1980), p. 320.
26 James Parkes, *Antisemitism* (Quadrangle Books, Chicago, Ill., 1963), ch. 3.
27 Léon Poliakov, *The History of Antisemitism*, vol. 3: *From Voltaire to Wagner* (Littman Library, London, 1975), p. 338.
28 Joshua Trachtenberg, *The Devil and the Jews* (1943; Meridian Books, Cleveland, Ohio, 1961).
29 Charles Tilly (ed.), *The Formation of National States in Western Europe* (Princeton University Press, Princeton, N.J., 1975); Bertrand Badie and Pierre Birnbaum, *Sociology of the State* (University of Chicago Press, Chicago, 1982); Peter Evans, Dietrich Rueschemeyer and Theda Skocpol, *Bringing the State Back In* (Cambridge University Press, Cambridge, 1985).
30 Pierre Birnbaum, *La Logique de l'État* (Fayard, Paris, 1982).
31 Hannah Arendt, *Sur l'antisémitisme* (Calmann-Lévy, Paris, 1973).
32 Ibid., p. 214.
33 Ibid., p. 48.
34 Ibid., p. 217.
35 Pierre Birnbaum, 'La modernisation étatique des juifs', *Traces*, 1986.
36 Claude Lefort, 'Hannah Arendt et le totalitarianisme', in *L'Allemagne nazie et le génocide juif* (Gallimard, Le Seuil, Paris, 1985), p. 527.
37 Byrnes, *Antisemitism in Modern France*.
38 John Higham, *Send These to Me* (Johns Hopkins University Press, Baltimore, Md., 1984), p. 95.
39 See David Gerber (ed.), *Anti-Semitism in American History* (University of Illinois Press, Urbana, Ill., 1986), p. 27.
40 Michael Doblowski, *The Tarnished Dream: The basis of American anti-Semitism* (Greenwood Press, Westport, Conn., 1979), ch. 1.
41 Richard Zweigenhaft and G. William Domhoff, *Jews in the Protestant Establishment* (Praeger, New York, 1982); Seymour Martin Lipset, 'The American Jewish community in a comparative context', in Peter Rose (ed.), *The Ghetto and Beyond* (Random House, New York, 1969).
42 Rudolf Glanz, 'The Rothschild legend in America', *Jewish Social Studies*, Jan. 1957. By the same author, *The Jew in Early American Wit and Graphic Humor* (Ktav Publishing House, New York, 1973). Norton Stern and William Kramer, 'Anti-Semitism and the Jewish image in the early West', *Western State Jewish Historical Quarterly*, Jan. 1974; Harold Quinley and Charles Glock, *Anti-Semitism in America* (Free Press, New York, 1979); John Appel, 'Jews in American caricature: 1820–1914', *American Jewish History*, Sept. 1981.
43 John Higham, 'American anti-Semitism historically reconsidered', in Charles Stember, *Jews in the American Mind* (Basic Books, New York, 1966).
44 Higham, *Send These to Me*, p. 113. On the other hand, they received a much more favourable reception in Catholic Quebec. See Michael Brown, *Jew or Juif: Jews, French Canadians and Anglo-Canadians, 1759–1914* (Jewish Publication Society, Philadelphia, Pa., 1986), pp. 134–6.

Hence the appearance of an anti-Dreyfus movement in Quebec which benefited from a widely disseminated press.
45 John Higham, *Strangers in the Land* (Atheneum, New York, 1972), pp. 282ff.
46 Robert Singerman, 'The American career of the *Protocols of the Elders of Zion*', *American Jewish History*, Sept. 1981.
47 Dennis Wrong, 'The rise and decline of anti-Semitism in America', in Rose, *The Ghetto and Beyond*, p. 328.
48 Colin Holmes, *Anti-Semitism in British Society, 1876–1939* (Edward Arnold, London, 1979), pp. 233–4.
49 See, for example, M. C. Salbstein, *The Emancipation of the Jews in Britain* (Associated University Press, London, 1982).
50 Claire Hirshfeld, 'The British Left and the "Jewish Conspiracy": a case study of modern anti-Semitism', *Jewish Social Studies*, Summer 1981.
51 Gisela Lebzelter, *Political Anti-Semitism in England, 1918–1939* (Macmillan, London, 1978), p. 173.
52 Geoffrey Field, 'A review of recent research on anti-Semitism in England', New York, 1982, unpublished article.
53 Abraham Gilam, 'Anglo-Jewish attitudes towards Benjamin Disraeli during the era of emancipation', *Jewish Social Studies*, Winter 1980.
54 Quoted by Holmes, *Anti-Semitism in British Society*, p. 146.
55 There is a vast literature on this subject; here, we shall only mention the most recent interpretation, by David Blackbourn and Geoff Eley, *The Peculiarities of German History: Bourgeois Society and Politics in Nineteenth Century Germany* (Oxford University Press, Oxford, 1984).
56 Moshe Zimmermann, *Wilhelm Marr: The Patriarch of Anti-Semitism* (Oxford University Press, Oxford, 1986).
57 P. G. Pulzer, *The Rise of Political Anti-Semitism in Germany and Austria* (John Wiley, London, 1964).
58 Werner T. Angress, 'Prussia's Army and the Jewish reserve officer controversy before World War I', *Leo Baeck Year Book*, no. 17, 1972.
59 There is a monumental body of literature on this crucial subject. We shall only mention the books by Ernest Hamburger, *Juden im öffentlichen Leben Deutschlands* (J. C. B. Mohr, Tübingen, 1968); Reinhard Rürup, *Emanzipation und Antisemitismus* (Vandenhock & Ruprech, Göttingen, 1975); Werner Mosse (ed.), *Juden in Wilhelminischen Deutschland, 1890–1914* (J. C. B. Mohr, Tübingen, 1976); and lastly, the *Leo Baeck Year Book*, no. 31, 1986, entitled 'From the Wilhelminian Era to the Third Reich'.
60 See Carl Cohen, 'The road to conversion', *Leo Baeck Year Book*, no. 6, 1961.
61 See Robert Wistrich, *Socialism and the Jews: The Dilemmas of Assimilation in Germany and Austria-Hungary* (Associated University Press, London, 1982), ch. 3.
62 George Mosse, *The Crisis of German Ideology* (Universal Library, Grosset and Dunlap, New York, 1964); Fritz Stern, *The Politics of Cultural Despair: A Study in the Rise of the German Ideology* (University of California Press, Berkeley, Cal., 1961); Shulamit Volkov, 'Antisemitism as a cultural code: reflections on the history and historiography of antisemitism in Imperial Germany', *Leo Baeck Year Book*, no. 23, 1978.
63 Galit Hasan-Rokem and Alan Dindes (eds), *The Wandering Jew: Essays in the Interpretation of a Christian Legend* (Indiana University Press, Bloomington, Ind., 1986).
64 Paul Mendès-Flohr, '*Fin-de-siècle* orientalism, the *Ostjuden* and the aesthetics of Jewish self-affirmation', in Jonathan Frankel (ed.), *Studies in Contemporary Jewry* (Indiana University

Press, Bloomington, Ind., 1984). See the large book by H. Mayer, *Outsiders* (Cambridge, Mass., 1982).
65 Jehuda Reinharz, *Fatherland or Promised Land: The dilemma of the German Jew, 1893–1914* (University of Michigan Press, Ann Arbor, Mich., 1975).
66 George Mosse, *Nationalism and Sexuality: Respectability and abnormal sexuality in modern Europe* (Howard Fertig, New York, 1985).
67 Walter Rathenau, 'Hear, O Israel!', in P. Mendès-Flohr and J. Reinhard, *The Jew in the Modern World* (Oxford University Press, New York, 1980), p. 232.
68 Donald Niewyk, *The Jews in Weimar Germany* (Manchester University Press, Manchester, 1980).
69 Otto Weininger, *Geschlecht und Charakter* (Wilhelm Braumüller, Vienna and Leipzig, 23rd edn, 1922), pp. 407 and 441.
70 See the superb book by Sander Gilman, *Jewish Self-Hatred: Anti-Semitism and the hidden language of the Jews* (Johns Hopkins University Press, Baltimore, Md., 1986).
71 Todd Endelman, 'Conversion as a response to anti-Semitism in modern Jewish history', in Jehuda Reinharz (ed.), *Living with Anti-Semitism: Modern Jewish responses* (University Press of New England, Hanover, N. H., 1987).
72 Peter Gay, *Weimar Culture: The outsider as insider* (Penguin Books, Harmondsworth, Middx, 1974). See also, Steven Aschheim, 'The myth of "Judaization" in Germany', in Jehuda Reinharz and Walter Schatzberg (eds), *The Jewish Response to German Culture* (University Press of New England, Hanover, N.H., 1985).
73 See Pierre Birnbaum, *Dimensions du pouvoir* (PUF, Paris, 1984), ch. 9.
74 See, for example, Stein Rokkan, 'Un modèle géo-économique de quelques sources de variations en Europe de l'Ouest', *Communications*, 45 (1987).
75 See Badie and Birnbaum, *Sociology of the State*; and Jean Leca, 'Individualisme et citoyenneté', in P. Birnbaum and Jean Leca (eds), *On Individualism* (Oxford University Press, Oxford, 1990).
76 Claude Nicolet, *L'idée républicaine en France* (Gallimard, Paris, 1982), pp. 398 and 459.
77 Ibid., p. 484. See also Guy Hermet, *Sociologie de la construction démocratique* (Economica, Paris, 1986), ch. 1.
78 Odile Rudelle, *La République absolue, 1870–1889* (Publications de la Sorbonne, Paris, 1986), pp. 282–3.
79 See Jacques Ozouf, *Nous les maîtres d'école* (Julliard, Paris, 1967).
80 Alexis de Tocqueville, *L'Ancien Régime et la Révolution* (Gallimard, Paris, 1952), vol. 1, p. 122.
81 Pierre Birnbaum, *The Heights of Power* (University of Chicago Press, Chicago, 1981); Christophe Charle, *Les Élites de la République* (Fayard, Paris, 1987), challenges the thesis of the separation of power.
82 Quoted in Michael R. Marrus, *The Politics of Assimilation: A Study of the French Jewish Community at the Time of the Dreyfus Affair* (Clarendon Press, Oxford, 1971), p. 91.
83 Paula Hyman, *From Dreyfus to Vichy: The Remaking of French Jewry, 1906–1939* (Columbia University Press, New York, 1979), ch. 2.
84 Eugen Weber, 'Un demi-siècle de glissement à droite', *International Review of Social History*, 1960, vol. 5 (1960).
85 Jean Touchard, 'L'esprit des années trente', in *Tendances politiques dans la vie française depuis 1789* (Hachette, Paris, 1960); J.-L. Loubet del Bayle, *Les Non-conformistes des années trente* (Le Seuil, Paris, 1969); Sternhell, *Ni droite ni gauche*.
86 Michael Marrus, 'Vichy before Vichy: antisemitic currents in France during the 1930s', *Bulletin of the Wiener Library*, vol. 33 (1980). See also, Kingston, *Anti-Semitism in France during the 1930s*.

87 The only other example of an unconverted Jew gaining power in a modern European state seems to be Luigi Luzzatti in Italy in 1910.
88 Hannah Arendt, *Condition de l'homme moderne* (Calmann-Lévy, Paris, 1983); Jürgen Habermas, *L'Espace publique* (Payot, Paris, 1978).
89 Colette Beaune, *Naissance de la nation France* (Gallimard, Paris, 1985).
90 See Pierre Nora (ed.), *Les Lieux de mémoire*, vol. II: *La Nation*, Part I (Gallimard, Paris, 1986).
91 See, for example, Anne-Marie Lecoq, 'La symbolique de l'État', in ibid.
92 Fernand Braudel, *L'Identité de la France* (Arthaud-Flammarion, Paris, 1986), vols 1 and 2.
93 Beaune, *Naissance de la nation France*, pp. 212–17 and 337.
94 Bernard Blumenkranz (ed.), *Histoire des juifs de France* (Privat, Toulouse, 1972).
95 It is therefore important to remember this specifically political use of the scapegoat which otherwise assumes a far too general character. On this, see Yves Chevalier, *Le Juif, bouc émissaire*, doctoral thesis, University of Paris V, 1986. The comparative sociology of anti-Semitism is thus separate from the history of ideas.
96 *L'Action française*, 3 March 1936.

Part I
The Fate of Franco-Judaism

Introduction
From Court Jews to State Jews

In both France and Germany at the beginning of the nineteenth century most of the Jews who had hauled themselves up the social ladder and shed their status as pariahs had done so through economic success. To adopt Hannah Arendt's typology, some of them looked like parvenus and in themselves embodied the image of the dominating Jew. From the Rothschilds to the Pereire brothers, from the Worms to the Foulds, the bankers gave rise to the myth of Jewish domination which would be engraved in the deepest level of collective consciousness for a long time to come. From the Restoration to the Second Empire, the sphere of high finance into which they integrated without undue difficulty was involved with the highest levels of political power. It advised princes, gradually replaced the old landed aristocracy and in return aroused immense animosity. From Toussenel to Pierre Leroux and, later, Drumont, this animosity hung heavily and fundamentally over their heads. Taken individually, the rich were already the Jewish bankers, with Rothschild as their archetype. From then on, economic anti-Semitism moved forward in leaps and bounds in modern France on both the Left and the Right. The wealthy banker, close to the seat of power, replaced the usurer of the Middle Ages in popular imagery influenced by innumerable inflammatory lampoons. In a centralized France, the court Jew, lording it in urban salons thronged with aristocrats who were themselves ready to strike up any sort of alliance, gradually overtook the rural Jew in anti-Semitic mythology. The denunciation of King Rothschild, of the rich, of the two hundred families or of stateless trusts threatening small-scale Poujadist merchants, were all evidence of the many facets of contemporary economic anti-Semitism, which originated in the rejection of court Jews.[1]

Perceived as court Jews – though only a few of them actually were – the Jews of France as a whole seem much more like loyal state Jews. Note the gulf between a man like Crémieux and someone like Bleichröder: the first was elected deputy as early as 1842 and became a minister of the Second Republic and a member of the provisional government in 1870; the second was Bismarck's banker and confidant, ennobled by the Emperor in 1872 'by the grace of God'.[2] One pursued the universalist ideal of the Republic and extended egalitarian emancipation to the Jews of Algeria. The other, outside the State, put his financial power at the personal service of Bismarck surreptitiously. In one case, power had an institutional and legitimate basis; in the other, it rested on a fragile personal and almost entirely illegal connection.

The difference lies in the fact that in France, since the Revolution, the Jews had become citizens. Since the last surviving discrimination, the '*more judaico*' oath, was abolished in 1846 they were identical to everyone else in every way. By law they possessed all the advantages of a citizenship which, on the other hand, continually diminished all the peripheral relationships of culture, language, common law and specific dialogue, as has already been mentioned. For the moment I simply wish to recall the logic inherent in this type of emancipation, using a few texts which are basic to our thesis.

On 26 August 1789 the Parisian Jews addressed the Assembly: 'We demand', they said, 'to be subject like all Frenchmen, to the same jurisprudence, the same police, the same courts, and we consequently renounce for the public good and for our own benefit, always subordinated to the general interest, the privilege which we were granted of having particular leaders drawn from our ranks and appointed by the government.' This desire for total integration in the structures of a strong state which was also the vehicle of the sole universalist legitimacy, closely foreshadowed the famous speech by the Comte de Clermont-Tonnerre which laid the foundations of the Jews' integration in the state. What the Comte maintained, in fact, was that 'everything must be denied the Jews as a nation and everything granted to the Jews as individuals: . . . they must no longer form either a political body, or an order in the State; they must be citizens individually. It is repugnant that there should be a society of non-citizens in a State, and a nation within the nation.' Emancipation took place on 27 September 1791. Granting their accession to the dignity of French citizenship, the National Assembly 'revoked all arguments, reservations, exceptions inserted in preceding decrees relating to Jewish individuals who take the civic oath, which will be regarded as a renunciation of all privileges previously introduced in their favour'.[3]

A few years later the incorporation of French Jews into the state was stressed still further. In 1806 Napoleon summoned the Great Sanhedrin which bluntly declared: 'Everything obliges [the Israelite] not to isolate his interests in any way from the public interest, nor his own and his family's destiny from the destiny of the great family of the state. Submission to the laws of the State in civil and political matters is a religious duty'. Things were now clear: the total integration into the state inherent in the model of the strong, secular state based on administrative law and the civil code, implied in return the complete disappearance of Jewish particularism and also of all other forms of non-universalist adherence. Now at last 'French Judaism took the form of a civil–religious appendix of the state in both fact and law'.[4]

French historiography has been severely critical of this integration into the state which submerged Jewish particularism. It was, it was claimed, a swindle: access to citizenship in a society which remained Christian severed the roots of all specific Jewish life.[5] In the framework of integration inherent in the strong type of state, it was in effect a zero-sum game. What was taken away from particularism was entrusted to a state which only recognized individual citizens, and denied all legitimacy to associations, intermediary groups, corporations or, later, political parties and pressure groups. The state claimed to be the sole instrument of legitimacy and, in return for its protection or the public order which it was its duty to maintain on a basis of equality, the citizens owed it total allegiance. In this sense, the incorporation of the Jews into the state formed part of a general process which affected all cultural, ethnic and social minorities. In France the bond between the state and its citizens took priority over all other ties.

A fine article by Jacob Katz shows how the formula of rejection of a state within the state was first applied in France to the Protestants and the Jesuits before Voltaire or even the Constituents used it apropos the Jews. It was also employed in Germany by Fichte and others, but in that case what was involved was the rejection of a Jewish nation or state within a society or state which remained Christian. In France, on the other hand, the denial of Jewish particularism took place within a state which untiringly affirmed its secular character even if the society remained largely Christian in its values and mode of organization.[6] Moreover, the use of this sort of formula could be found in such disparate societies as Great Britain and Russia, where again it assumed very different significance. What must be remembered for the moment is that in France – a society where the state came closest to the ideal type of strong state – rejection of the existence of a state within the state flowed from a specific idea of representation: representation was entrusted solely to the state and was consequently incompatible with the maintenance of a significant degree of particularism.

To combat the presence of a nation within the nation, or of a state within a state, as did the Constituents, who created the most extreme universalist mode of Jewish emancipation, also involved at that period adherence to a rationalist and progressive vision of the world. This envisaged liberating individuals from the influence of the many groups which could exert immense control over them, and restricting to the private sphere the hold exercised by religion. In public life, the Jews appeared merely as ordinary citizens equal with all the rest, enjoying the same rights and constrained by the same obligations. The republican ideal by definition emphatically turned its back on anti-Semitism[7] since it finally allowed the integration of the Jews in the state. Those who later professed hatred of the Jews yearned therefore for an end to the republican

State and the return of the dominant Christian particularism. Yet this same ideal founded Franco-Judaism, the herald of complete emancipation, which in return was long regarded as the cause of a seemingly inexorable decline in Jewish life and culture.

Franco-Judaism triumphed in the nineteenth century: suffice it to quote a few of its most famous expressions. For Léon Halévy, 'It is necessary, in a word, that for them the name of Jew become accessory, and the name of Frenchman principal.' Similarly, according to H. Prague, the influential editor-in-chief of the *Archives israélites*, 'The Jews, since they have ceased to be treated as pariahs, must cease to be a dispersed nation, and henceforth be considered only a religious denomination.' The historian Darmesteter presented a more theoretical interpretation at the end of the nineteenth century: Franco-Judaism, he claimed, led to a sort of general humanism resulting from the teaching of the prophets. Joseph Reinach remained loyal to it. Faced with the dual challenge of the virulent anti-Semitism which erupted at the time of the Dreyfus Affair and the Zionism which responded to it with a return to particularism, he declared: 'The French fatherland was given to the Jews by the Revolution – the anti-Semites will not take it away from them, and the Zionists of Basel will not determine any Jew to renounce it. We are French, and French we shall remain. All our efforts, all our intellectual activity, all our love, the last drop of our blood belongs to France, and to her alone.'[8]

Franco-Judaism, embodied by Durkheim and, later, by the historian Marc Bloch, when he was shot during the Second World War, remained the ideology in which most French Jews recognized themselves – until the shock of Vichy and the betrayal of the emancipating state. The French Jews pursued to its logical conclusion a concept which involved relinquishing all attachment to a Jewish nation in favour of a single attachment to citizenship of the state. They had become state Jews through the medium of Franco-Judaism. According to Hannah Arendt and Michael Marrus, they had long since abandoned all Jewish life and only resumed their particularism in the contemporary period when they gradually rejected the universalist vision of Franco-Judaism.[9] This accusation is challenged today. Some commentators emphasize that French Jews preserved their ethnic identity despite Franco-Judaism and, on several occasions, demonstrated real Jewish solidarity beyond the Hexagon. In this sense, integration into the State, however total, did not involve complete acculturation.[10] Moreover, this revised view of the consequences of Franco-Judaism is compatible with recent work which attempts to show that in the modern period the modernization of the Jews resulting from industrialization and the change in type of employment, or from urbanization and the change in where they lived, did not really destroy their ethnic solidarity.[11] This viewpoint, consistent with the more general reinterpretations found in developmental theories,[12] takes all its applied meaning from the purely political domain. It is now a question of enriching this debate by examining the attitudes of those most famous state

Jews, Léon Blum and Pierre Mendès France, often making use of the original material available.

NOTES

1 Pierre Birnbaum, *Le Peuple et les gros: Histoire d'un mythe* (Grasset, Paris, 1979).
2 Fritz Stern, *Gold and Iron: Bismarck, Bleichröder and the building of the German Empire* (Allen & Unwin, London, 1977), p. 167.
3 These texts are quoted in Beatrice Philippe, *Être juif dans la société française* (Éditions Pluriel, Paris, 1979), ch. 4. See also, David Feuerwerker, *L'Émancipation des juifs en France, de l'Ancien Régime à la fin du second Empire* (Albin Michel, Paris, 1976), ch. 2; and Patrick Girard, *Les Juifs de France de 1789 à 1860* (Calmann-Lévy, Paris, 1976).
4 Éric Smilévitch, 'Halakha et code civil: questions sur le Grand Sanhédrin de Napoléon', *Pardès*, 3 (1986), p. 23.
5 On this debate, see François Delpech, 'Les juifs en France, 1780–1840', in Bernard Blumenkrantz and Albert Soboul, *Les Juifs et la Révolution française* (Privat, Toulouse, 1976). More recently, Shmuel Trigano, *La République et les juifs* (Les Presses d'aujourd'hui, Paris, 1982).
6 Jacob Katz, 'A state within a state: The history of an antisemitic slogan', in J. Katz, *Emancipation and Assimilation: Studies in modern history* (Gregg International Publications, Farnborough, Hants., 1972; see also, Arthur Herzberg, *The French Enlightenment and the Jews* (New York, 1968).
7 For S. Trigano, on the other hand, 'French and European antisemitism in the nineteenth and then in the twentieth century, had its [secret] sources in the eighteenth century revolutionary republican myth, in the very principle of the Declaration of the Rights of Man and of the citizen; I would add: despite itself.... Antisemitism soiled its hands, something the Republic never did, but which it made possible, abstractly and in principle', in *La République et les Juifs*.
8 These three texts are quoted in Michael Marrus, *The Politics of Assimilation: A study of the French Jewish community at the time of the Dreyfus Affair* (Clarendon Press, Oxford, 1971), pp. 90, 94 and 276.
9 See, for example, Patrick Girard, 'Les petits-neveux du Grand Sanhédrin', and Shmuel Trigano, 'La statue de Napoléon est renversée', in *L'Arche*, June 1980.
10 See, for example, Phyllis Cohen Albert, 'Ethnicité et solidarité chez les Juifs de France au XIXe siècle', *Pardès*, 3, 1986.
11 Calvin Goldscheider and Alan Zuckerman, *The Transformation of the Jews* (University of Chicago Press, Chicago, Ill., 1984).
12 Bertrand Badie, *La Développement politique* (Economica, Paris, 1978).

1
Between State, Republic and Socialism

While remaining true to their common Jewish origins, both Léon Blum and Pierre Mendès France personified on several occasions the legitimacy of the republican State. Both, for more reason than one, were in their own persons living proof of the reality of Franco-Judaism. However, although they both adhered to the republican ideal and justified their actions by an almost eschatological vision of citizenship, they diverged on a number of *a priori* judgements in ethics and politics, so much so that in January 1946, when they held different opinions on the need to resort to the decree laws condemned by Léon Blum, Mendès France noted: 'I think I detect that he regrets certain severe remarks I made on the demagogy of the parties, the mediocrity of the Assembly.... my remarks must have seemed undemocratic and unparliamentary to him.'[1] Léon Blum was a senior civil servant in the republican state, but he also wanted to be the man of democratic socialism, the guardian of all pluralism. Pierre Mendès France was a lawyer, from a professionalized political background, but none the less he compiled for himself an entirely Jacobin moral code of the general interest, represented above all by the state. Although they argued in similar universalist terms and based their authority on an exemplary citizenship, one was inspired by a prophetic tradition leading to socialism; the other turned more towards reason.

A LONG WAY FROM MARX?

Since the end of the nineteenth century, Jews in many countries have confused their own emancipation with the emancipation of mankind as a whole by blindly enrolling in the socialist ranks. In Eastern Europe, but also in Germany and the Austro-Hungarian Empire, they were often in the forefront of the revolutionary movement inspired by Marxism, aiming to regenerate the world by abolishing the unjust class relationship. The social emancipation they sought as the sole form of assimilation drove them to reject violently any form of cultural particularism by denying their former Jewish identity. Many 'non-Jewish Jews'[2] who emerged in East and Central Europe claimed Marxism as the justification for ending their own history. Marxism was far from being solely the sublimation of Jewish messianism. It was its final negation both theoretically and in almost all its historical applications which, in the last analysis, imposed a return to particularism within the working-class movement.[3] In France, on the other hand, the Jews were always very cautious about a Marxism which threatened to divert them from the path of republican emancipation by introducing class conflict over and above common citizenship. They took this so far that at the turn of the century the Guesdist movement, on the basis of class logic, ranged itself in the anti-Dreyfusard camp.

This meant that the relationship with Marx and with the movement inspired by him was vital to the adherents of Franco-Judaism. But Léon Blum's attitude differed considerably from that of Pierre Mendès France. Blum may have followed in the tradition of Jaurès and rejected the Bolshevization of French socialism in 1920 as incompatible with maintaining the republican tradition created in 1789. He none the less stated as late as 1945, for example: 'We accept Marx's analysis of capitalist society in its entirety – the essential principles of Marxism remain.'[4] Pierre Mendès France, on the other hand, declared roundly: 'I am the first of the anti-Marxists.'[5] In 1952 he was lent some of Marx's books and 'read them without finding them very interesting'.[6] He can thus be regarded as 'a pre-Marxist man'.[7] Whereas Léon Blum turned towards socialism very early on, when he joined Jaurès in his struggle, it was not until 1959 that Pierre Mendès France adopted this viewpoint, inspired by 'the humanist tradition of Jaurès and Blum'.[8] He remained no less true to the radical 'Young Turk' he had been in the inter-war period, concerned much more with the general good than with the specific interest of the working class – to which Léon Blum ceaselessly proclaimed his 'attachment'.[9] After the Liberation, he considered that the communist ministers 'had acted like "Trojan horses", working exclusively for the communist party and not for the country',[10] and refused to count their votes in his majority when he formed his government in June 1954. Léon Blum, on the other hand, was 'convinced that it was impossible to defend republican liberties in France by excluding from the effort the working-class masses and the fraction of the working-class elite still grouped around the communist concept'.[11]

Unquestionably far removed from Marx but in accord with the emancipating vision of the French Revolution which also founded Franco-Judaism, Pierre Mendès France emphasized that 'true democracy is the intimate association, the fusion, of the state and the citizen'.[12] This method of managing society left very little room for political parties which were the vehicles of particularism and which acted through 'sectarianism' in the name of 'particular interests'. In this sense it was appropriate that the government should be 'neither that of a coterie nor that of a party, but the government of France'.[13] In Pierre Mendès France's political thought, the citizens recognized themselves in a republican state and not in a class relationship for which certain political parties became the spokesmen. Léon Blum preferred a theory of representation that implied the pre-eminence of parties in transmitting class action, to this image of a nation of citizens who were motivated by a concept of Reason directly descended from the Enlightenment. 'When one defines a socialist party', Blum said, 'as a class party, one actually means that that party practises class action. This means that its object is the conquest of political power in the name and by the means of the organized proletariat that it represents.'[14] Whereas Pierre Mendès France intended to change society through the medium of rational state action, Léon Blum gave a great deal of thought to reconciling Jaurès and Marx, the Republic and Marxism. Rejecting both Blanquism and Bolshevism for their denial of liberty, he formulated subtle distinctions between conquest, the exercise and the possession of power to make 'the revolutionary conquest of power' compatible with the survival of republican traditions[15] and resort to the dictatorship of the proletariat with the maintenance of democracy. 'Dictatorship by one party, yes; dictatorship by one class, yes; dictatorship by a few individuals, known or unknown, no . . . it must exalt the freedom of thought, freedom of assembly, freedom of discussion' of the proletariat as a whole and not of a small minority.[16] In a word, Léon Blum set himself the task of fulfilling his 'duty as a socialist, as a republican, and as a Frenchman', all at the same time,[17] whereas Pierre Mendès France appealed solely to the Jacobin tradition which brought him close, at least for a while, to General de Gaulle[18] with whom he shared a common vision of the pre-eminence of the state.

RESORT TO THE STRONG STATE

Léon Blum was a senior civil servant. He was a member of the Council of State, one of the most prestigious of the great state bodies. Starting with his entry into the *École normale supérieure*, he achieved his integration into the state through its most noble institutions. None the less, he remained sensitive to a messianic tradition shared by many Jews who also identified their destiny with the destiny of the labouring masses.

Paradoxically, Pierre Mendès France, the lawyer who had not been socialized for the state in one of its educational institutions where republican elitism ruled supreme, had greater faith in the 'sanctity' of the state.[19] This, as François Bloch-Lainé clearly states, 'made him a senior civil servant rather than a politician'.[20] It is therefore not surprising that careful study of Pierre Mendès France's writings reveals several references to this idea of the strong state, as expressed in the comparative sociology of states and freely applied to France. As early as 1928, in a text which formed his first major political article, he claimed outright: 'We too want a strong state, but a state which is above all the political, social, spiritual or economic organizations, an autonomous, liberated state, free of the sclerosis of specific interests which live off it by stifling it.'[21]

From this point of view, the institutionalization and differentiation of the state seemed to be preconditions for the pursuit of the general good, for the exercise of public service and also for the flowering of democracy. This in no way implied the advent of an authoritarian power providing legitimate cover for a 'Bonapartism of businessmen'.

Pierre Mendès France still continued to hammer out his own opinion in the inter-war period when the dangers of fascism were becoming more apparent. For him it was indispensable to favour 'the strong state over strong money'[22] because it alone kept democracy alive. This vision was so constant a theme that in 1954, for example, he explicitly established an equivalence between the strong state and the strong Republic. 'We must no longer resign ourselves to seeing the state torn apart, unravelled, dislocated by so many centrifugal forces ... the Republic demands to be great and strong again.'[23] This vital identification of state with Republic is rooted in the Jacobin revolutionary tradition of public safety through national mobilization, suppressing particularisms in the name of a positive cult of emancipating Reason, the vehicle of progress. Individuals are transformed into citizens, forgetting their social and cultural affiliations, wishing only to serve the public good. The author of *La République moderne* always showed himself to be an exemplary citizen in his personal conduct as deputy, minister and president of the Council, and also as prisoner and fighter. He himself adhered totally to the republican identity and he conceived his own actions in austerity, a quasi-asceticism, not acknowledging the existence in the public arena of the various particularisms.[24] Standing aloof too from ideologies, he was only concerned with the obligations inherent in civic duty. As Raymond Aron notes, he wanted simply to be 'a statesman'[25] who belonged to the line running from Gambetta to Clemenceau and, in certain respects, to General de Gaulle.[26]

It is therefore not at all surprising that Pierre Mendès France – a state Jew by destiny if not by function, who lauded public service, and who as a citizen was comparable to the hermits of Port-Royal[27] – was able to influence generations of civil servants to such an extent that they copied his virtues.[28] Later on, in the service of the state, these senior civil servants, imbued with a strong self-assertive rationalism, favourable to economic planning for example, had no qualms about joining Michel Debré's government which had set itself similar tasks.[29] The Mendès-ist political concept, therefore, was perfectly adapted to the type of strong state born from the remote past of French society.

Entirely different was the socialist viewpoint inherent in Léon Blum's school of thought. It showed more concern for the specific needs of certain groups in society, such as the working class, that his own party wished to defend. Hence, by comparison, a certain mistrust on the part of senior civil servants, particularly perhaps those wielding authority who were concerned to demonstrate the pre-eminence of the State, such as the prefects, and those involved in foreign affairs and the colonies.[30] The exercise of power in accordance with Léon Blum's doctrine thus came up against certain recalcitrant senior civil servants who were disturbed by the ideological proclamations which proliferated from the pens of the socialist leaders of the day, aiming to purge the upper levels of administration of the state. These proclamations were sometimes ill-adapted to the structures of a strong state whose main aim was functional.[31]

The fact was that Léon Blum, unlike Pierre Mendès France, began by adopting a socialist interpretation of the state, deprived at the same time of all legitimacy within capitalist society. He immediately attacked the idea of the strong state on the Jacobin or Napoleonic model, and the extreme centralization it implied. For him, 'it is not possible both to restore the historic type of state and to prepare the way for the new state which will no longer be an authoritarian power but the organ for the co-ordination and regulation of professional groups'.[32] He even went so far as explicitly to compare this idea of a strong state with the national socialism which the neo-socialist trend, led by Adrien Marquet, wished to plagiarize. In his eyes, wherever fascism prevailed, 'the Caesarist or Jacobin type of strong state was established'.[33] Having become a socialist, Blum saw in the state either the spectre of despotism or a power entirely dedicated to the ruling class.

Thus he moved away from the very different viewpoint that he had expressed in 1897, for example. At that period he maintained that 'it is in a centralized, unified, levelled nation that individuals are truly free. And the Montagnards of '93 had truly seen it in opposition to those Girondins with whom Barrès claims kinship.'[34] Hostile to that author's ideas on the primacy of rootedness in the land, Blum this time appealed to Reason which the revolutionary state employed. Later, he saw socialism as the best form of universalism, and this obliged him to change his assessment of both Jacobin power and the state itself. When he now maintained, in opposition to Pierre Mendès France, that it was 'the bourgeoisie considered as the ruling class or as the political expression of capitalism' which dominated French society and not a universalist Jacobin-type state, he was often attacking the body of civil servants perceived as being 'exclusively bourgeois in France'.[35]

Pierre Mendès France consequently subscribed more to a pure logic of the strong state. Léon Blum, on the other hand, after his adoption of socialism, wanted to ensure the pre-eminence of civil society by bringing the political parties into the state, which would thereby become 'democratic',[36] and abolish its discrimination at the same time. Mendès France wanted to ensure the pre-eminence of the unitarian, emancipating state, while Blum looked to Switzerland or the United States for appropriate models of federalism (which could include the parties) to limit the state's grip on society.[37] Except for the lowest common denominator formed by their identical adherence to the republic of citizens, which was extended by an unchanging struggle for complete secularism,[38] these two state Jews seemed to set out on divergent paths, one leading to the state, the other to society.

However, these differences must not be exaggerated. They indicate how much these two state Jews, despite a common destiny, adopted dissimilar values. Enemy of the strong state which reinforced the domination of the bourgeoisie, Léon Blum still came to the conclusion that 'the modern state progressively detaches itself from capitalism and that is why it is possible for the socialist parties to manipulate it without subjugating it and, with even greater reason, without themselves being subjugated by capitalism'.[39] After the Second World War he returned increasingly to a quasi-Jacobin concept of an emancipating state. He may have given a provocative answer to the AFP correspondent in Washington, 'But of course I remain a convinced Marxist, my friend',[40] yet his conversion to a non-instrumental vision of the state is glaringly obvious. 'Today', he said, 'capitalism no longer dominates the democratic state like a master; the working force has been formed and has grown continually; the two forces thus counterbalance and neutralize each other.'[41] Léon Blum rediscovered a sort of Bonapartist theory of the state, particularly well-adapted to the type of strong state built up in France. From the time of the absolute monarchy, the state had claimed to dictate to the various social forces from an external position. When it became republican, it enjoyed immense legitimacy and the loyalty of citizens, whatever their class origin.

Léon Blum thenceforth placed emphasis on the virtues of the welfare state, the protective state, 'Here we are', he said, 'pitched into full state socialism since, on all the evidence, the power of the state should be deployed to define, protect, guarantee the condition of the workers.'[42] At the same time, he rediscovered the Jacobin theories which attributed to the state a vital role in the achievement of public well-being. At other times, as government representative at the Council of State, he himself helped to strengthen these same theories. He demanded the extension of state responsibility when the famous Lemonnier judgment was given (26 November 1918), marking a decisive turning-point in jurisprudence on questions of misconduct by an official.[43]

All in all, Blum was a long way from the reductionist theories of the state. As a state Jew, he fits much better into the republican trend which, since Gambetta, wanted the state's apparatus to become ever stronger, public services extended, and absolute respect shown towards the protective legislation of the Council of State, the supreme authority watching over the general good.[44]

Pierre Mendès France, on the other hand, was a convinced supporter of a strong state. After a late conversion to socialism, he maintained in *La République moderne* that the ruling class 'impressed its own values on the state'.[45] Later, reverting to the vocabulary of the Popular Front which he himself did not use much at that time, he wrote that in our days, 'the Bastille to be taken is the state in its entirety, real, total power'.[46] All in all, 'the efficacy of the state must come from the mass as a whole'.[47] It could not flow from the actions of high officials who, under the Fifth Republic, ran the risk of developing 'into a caste, an oligarchy'.[48] And Pierre Mendès France himself postulated a turn towards self-administration or decentralized socialism, modes of organization hardly compatible with a logic appropriate to the strong state. The paths of Blum and

40 The Fate of Franco-Judaism

Mendès France could meet at that point because they both led to integration in the state and shared in the recurrence of concern for ethical matters.

NOTES

1 Pierre Mendès France, *Oeuvres complètes*, vol. 2 (Gallimard, Paris, 1985), p. 167.
2 Isaac Deutscher, *Essais sur le problème juif* (Payot, Paris, 1969).
3 Robert Wistrich, *Revolutionary Jews from Marx to Trotsky* (Harrap, London, 1976).
4 Léon Blum, 'Le socialisme maître de l'heure', in *L'Oeuvre de Léon Blum, 1945–1947* (Albin Michel, Paris, 1958), pp. 66–7. See also his 'Préface pour une nouvelle édition du "Manifeste communiste"', in *L'Oeuvre de Léon Blum, 1947–1950* (Albin Michel, Paris, 1963), pp. 431–5.
5 *L'Express*, 7 April 1960.
6 Interview, *Institut d'Histoire du temps présent* (IHTP), with Roger Stephane.
7 Interview, IHTP, with Simon Nora, 93. In an oral contribution at the colloquium organized by IHTP on Pierre Mendès France, in 1984, Gilles Martinet also considered that Mendès France was 'anti-communist because he did not acknowledge Marxism'. For this colloquium and the interviews organized by IHTP (CNRS), see François Bédarida and Jean-Pierre Rioux (eds), *Pierre Mendès France et le mendésisme* (Fayard, Paris, 1985).
8 Speech at the *Mutualité*, 14 October 1959, quoted in Daniel Salem, *Pierre Mendès France et le nouveau socialisme* (PUF, Paris, 1967), p. 15.
9 Léon Blum, 'La prison et le procès', in *L'Oeuvre de Léon Blum, 1940–1945* (Albin Michel, Paris, 1966), p. 313. 'I am a chauvinist in that respect: the French working class is probably the most intelligent of any people' (ibid., p. 452).
10 Pierre Mendès France, 'Gouverner, c'est choisir', in *Oeuvres complètes*, vol. 2 (Gallimard, Paris, 1986), p. 358.
11 Blum, 'La prison et le procès', p. 323. Similarly, in 1936 he confirmed that 'every time that the Republic has been threatened, it has been saved by that union of the Republican bourgeoisie and the people, the body of workers and peasants' (*L'Oeuvre de Léon Blum, 1934–1937* (Albin Michel, Paris, 1964), p. 282).
12 Pierre Mendès France, 'Discours à l'Assemblée nationale', 2 November 1955. Quoted in Salem, *Pierre Mendès France et le nouveau socialisme*, p. 94.
13 Mendès France, *Oeuvres complètes*, vol. 2, pp. 246 and 287.
14 *L'Oeuvre de Léon Blum, 1945–1947*, p. 275. In the same spirit, see p. 280.
15 Léon Blum, 'Le programme du Rassemblement populaire', in *L'Oeuvre de Léon Blum 1934–1937*, p. 192–6.
16 Léon Blum, 'Le Congrès de Tours', in *L'Oeuvre de Léon Blum, 1914–1928* (Albin Michel, Paris, 1972), pp. 155 and 247–51. On these distinctions, see Gilbert Ziebura, *Léon Blum et le Parti socialiste, 1872–1934* (A. Colin, Paris, 1967); and Gilbert Ziebura, 'Léon Blum à la veille de l'exercice du pouvoir', in Pierre Renouvin and René Rémond (eds), *Léon Blum, chef de gouvernement, 1936–1937* (Presses de la Fondation nationale des sciences politiques, Paris, 1981).
17 Léon Blum, 'Mémoires', in *L'Oeuvre de Léon Blum, 1940–1945*, p. 70.
18 Pierre Mendès France, 'De Gaulle', in *Oeuvres complètes*, vol. 2, pp. 155–7.
19 Interview by Jean Lacouture, IHTP, 60.
20 Interview with François Bloch-Lainé, IHTP, 283.
21 Pierre Mendès France, 'Restaurer l'État', in *Oeuvres complètes*, vol. 1 (Gallimard, Paris, 1984), p. 99.
22 Pierre Mendès France, 'L'État fort contre l'argent fort', in ibid., p. 104.

23 Pierre Mendès France, 'La République se veut grande et forte à nouveau', in *Oeuvres complètes*, vol. 3, pp. 409–10.
24 See Alain Pellet, *Une morale de la République: Pierre Mendès France et les institutions républicaines*, diploma in études supérieures, Institut d'études politiques, Paris, 1968; Claude Nicolet, 'Mendès France, le(s) mendésisme(s) et la tradition républicaine', in *Pouvoirs*, 27 (1983); and Odile Rudelle, 'Pierre Mendès France et l'identité républicaine', in Bédarida and Rioux (eds), *Pierre Mendès France et le mendésisme*.
25 Raymond Aron, interview, IHTP, 286.
26 François Goguel stresses the similarities between Gaullism and Mendés-ism, in interview, IHTP; Yves Canac also considers that they had a common conception of the state: interview, IHTP, and Léo Hamon likens Mendès France to Clemenceau, Gambetta and Waldeck-Rousseau, when emphasizing that he, like them and unlike the socialists, had 'the feel of the republican state': interview, IHTP, 561.
27 Jean Lacouture,'Pierre Mendès France: notes sur l'homme', in Bédarida and Rioux (eds), *Pierre Mendès France et le mendésisme*, p. 21.
28 See Bloch-Lainé, interview, IHTP, 55, 179; Nora, interview, IHTP, 112.
29 Michel Debré, interview, IHTP, 350.
30 See Renouvin and Rémond, *Léon Blum, chef de gouvernement, 1936–1937*, pp. 39 and 424.
31 See Irwin Wall, 'Socialists and bureaucrats: the Blum government and the French administration, 1936–1937', *International Review of Social History*, vol. 19 (1974). A similar ambiguity appeared later, in 1981, in response to the new experience of socialist change in contemporary France: see Pierre Birnbaum (ed.), *Les Élites socialistes au pouvoir, 1981–1985* (PUF, Paris, 1985).
32 Léon Blum, *L'Oeuvre de Léon Blum, 1928–1934* (Albin Michel, Paris, 1972), pp. 19 and 20.
33 Ibid., p. 565. In the same vein, he refused the reform of the state which Doumergue and Tardieu wanted because, for him, 'the state would cease to be a republic', *L'Oeuvre de Léon Blum, 1937–1940*, p. 424.
34 Léon Blum, 'Nouvelles conversations de Goethe avec Eckermann', in *L'Oeuvre de Léon Blum, 1891–1905* (1954), p. 220.
35 Léon Blum, 'À l'échelle humaine', in *L'Oeuvre de Léon Blum, 1940–1945*, pp. 449 and 437.
36 Blum, 'La prison et le procès', ibid., p. 381.
37 Blum, 'À l'échelle humaine', ibid., p. 469. On these differing approaches to the state, see Oliver Duhamel, *La Gauche et la Ve République* (PUF, Paris, 1980).
38 On Blum and secularism, see *L'Oeuvre de Léon Blum, 1914–1928*, pp. 26 and 211; see also, p. 35 in the *1934–1937* volume.
39 *L'Oeuvre de Léon Blum, 1945–1947*, p. 436.
40 Jean Davidson, *Ce que je n'ai jamais câblé* (Paris, 1954), p. 15.
41 Léon Blum, *Oeuvres complètes*, vol. 9, p. 57.
42 Ibid., vol. 7, p. 470.
43 P. Juvigny, 'Un grand commissaire du gouvernement: Léon Blum', in *Le Conseil d'État* (Livre jubilaire, Paris, 1952).
44 Léo Hamon, 'État, socialisme et pouvoir dans l'oeuvre de Léon Blum', in 'Jean Jaurès et Léon Blum', *Cahiers Léon Blum*, no. 11 (1982). See also Julien Lévy, *Responsabilité des fonctionnaires et idées d'État*, D.E.A. de sociologie politique, University of Paris 1, 1986.
45 Mendès France, *La République moderne*, p. 58.
46 *Tribune socialiste*, Feb. 1961.
47 Quoted by Salem, *Pierre Mendès France et le nouveau socialisme*, p. 135.
48 Mendès France, *La République moderne*, p. 206.

2
Israelite, Jew or Zionist?

A traditional presentation of Franco-Judaism makes a careful distinction between two categories of Jews. There are, first, the Israelites who accepted completely the conditions of emancipation which submerged particularisms and involved complete de-Judaization. Secondly, there are those who continue to see themselves as Jews both by observing religious practices and by performing a specific type of public activity. The French Israelites were assimilated. From the turn of the century they had kept aloof from the new immigrants from Eastern Europe who maintained their relationship with Judaism and strove to strengthen ethnic solidarity in the community.[1] The first group took pains to differentiate themselves from the second by continually seeking assimilation which, for example, separated them from the strong socialist or Zionist aspirations of the second.

In France at the beginning of the twentieth century the Israelites strongly rejected anything that struck a blow at consensus and reintroduced conflict or evidence of difference. They fought against both the doctrines of the class-struggle and the idea that the Jews had a specific destiny involving an inevitable return to Palestine. Both were conceived as attacks on the character of a unified citizenship. These Israelites were solely concerned with giving strong confirmation of their patriotism by strengthening their allegiance to the Republic and appearing as what we call state Jews. They deliberately turned their backs on Zionist doctrines and even took direct action, with the public authorities, for example, to limit their impact.[2]

BORN A JEW

Did those state Jews *par excellence*, Léon Blum and Pierre Mendès France, conform to this traditional image of the French Israelites? Some commentators, Albert Memmi for example, think that both 'tried to forget their Jewishness, in order the better to devote themselves to their electorate'.[3] In that case, what is

Israelite, Jew or Zionist? 43

the explanation of Léon Blum's public statement on 11 January 1923 in the Chamber of Deputies, a place which embodies significantly the most sovereign majesty of the emancipating Republic:

> I am a Jew ... That is a fact. You are not insulting me when you remind me that I belong to a Jewish race, that race I have never denied, and I have only feelings of gratitude and pride towards it.[4]

And what caused him to add even more explicitly:

> I was born in France, I was brought up as a Frenchman in French schools. My friends are French ... I have a perfect command of the French language without the slightest trace of a foreign accent. Even my features have none of the characteristics of my race of origin. I have the right to consider myself perfectly assimilated ... And yet, none the less I feel that I am a Jew. And I have never felt the slightest contradiction, the slightest conflict between these two areas of my consciousness.[5]

There are in fact innumerable quotations which confirm his complete lack of self-hatred as well as his constant hostility to the Israelites who clung to an unequivocal Franco-Judaism. At the LICA congress in December 1938, he again stated: 'I am a Jew, I am a Jew who has never flaunted his origins but who never blushed for it, a Jew who has always borne its name.'[6] And what made *Tribune juive*, the traditional organ of Alsatian Judaism, comment: 'Read this speech again. It expresses the thoughts of a man who loves his unhappy Jewish people'?[7] Léon Blum intended to remain loyal to his Jewish origins, and even expressed, albeit humorously, the desire to die a Jew. When he left the *École normale supérieure*, the young Blum, then aged 19, mockingly imagined the version of his life-story that Guy Perrot, director of the *École*, would pronounce over his grave. Perrot, telling of the funeral of his former pupil, would solemnly say: 'It is customary in the Jewish religion to which the deceased belonged ... '.[8] Born a Jew, Blum, emerging from adolescence, quite unambiguously envisaged dying in accordance with the faith of his ancestors.

But does Pierre Mendès France fit into the model of a Franco-Judaism which produced Israelites who were anxious to forget their origins as far as possible? We have already stressed his constant concern to adhere to the logic of the strong state. 'I am not religious, nor do I observe religious practices', he declared:

> On the other hand, I am deeply aware that I am Jewish and my children know it too. ... I remain intrigued and impressed by the fact of Jewishness. This is not a religious fact since there are a large number of men who do not have faith, do not practise the religion but who still feel Jewish. Neither is it a racial fact. ... So what precisely is it? It is a sensation, a very intense feeling that I experience, and therefore a reality. I do not claim to give a rational or scientific definition of it.[9]

This feeling never left him throughout his life and traces of it can be found from the time of his first electoral compaign in Normandy until his death in

1982. Thus, in April 1932, during the first electoral campaign in the Eure (which he was to represent in Parliament for many years), he was careful to reply in public to direct personal anti-Semitic attacks:

So I am being blamed for being a Jew. So what? I imagine it is not a blemish and I do not blush for it. From 1914 to 1918 the Jews were not treated as second class citizens and denied the dangerous honour of defending the threatened homeland. . . . And my father did his duty from 1914 to 1918, as did my two grandfathers who volunteered in 1870.[10]

If the slanderers were not satisfied, he kept hammering away at the same idea, in keeping with a non-reductive Franco-Judaism: 'Monsieur le Comte', he remarked on another occasion, 'let me stress that while my family left Alsace after the 1870 war in order to remain loyal to France, your ancestors joined the Duke of Brunswick in 1792 to fight against France.'[11] Frenchman and Jew: these two characteristics lay at the roots of his existence, as they did of Léon Blum, who was forced by a wave of anti-Semitic hatred to publish an article in *Le Populaire* entitled 'I am a Frenchman'. Here, once again, he patiently repeated his own life-story:

I was born in Paris on 9 April 1872, of French parents. My father was born in a village in Alsace, called Westhoffen, more than a century ago now, French of French parents. My mother was born in Paris of French parents. My four grandparents were born French on Alsatian soil. . . . Ever since French Jews have possessed civil status, my paternal ancestors have borne the name that I bear today.[12]

Both were, in fact, Frenchmen and Jews and, in some respects, in the same way.[13] Pierre Mendès France himself was keenly interested in genealogical research into his ancestry and throughout his life wanted to know more about his background. 'I find it passionately interesting', he exclaimed.[14] As early as 1938 he wrote to the Chief Rabbi of the Gironde asking for help. He received the following reply:

Monsieur and eminent co-religionist,
I am infinitely grateful for your very friendly letter of September 30. Let me assure you again of my complete co-operation with the research into your family that you have undertaken. Unfortunately, our old Bordeaux Jewish families which formed the first French Jewish aristocracy have practically disappeared from our local registers. That is why – and I am sure I speak for the whole of our community in this – I ask you to be so kind as to try and renew your connections with Bordeaux by authorizing our *Consistoire* to count you amongst its adherents.
I have been persuaded by the events through which we have just lived to allow foreigners who are our co-religionists to make a fine gesture: they have all signed a document calling for their voluntary enlistment in case of general mobilization. And despite my age and other considerations which would otherwise have made it my duty to remain at my post, I have sworn to leave with them to set an example. Thank God! You have been a true prophet and everyone has remained at home at peace. I send you my greetings and my blessings and beg you to accept the homage of my high esteem and religious devotion.

J. Cohen, Chief Rabbi[15]

Pierre Mendès France had a genuine and passionate interest in the history of the marranos, which he pursued throughout his life. He carried this so far that the files he built up on marranos in general and on his own family – who were descended from them – could well form the basis for scholarly research. Everything is carefully arranged, files of archives, registration of births, deaths, marriages, professions, the whole forming a gigantic family tree of the Mendès Frances. It traces successive generations of Jews from the sixteenth century, almost all with biblical first names (Abraham, Judith, Isaac, Rebecca, Moses and so on). In addition, it is backed up by scholarly documentation, abounding in academic articles, often in English.[16] These extensive files give an exhaustive history of the Mendès France family, up to about 1684 when, they claim, Luis Mendès de Franca arrived in France and settled in Agen. He had seven children, including Jean Mardochée Mendès France, born in 1687, from whom Pierre Mendès France was directly descended.[17]

Between 1961 and 1964 the former President of the Council corresponded regularly with Portuguese organizations specializing in this type of genealogical research.[18] Again, in 1966 he sent a letter to the President of the Israelite Consistory of the Gironde asking for help and enclosing a cheque as a contribution to the upkeep of the cemetery containing the graves of some Mendès Frances not directly related to his own family.[19] In August 1967 the president of the Israelite Cultural Association of Bayonne, P. Abraham, wrote to him to inform him of a Mendès France who had been guillotined on 2 Thermidor at Bayonne.[20] Likewise, on 16 October 1969 Pierre Mendès France replied to the president of the Association who had sent him new information on his distant forebears who had lived at Port-au-Prince in the eighteenth century.[21] He was, in fact, descended on his father's side from a long line of Portuguese marrano Jews, his family having settled, he said, in Bordeaux, in 1683. But, like Léon Blum, he also had links with Alsace through his maternal grandparents. This was an area favoured by Jews who were deeply attached to France, many of whom had settled in the capital after the defeat of 1870. From that time they provided a significant proportion of the new graduates of the Republic, those scholarship-holders who hoisted themselves up the social ladder and who, in particular, formed the new political cadres of the Third Republic, against which every adherent of the old order would later violently rise.

Both Blum and Mendès France were born in the heart of Paris and spent their adolescence between rue Réaumur, rue du Quatre-Septembre, Porte Saint-Denis and the square des Arts et Métiers, where successive generations of Jews traditionally settled, from the Sentier to the *Pletzl*, when they arrived in the capital.[22] Their parents ran businesses in textiles (Mendès France) and ribbons and silks (Blum), situated, after two changes of address, in the rue Réaumur. They both had barmitzvahs; learned Hebrew; took part in the most important religious festivals; one attended the *Lycée Charlemagne* (Blum), the other the *Lycée Turgot* (Mendès France) right in the heart of the Jewish quarter of Paris. In both cases, as is customary in Jewish tradition, they learnt Judaism from their mothers, who fasted on Yom Kippur, for example. Madame Abraham Blum was particularly attached to religious tradition. Note, too, that they both married Jewish women. When Pierre Mendès France married Lily Cicurel in December 1938 the religious ceremony was conducted by a rabbi, and a religious marriage contract – a ketuba – was drawn up.

Steeped in a Jewish environment, reciting their prayers (Blum), and even going through a brief mystical period (Mendès France), they never the less soon abandoned religious values so that they could identify more closely with a rationalist and anti-clerical humanism which the laicism of a strong State and the ideals of the Republic demanded. These latter values had in any case been passed on to them by members of their families who supported the Commune or the Dreyfusard conflict. They were therefore both totally Frenchmen and Jews, and they saw no point in hiding it because they perceived no disparity between those two vital aspects of their existence. Henceforth for them, the assimilation produced by Franco-Judaism no longer implied denying their loyalty to Judaism. This view was shared at the turn of the century and during the first half of the twentieth century by other Jews who had entered state service in considerable numbers after passing through the Republic's most prestigious schools, such as the *Polytechnique* and the *École normale supérieure*.[23]

One last example of this fundamental point: when Léon Blum was President of the Council, he told the inaugural assembly of the Jewish Agency, 'In feeling that I am a real Frenchman, I know that I am at the same time an Israelite. I have never been able to discover the slightest contradiction between these two aspects of my consciousness. We can belong body and soul to Judaism and remain wholly French in our feelings. There is no difficulty or contradiction in this.'[24] Being an Israelite, in his opinion, was simply being Jewish, and there was for him no longer any difference between these two concepts which other people often chose to distinguish. His famous public speech in Luna Park on 6 September 1936 ensured that no one remained in ignorance of it, in that France of the Popular Front, rumbling with every type of intolerance. 'I am a Frenchman', he cried, 'proud of his country, proud of his history, nourished like anyone else, despite my race, on its traditions'.[25] Pierre Mendès France was more sparing in his use of this type of public declaration, but they none the less illustrate his feelings. 'I am', he said, 'a French republican atheist, but I am also very attached to Judaism ... that's how it is'.[26]

It is also possible to find proof of their life-long participation in the life of the Jewish world. From his youth, when he was writing regularly for *La Revue blanche*, Blum had shown an interest in authors with Jewish connections, such as Marcel Proust, Marcel Schwob, Tristan Bernard and even Porto-Riche. He did not try to hide certain affinities for which he was later criticized.[27] And it is easy to pick out one or two little-known examples which brought him into contact with the everyday life of the Jews in France or abroad, without mentioning his participation in the Zionist adventure. On 4 April 1933, together with Bernard Lecache, Chief Rabbi Julien Weil and Rabbi Louis

Germain Lévy, he took part in a meeting in the Salle Wagram organized by the *Union universelle des jeunesses juives*.[28] In 1936 he was invited as President of the Council to a Jewish students' ball.[29] In 1937, when he visited Prague as Vice-President of the Council, it was public knowledge that he went openly to the synagogue to examine old Jewish religious objects.[30] And in 1950 he sent a long message of solidarity to the *Fonds social juif unifié*, marking his approval of its activity within 'the Jewish community of France'.[31]

Apart from the struggle against anti-Semitism and his relationship with Zionism, such interventions by Pierre Mendès France were less frequent, and in that respect again he remained more withdrawn than Blum. None the less, in his personal life he considered that 'he mixes mainly with Jews', without pursuing 'any premeditated plan'.[32] The private archives of Marie-Claire Mendès France show that when he was a student, he was president of the festivals commission of the Association of Israelite Students in Paris. He became increasingly involved in later life. Thus he had no hesitation in congratulating the monthly *L'Arche* on its 'untiring fight in the service of the values to which [he is] most attached', emphasizing in his turn the existence of 'so diverse a community as that of the French Jews, [which] today shares the same anxieties and the same hopes'[33] and with which, he openly confirmed, he identified.

JUDAISM, SOCIALISM AND REPUBLIC

Léon Blum and Pierre Mendès France were both Jews but they were Jews in different ways both as regards personal involvement in the French Jewish community and in the significance they assigned to Judaism in implementing their actions in the public sphere. Blum saw Judaism as one of the basic sources of his adherence to socialism, whereas Mendès France remained strictly within the emancipating republican framework. 'I am a Marxist, I am a Jew', Léon Blum replied to Hitler's envoy, Dr Schacht.[34] And he explained his refusal to leave France in June 1940, despite Churchill's insistence, simply by stating, 'I am a Frenchman, I am a socialist, I am a Jew.'[35] Reversing the order of this statement, Ben Gurion merely noted that Hebrew was read from right to left.

As for Pierre Mendès France, on 21 June 1944, when he escaped from Clermont-Ferrand prison, he left a letter in his cell addressed to Marshal Pétain. At that particularly dramatic moment in his life he wrote, 'The punishment was not intended for the officer. It was the politician, the left-wing deputy, the Jew who was the target'.[36] As an unashamed patriot, he was aware, like Léon Blum – but to a lesser degree that corresponded to his reservations at that time about socialism as an ideology – that the symbiosis between Judaism and left-wing leanings provoked the most intense hatred, even within the republican framework.

Léon Blum and Pierre Mendès France were both left-wing Jews who at times engaged in the same political conflicts. Blum personified the socialist struggle; Mendès France identified more with the virtues of a republican and reformist radicalism, by virtue of which he agreed to take office in the second Blum government of 1938. At various times in contemporary French history these two Jews, both left-wing but with distinctly different political ideals, personified absolute evil. Yet other Jews, unconverted but situated on the opposite side of the political chessboard, did not provoke this reaction. From this point of view, it is essential to compare (and we shall return to this on several occasions) Léon Blum and Georges Mandel on the one hand, and Pierre Mendès France and René Mayer, on the other. State Jews attached to the existing order were, so to speak, immunized, sheltered from anti-Semitic hatred, at least for a time. Can it be argued that Israelites who tried to maintain a more traditional order avoided the castigation meted out to those Jews who were more concerned with social justice, even though both types were firmly integrated in the state? Mendès France showed that he was aware of this when he himself stressed that 'in France, no one found anything wrong with it when a Jewish President of the Council was right-wing. When he was left-wing, he stirred up passions. Léon Blum was violently attacked, and it did not matter what weapon was used.'[37] As Pierre-Henri Simon shows, this time apropos Mendès France: 'He was a Jew. This has to be recognized: anti-Semitism remains a constant in French political consciousness. . . . When one enters high politics with the handicap of Semitic blood, it is safer to be Tory than Whig; one must be Disraeli or fall.'[38]

Disraeli himself would not have been protected in France in the inter-war period, so violent were the conflicts that raged. And, after a period of respite, that energetic Israelite Georges Mandel had to face the outburst of anti-Semitism in his turn. For a time, Charles Maurras and the whole royalist movement admired him. He was 'a high class Israelite',[39] Pierre Gaxotte wrote in the anti-Semitic journal *Je suis partout*. Mandel was a possible candidate for President of the Council. He was appointed to highly symbolic posts: high commissioner for Alsace-Lorraine, then Minister for the Colonies, and, most importantly, Minister of the Interior, specifically charged with maintaining order.[40] Yet Mandel, who was a disciple of Clemenceau, also became the target of the most obscene personal anti-Semitic attacks. After that, his friends no longer regarded him as any different from the Jew Blum. By a strange freak of history, the Israelite Tory met an even more tragic fate than the socialist Jew: he was assassinated by the Militia, a fate which the former President of the Council miraculously escaped, despite deportation to Buchenwald.

Léon Blum was not, however, connected with the whig – liberal – tradition, since to his way of thinking the socialism he identified with originated in Jewish messianism and went far beyond simple liberal reformism. During his entire life, from the period of the Dreyfus Affair, through Vichy and until his last moments, he closely associated these two aspects of his own commitment to greater justice.⁴¹ Thus, recalling the vital role of Bernard Lazare in reopening the question of Captain Dreyfus's alleged guilt, Léon Blum added 'He had within him a Jew of the great race, the prophetic race, the race which says "a just man" where others say "a saint".'⁴² While he was still a young man he fought against the determinist theories of Taine, Barrès and Maurras on the grounds that they overestimated the existential significance of rootedness in the soil. Blum, like so many Jews who venerated the French Revolution, placed his confidence in Reason to break down the injustices which these traditionalist theories legitimized. And he added:

To the extent that I discern the collective thrust of their race, it is leading them towards the Revolution. The critical force is powerful in them. . . . It is this world, this present, living world, with its ancient people and its ancient pedigree, which must be set to rights one day in accordance with Reason; which must be made to prevail over every rule; which must be made to return to each person his due. Is not that the spirit of socialism? It is the ancient spirit of the race. . . . It is by no means an accident of Providence that Marx and Lasalle were Jews.⁴³

Paradoxically, Blum himself drifted into a sort of anti-Semitism from vexation when he reverted – though temporarily – to the tone Marx used in *The Jewish Question* against Jewish capitalism, adopted the arguments of certain French socialist leaders, and anticipated Hannah Arendt's violent diatribes against Jewish bankers who devoted all their energy to the unbridled pursuit of profit in a Third Republic historically prone to financial scandals. Blum was also disappointed that some Jews dared to turn away from socialism towards which they should all be naturally drawn. Like the most mechanical Marxist theoreticians of that era, he in his turn attacked the 'rich bankers', indicted 'Jewish capital' for not putting itself 'at the service of international socialism' and concluded in familiar terms:

However, given what they are, the Jewish financial millionaires would not be stubborn adversaries of the Revolution. . . . They would be the first to give way. . . . That is a characteristic of the race. It is clearsighted, it is able to foresee. . . . The Jews are resigned. . . . I do not think they would mourn their gold for long.⁴⁴

Better still, Blum, a state Jew who had gone through elitist institutions like the *École normale supérieure* and the Council of State and who knew the extent to which republican Franco-Judaism was based on a meritocratic public service open to Jews, now seemed to regret that integration into the state which he thought had helped to turn the Jews away from socialism. 'Too many Jews', he stated, 'plunged into public office at the same time. It is no bad thing if they keep away from it, even if only in self-defence. The status of civil servant is unsuited to the fundamental characteristics of their race.'⁴⁵

Léon Blum briefly adopted Bernard Lazare's viewpoint and embarked on a war against the Israelite establishment because it was ignorant of, or fought against, the socialism with which every Jew should identify. He did this just when the anti-Semitic movement was gathering strength – that movement which, from Drumont to Vichy, untiringly aimed to exclude Jews from the state – and when in the violently anti-Semitic atmosphere of the Dreyfus Affair the resignation of certain Jewish officers seemed to foreshadow the exclusion of Jews from all public office in 1940. This lovers' quarrel did not last. Blum abandoned such anathemas as soon as he reverted to the republican synthesis. Although he maintained particularly close contact with left-wing Jewish political organizations, he none the less drew closer to the community, even if he still did not forge any close bonds with those who led it.

FIGHTING ANTI-SEMITISM

Those two French citizens, Jews and left-wingers, Léon Blum and Pierre Mendès France, were far from adopting the same viewpoints on strengthening the state or even on the blossoming of socialism. But they agreed on the main aims: they pursued the same struggle against anti-Semitism in general. However, they confronted it in different ways throughout their lives: one as a republican socialist, the other as a republican who had confidence in the omnipotence of Reason.

Léon Blum, following Jean Jaurès and Lucien Herr,[46] felt that anti-Semitism, that prejudice of times past, could only be conquered by the triumph of socialism. He drew a parallel between the anti-Semitism which erupted at the time of the Dreyfus Affair and the even more savage anti-Semitism unleashed during the inter-war period. 'Must an explanation for it be sought in the materialist philosophy of history?', he reflected. Did the survival and even the spread of anti-Semitism really illustrate the fact that 'social distinctions had not been broken down, that social relationships had not been changed'?[47] Here again, therefore, it was as a Marxist that Blum was trying to explain the continued existence of anti-Semitism. As a convinced socialist, he harshly attacked the Jewish bourgeoisie, accusing it of indifference to the fate of Captain Dreyfus in order the better to protect its class interests. Describing himself somewhat strangely as 'an average Jew', he joined the Dreyfusard camp under the socialist flag and embarked on a war against the traditional ruling class in general but also and above all – as he had already done nearly 40 years before in the *Nouvelles Conversations de Goethe avec Eckermann* – against the Israelite bourgeoisie. It remained deaf, he claimed, to the liberating appeals of socialism and strove vainly to conceal its own particularism. For him,

the Jews did not want anyone to think that they defended Dreyfus because Dreyfus was a Jew. They did not want their attitude to be attributable to racial difference or solidarity.... The Jews of the Dreyfus period, those who belonged to the same social stratum, who, like him, had passed difficult examinations, penetrated the cadres of staff officers or the most sought-after corps of the civil administration, were exasperated by the idea that hostile prejudice might limit their irreproachable careers.... The rich Jews, the Jews of the middle bourgeoisie, the Jewish civil servants were frightened of the struggle for Dreyfus just as they are frightened of the struggle against Fascism today.... They imagined that they could avert anti-Semitic passion by their cowardly neutrality.[48]

Léon Blum here touched on a basic and tragic aspect of the Jews' integration into the state. In France as in Germany, particularly during the Weimar Republic, they vied with each other in patriotism, shut their eyes to the rise of anti-Semitism within social groups opposed to the republican synthesis, and retained their confidence in the ability of a supposedly secular state to protect them. Here again, the socialist Jew in the innermost depths of his being attacked again the republican state Jew whom, despite everything, he himself wanted to personify. 'As socialist militants', he said on several occasions, 'we will continue to appeal to Reason against the aberrations of instinct.'[49]

None the less, by appealing to Reason against the anti-Semites, Blum aligned himself with the strategy of Jews who adhered solely to Franco–Judaism and based their actions on the defence of the rights of man in general and not of Jews in particular. Blum's reactions shared some common ground with Durkheim. When Durkheim was attacked as a Jew at Bordeaux during the Dreyfus Affair, he chose a universalist response by starting the local branch of the *Ligue des droits de l'homme*.[50] When the emergency came, Léon Blum in the end also turned to the *Ligue internationale contre l'antisémitisme* (LICA) to proclaim his solidarity with persecuted Jews abroad. On 26 November 1938, at the congress of LICA, held under his presidency, he declared 'Nothing in the world would be more painful or more dishonourable than the sight of French Jews striving to close France to Jewish refugees from other countries.'[51] Assimilated Jew *par excellence*, Blum was bent on marking his solidarity with all other Jews, dismissing the fears of some Israelites, as on so many other occasions. As a result he brought upon himself the main thrust of the anti-Semitic charge.

Pierre Mendès France's attitude fits totally into the republican and, consequently, rationalist framework. He was a member of the *Ligue d'action universitaire républicaine et socialiste* (LAURS), and in 1926 became general secretary of its Paris branch. Within the framework of this organization, basically orientated towards defending the Republic, he gave the clenched fist sign in the streets of the Latin Quarter against the anti-Semitic Camelots du Roi, young royalists grouped around the royalist paper, *L'Action française*.[52] Faced with constant anti-Semitic attacks both in Normandy and in the capital, Pierre Mendès France was forced to recognize that 'there is a base of latent anti-Semitism, of racialism in general, in France. Sometimes there is a spasm, sometimes the base is more or less camouflaged, silent. But there is a base. It will take a long time for this eventually to disappear.'[53] He responded to these attacks by resort to the law because these personal threats could constitute an 'attack on the Republic' which he represented in his capacity as President of the Council.[54] He constantly backed up the LICA with many messages of support[55] and he helped victims of anti-Semitic discrimination who came to him for reassurance. Again, he advised them to trust in the justice of the Republic.[56] None the less, he himself was greatly saddened by these attacks which wounded him deeply, as the Pierre Mendès France Institute archives show. Anti-Semitic abuse often 'moved' him.

ZIONISM AND ISRAEL

Blum and Mendès France, both republican state Jews, had not only different perceptions of socialism, as we have seen, but also of Zionism. Blum, from the first and unflaggingly, seems the more ardent, sparing no effort. He appears almost militant, acting with almost the same enthusiasm that he felt for socialism. Mendès France was always concerned about Israel's destiny, more so after he had given up political power; but here again he based his actions much more on law and reason than on some sort of essential sense of history. Heirs as they were to a Franco-Judaism which was disinclined to tolerate public expressions of difference, they were none the less, each in his own way, loyal supporters of the legitimacy of the Zionist cause. But this cause still shattered the unequivocal link binding every citizen to the state, because it revived the idea of a Jewish nation with its own history like any other nation.

It is well-known that French Jews, firmly integrated in the structure of the republican state, were for a long time cautious about the Zionist revival. In fact, they could not conceive of their own destiny apart from the destiny of the French nation which already seemed itself to be the new, rebuilt Zion. Zionism also met a weak response in countries with weak states where representative democracy had flourished, to the extent that Jews in Britain and the United States had their own representative, legitimate communal structures. Social integration, like integration into the state, reduced the attraction of Zionism. Citizenship of the state and particularist representation in the specific framework of the nation-state, reduced the significance of the Zionist ideal. On the other hand, it met an immediate response in Germany where aristocratic authoritarianism and the institutionalization of the state co-existed, the Jews then being understandably divided between love of *Vaterland* and the ideal of the return to Zion. It was, however, in Eastern Europe, where autocratic power allowed no room for the expression of particularisms but where communal structures were powerful – which on the whole prevented the formation of the state–citizen bond of allegiance or of loyalty to the czar – that Zionism really flourished. To the Jewish masses it seemed like a mode of collective, and not individual, escape. The latter nevertheless attracted hundreds and thousands of immigrants, notably towards the United States, where individual mobility had a double value: it meant escape not only from the repressive structures of the global society but also from the community itself.[57] In this sense, the standard model of anti-Semitism as the variable that affected the attraction of Zionism depended largely on the particular mode of construction of the state in Europe.[58]

It has long been thought that followers of Franco-Judaism, the French Israelites, felt little more than a vague sentimental sympathy with the Zionist movement. In their opinion it could at the most only concern the Jews of Eastern Europe, Poland or Russia, or those who had emigrated – notably to France – after the pogroms. It is true that the leaders of the Israelite community, as well as the *Alliance israélite universelle*, placed greater value on the process of assimilation than on the return to a particular form of Jewish nationalism. In an important declaration, *L'Association des rabbins de France* stated that 'the French rabbinate considers that the national and political doctrines of Zionism, of which they recognize the moral and ideal value for millions of their brethren, cannot be reconciled with the principles of French Judaism'.[59] However, even before the 1914–18 war, the two main communal newspapers, *L'Univers israélite* and *Archives israélites*, were adopting a more favourable tone. Chief Rabbi Zadoc Kahn also passed a less-negative judgement. Minority groups were formed which agitated in favour of Zionism, and some totally assimilated Jews, like André Spire, Edmond Fleg and Victor Basch, even went as far as acknowledging the Zionist ideal publicly.[60]

These examples could not have revealed more clearly the deep-seated changes which were affecting the adherents of Franco-Judaism, in as much as André Spire and Victor Basch were Israelite members of the state apparatus who had reached the highest echelons of politico-administrative power by the traditional route. Nevertheless, the case of Léon Blum seems to illustrate best the new tendencies appearing amongst French Jews. Yet most biographies of Blum are extremely discreet on this subject, although there is no shortage of proof of his growing involvement.

We shall mention some of them briefly. It is a well-known fact that the Dreyfus Affair acted as a catalyst for the birth of Zionism. It seemed to indicate that, even in the West, where the Franco-Judaism synthesis was established, emancipation, which favoured assimilation and the apparent disappearance of all awareness of identity and all forms of particularist life, none the less proved propitious to the appearance of a particularly serious form of anti-Semitism within the Republic. As the Jews became identical with other citizens, their absence of visibility conjured up even more frenzied horror stories. These were publicized by Drumont's *La France juive*, *La Libre Parole*, *La Croix* and many other inflammatory newspapers and lampoons. When Herzl turned to Zionism, he was drawing what he thought were definitive conclusions from this unprecedented crisis that was shaking the emancipating Republic. Far from the pogroms of the East and the reductive emancipation of the West, both of which were proving equally incapable of preventing anti-Semitic mobilization, the Jews' destiny henceforth lay in an inexorable return to Zion.

54 The Fate of Franco-Judaism

The period of the Dreyfus Affair was vital because the temporary failure of the republican synthesis left the way open for both socialism and Zionism. At first Blum, like many French Jews, was indifferent to the Captain's fate and barely felt involved. As he himself recounts, it was Lucien Herr who shook him from his apathy and drew him into the Dreyfusard camp. Then, as has already been noted, he sought to solve the problem of anti-Semitism via socialism and the most reductive Marxism. However, on several occasions his path crossed that of Bernard Lazare, the moving spirit of the Dreyfusard camp, and Lazare even visited him. Blum considered him 'a Jew of the prophetic race' but at that period he did not seem to see that Lazare looked more towards Zionism for a solution, which for a time he thought was identical with Herzl's.[61] Nowhere in his *Souvenirs sur l'Affaire* does Léon Blum mention Zionism. He waged his war alongside Jaurès and Lucien Herr and, oddly enough, on the way he even absolved Jules Guesde, who introduced Marxism into France, 'of any sympathy with anti-Semitism'.[62]

If Blum thus passed through this dramatic crisis without encountering the Zionist hypothesis, it was because Zionism remained a peripheral concern in France at that time. But although he turned first to socialism to put an end to anti-Semitism, he does also mention Zionism very early on. Describing Maurice Donnay's play, *Le Retour de Jérusalem*, he suggested the following definition of Zionism: 'Those Jews who want to gather their dispersed co-religionists in one homogeneous state around the traditional capital, are called Zionists. For them, Zion is the true homeland.'[63]

The testimony of Marc Jarblum, who was close to him for a long time, sheds light on the path that led Blum to Zionism. He recounts in detail how Blum was part of a delegation led by Marcel Sembat which visited the United States during the First World War. On this occasion, he had the chance to explain the situation of the Jews of Eastern Europe and to intervene, in the hope that France would support the Zionist claims. Weizmann was kept informed of these conversations and from then on close ties existed between him and Blum.[64] So accurate was this account that later, during a ceremony in Weizmann's honour, organized in Paris on the occasion of the creation of Israel, Blum could proclaim,

I knew nothing about Zionism when I met him. He made me aware of the work and he won me over. In the aftermath of the First World War, he [Weizmann] enrolled me in the service of his plans, sometimes drawing on my advice. It is a source of great pride and great satisfaction to me to think that I was able to help him in the difficult negotiations on which the creation of the national home depended.... I am a French Jew, born in France from a long line of French ancestors. I only speak the language of my country, and I refused to leave it when I was in the greatest danger. Nevertheless, I share with all my soul in the admirable effort – miraculously transformed from a dream to historical reality – which henceforth assures a homeland, worthy, equal and free, to all Jews who unlike me, have not had the good fortune to find one in their native land. I have followed this effort since President Weizmann explained it to me.... I have always felt and I feel now more than ever part of it.[65]

Three years earlier, at the time of the Exodus drama, Blum had expressed himself in practically the same terms to support the right of Jews from the German camps to 'seek their homeland on biblical soil, the soil which is the site of their history'.[66] But it is of primary importance to emphasize that Blum retained his socialist outlook throughout the long journey that led him towards Zionism after the First World War. In August 1922 he presided over a crowded meeting at the *Mutualité* when the mandate over Palestine was ratified. 'The socialists of the world and we the French socialists', he said, 'will help you by all means within our power, because Zionism can be reconciled with international socialism, in that it began with the suffering classes. Jaurès would love your work. It is socialist because it is popular, just and humane.'[67] Thereafter Blum abandoned the reductionist Marxism which antagonistic communist brothers brought to bear on this subject and adhered to this synthesis between socialism and Zionism, which he still did not regard as having validity for the emancipated Jews of France.

In 1925 he sent a message to Jerusalem on the occasion of the inauguration of the Hebrew University which 'doubly touched [his] Jewish and French heart'. 'The new Judea', he thought, 'will always remember the blessings of the Great Revolution. It will not forget that it was the armies of the Republic which broke the chains of its sons. A socialist cannot but hope for fine fruits from the renaissance of a Jewish culture.'[68]

This little-known declaration was not the only one. In 1929 he attended a meeting of the Jewish Agency as a non-Zionist delegate representing a new Jewish workers' organization, the *Ligue des amis de la Palestine ouvrière*.[69] In a public speech on that occasion he set out the same argument: 'Being a Zionist', he declared, 'because I am French, because I am a Jew and because I am a socialist, because modern Jewish Palestine is the unprecedented and unique meeting-place of the oldest traditions of mankind and of its newest and most daring search for liberty and social justice.'[70] This unconditional support for the socialist branch of the Zionist movement never weakened. It even brought him into conflict with the British Labour government when it still opposed Jewish immigration into Palestine after the war.[71]

Thereafter, he threw his full weight as a statesman and all his international stature into the attempt to influence the course of events. 'Differing in this respect also from many French Jews', as he himself stressed, he was therefore 'passionately interested in the Zionist cause',[72] and did not hesitate to intervene personally. From 1925 he was a member of the executive of the *Association France–Palestine*, together with André Spire, Charles Gide and Henri Hertz, other Jewish members in high public office and higher education, and he was active in the ranks of the Committee for Keren Hayesod in France.[73] In these capacities, Blum was worried about the practical effects of immigration. Once a considerable number was involved, would it be capable of 'imposing the ascendancy and the influence of the Jewish enterprise through "compromises" with the Arab population'?[74] When he became President of the Council, he continued to monitor the fate of Palestine and kept up his close links with Weizmann who asked him to intervene with the French government in the vote on Partition in November 1947. In May 1948 Blum advised against postponing the proclamation of the State of Israel because of the risk of offending public opinion in the United States, and then he opposed the UNO decision to internationalize Jerusalem.[75] The foundation of Kibbutz Kfar Blum in 1943, after his deportation to Germany,[76] was a clear acknowledgement of his actions which were based on his ideals as a state Jew, as a socialist and, none the less, as a Zionist; proof, if any were needed, of the evolutionary character of a French Judaism which also identified with values not inherent in the republican consensus. But this viewpoint was anathema to the bitter adversaries of the republican synthesis who thought this evolution provided their anti-Semitic campaigns with new arguments against the dual allegiance.

Pierre Mendès France seemed more anxious to remain within the traditional framework of Franco-Judaism. Just as he was more cautious than Léon Blum about Marxist-inspired socialism, for reasons already shown (did it not undermine the republican consensus by re-introducing conflict as a structural phenomenon?), he also avoided any over-emphasis in his adherence to Zionism. Nowhere in his writings does he show an attachment to the fate of Israel as deep-seated as Léon Blum's. Moreover, his declarations on the subject came later and, it seems, only after he became head of government. Although he became immersed in political life at the beginning of the 1930s, the first texts – and these were in any case more concerned with Israel than with Zionism – do not seem to have been published until 1957 and primarily dealt with developments relating to war and peace in the Middle East.

In the volume published by 'The Friends of the French Republic in Israel' on 14 July 1957, Pierre Mendès France stressed that he had been 'sympathetic' to the creation of the State of Israel. 'We thought', he said, 'that the past trials, still fresh in every memory, and the totally peaceful motives of the founders of the new state, would arouse broad solidarity throughout the world which would ensure its survival.'[77] Like Léon Blum, Mendès France justified the creation of Israel by the genocide of the Jews but, unlike Blum, he did not refer to a history which was specific to the Jewish people. He would speak to the Israelis 'as a friend', he repeated later,[78] not as a 'passionate' Zionist, as Blum would have done, or even as a Jew. He unswervingly confirmed his conviction that Israel had a right to exist via a more normative process, based (as earlier, when he opposed anti-Semitism) on law and, more specifically here in the framework of international relations, on the pursuit of peace.

He employed no ideas arising from Judaism to justify his concern when, for example, Israel was threatened during the various wars it faced. He seemed to take care to limit the use of the terms 'Jew' or 'Judaism' to statements of his own feelings of identity solely in the framework that he acknowledged was constrictive: that of Franco-Judaism. Unlike Blum, he never called himself a Zionist even though, as a republican revering the strong state, he none the less turned to socialism late in the day, even acknowledging Blum's legacy. The birth of Israel was 'a miracle' responding to the wishes 'of innumerable generations' and resulting in the formation of a 'strong nation' which he did not perceive as specifically Jewish.[79] One of Pierre Mendès France's most significant declarations was made at the colloquium on 'The universalism of Islam and the fate of the Jews'. Speaking to Colonel Kadhafi on 27 November 1973, he wondered: 'Is Judaism a nationalism or a religion? To be honest, I don't know. But there are a certain number of men who want to gather in Israel and have undertaken to build a home together there. It is their right, no one has the right to prevent them. If the Palestinians want to build a nation, it is their right too. There is enough room in the world and in the Near East for the Israelis to have a home in one part and the Palestinians a home in their part.'[80]

This statement which loudly and clearly proclaims the existence of a relationship between Judaism and Israel seems to be a complete exception and was probably only provoked by the subject of the colloquium.

But another declaration – and one which caused a number of repercussions – should be recalled in this context. It was signed by Mendès France jointly with Nahum Goldmann and Philip Klutznick following Israel's entry into Lebanon in 1982. In it, these three leading figures in the Jewish world thought that 'our sense of Jewish history and the demands of the moment lead us to affirm that the time has come for the mutual recognition of Israel and the Palestinian people'.[81] Here again, and probably because he signed this important declaration in company with the president of the World Jewish Congress and his predecessor, Pierre Mendès France acknowledged the reality of a Jewish history and proved that he was guided by it when he formulated judgements on the destiny of Israel and the Middle Eastern conflict.

However, this explicit acknowledgement of links going beyond the framework of Franco-Judaism remains isolated. It was, in fact, solely 'as a Frenchman' that the former President of the Council wished to examine relations between Israel and her Arab neighbours,[82] as a man who had 'never considered himself unwavering in respect of Israel' and preferred to formulate his own opinions by virtue of the 'rights of man'.[83] His actions were determined by a stern rejection of chauvinism and he later intervened on several occasions to facilitate peace between Israel and the Palestinians on the basis of reciprocal recognition of the rights of the two peoples.[84] It was as if there was an urgent need to reaffirm the validity of an emancipating Franco-Judaism in a France where the desire for a return to particularisms of identity was asserting itself increasingly openly.

NOTES

1 See Michael Marrus, *The Politics of Assimilation* (Clarendon Press, Oxford, 1971); David Weinberg, *Les Juifs de Paris de 1933 à 1939* (Calmann-Lévy, Paris, 1974); Dominique Schnapper, *Juifs et Israélites* (Gallimard, Paris, 1980).

58   *The Fate of Franco-Judaism*

2 In this context, see Paula Hyman, *From Dreyfus to Vichy: The Remaking of French Jewry, 1906–1939* (Columbia University Press, New York, 1979), ch. 5; and Nelly Las, *Les Juifs de France et le sionisme: De l'affaire Dreyfus à la Seconde Guerre mondiale*, doctoral thesis from the 3rd cycle, Paris, université de Sorbonne nouvelle, 1985.
3 Albert Memmi, *Portrait d'un Juif* (Gallimard, Paris, 1962), p. 267.
4 Chamber of Deputies, *Débats parlementaires*, 11 Jan. 1923.
5 Quoted in Marc Vichniac, *Léon Blum* (Flammarion, Paris, 1937), p. 10.
6 *Le Droit de vivre*, 3 Dec. 1938.
7 *Tribune juive Strasbourg–Paris*, 9 Dec. 1938. The same journal added: 'The man who is in charge of the destiny of France at this grave time remembers whence he came' (27 Dec. 1936).
8 Bibliothèque nationale, *Nouvelles Acquisitions françaises*, 24953 607.
9 *L'Arche*, March 1976.
10 Pierre Mendès France, 'Lettre ouverte à mes amis sur les calomnies', in *Oeuvres complètes*, vol. 1 (Gallimard, Paris, 1984), p. 176.
11 Quoted in Alexander Werth, *The Strange History of Pierre Mendès France and the Great Conflict over French North Africa* (Barrie Books, New York, 1957), p. 4.
12 *Le Populaire*, 19 Nov. 1938.
13 For this aspect of Léon Blum, see Vichniac, *Léon Blum*; Zachariah Shuster, 'As Léon Blum began to Reign', *Menorah Journal*, Oct. 1936; Richard Stokes, *Léon Blum, Poet to Premier* (Coward McCann, New York, 1937); *L'Oeuvre littéraire de Léon Blum* (author unknown) (Edition de l'Avenir Socialiste, Lyon, 1937); Geoffrey Fraser and Thadée Natanson, *Léon Blum: Man and Statesman* (J. B. Lippincott, Philadelphia, 1938); André Blumel, 'Léon Blum, juif et sioniste', *Revue de la pensée juive*, no. 9 (Autumn 1951); James Joll, *Three Intellectuals in Politics* (New York, 1971); Louise Dalby, *Léon Blum* (Thomas Yoseloff, New York, 1963); Joel Colton, *Léon Blum* (Fayard, Paris, 1967) (the new edition – Duke University Press, Durham, 1987 – of this book adds nothing on the question of anti-Semitism); William Logue, *Léon Blum: The formative years, 1872–1914* (Northern Illinois University Press, De Kalb, Ill., 1973); Jean Lacouture, *Léon Blum* (Le Seuil, Paris, 1977); Israel Eldan, 'The main features of the Jewish condition in Léon Blum's biography', *Yalkut Moreshet*, no. 40 (in Hebrew); Helmut Gruber, *Léon Blum, French Socialism and the Popular Front: A case of internal contradictions* (Cornell Studies in International Affairs, New York, 1986). On Pierre Mendès France, see Jacques Nantet, *Pierre Mendès France* (Édition du Centurion, Paris, 1967); Pierre Mendès France, *Choisir: Conversations avec Jean Bothorel* (Stock, Paris, 1974); Alain Gourdon, *Mendès France ou le rêve français* (Ramsay, Paris, 1977); Jean Lacouture, *Pierre Mendès France* (Le Seuil, Paris, 1981).
14 Interview with Claude Nicolet, IHTP, 272, 2nd side.
15 *Fonds Pierre Mendès France*, BAIU, M.1.
16 For example, these boxes contain most of Zosa Szajkowski's articles on the marranos, published in various specialist American Jewish journals.
17 These 45 boxes of unpublished archive material can be consulted at the library of the *Alliance israélite universelle*.
18 See *Fonds Pierre Mendès France*, BAIU, M.1.
19 *Archives de l'Institut Pierre Mendès France*, letter, 16 Oct. 1969.
20 See *Fonds Pierre Mendès France*, BAIU, M.1.
21 *Archives de l'Institut Pierre Mendès France*, letter, 16 Oct. 1969.
22 Nancy L. Green, *Les Travailleurs immigrés juifs à la Belle Époque: Le 'Pletzel' de Paris* (Fayard, Paris, 1985).
23 On this, see Perrine Simon, *Contribution à l'étude de la bourgeoisie intellectuelle juive à Paris entre 1870 et 1914*, D.E.A., Institut d'études politiques, Paris, 1982.

24 *Bulletin du Comité de vigilance*, 4 Feb. 1937.
25 Quoted in Blumel, 'Léon Blum, juif et sioniste', p. 8.
26 Quoted in Claude Nicolet, interview, IHTP, 272, 2nd side. As H. Caillavet clearly puts it, 'he remained a Jew as he remained a Frenchman' (interview, IHTP). Likewise Jean Bothorel notes: 'He was not of the Jewish religion, he was agnostic, the product of a tradition, despite everything, like Blum, he had that same sense, that same idea of a history which was continuing despite everything' (interview, IHTP, 367).
27 See A. B. Jackson, *La Revue blanche* (Minard, Paris, 1960), pp. 86–7. See also W. Rabi, 'Léon Blum adolescent', *La Terre retrouvée*, 15 Oct. 1954.
28 *Le Volontaire juif*, April 1933.
29 *Samedi*, illustrated weekly journal of Jewish life, 6 Oct. 1937.
30 Ibid., 16 Oct. 1937.
31 FSJU, March 1954.
32 Mendès France, *Oeuvres complètes*, vol. 1, p. 688.
33 *L'Arche*, no. 238, Jan. 1977.
34 *L'Oeuvre de Léon Blum, 1940–1945*, op.cit., p. 307.
35 Dalby, *Léon Blum*, p. 89.
36 Mendès France, *Oeuvres complètes*, vol. 1, p. 334.
37 *L'Arche*, no. 228, March 1976, p. 39.
38 Pierre-Henri Simon, preface to Claude Nicolet, *Pierre Mendès France ou le Métier de Cassandre* (Julliard, Paris, 1959), p. 14. Alain Gourdon notes that Mendès France 'is a Jew and will never be an Israelite like Michel Debré or even René Mayer', in *Mendès France ou le rêve français*, p. 70. See also Maurice Le Ruel, 'Karl Marx ou Disraeli? Léon Blum vu par un de ses camarades d'études', *Le Monde illustré*, 13 June 1936, p. 491.
39 *Je suis partout*, 30 Sept. 1930.
40 See John Sherwood, *Georges Mandel and the Third Republic* (Stanford University Press, Stanford, Conn., 1970).
41 See, for example, his 'Mémoires', written in prison in 1940, in *L'Oeuvre de Léon Blum, 1940–1945*, p. 61, as well as his article, 'Les juifs devant le problème allemand', in *L'Oeuvre de Léon Blum, 1947–1950* (Albin Michel, Paris, 1963), pp. 310–11.
42 Léon Blum, 'Souvenirs sur l'Affaire', in *L'Oeuvre de Léon Blum, 1937–1940*, p. 518 (re-issued Gallimard, Paris, 1981).
43 Léon Blum, 'Nouvelles Conversations de Goethe avec Eckermann', in *L'Oeuvre de Léon Blum, 1891–1905* (Paris, 1954), pp. 266–7.
44 Ibid., pp. 265–6.
45 Ibid., pp. 263–4.
46 See Daniel Lindenberg and P.A. Mayer, *Lucien Herr, le socialisme et son destin* (Calmann-Lévy, Paris, 1977).
47 Léon Blum, *Souvenirs sur l'Affaire*, p. 578.
48 Ibid., p. 520.
49 In *L'Oeuvre de Léon Blum, 1928–1934* (Albin Michel, Paris, 1963), p. 491.
50 On this point, see Pierre Birnbaum, *Dimensions du pouvoir* (PUF, Paris, 1984), pp. 23–4.
51 *Bulletin du Comité de vigilance*, 1 Dec. 1938.
52 See Lacouture, *Pierre Mendès France*, pp. 50–5; and Maurice Rolland, 'Pierre Mendès France résistant', in 'Hommage à Pierre Mendès France', *Droit et Démocratie*, Jan. 1984, p. 36.
53 *Le Nouvel Observateur*, 14 Aug. 1982.
54 See, for example, 'A propos des jugements rendus contre les auteurs des diffamations visant le chef du gouvernement. Lettre à René Coty, Président de la République', in Pierre Mendès

60 The Fate of Franco-Judaism

France, *Oeuvres complètes*, vol. 3 (Gallimard, Paris, 1986), pp. 740–1.
55 In this context, see *Le Droit de vivre*, June 1957, Nov. 1958, Nov. 1966, as well as a letter Pierre Mendès France wrote to Pierre Bloch, president of LICA, 24 Dec. 1971, in *Archives de l'Institut Pierre Mendès France*.
56 See, for example, the exchange of letters between Pierre Mendès France and Mme Maud K., in March–April 1978, when Mendès France says he is 'worried by the reappearance and resurgence of anti-Semitism in French life' (in *Archives de l'Institut Pierre Mendès France*).
57 The reference here is to the general perspective presented by Alfred Hirschman, aiming to explain all social phenomena by concepts of 'exit', 'voice' and 'loyalty', in *Face au déclin des entreprises et des institutions* (Édition Ouvrière, Paris, 1970).
58 For a global presentation, see Pierre Birnbaum, 'Nation, État et culture: l'exemple du sionisme', *Communications*, 45 (1987). There is a vast amount of literature on the subject; on Great Britain see, for example, Stuart Cohen, *English Zionists and British Jews* (Princeton University Press, Princeton, N.J., 1982); on the United States: Naomi Cohen, *American Jews and the Zionist Idea* (Ktav Publishing House, New York, 1975); on Germany: Marjorie Lamberti, *Jewish Activism in Imperial Germany* (Yale University Press, New Haven, Conn., 1978); and Yehuda Reinharz and Walter Schatzberg (eds), *The Jewish Response to German Culture* (University Press of New England, Hanover, N.H., 1985); on Russia: Jonathan Frankel, *Prophecy and Politics: Socialism, nationalism and the Russian Jews, 1862–1917* (Cambridge University Press, Cambridge, 1982).
59 Quoted in Hyman, *From Dreyfus to Vichy*, p. 168. In the same context, see the numerous statements mentioned by Marrus, *The Politics of Assimilation*, ch. 9.
60 See Catherine Levigne, 'Les juifs français et le sionisme de 1896 to 1920', *Yod*, no. 6; and Catherine Nicault, 'La France et le sionisme, 1896–1914', doctoral thesis, University of Paris I, 1985. The author describes the 'hostility' and 'anti-Zionism of French Jews', pp. 139–53.
61 See Nelly Wilson, *Bernard-Lazare: Antisemitism and the problem of Jewish identity in late nineteenth-century France* (Cambridge University Press, Cambridge, 1978), ch. 1.
62 Blum, *Souvenirs sur l'Affaire*, p. 555. On the relationship between Guesdism and anti-Semitism, see Claude Willard, *Le mouvement socialiste en France, 1893–1905: Les guesdistes* (Éditions Sociales, Paris, 1965), pp. 410–11; Michel Winock, 'La gauche et les juifs', *L'Histoire*, May 1981, pp. 13–25; and Zeev Sternhell, *La Droite révolutionnaire* (Le Seuil, Paris, 1978), pp. 239–41. Blum, in his *Souvenirs sur l'Affaire* (1935), makes no mention whatsoever of the vacillating position of Jaurès who was at first very hostile to Dreyfus; see Harvey Goldberg, 'Jean-Jaurès and the Jewish Question: the evolution of a position', *Jewish Social Studies*, 20 (April 1958).
63 *Le Gymnase*, 3 Dec. 1903.
64 See the little-known article by Marc Jarblum, 'Léon Blum, le sioniste', published in *Renaissance*, first year, no. 3 (Oct. 1956).
65 Léon Blum, 'Hommage à Weizmann', in *L'Oeuvre de Léon Blum, 1947–1950*, pp. 391–2.
66 Léon Blum, 'Le drame de l'Exodus', in ibid., p. 391. 'I was born a Jew', he said; 'for twenty-five years, I have helped to the best of my ability the formation of the "Jewish National Home" in Palestine and I have never dreamt of leaving France' (ibid., p. 392).
67 *L'Univers israélite*, 11 Aug. 1922.
68 *La Revue juive*, 15 March 1925.
69 See Hyman, *From Dreyfus to Vichy*, p. 170; and Las, *Les juifs de France et le sionisme*, p. 217.
70 *La Terre retrouvée*, March 1930. Note that the Poale Sion-Histahdrout, the socialist Zionist movement, in France was led by Marc Jarblum, a close associate of Léon Blum.
71 See, for example, his article in *Le Populaire*, 'L'Affaire de Palestine', in *L'Oeuvre de Léon Blum*,

1945–1947 (Albin Michel, Paris, 1958), pp. 243–5. On this point, see also Jarblum, 'Léon Blum, le sioniste', p. 6.
72 See his declaration at the congress of LICA in 1938, in *La Tribune juive Strasbourg–Paris*, 9 Dec. 1938. And the journal commented, 'Is this a return to the fold? Has this interest brought him back to us?' (p. 254).
73 See Las, *Les Juifs de France et le sionisme*, pp. 141 and 175.
74 Catherine Levigne points out a very interesting letter on this point from Blum to Marc Jarblum in Oct. 1929, 'A propos de Léon Blum', *Le Monde juif*, no. 90 (April–June 1978), p. 94. She also quotes other texts from the Jarblum archives in Jerusalem.
75 See Jarblum, 'Léon Blum, le sioniste', pp. 6–7.
76 Blumel, 'Léon Blum, juif et sioniste', p. 12.
77 *Archives de l'Institut Pierre Mendès France*.
78 *Le Nouvel Observateur*, 5–11 Dec. 1977.
79 *Amitiés France–Israël*, April–May 1958.
80 *Le Monde*, 27 Nov. 1973.
81 *Le Monde*, 3 July 1982.
82 Statement to the colloquium organized by the journal *New Outlook*, *Cahiers Bernard-Lazare*, Feb.–March 1978, p. 2.
83 *Le Nouvel Observateur*, 14 Aug. 1982.
84 His statements from this point of view are very numerous. See, for example, *Le Monde*, 5 June 1967; *Le Nouvel Observateur*, 14 June 1967 and 17 May 1976; *Cahiers Bernard-Lazare*, no. 47 (Feb. 1968) and no. 46 (April 1974); *Regards*, May 1978. Letter to Claude Nicolet, *Archives de l'Institut Pierre Mendès France*, 10 Aug. 1982.

3
The Jews of France *vis-à-vis* the Blum and Mendès France Governments

Devotees of a strict Franco-Judaism, nationalists, sometimes nationalists of the extreme Right, traditionalists, socialists, communists or those basically attracted to the Zionist idea – the Jews of France were far from a homogeneous body. This lack of homogeneity was accentuated by the long-standing division between the old-established Israelite families and the immigrants who sought refuge in the Hexagon in increasing numbers in the inter-war period. As they represented the whole political spectrum and were associated with very varied ideological trends and organizations, their reactions to, first, Léon Blum's and then Pierre Mendès France's advent to power varied greatly. Examination of these reactions is all the more interesting because they reveal heterogeneous attitudes regarding the secular framework defined by Franco-Judaism and its limits.

THE COMMUNAL INSTITUTIONS

A brief outline of the reactions of the principal organs of the community press shows the strength of Franco-Judaism during these periods of disturbance and ideological confrontation. As early as 22 May 1936, Raymond-Raoul Lambert, moving spirit of *L'Univers israélite*, who exerted considerable influence on all Jewish circles – to such an extent that he later led the UGIF – expressed the community's official position:

> We have never faltered in our doctrine of maintaining Judaism at a purely spiritual level. We have always protested against right- or left-wing agitators ... We have always stated that the Israelites of France had the right to belong to the political grouping that suited them, as free citizens, and that none of us had the right to commit his co-religionists by giving Jewish significance to a personal attitude ... Tomorrow M. Léon Blum will be called on to direct the policy of France. He belongs to our faith, through his family and through his declarations. He emerged from the ranks of our community to lead a political party. In that capacity, it was not fitting for us either to criticize or

judge him, even here. In a few days, when he is head of the government, we shall have no more rights or duties towards him than any other spiritual family in France. But it would not be held against us if we emphasized what lesson history will draw from this French liberty. France in 1936 no more dreams of enquiring into the faith of its ministers than the leader of an infantry division on the parapet of a trench 20 years ago thought of enquiring into the origin of the men waiting for the signal to go out to attack or die... What an admirable nation is ours![1]

Even if *L'Univers israélite* had some cruel disappointments in store, and even though it showed a certain *naïveté*, its point of view was a perfect illustration of a Franco-Judaism which was firmly integrated into the nation and which jibbed at seeing religious and cultural differences being dragged into the public arena. When that 'Israelite of France', Léon Blum, moved away from the purely spiritual dimension with which Judaism wished to be identified, he simultaneously 'left' the community which sought to maintain its political neutrality towards all 'agitators' and retain its place in a unified nation. Had not the seal on this unity been set for all time by the French Revolution and confirmed in the face of extreme danger in the trenches during the Great War? The reaction was the same later when Pierre Mendès France came to power. Thus Rabbi J. Grunewald, editor of *Tribune juive*, thought that 'the Jews of France proudly saw this prime minister, infinitely respected by the nation, as the most perfect expression of the union of their patriotic feelings and the moral demands of Judaism'.[2]

When the Blum government was formed, *Samedi*, which succeeded *Archives israélites*, the oldest organ of the community, to show even greater neutrality, wrote in the same spirit as *L'Univers israélite*:

We are concerned only with Judaism because we are a Jewish paper. We did not put M. Léon Blum at the head of the government of the French Republic and not all French Jews find this choice satisfactory.... Our pleasure is to note that the sons of the '89 Revolution make no distinction whatsoever between any of the children of the same nation... France offers the world an example of fraternity, agreement and harmony.[3]

As this paper repeated in June 1937 in a more restrained key, the formation of his government did 'nothing to send us into excesses of joy, nor, on the other hand, to embarrass us: this is to speak from the point of view of Jews, solely concerned with Jewish interest: A new conquering Disraeli, we will not ask for any specific advantage, nor draw any ostentatious glory from M. Léon Blum's success.'[4] The rules of the game were thus made clear: the French Israelites, as a specific spiritual community, intended to remain distanced from the socialist experiment conducted by one of its members who had left it to enter the public domain.[5]

None the less, a different opinion seems to emerge from the columns of *La Tribune juive Strasbourg-Paris*, the important organ of the Alsatian Jewish community. It pointed to the contrast with Great Britain which had in earlier times entrusted its fate to Disraeli, a baptized Jew:

For the first time we are seeing a great European power entrusting the conduct of its destiny to a Jewish citizen.... France, noble and generous France, is leading the democratic states.... We consider it a privilege to belong to France. The world knows that there are no better patriots than the French Israelites – M.Léon Blum is very well aware that if a person is born Jewish, he is not just a socialist and nothing but a socialist. He is not just a free-thinker and nothing but a free-thinker. The man who does not abandon the Jewish community is burdened with a whole past, a whole ambience and, above all, a heavy responsibility towards the community.... Although the assimilation, which has been taking place for a hundred and fifty years has almost entirely diluted French Judaism, it has not caused it to disappear.... The actions of a public figure particularly involve accountability to the community. We do not believe that this wise reticence will make anti-Semitism disappear – it will live as long as Satan – but politics is such a delicate area that the representative of a minority runs too great a risk.... The Jews are not expressing their joy by shouting hosanna. Moreover they did not display any enthusiasm when M. Léon Blum became President of the Council.... No, the French national socialists are wrong to think that we regard M. Léon Blum as someone sent to us by Heaven. When we see the malice, the baseness, the hatred, the passions unleashed by the socialist leader's advent to power, we are more tempted to recite the prayer reserved for the festival of Tabernacles: Hocha'na! Save us, oh Lord, our God, save us, our Creator, save us, our Redeemer, save us, our Protector![6]

Alsatian Judaism had more experience of persistent anti-Semitism. This time, it showed greater awareness of the real stakes confronting the Jews of France. Contrary to what *L'Univers israélite* and the communal establishment had thought since the nineteenth century, assimilation and integration into the state, however strong, had not entirely submerged the sense of identity. So whatever a Jew said about this very strongly institutionalized state – and much was said – he could not solely appear as the embodiment of Left or Right. Contrary to the assumptions of Franco-Judaism, there was always the risk that his involvement in public life would be seen by some people as having a particularist dimension. This in turn could endanger the whole community, of which he became an involuntary representative. Would not Léon Blum, Frenchman and socialist, none the less awaken the demons and unleash anti-Semitism against himself and the whole community? *L'Univers israélite*, in this difficult situation, thought that it was possible to maintain 'Israel above party' at any price.[7] Similarly, *Paix et Droit*, the organ of the *Alliance israélite universelle*, also believed that 'it is even commonsense' to honour Léon Blum as a socialist and a Jew for his presence at the head of the government. But at the same time 'the very great majority of French Israelites know their duty towards their homeland',[8] and were aware that they must not deal a blow to that Franco-Judaism which, by carefully differentiating between spheres and roles, could give ultimate proof of its capacity to integrate.

The *Consistoire* does not seem to have been convinced by this optimistic argument. There is evidence to suggest that it strove to persuade Léon Blum against agreeing to become President of the Council. But there does not seem to be any definite proof of this unusual intervention which overstepped the boundaries. None the less, it is claimed as fact by a few important witnesses – people close to Léon Blum – who on several occasions made public the attempt by the Chief Rabbi of Paris[9] to dissuade the socialist leader. If this move really took place, it would be very significant. Since the period of emancipation, the consistorial structure effectively paralleled the centralization of the state. '[The *Consistoire*] served two essential purposes: it guaranteed to the state that the Jews were trustworthy and patriotic citizens, and it afforded the Jewish population a sense of security as a recognized religious group.'[10] For nearly one and a half centuries, the political modernization of the Jews took place by respecting this separation of the roles of the state and the *Consistoire*. But, by creating a political space for the parties, the Third Republic strengthened the principle of representation. Now, side by side with state Jews imbued with the sense of public power, or intermingled with them were Jews who had entered the political arena through the medium of the parties and who risked shaking the foundations of Franco-Judaism, which sought to practise the utmost neutrality. Suddenly, danger threatened this whole beautiful structure!

No irrefutable proof has been found of this unheard of process, motivated, if it really took place, by the seriousness of the conflicts at home and the rise of fascism abroad. None the less, the symbolic importance of the *Consistoire* in this context is borne out by the relevant correspondence. In June 1937, in a letter to the Chief Rabbi of France, Jacques Bonhomme – the pseudonym used by a group of Israelites, Catholics and Protestants – deplored 'with deference' the formation of a

government with a Jew at its head. . . . Is M. Léon Blum a sick and sadistic man who gets a Neronian pleasure from setting his compatriots against each other? . . . No doubt people murmur that you are acting and have acted. But if your co-religionists were threatened with the terrible curse of Israel, we are convinced that their deadly work would cease. By not acting publicly, you become to some small extent their accomplice.[11]

The very confused letter that Jules Blum sent to the *Consistoire* on 6 May 1934 is also relevant here. Without explicitly naming the socialist leader, its author first attacked 'wicked Jews, of the Dreyfus ilk'. He criticized the 'handful of Jews from Alsace and elsewhere who are shooting our regime in the back because they fear for their money. . . . All the vandals have a preponderance of Jews at their head, particularly when compared with the small number of Jews in France. In addition, our honest Jews will fight anti-Semitism, without the help of these indefensibly bad Jews who are a danger to the homeland.'[12] The meaning of this last missive is anything but crystal clear. It is enough merely to recall that many people thought that the *Consistoire* played a potentially crucial role in resolving the difficult crisis which threatened. The Chief Rabbi received several letters hostile to Blum. One of them stated, 'his attitude is infinitely harmful to French Israelites . . . it would be a good thing if his co-religionists disowned him.'[13] Someone else wrote a letter to Léon Blum and sent a copy to the Chief Rabbi. 'I am a Jew', he said. 'But first of all I am a Frenchman by my blood and in my heart. The policy you direct has done, does and will do enormous harm to your co-religionists. . . . I ask you personally in the expectation that the body of your co-religionists will demand it of you in the near future, to cease all political activity that is contrary to the attempt at unity which is sought by all and accepted by the majority, except by yourself.'[14]

Another Jew in Marseilles wrote to the Chief Rabbi of France on 16 February 1934, asking him, in the name of his 'deeply Jewish but also deeply French views . . . to dissociate the Jews from M. Blum'.[15]

Likewise, when Xavier Vallat uttered anti-Semitic insults against the head of government in the Chamber of Deputies in February 1934, a Jew who was a foreign trade adviser, a reserve lieutenant in the infantry and a holder of the *Croix de guerre*, wrote to him and sent a copy of his letter to the rabbinate:

No, Sir, it was no more the voice of Israel that the Chamber heard yesterday when listening to M. Léon Blum than the voice of Jesus Christ when listening to you. Twenty years ago, we were probably side by side in the trenches. And the German bullets did not discriminate between either our religions or our political opinions. . . . Do not be surprised therefore that I am protesting so strongly, and be sorry, Sir, that you have offended good Frenchmen who were your comrades in battle and who are prepared, if necessary, to 'have another go' with you with the same good heart.[16]

Many letters could be cited, and the *Consistoire* archives seem so rich that they should themselves be the subject of proper study. One final extract, again about the altercation between Blum and Xavier Vallat: here we have another Jew writing to the Chief Rabbi:

since none of the fifteen – more or less shameful – Jews who sit in Parliament has had the courage to rise in our defence, it is up to the 'Voice of Israel' to do so without delay because there is always the fear that an anti-Semitic movement may flourish in France. Unfortunately, too many Jews are working to create this movement; and it is urgent that French Judaism state *urbi et orbi* its indestructible attachment to the country which was the first to release Israel from its thousand years of slavery. And it is also necessary to disavow all solidarity with politicians elected not by Jews but by Christians.[17]

Moreover, from age to age the Chief Rabbi of Paris had retained this symbolic function. In 1956 he received the following letter:

I had the honour to be a family friend of your predecessor, Chief Rabbi Zadoc Kahn, and I have great respect for his memory and for his wife's. They did not like to be called Israelites. They did not like their co-religionists who exchanged the name of their ancestors for the name of a French village. . . . I got the impression that you disapproved of Pierre Poujade's attacks on Monsieur Mendès Antifrance. That a Chief Rabbi, a pious Jew should defend a renegade who is a traitor to his race, the religion of his fathers, is incomprehensible. You would view Mendès's demoniacal, destructive, anti-French activity quite differently if you had seen, as I saw 35 years ago, the Tunis Arabs devastate and pillage Jewish shops. . . . And what can one say, sir, about the wave of anti-Semitism that this madman is going to provoke. . . . Mendès's case is different, Dreyfus was innocent. But had he been guilty, his crime would not have been fratricide. . . . Sir, this man is not a Jew, he is an Arab in disguise. . . . He works for Moscow.[18]

Willy-nilly, the *Consistoire* found itself caught up in the political conflicts that ravaged France in the inter-war period, as they did later during the decolonization of North Africa. But at the time of Léon Blum's nomination to the Presidency of the Council, a commemorative service took place in the Temple in rue de la Victoire. It was dedicated to the Croix-de-Feu and organized by Rabbi Kaplan. The congregation included Colonel de La Rocque, the members of the executive committee of the Croix-de-Feu, Baron Robert de Rothschild, president of the Paris *Consistoire*, as well as other members of the rabbinate and the central *Consistoire*. In a long speech during the service, Rabbi Kaplan stressed that

above parties, there is France; above individual faiths, there is God – for everything that we have in common, that we hold most dear, I entreat you, my brethren, like the old soldier I am, to work for the triumph of the sacred union around you. . . . What have they not said about us? That the Jew is working for the break-up of France, that he is the enemy of mankind, that he is intolerant, that he incites war! The exact opposite of our most infallible, most revered doctrines.[19]

Taking up some of the criticisms which extreme Right-wing organizations unremittingly directed at Léon Blum, Rabbi Kaplan tried above all to dissociate himself from Blum in the name of Judaism. Incidents broke out at the conclusion of the service when a large number of Jews seemed to be in the grip of very powerful emotions, shocked at the conduct of the ceremony which had taken a strongly anti-Blum line. However, the editor of *L'Univers israélite* came to the *Consistoire*'s rescue:

The demonstrations at the synagogue are unacceptable. No doubt the *Consistoire* could have decided that it was no longer able to accede to the requests of any organization while the whole country is in turmoil. But what dangerous conclusion would have been drawn from this by those who claim that the service gave the lie to accusations of racism? It will probably be easy in future for factional propaganda to claim that the synagogue gives its allegiance to the Croix-de-Feu. . . . As a French citizen, I use the freedom my ballot paper gives me; I belong to the political party that pleases me; I use my right to be communist, socialist, radical, moderate or Croix-de-Feu. But when I climb the stone steps to say the prayer for the dead, I acknowledge no one's right to wear an insignia in his buttonhole which might offend the man praying next to him.[20]

Writing in the left-wing paper *Vendredi*, André Wurmser reacted quite differently. 'It is the Frenchman in me rather than the Jew who is revolted by anti-Semitism', he said. '. . . I leave the task of stigmatizing it to my Aryan friends, Andrée Viollis and Paul Nizan. . . . It is natural that the members of the Croix-de-Feu should be anti-Semites. . . . Those who attended a "service to the memory of the war-dead" at the synagogue de la Victoire, at the request and in the presence of the Croix-de-Feu, were those trembling "Israelites", well known to M. de La Rocque.'[21] Unlike everyone else, the *Consistoire* and the communal leaders thought that they could remain detached from the anti-Semitic conflict that was tearing both society and political personalities apart. In order to keep Franco-Judaism out of it, care was taken to stress that, as Blum

68 The Fate of Franco-Judaism

was not a practising Jew, his activities did not involve the *Consistoire* in any way.[22] 'Astonished' by Léon Daudet's violent speeches, *La Tribune juive Strasbourg-Paris* 'thinks that the Jewish question does not arise. Moreover, M. Léon Blum's appointment as President of the Council is not a Jewish concern.'[23] And it went on, 'what is the connection between Judaism and the political struggle against M. Léon Blum who is a socialist, an atheist and completely detached from our religion?'[24] Criticism was becoming increasingly sharp because 'the leader of the socialist party laughs at his co-religionists and has surrounded himself with his socialist friends, as far from the mass of French Israelites as Marxism is from Judaism'.[25] So much acrimony revealed that the divorce was to be final.

In so far as he kept strictly within the rigid framework of Franco-Judaism by identifying his activities with those of the modernizing state, Pierre Mendès France, on the contrary, received warm but distanced support from the spokesmen of the community, as has already been noted. During the very short period of his government, with the benefit, unlike Léon Blum, of national quasi-unity, he exemplified the integration of state Jews. This time, the communal institutions remained almost totally silent, although they had taken pains to dissociate themselves from the Popular Front experiment. Apart from a few rare statements, the institutions remained almost mute.[26] But later, things changed radically. When the Algerian war again inflamed passions, Pierre Mendès France's open commitment to decolonization again allowed anti-Semitism free play. In the newly threatening atmosphere of 1965, when the PSU (*Parti socialiste unifié*) considered nominating him for future presidential elections, Pierre Mendès France refused outright. In a fashion almost identical to Léon Blum in 1936, he received letters from Jews begging him to do nothing that would fan the flames of anti-Semitic hatred any further.[27] But here again the leaders of the communal institutions remained cautious. They did not come forward and applied no pressure such as the rabbinate had applied to Léon Blum. Later the leaders intervened on the proposals which Pierre Mendès France drew up for a peaceful solution to the conflict between Israel and her Arab neighbours, particularly the Palestinians. Thus, in July 1982 CRIF (*Conseil représentatif des institutions juives en France*) 'formally dissociated itself' from the joint declaration signed by Mendès France, Nahum Goldmann and Philip Klutznick.[28] But these divergences were in no way concerned with the basic foundations of Franco-Judaism.

THE CASE OF THE NATIONALIST JEWS: THE EXAMPLE OF MAÎTRE EDMOND BLOCH AND SOME OTHERS

If the communal institutions had differing views on the Blum and Mendès France experiments, the two episodes aroused identical reactions from nationalist Jews opposed to their policies.[29] Strange alliances between some Jews and traditionalist, or even extreme right-wing, organizations were formed in opposition to the two left-wing Jewish politicians. Is it possible that they were encouraged by the *Consistoire's* nationalist attitude?

The ceremony at the Temple de la Victoire was only one symptom of the *Consistoire's* propensity to show understanding towards the Right. In the run-up to the elections to the legislature in 1936 a confrontation took place in the heart of Paris, in the Jewish quarter, between the Popular Front candidate – himself a Jew – and Maître Edmond Bloch, sympathetic to the Croix-de-Feu. Bloch had been received with great ceremony by Rabbi Kaplan, and this lit the fuse amongst the Jewish population. This election showed particularly the opposing strands of opinion running through the community. Now according to numerous witnesses, it seemed that the *Consistoire* had no hesitation in discreetly encouraging Maître Bloch's election.[30] Note moreover that, as in Germany at the same period, some Jews were supporting Colonel de La Rocque, whose followers in France, and even more in Algeria, were showing evidence of anti-Semitic activity, though their leader remained much more restrained in this respect. At Strasbourg, for example, Jews applauded him at a meeting at which Léon Blum was sharply attacked.[31]

The example of Edmond Bloch is an illustration of how Franco-Judaism had lost its way. This time it was not identifying with the republican nation but with the worst reactionary and aggressive right-wing nationalism, which in the long term ran the risk of carrying along with it a *Consistoire* that was merely traditionalist. Remember, first of all, that Edmond Bloch took part with ex-soldiers in the riots of 6 February 1934, until late into the night.[32] Again, in January 1937 right-wing veterans organized a meeting to promote the 'protection of French civilization'. The *Rassemblement français* not only invited Rabbis Kaplan and Louis Germain Lévy to this demonstration which took place in the Salle Wagram; it also invited Maître Edmond Bloch. The situation became so explosive and the indignation of several Jews so fierce that Rabbi Kaplan, at the explicit request of the *Consistoire*, refused to attend this strongly nationalist meeting. It was as well he did. While Rabbi Louis Germain Lévy and Maître Bloch 'stayed placidly on the rostrum', the hall resounded with cries of 'Down with Blum!', 'Down with the Jews!'.[33] As *Parizer haynt*, a moderate Yiddish-language daily paper, soberly commented: 'Getting together with a band of anti-Semites and fascists, the best of Hitler's friends, to fight a supposed danger. . . . is doing dirty work.'[34]

The lawyer Edmond Bloch appears to have been rabidly anti-Blum, translating into action and expanding a nationalist tendency which was emerging into the open. It can even be seen in *L'Univers israélite*, a paper with quasi-official standing, in which a Jewish reader, the head of a clinic at the Faculty of Medicine in Paris, had no hesitation in writing: 'there is no theoretical contradiction between the religion and the political doctrines known as right-wing; on the contrary, they are close to one another through the similarity of their objectives and their spiritual outlook'.[35] Maître Bloch was simply taking such an ideological choice to absurd lengths in the conflict-filled context of the 1930s when the Jews were under attack from a number of right-wing groups. In *Le Temps* in June 1936, together with other Jews who were officers of the *Légion d'honneur* and holders of the *Croix de guerre*, he published the *Manifeste de l'Union patriotique des Français israélites*, which merits attention from historians of modern Judaism. 'Strong in its loyal and healthy doctrine', the manifesto announced that 'Judaism and the Israelites have two declared enemies against whom we have struggled since the first day of our constitution and which we do not separate: Hitlerian-type racism; materialism on the Soviet model. . . . We have always proclaimed that the nation has priority over race, that religion comes after homeland. Frenchmen of the Israelite persuasion maintain, as they have always maintained, that the first human solidarity they practise is national solidarity.'[36]

This time it was too much. Community spokesmen were quick to dissociate themselves from this movement which they had rather more than tolerated. To begin with, Raymond-Raoul Lambert took up a hostile stance. After dealing a blow to the Left by severely criticizing Bernard Lecache's action in leading the *Ligue contre le racisme et l'antisémitisme*, he harshly attacked Edmond Bloch and his manifesto:

There is good and bad, as in all manifestos, but this time I think that the bad is predominant. . . . we used to criticize the Judaism of the extreme Left; from now on, we will criticize the Judaism of the extreme Right, because the comments on these ideas by *L'Action française* are – I regret to say – such as to render them suspect in the future. . . . There is one phrase that sticks out. 'Religion comes after homeland' is written with a somewhat pretentious slickness. The problem could not have been worse-stated than by justifying all the confusion in advance. . . . . Therefore let us not mix up spiritual duties with freely accepted obligations to the State. Finally, except for our rabbis and our teachers, we do not recognize anyone's right and authority to talk about religion in the public domain. If that were not the case, we would be justified in requiring proof that those who are speaking keep a Jewish home.[37]

L'Univers israélite solemnly intended to reaffirm the validity of the framework bounding Franco–Judaism, which Edmond Bloch had transgressed by bringing politics into religious matters and introducing it into the public domain.

In the same spirit, *La Tribune juive* reported favourably on the creation of the *Union patriotique des Français israélites* and invited Jews to support it.[38] Now, faced with the contents of the *Manifeste*, it abruptly changed its mind.

To warn our co-religionists against the demon which is taking them on the slippery slope towards subversive doctrines, we do not need an organization, an office, a president with advisers. Their religious law, their commonsense and the organs of French Judaism are more than sufficient . . . M. Edmond Bloch wants to unite the Israelites, whom he calls patriots, to lead them to a victory, which would be his victory if he overcomes those whom he calls anti-national. . . . As Israelites, we belong to no party. All Israelites have a deep love of their homeland. . . . Our religious opinions are independent of our political opinions. . . . M. Edmond Bloch is a total stranger to Judaism. He knows neither our traditions nor our history. . . . He wants to play a political role and draw our co-religionists into the right-wing parties. But he is doing it badly. . . . Because M. Léon Blum has now come to power, the national parties' polemic has become so violent that they do not flinch from jeopardizing national unity or shaking the whole edifice of French ethos.[39]

Positions were now fixed. There was no further question of turning to the national parties and their Jewish imitators under the guise of fighting the socialist movement led by Léon Blum, who as a Jew was the provocation for a strong anti-Semitic revival. For the extremism of the nationalist faction ran the risk of 'shaking the whole edifice of the French ethos' and bringing the essential element – that is, Franco-Judaism – down with it. *Tribune juive* did not let up:

Maître Bloch has adopted the habits of his non-Jewish friends. . . . For over a hundred years, the Jews have done nothing but assimilate, but this does not appease the Maurras and the Vallats and Maître Edmond Bloch's other friends. Is it because Léon Blum and Georges Mandel are not assimilated Jews? The National Front and the other anti-Jews do not regard them as Frenchmen. Maître Bloch is proud of having been welcomed by these anti-Semites because they kept a place for him on the platform.[40]

This is a long way from the ceremony at the Temple de la Victoire! The split was complete: from then on people were no longer afraid to declare their complete solidarity with Léon Blum even though they had previously rejected him. The full importance of this turning point must be emphasized, because it very largely exonerates the communal institutions, which some historians of French Judaism in the inter-war period are too quick to condemn.

None the less Maître Edmond Bloch continued on his chosen path. He expressed complete agreement when Henri de Kerilis, who was himself attacked by the extreme Right for defending anti-Munich policies, criticized Jules Moch's appointment as Under-Secretary of State to the Blum government. 'Cousin or not', de Kerilis exclaimed, 'he definitely belongs to the family. . . . One might say that by his excesses M. Léon Blum wants to revive one of those violent outbursts of anti-Semitism which have sometimes broken out in the country.'[41] Edmond Bloch was quick to respond: 'Alas, how right you are. I can not disagree with a word of anything you say.'[42] Charles Trochu, president of the *Association nationale des officiers combattants*, appealed to Bloch in the following terms: 'Our ancient Gallo-Roman nation is governed by a Jew, and surrounded by a band of insolent Jews. Are you ready, Edmond Bloch – and I am apppealing to you, the proudest of well-born Jews, as to a living symbol of the Jewish heroes of the Great War – are you ready to drive out, as they deserve, the Blums, the Zays, the Abrahams and the whole greedy tribe squatting in our national palaces?'[43] Despite all the clouds which were gathering, and the growing anti-Semitic hysteria, at meetings in July 1938 Edmond Bloch still sat beside Doriot, Maurras, Daudet and even Xavier Vallat.[44]

However, he was not the only Jew to join the extreme right-wing camp and to agitate within it. Some of them were particularly active in the ranks of *Action française* where the most obscene anti-Semitism was expressed every day. The subscription list for the sword of the Academy that French nationalists offered to Charles Maurras contains an impressive number of Israelites, almost all natives of Alsace-Lorraine.[45] And Maurras was the man who led *Action française* and reserved all his anti-Semitic hatred for Léon Blum, whose most ferocious adversary he had become. In the same spirit, Paul Lévy, editor-in-chief of the journal *Aux écoutes*, hotly defended Maurras: '*Action française* is big and beautiful. M. Charles Maurras is not an "aged" man as that ridiculous fellow Emmanuel Berl writes, he is a man of surprising youthfulness with an unconquerable civic courage.'[46] And he added: 'If M. Blum is tuned into French reaction, he must prevent M. Maurras going to prison.'[47] Léon Daudet, the vehement anti-Semitic spokesman for *Action française* wrote:

M. Léon Blum hates patriotic Frenchmen. Everyone knows that. . . . I turn to those who are Jewish by race but French at heart, who have fought, or worked a long time for France, in our faculties or elsewhere, and who write to us daily to regret the new acuteness of the Jewish question. What do they think of articles like Léon Blum's, whether they be inspired by that dandified fool Paul-Boncour or by the secret funds of the pro-German janissaries of the SG, or even if they be a hideous discharge from the Germanic sores of that circumcised hybrid?. . . . Do they not think that the worst risk to the Jewish community would be a Dreyfus-type attack, renewed in 1900, 1901, 1902, against the French general staff?. . . . His compatriots in Sem should really advise him, in the general interests of the Jewish people, to stop talking and quickly. '*Maul zu!*', say the Germans, which in good French means 'Shut your gob!'[48]

Charles Maurras published a letter from a French Jew which again referred to Edmond Bloch's manifesto, and added: 'A Jewish patriot repudiates the stateless and anti-patriotic mystique. . . . which has never ceased to animate Léon Blum and all socialist Israel. Well-born Jews. . . . will understand that the common safety, that of France and their own, is at the price of an effort of legitimate purification. And they will thank you for it with all their heart.'[49] Other Jews chose to write to papers which vied with *L'Action française* in anti-Semitic violence, like *Choc*, in which Édouard Helbronner, on 18 June 1936, chastised Léon Blum in the following terms:

This absolutely impartial and independent paper permits me, a Frenchman of the Israelite religion, a nationalist, who does not hide the fact that he is an Israelite and a nationalist, to give you some simple advice: live where you belong; do not differentiate yourself from other Frenchmen; think French, do not think international. Therefore do not try and take responsibility for the 'France' Society and if by chance or deliberately, you find yourself caught up in political life, work for the greatness of France.[50]

This letter had immediate repercussions nationally, and Jewish circles took up a large number of contradictory positions in response. Some were enthusiastic, others severely condemned this hostile judgement on Léon Blum which had been published in a paper which made no secret of its anti-Semitism. In Algeria, in *Le Petit Oranais* which daily discharged an uninterrupted stream of anti-Jewish hatred at Léon Blum, an Israelite schoolmistress published an article in which she expressed the wish that the text of Helbronner's letter should be posted up everywhere. Together with 'the Israelites of Oran worthy of the fine name of Frenchmen', she offered to organize a collection for this purpose. At the same time, she harshly criticized Jews like Bernard Lecache who did not conceal their socialist sympathies and acted openly as Jews in public life.[51] Finally, others even ended up joining movements in the vanguard of extremism, such as *Franciste*.[52]

Disillusion with collaboration pursued with Vichy's active and deliberate participation, only lasted for a while. Again, during the Mendès France experiment, and above all during the Algerian war, nationalist Jews co-operated with the most intolerant movements which were not above singing the old anti-Semitic songs. From this point of view, Pierre Mendès France now found himself almost in the same boat as Léon Blum.

The inevitable Edmond Bloch had learned nothing. Twenty years on, beyond the tragedies of collaboration to which several of his then friends had surrendered, he remained true to himself. On 1 October 1954, faced with the peace process pursued by Mendès France to end the Indochina war and on the subject of what he, along with many others, was already calling 'the abandonment' of North Africa, he wrote: 'It is important that you know, Sir and dear compatriot, that M. Mendès France commits no one but himself, that his policy is his personal policy, that he has no capacity to represent anyone but himself and the politicians who support him, and that his co-religionists in particular have no wish to share either the glory or the opprobium with him.'[53] The vocabulary has stayed the same. The terms of the accusation have not changed.

The nationalist Jews, whom Bloch personified, had no wish to be confused with Mendès France any more than with Léon Blum. The nationalist movements were recruiting fewer people then than in the inter-war period. They were both less powerful and less in evidence in public life. In addition, Pierre Mendès France's particular characteristics, his concern for the maintenance of Franco-Judaism and the fact that for a time he symbolized for everyone a sort of Jewish De Gaulle, provided, despite everything, less encouragement for the form of self-hatred – quite exceptional in France – practised by Jewish members of extremist movements. For example, no denunciations of Pierre Mendès France's actions by hypothetical Jewish Poujadists seem to have appeared in *Fraternité française*. It was Pierre Poujade himself who frequently interrogated Jews, demanding that they clearly dissociate themselves from Mendesian policy and the policy of capital.[54]

Note, however, that after his declarations in favour of peace in the Middle East, Pierre Mendès France was sent the yellow star worn by an anonymous Jew during the Vichy period. The sender meant it as an expression of extreme disapproval.⁵⁵ The incident, which is very revealing of the strong emotion Mendès France aroused in certain Jews, irresistibly recalls the accusations uttered in Léon Blum's day. Just as certain Jews under the Popular Front adopted the assertions of the extreme Right, of some factions of the Right wing and even of the Socialist party, that the proportion of Jews in the socialist leader's entourage was far too high, so now other Jews said the same thing about Pierre Mendès France. It happened moreover, that Georges Boris, the man principally accused, was the faithful associate of both Blum and Mendès France. He certainly provided the link between one period and the next. He was the object of violent anti-Semitic attacks at the time of the Popular Front. He was once more the target during the Mendès France experiment.

The attack was led by a great Jewish notable, René Mayer, former President of the Council. In a much-publicized letter to Emmanuel Astier de la Vigerie, he declared apropos Georges Boris, the man who manifestly played a decisive role in implementing Mendès France's policy:

I do not think I need a lesson from this character, either in patriotism or as a Frenchman of the Israelite persuasion. I maintain only that, after eight years, M. Boris has not understood the harm that he and his peers did to their co-religionists by their indiscreet invasion of political power in Léon Blum's train, much more than the policy of the then President of the Council, but which sowed the seed without which Hitler's propaganda could never have had the effect in France that, as you know, it unfortunately did.⁵⁶

René Mayer, who contributed decisively to the fall of the Mendès France government by inspiring the strategy of the right-wing parties, thus revived one of the most well-worn themes of traditional anti-Semitism: that the role of Jews in the state was excessive. The metaphor of 'invasion', used by large numbers of extremist authors, is the anti-Semitic version of the Jews' integration into the state. Observers took considerable note of this confrontation. For *Combat*, 'this avowed hatred is coloured – why not say it outright? – by an unpleasant whiff of whispered anti-Semitism which Monsieur René Mayer has just unexpectedly underwritten'.⁵⁷ The extreme right-wing press gloated at the sight of French Jews tearing themselves apart: 'But the funniest thing about this whole episode, Sir', Jean Pleyber emphasized in *Rivarol*, 'is that Mendès's opponent is Mayer, the Rothschilds' rabbi. Here we have two Jews, two free-masons, two radicals, two Gaullists from London and Algeria who should have got on together like the best of pals. Really, Sir, you can't bet on anything anywhere....'.⁵⁸ Barnet Litvinoff has the last word in the story: 'The Sephardi was defeated by his old "Ashkenazi" enemy, René Mayer.'⁵⁹

THE CASE OF THE LEFT-WING JEWS: THE EXAMPLE OF BERNARD LECACHE AND SOME OTHERS

Left-wing Jews were divided amongst an even greater number of political parties and associations. They could sometimes be found in the large mass parties, such as the socialists or communists, or in groups engaged in the struggle to defend liberties, like the LICA or the MRAP. Sometimes they were members of specifically Jewish movements, like the Bund; or else they made their views known through Yiddish-language papers, directed more at immigrants from Eastern Europe. It would be deeply interesting to carry out systematic research into their reactions to the appointments of Léon Blum and Pierre Mendès France and their assessments of the policies implemented by the two ministers. The result would then serve as a counterpart to the foregoing brief exposé of the reactions and assessments of the *Consistoire*, the traditionalist institutions and the nationalist Jews. Even though it means neglecting a large number of sources, the emphasis here will be primarily on the positions taken up by the LICA, the MRAP and papers close to the communist party, like *Naie Presse*.

Bernard Lecache, who was always very active in both the inter-war years and the decolonization period, stands out from the start as an important figure in left-wing Judaism. The crucial role he played over such a long period of time makes him a symbol. Constantly active, signing manifestos, organizing meetings and demonstrations, travelling around mainland France and Algeria to encourage discussion everywhere, making his officials available to maintain order when the need arose, and having no hesitation in forming his own defence groups to oppose the extreme right-wing leagues, Bernard Lecache deserves a long biographical study to himself. The LICA fulfilled such an important role that he is the perfect illustration of the hopes and fears not only of the Jews of France but also, on the even wider stage, those of the whole Left.

Lecache was the anti-Edmond Bloch *par excellence*. At the outset, no sooner had the Popular Front won their victory, than the editor of *Droit de vivre* asked the new head of government to take not only Matignon but also the Quai d'Orsay in hand: 'In the name of the Frenchmen of the Popular Front, Léon Blum, you have a mission to fulfil. It is you who must speak to the fascists. It is you who must conquer them. It is you, just because you are Blum, who must unite men everywhere in peace, in the face of and against a Hitler.'[60] Rejecting the balanced and cautious behaviour of the *Consistoire* and the representative organs of the community, he openly and strongly appealed for complete support for Léon Blum who 'has never denied his race. . . . and has an unusually lofty conception of the homeland'.[61] There was only one strategy open to the Jews faced with the rise of fascism abroad and the challenge to the Republic made by the allies of fascism within the Hexagon. Jews had to rely on the forces of the Left: they alone were capable of blocking the violence of the extreme Right which threatened to sweep away the Republic and thereby deal a fatal blow to the Jews. That is why Lecache spoke out vehemently against the *Consistoire*'s behind-the-scenes support of Edmond Bloch in the 1936 legislative elections. At times of danger, such compromises were not acceptable. Lecache and the militants of the LICA enthusiastically supported Léon Blum to the end.[62]

Curiously, the grotesque conflict between Edmond Bloch and Bernard Lecache which emerged during the Popular Front period and which revealed the deep-seated discord amongst French Jews, was repeated at the time of the Mendès France experiment. Bloch attacked the President of the Council and put all his efforts into alienating the Jews from him. Lecache, on the other hand, helped Mendès France and took up the battle against the anti-Semitism which was now attacking the radical leader. 'I am not', he said, 'part of the Mendès France entourage, though I still esteem and, in certain respects, admire him. . . . Racists are like wasps. You drive them out. They reproduce, return, finally sting you. I support the fly-tox policy.'[63] As in the *Je suis partout* period, he now attacked *Aspects de la France* which was waging a vigorous anti-Semitic campaign under the signature of Pierre Boutang. 'Professional racists have not changed' since the Blum period, he commented. 'Their brains have simply softened.'[64] As in the 1930s, the German question again provoked dissent. This time it concerned the attitude which should be adopted to the problem of German rearmament. This was the crucial question of the day, which aroused so many nightmares and contradictory fears, with the need for international balance between the West as a whole and the East. The Paris agreements threatened to split the government coalition, provoked angry outbursts in all parties and, on the Left, aroused the wrath of the Communist Party. The Jews for their part, also hesitated and, depending on their political allegiance, took up differing positions on Pierre Mendès France's policy, in a situation, moreover, where he was simultaneously faced with a strong anti-Semitic campaign.

A comparison of the analyses of *Droit de vivre* and *Droit et Liberté*, the organ of the MRAP and close to the Communist Party, is sufficient to show how greatly left-wing Jews were divided on this fundamental point. Lecache wished Mendès France a similar fate to Disraeli in the success of his policy, but added: 'We will not switch on the illuminations, we will not shout out in triumph', reckoning that reconciliation with Moscow was essential.[65] Contrary to this understanding attitude, *Droit et Liberté* declared itself totally opposed to the London agreements and strongly denounced the anti-Semitic campaign that *Rivarol* and *Aspects de la France* were waging against the President of the Council. On 25 August 1954 the MRAP even sent an open letter to Pierre Mendès France, establishing a direct connection between German rearmament and the resurgence of anti-Semitism.[66] In the same paper, the *Union des sociétés juives de France* also came out against the rearmament favoured by the President of the Council.[67]

The tone of *Droit et Liberté* became ever sharper, equalling that of *L'Humanité*, but it placed more stress on Mendès France's Jewish allegiance which it found incompatible with his foreign policy. The 15 January 1955 issue was absolutely typical of this point of view. 'Read this list carefully', *Droit et Liberté* demanded. 'These are the 287 deputies who voted on December 30 for the rearmament of the Nazi executioners who assassinated your parents, your neighbours, so many of your innocent loved ones.' Mendès France figured on that list as did Jules Moch and Daniel Mayer. The whole issue of the paper appeared to emphasize this adherence to Judaism which seemed totally at variance with German rearmament. Henry Bulawko, president of the Hashomer Hatza'ir group, and André Blumel signed declarations opposing Mendès France's policy and for once the paper also published a statement from the CRIF denouncing it. *Droit et Liberté* concluded:

Six million Jews, including two million children, were exterminated by the Nazis. The anger and indignation of the survivors at the rearmament of the former executioners is understandable, even if this time by the chance combination of political circumstances, a Mendès France or a Jules Moch stand surety for this monstrosity.... The vote of a Jew [and this is explicitly aimed at Mendès France] in favour of the assassins of six million Jews appears more odious perhaps than the same vote by non-Jewish deputies. This fact is not less scandalous for being comprehensible.[68]

The communist Jewish press in Yiddish all followed the general policy drawn up by the Communist Party. But, like *L'Humanité*, the favourable or hostile opinions it expressed on Léon Blum or Pierre Mendès France never mentioned their adherence to Judaism. *Naie Presse* came out against French fascism and stated that 'the Jewish workers stand beside the Popular Front because they are hostile to fascism, because they do not want to experience again the fate of their ancestors in the Middle Ages'.[69] Adopting the same phraseology as all the communist press, it waged war on the 200 families and the 'men of money', strongly opposed the reactionary Jewish candidate during the election campaign, and in both 1936 and 1938 begged Léon Blum to pursue the policy of the Popular Front with the CP.[70]

At the time of the Mendès France experiment, *Naie Presse*, in accordance with the guidelines defined by Maurice Thorez, supported the new President of the Council and later explained his fall by the fact that Mendès France 'was no longer useful to the bourgeoisie'.[71] The paper later found itself in a difficult situation when, in the presence of witnesses, Jacques Duclos gave vent to anti-Semitic abuse of Pierre Mendès France. Mendès France had just refused to include the communist votes supporting his investiture; Jacques Duclos lost control. 'He is a coward', he declared, 'a little scared Jew who chatters away and is afraid to act! He is a shit but without the silk stockings.' A war of words ensued between the different Yiddish-language papers of opposing political persuasions. For *Unzer Shtime*, 'racist remarks from the mouth of an associate of *Nouvelle Presse*. . . . I beg your pardon, of *L'Humanité*! What will the Jews who (still) read the *Nouvelle Presse* say about this Nazi insult by Monsieur Jacques Duclos?'[72] In the same spirit and on the same day, *Unzer Vort* carried a front-page headline: 'Jacques Duclos: An Anti-Semite' and considered that 'in anger, in a sincere outburst, Duclos has revealed the anti-Semitic thoughts which he habitually masks for reasons of tactics and discipline'.[73] *Unzer Vort* carried on the polemic for almost a fortnight with any number of framed inserts on the front page, putting *Naie Presse* in an impossible position and forcing it to react with a particularly ill-timed choice of words recalling the most tragic times in the history of the Jews of France: '*Unzer Vort*'s calumnies against the French Communist Party, worthy of the *Judenrat*, are arousing a mighty anger amongst the Jewish masses.'[74]

Bulletin de nos communautés, one of the quasi-official mouth-pieces of the Jews of France, compared Pierre Mendès France to Moses, so 'fair and true is his policy'.[75] Because of his Jewish origin, Mendès France, like Léon Blum before him, was at the centre of innumerable controversies rending the Jewish world. As there were Jews belonging to both the extreme Right and the extreme Left, they even reached the point, through political loyalty and perhaps in self-defence, of reviving genuinely anti-Semitic slogans or, at least, of defending those who uttered them.

NOTES

1 Raymond-Raoul Lambert, 'M. Léon Blum, président du Conseil', *L'Univers israélite*, 22 May 1936.
2 *Tribune juive*, 28 Oct. 1982.
3 *Samedi*, 23 May 1936.
4 *Samedi*, 19 June 1937. Rabi made the following comments on the fall of the Blum government in *Samedi*: 'This failed policy has done more for anti-Semitism than ten Dreyfus Affairs. This Disraeli was nothing but a frequenter of socialist meetings. He would have done better to stay on the Council of State' (quoted in *Tribune juive Strasbourg–Paris*, 6 Jan. 1939).
5 The Zionist position is quite original from this point of view. For *La Terre retrouvée*, 'only Zionists would have the moral right to be displeased that Blum should be President of the Council today, because from the Zionist point of view, his is a great talent which can no longer belong entirely to the Jewish people. But that this displeasure should come from French, very French, Jews who are French before all else, and who advocate integration into the French nation, this is unbelievable on all counts! It is they who should be pleased and proud that a French Israelite is the full expression of Jewish integration in the bosom of the French nation' (25 June 1936).
6 *La Tribune juive*, 12 June 1936.
7 *L'Univers israélite*, 19 June 1936.
8 *Paix et Droit*, June 1936.
9 Again in 1965, during a colloquium on Léon Blum organized by the *Fondation nationale des science politiques*, André Blumel, one of the closest associates of the socialist President of the Council, declared: 'It was at that time that the Chief Rabbi of Paris took a most unusual step

The Jews of France 79

vis-à-vis Léon Blum – Léon Blum never knew exactly who provoked this step – the Chief Rabbi of Paris came to see him to say: "If you do not take the Presidency of the Council, 'one' pledges to grant you a pension for your whole life equivalent to the President of the Council's salary" ' (in Pierre Renouvin and René Remond (eds), *Léon Blum, chef de gouvernement 1936–1937* (Presses de la Fondation nationale des sciences politiques, Paris, 1981), p. 46. In his earlier article, 'Léon Blum, juif et sioniste', *Revue de la pensée juive*, no. 9 (autumn 1951), p. 9, André Blumel describes this step as 'a base and vile insult had it not been covered up by a childhood friendship'. On the subject of Jewish reactions in general, see P. Aubery, *Milieux juifs de la France contemporaine* (Edition de Minuit, Paris, 1957), pp. 180–3.

10 Phyllis Albert Cohen, *The Modernization of French Jewry: Consistory and community in the nineteenth century* (Brandeis University Press, Hanover, N.H., 1977), p. 314.
11 *Bulletin du Comité de vigilance*, no. 51.
12 *Archives du Consistoire central israélite de Paris*, Box 130. This document and those which follow have been kindly provided by the curator, M. Philippe Landeau.
13 *Archives familiales Philippe Landeau*, 18 Feb. 1933.
14 Ibid., 11 Feb. 1934.
15 *Archives du Consistoire israélite de Paris*, file B.133.
16 Ibid., 16 Feb. 1934.
17 Ibid., 24 Feb. 1934.
18 'Letter to the Chief Rabbi of France', *Rivarol*, 8 March 1956.
19 *L'Univers israélite*, 19 June 1936.
20 Raymond-Raoul Lambert, 'Israel au-dessus des partis', *L'Univers israélite*, 19 June 1936. Note that in 1932 a group of Jews from Narbonne, where Blum had been elected deputy, accused *L'Univers israélite*, in view of the stand it had taken, of no longer appearing 'as a journal of the conservative principles of Judaism, but solely as a journal of conservative principles', *L'Univers israélite*, 29 April 1932.
21 *Vendredi*, 19 June 1936. At a meeting in which André Wurmser, René Cassin, Léon Brunschvicg and Lucien Lévy-Bruhl participated, Henry Bernstein declared: 'Léon Blum's friends claim that Bernstein is fascist. We are as divided as the rest of the nation.... We can support Léon Blum and the communist Jews.... let us join together as men of the same blood' (*Centre de documentation et de vigilance*, BAIU, Sept. 1936). Nonetheless, *L'Univers israélite* stuck to its guns. Describing the violent anti-Semitic attacks on Blum by Maurras, Daudet and Pujo, the paper added: 'Of course, their fury in the presence of the most advanced government the Republic has ever had is comprehensible. But it is another thing to make a whole religious collectivity jointly responsible with its leader, who by chance is of Jewish origin. Their opinions, shades of opinion, as well as their legitimate interests are infinitely varied, essentially dissimilar. As M. Maurras knows as well as anyone else' (7 Aug. 1936). On the episode of the rue de la Victoire, see Zachariah Schuster, 'As Léon Blum began to reign', *Menorah Journal*, Oct. 1936, pp. 312–13.
22 Maurice Rajsfus emphasizes that 'When Léon Blum was defeated and resigned in June 1937, a great sigh of relief was heard between rue Saint-Georges and rue de la Victoire; between the seat of the Consistory and the synagogue where Jacob Kaplan, the friend of the Croix-de-Feu officiates' (in *Sois Juif et tais-toi*, EDI, 1981, p. 35).
23 *La Tribune juive* Strasbourg–Paris, 5 June 1936.
24 Ibid., 6 May 1938. See also the issue of 1 April 1938: 'But why are we fighting M. Léon Blum, Jew? He is so little a Jew'; and of 20 Jan. 1939 where it is stressed that 'these men [Blum, Moch, etc.] are a long way away from the Israelite religion'. On 21 Feb. 1936, after Blum was violently attacked in the boulevard Saint-Germain by members of *Action française*, *La Tribune juive* made

80   The Fate of Franco-Judaism

the following comments: 'The socialist leader, Léon Blum, victim of aggression provoked by his political opponents, is not a fighter for Judaism and puts his dazzling talent and his remarkable intelligence at the service of a cause which is not ours. Therefore, we need not concern ourselves here with this affair which is stirring up the world of politicians.... As a politician, M. Blum represents a political idea which is not a Jewish idea.' In the same spirit, see *L'Ancien Combattant juif*, no. 2 (May 1938).

25 Ibid., 18 Nov. 1938. In the same spirit, see also the issue of 8 April 1938.

26 Thus, the journal *FSJU*, which preceded *L'Arche*, did not mention Mendès France once in 1954–5. Similarly *Les Cahiers de l'Alliance israélite universelle* did not devote a single article to him during the same period. *Tribune juive* only wrote one article – very favourable, moreover – on this subject. Only *La Terre retrouvée*, the Zionist organ, seemed to be fighting the anti-Semitism which raged against Pierre Mendès France in 1954–5 even more keenly than it had the much more intense variety displayed against Léon Blum.

27 This emerges from Gilles Martinet's statement to the colloquium on Pierre Mendès France organized by the IHTP in Dec. 1984.

28 *Le Monde*, 7 July 1982. See also *L'Express*, 9 July 1982.

29 Note here that, according to right-wing observers, certain Jews in the banking sector were equally upset by the Popular Front's advent to power, led by a socialist Jew. According to *Le Rire*, 'his own co-religionists in finance, after weighing up the pros and cons, were not keen on one of theirs taking on such a responsibility, the eventual defeat of which could have serious consequences' (16 May 1936). *Je suis partout* took a slightly different point of view: 'We do not know', declared this anti-Semitic paper, 'how the Jews send out distress signals, but we do know that they are actually doing so from France to America. The Meyers in New York must promise Blum, Moch and Lévy in Paris to save face' (30 May 1936).

30 This, for example, is what *Le Droit de vivre*, the organ of the LICA states very clearly, 16 May 1936.

31 *Le Droit de vivre*, 19 Dec. 1936.

32 *Archives de la préfecture de police*, BA 1853. Edmond Bloch was very active in old-soldier circles. See also BA 1860.

33 *Le Droit de vivre* reported this meeting and stated that if Rabbi Kaplan did not come, it was because 'a certain number of the leaders of the *Consistoire* were aware of the gaffe'. It then described Rabbi Louis Germain Lévy and Maître Bloch as 'Jewish fascists' (30 Jan. 1937).

34 Quoted by Paula Hyman, *From Dreyfus to Vichy: The remaking of French Jewry, 1906–1939* (Columbia University Press, New York, 1979), p. 228.

35 *L'Univers israélite*, 24 April 1936.

36 *Le Temps*, 16 June 1936.

37 *L'Univers israélite*, 26 June 1936.

38 *La Tribune juive Strasbourg–Paris*, 1 May 1936.

39 *La Tribune juive Strasbourg–Paris*, 26 June 1936. See Lazare Landau, *De l'aversion à l'estime: Juifs et catholiques en France de 1919 à 1939* (Édition Le Centurion, Paris, 1980), pp. 299ff.

40 *La Tribune juive Strasbourg–Paris*, 22 July 1938.

41 *L'Écho de Paris*, 28 May 1937.

42 Ibid., 29 May 1937. The Committee of Vigilance commented: 'One would not know how to accept the privilege of collective responsibility for Judaism... Are all Corsicans solidly behind M. Chiappe and all Bretons behind M. Cachin?' (3 June 1937).

43 *Par l'Effort*, April 1937.

44 See *La Tribune juive Strasbourg–Paris*, 1 July 1938.

45 See the list published in *Tribune juive Strasbourg–Paris* which repeated Bernard Lecache's argument in *Le Droit de vivre*, and then added: 'M. Bernard Lecache notes that one might think one were reading a list of subscribers to *L'Univers israélite*. Is he exaggerating?' (24 March 1938).
46 Quoted by *La Tribune juive Strasbourg–Paris*, 6 March 1936. The journal's comments are clear: 'This is what one French Jew is writing in an anti-Jewish paper against another French Jew who does not seem to him to be French enough because he allowed himself to attack Action française.'
47 *Aux écoutes*, 23 Oct. 1936.
48 *L'Action française*, 11 Oct. 1933.
49 Ibid., 18 June 1936.
50 *Choc*, 18 June 1936.
51 *Le Petit Oranais*, 25 June 1936.
52 In *Kadimah*, 25 May 1934, a Jewish reader wrote: 'No, my brothers in Alsace, no! France-ism is not anti-Semitic. France-ism is the fascism of France. France-ism is patriotic and anti-foreigner, yes! but anti-Semitic . . . never. I am an enthusiastic Francist as hundreds of Jews like me have become Francists.'
53 *Nouveaux Jours*, 1 Oct. 1954. In the same issue, M. René Lignac declared that Mendès France 'by himself does not represent all the Israelites'. On 1 Jan. 1955 *Nouveaux Jours* published an article on the Indochina disaster by M. Maurice Weil, former president of the Dijon court of appeal, though without mentioning Mendès France's name.
54 See, for example, the solemn appeal to the Israelites by Pierre Poujade in *Fraternité française* on 11 Feb. 1956. Moreover, on 14 January 1956, *Fraternité française* declared: 'I would like Mendès to interrogate his simple North African co-religionists who have African soil on their shoes on this subject' (that of the Israelite soldiers killed by the FLN).
55 *Archives privées Simone Gros*.
56 Letter reprinted in *Crapouillot*, Jan. 1959, and in Alfred Fabre-Luce, *Vingt-cinq années de liberté* (Julliard, Paris, 1964), vol. 3, p. 194; and in E. Astier de La Vigerie, *Les Dieux et les hommes* (UGC, Paris, 1964), p. 185. On this point, see also Marie-France Toinet, *Georges Boris (1888–1960): Un socialiste humaniste*, thesis for the *Fondation nationale des sciences politiques*, Paris, 1969.
57 *Combat*, 4 Feb. 1955.
58 *Rivarol*, 17 Feb. 1955. On the same point, see also the issue of 24 June 1954.
59 Barnet Litvinoff, *A Peculiar People: Inside the Jewish world today* (Weidenfeld & Nicolson, London, 1969), p. 127.
60 *Le Droit de vivre*, 23 May 1936.
61 Ibid., 15 Feb. 1936.
62 See ibid., 5 Dec. 1936, which has the front-page headline: 'Popular Front 100%. Léon Blum must stay'.
63 Ibid., 30 June 1954.
64 Ibid., 30 Sept. 1954.
65 Ibid., 30 Oct. 1954.
66 *Droit et Liberté*, 25 Aug. 1954.
67 Ibid., 7 Oct. 1954.
68 *Le Droit de vivre*, 15 Jan. 1955.
69 *Naie Presse* (The New Press), 14 July 1935. (The translation from Yiddish is by Jacques Mandelbaum.)

70 See, for example, the issues of *Naie Presse* for 5 May, 22 and 23 June 1936 and 10 April 1938.
71 Ibid., 19 June 1954 and 8 Feb. 1955.
72 *Unzer Shtime* (Our Voice), 19 June 1954.
73 *Unzer Vort* (Our Word), 19 June 1954.
74 *Naie Presse*, 22 June 1954.
75 *Bulletin de nos communautés* (the title which preceded *Tribune juive*), 13 Aug. 1954.

Part II
Drumont's Legacy: Jewish Money, Perversion and Nomadism

Introduction
Neither Right nor Left?

The electoral campaign had just ended. The results had been announced and the happy winners included, noted *L'Univers israélite*, Léon Blum, Pierre Mendès France, Jean Zay, Georges Mandel, Léon Mayer, Pierre Bloch and many other deputies whom it regarded as Jews. And the paper proclaimed its satisfaction: 'The electoral campaign in France has not been marked by a single display of anti-Semitism. The days of Édouard Drumont are gone for ever... there are poisonous plants that can not grow in the free soil of France.'[1] *La Tribune juive*, which loudly proclaimed 'we do not believe in an explosion of anti-Jewish hatred',[2] also thought that the era of contempt, personified in the very name of Édouard Drumont, appeared to be completely in the past. Never again would France know such a period of conflict as when the author of *La France juive* encouraged anti-Semitic hatred by using the Dreyfus Affair to challenge the Jews' emancipation and their integration into the Republic.

This hope rapidly proved vain. In 1920 Léon Daudet, himself closely associated with Drumont's struggle, set the tone. While 'Léon Blum, spokesman of high finance and the Semitic raiders... a Semite with a girlie head and little excited gestures... was talking, talking; I detected above him the prophetic laughter of Drumont who forewarned us of this type of nomad in 1886.'[3] Curiously, the same small group of zealots preaching extreme anti-Semitism continued to exist, with astonishing perseverance and immovable stubborness, from *La France juive* to *Lectures françaises*, from the Dreyfus Affair to the Mendès France government and even into the present time. Endowed with astonishing longevity, as if anti-Semitism were a source of life, Drumont's companions rode buoyantly over the most tragic crises in contemporary French history. Some of them, such as Jean Drault, Urbain Gouhier, Lucien Pemjean and Albert Monniot, obstinately carried on their anti-Semitic manoeuvres from the turn of the century to Vichy, naturally attacking Léon Blum in the process. They thus ensured that Drumont's struggle continued beyond the grave, as Léon Daudet noted, himself in the van of those obsessed with anti-Semitism as practised according to the precepts of *La Libre Parole*.[4]

This paper, created by Drumont, guaranteed the continued existence of a scheme backed by a few loyal supporters already expert in mass communications. It disappeared in 1924, reappearing in 1928 under the editorship of Jacques Ploncard, who attacked Léon Blum in a violently anti-Semitic libel.[5] (Today Jacques Ploncard d'Assac attacks Laurent Fabius.[6]) Ploncard was followed by Henry Coston, who was part of the Francist movement, rivalling Marcel Bucard's movement. Coston stood in the 1936 legislative elections in Algiers for Drumont's old constituency. He stirred up anti-Semitic movements and, from Vichy until the present day, has published *Les Documents maçonniques*, *Lectures françaises* and other writings which uphold the same traditions, though now in a more moderate tone.[7]

In May 1936 *La Libre Parole* celebrated the fiftieth anniversary of *La France juive*. Jean Drault, Drumont's friend, wrote: 'The elections of May 3 last are the direct victory of Judeo-Masonry, financed by money from Moscow'.[8] In the same issue, Henry-Robert Petit, who became one of the most important lampooners under Vichy, added: 'The die is cast. France as a whole has voted red. The Judeo-Masonic block is now master of our country. Israel is king of the land of France. The Talmudic Jew Léon Blum will be arbiter of our destiny.'[9]

Another anniversary occurred on 20 April 1942: the fiftieth anniversary of *La Libre Parole*. In the special issue, which consisted mainly of old articles, Henry Coston wrote: 'It has required the most stinging defeat in our history for a truly French government finally to take the revenge on Israel that Drumont proclaimed half a century ago.' Further on, Blum was named as one of those parasite Jews.[10] A few months before the end of the war, on 20 June 1944, Henry Coston again celebrated Drumont's glory by publishing a final facsimile edition of *La Libre Parole*.

In the same vein in 1890, Jean Drault, one of Drumont's most faithful friends, had given his name to a piece of work entitled *Youtres impudents* and, in 1935, true to himself, he wrote: 'Drumont did not foresee Hitler. However, my old master would perhaps have thought it possible, if not probable, that a Hitler could one day arise when he repeated ... "The Jews will miss me".'[11] In 1942 he was more confident in his judgements: 'When Drumont launched the first issue of *La Libre Parole* on April 20 1892, the avenger was on his way. He was three years old to the day at the time. A. Hitler was born on April 20 1889.'[12] The 'inspired forerunner of French national-socialism', in Robert Brasillach's memorable expression,[13] saw anti-Semitism as 'the link able to reunite the castes of France which the class struggle, organized by Léon Blum's predecessors, had perfidiously divided'.[14] And in 1944 Lucien Rebatet was not afraid to announce: 'I admire Hitler. We admire Hitler. In the fight against all the rubbish of the nineteenth century, Hitler has had innumerable precursors, analysts, dialecticians, more brilliant and more quick-witted than he, including Drumont.'[15] Hitler – and consequently Drumont – was preferable to Blum, as many of his contemporaries so bluntly said.

Continuity from one period to the next was therefore ensured. Drumont's vehement denunciations led directly to anti-Semitic hatred, which was particularly directed at Léon Blum in the inter-war period and during the Vichy episode, and later at Pierre Mendès France, in the attacks made by Henry Coston.[16] In a symbolic sense, it was Drumont himself, through his direct successors, who was attacking these two distinguished state Jews. A few final examples demonstrate this. In 1941 *L'Institut d'études des questions juives* was created in Paris, charged with promulgating racially based anti-Semitic propaganda. The sadly famous exhibition. 'The Jew and France' was held from September 1941; 300,000 people had bought tickets to visit it by September 5.[17] Both Léon Blum and Pierre Mendès France took pride of place among the famous Jews stuck up on the walls of the Berlitz Palace. The exhibition catalogue described Léon Blum's vile personality at length, and lingered over the Jews who gravitated to him, like 'Mendès France (yes, really, France!)'.[18]

Now, on 24 September 1941 an important ceremony in memory of Drumont took place in that same Berlitz Palace, marked by the attendance of M. de Brinon and Xavier Vallat. A visit to the central exhibition on the Jews was particularly planned.[19] Note, as another illustration of this consistency over time, that Xavier Vallat, for example, attacked Léon Blum in the Chamber of Deputies by expressing surprise that a Jew should now be able to lead an ancient Christian country. He later became commissioner-general for Jewish questions under Vichy and in that capacity visited this exhibition in Drumont's honour as well as the rooms where the portraits of Blum and Mendès France were on display. In 1955 under the Mendès France government, stating that 'he had not altered a line in his conception of the Jewish problem', he published a very cautious article on the President of the Council in *Aspects de la France*, though in the framework of a column entitled 'Correspondence on Israel'.[20]

So many encounters do not occur by chance. Drumont's legacy over the years also weighed heavily on the destinies of Léon Blum and Pierre Mendès France. Céline made clear how convinced he was when he devoted ferociously anti-Semitic pages to Blum in *Bagatelles pour un massacre* and judged that 'every Aryan should have read Drumont, Montandon, Darquier de Pellepoix and Henry Coston'.[21] The matter was now clinched and the anti-Semitic tradition appeared as a coherent whole. This was even more the case in 1968, when E. Beau de Loménie, in his turn, published *Édouard Drumont ou l'anticapitalisme national*.[22] He had earlier joined with Jacques Ploncard d'Assac, Maurice Bardèche, J.-M. Rouault, Xavier Vallat and Pierre Dominique in founding a society called '*Les amis de "La Libre Parole"*' in 1963.[23] They were all sympathetic to Drumont's cause; their names will recur on numerous occasions throughout this book. Finally, in January 1986 *Présent*, sympathetic to the National Front, celebrated its thousandth issue by publishing a big article on Drumont, 'the anguished witness of the obliteration of France'.[24] The same weekly had acknowledged this affiliation two years earlier, when the statue of Pierre Mendès France was unveiled. 'There we found', it noted, 'Madame

Mendès France, née Servan-Schreiber, Madame Giroud, Laurent Fabius, François Jacob, and I give up on the Meyers (Daniel).'[25]

When Blum and Mendès France appeared before their judges at the trials of Riom and Clermont-Ferrand under Vichy, they still faced the same adversaries or their intellectual heirs. Also it should not be forgotten that Pétain, like Maurras, opposed Dreyfus at the turn of the century, while Blum plunged into his first political battle alongside Dreyfus's supporters. In this sense, it really was the old 'ghosts who dance in France from 1940 to 1944'.[26] But if, by a curious combination of circumstances, the most rabid followers of anti-Semitism looked as if they were joining hands across the generations, were their frenzied ravings the same, was their paranoid interpretation of Jewish domination unchanged behind the profound transformations that had affected French society over such a long period of time?

This interpretation of Drumont's legacy has some notable supporters, the historian Michel Winock, for example. According to him 'a series of correspondences with, if not reproductions of, the Dreyfus Affair can be observed right through the twentieth century'. The Dreyfus conflict is depicted as a real 'historical paradigm' of anti-Semitism, with first Dreyfus himself, then Léon Blum, and finally Pierre Mendès France, as successive scapegoats.[27] Michel Winock with this article is the only historian to establish the broad outlines of the sort of connection which lies at the heart of this book. He takes the precaution of emphasizing that 'the Dreyfus Affairs' had neither the same scenario nor similar content; there were important variations, for example, in the army, the Church and in anti-Semitism itself.[28] Nevertheless, for him, 'two opposing ethnocentrisms (it might perhaps be better to say "culturocentrisms") have converged to create or aggravate antisemitism: singularist ethnocentrism and universalist ethnocentrism'.[29] The first was the effect of the counter-revolutionary trend which rejected the Jew as other and different from national and religious singularities. The second, on the other hand, was put forward by left-wing men who rejected particularism on the basis of Reason and in their turn sought to re-establish a homogeneous society in the universalist mould.

On this specific point Zeev Sternhell also thinks that the source of anti-Semitism in France can be found on both extreme Right and extreme Left. However, his interpretation of this latter trend differs from Michel Winock's, since he sees it as a component of fascist ideology. For him 'the Jew mirrored the nation's decadence.... There would have been no Dreyfus Affair, no Bloc, no Popular Front, had France not already been on the downward path for many years. Thus anti-Semitism was one aspect of the great revolt against materialism – against liberalism and Marxism – against the core of the intellectual heritage on which Europe had been living since the eighteenth century.'[30]

This is no small divergence of opinion. For Michel Winock left-wing anti-Semitism was an extension of rationalist universalism and consequently, implicitly, Marxism. For Zeev Sternhell it essentially constituted, if not the rejection of rationalist universalism, at least necessarily its profound revision. For Sternhell, 'the 1930s generation more or less adopted and extended the concerns which were those of the men of the 1890s.... Fascism in France drew its sources and its men both from Left and Right, very often much more from Left than from Right.'[31] Fascism and anti-Semitism, then, seem to be inextricably intertwined from one period to the next, even if, as Sternhell is careful to point out, anti-Semitism on the Left survived only in non-conformist ranks after 1914.[32]

Though their approaches are fairly distinct they none the less lead both historians to believe that they can establish the recurrence of certain myths which they claim have endured in modern France. But the moment one turns towards the state, it is apparent that it is nothing of the kind. For us – and this is a crucial point in our overall view which neither of the two authors envisages – *Drumont closed a period*. His successors, even if they sometimes claimed kinship with his work, broke with him, usually unconsciously, on the central point: that of the state. Drumont's anti-Semitism was still crude, mechanistic and economic, and therefore easily reconcilable with left-wing anti-Semitism. It too rested on the myth of the rich, on the demonology of money, to which one trend in nineteenth-century socialist thought all too often adhered, and which was close to a reactionary and Catholic interpretation of history. Like Proudhon, Leroux, Toussenel and Marx on the one hand, but also like Gougenot des Mousseaux or Abbé Chabauty on the other, Drumont saw possession of money as the ultimate source of all power. Money or gold lay at the centre of his cosmology, not the state. In utter opposition to Tocqueville who, from the early nineteenth century, was aware that the strong institutionalization of the state was the result of the singularities peculiar to French society, Drumont knew only the power of money. Ignoring generations and political traditions, it could be said, simplistically of course, that the enemy in Drumont's eyes was already that famous monopolistic state capitalism – that symbolic figure which at the time of the Third International drove the Communist Party, particularly in France, to proclaim *urbi et orbi* that the bankers had infiltrated the state; that the most powerful of them, the Rothschilds, directed the apparatus of the state in the same way as monopolistic capitalism was oppressing the whole nation. Should we see in Drumont's strong influence a sort of predisposition to such simplistic and reductionist visions in a country where, moreover, Marxist-inspired theoretical research has been relatively weak and tardy?

Basically, if Drumont believed that everything, the state included, could be bought, this was really because money made it possible to take possession of the state:

The Jew sheltered under the same umbrella as the bourgeoisie: the principles of '89 ... in reality it was he that the bourgeoisie worked for and, above all, made others work. The fox waits until the chickens have grown fat before gobbling them up. The Jew waited until the pile was made before removing it with a smooth gesture and a smile ... The bourgeoisie exploiting the People and then, in its turn, being stripped by the Jew – there you have a summary of the economic history of this century.[33]

It has rarely been noted that Drumont's nightmare hinged on an economic interpretation of society which could not fail to seduce socialist theorists with an equally mechanistic approach. In this sense, the key to history was not the class struggle but the battle which the people waged against a bourgeoisie subjected to the power of the Jew. The state had no place in this strange social stratification: it was the power of the Jew in action. For Drumont, 'the Judaized Bourgeoisie operates everywhere, either through its representatives or its officials. In France, it has re-established slavery in the industrial regions.'[34] It was not the bourgeoisie, as in the strictly Marxist interpretation, who controlled the state. It was the Jews who led it and enslaved, through their agency, industrial society as a whole.

An obsessive leitmotif runs right through Drumont's work: 'the Jews have come to command all the enterprise of the State', he noted;[35] or again, 'France fell into dissolution as a result of the principles of '89, skilfully exploited by the Jews. The Jews had monopolized all public wealth, invaded everything, except the army.'[36] For him, 'the Jew appears as master ... he has bought all the statesmen who were for sale and removed from their posts those he could not corrupt'.[37] Consequently, 'the Jew-official has invaded everything ... [the Jews] have entered public office like a hunted robber enters a house when he sees the front door open'.[38] In the legislative elections in February 1890, Drumont canvassed votes for Laur, the candidate for the Neuilly constituency: 'A vote for Laur is a blow struck at the heart of financial Jewry which imagines that, because it has bought everything in the Government and the Chambers that is for sale, everything in France is up for sale.'[39]

On 1 May 1891 brawls broke out at Fourmies between striking and non-striking workers and the employers who had pressured the opportunist mayor Bernier into persuading the young sub-prefect of Avesnes, Ferdinand Isaac, to send in troops. The crowd abused the soldiers, who responded by firing. Nine deaths were reported, including two children, two youths, and four girls, and 35 people were injured. The workers blamed the employers. The employers said the socialists were responsible. But Drumont greedily seized on this affair as symbolic of the cruel domination of the working class by the Jews. 'Perhaps this was simply Isaac's own way of celebrating the centenary of the emancipation of the Jews in 1791.... Isaac can be considered one of the most curious specimens of the officials of the Hebraic Republic which is dishonouring and ruining France.'[40] What was more, he had been appointed 'sub-prefect without taking any examination'.[41] Now all was clear: thanks to their gold, the Jews were invading the state; they did not respect the rules of the administrative profession since, from the outset, their appointment did not rest on universalist-type meritocratic criteria. At Fourmies, and at Belfort as well, the prefectorial body, the guarantor of state order, was the creature of the Jews: 'Go into that Belfort synagogue now', Drumont advised. 'You will find the prefect there. At Belfort, the prefect is a Jew, naturally. Belfort will be crucially important in time of war and the Jews will always be in the right places. It is Yom Kippur and, clad in the tallit, phylacteries on his head and arms, the prefect is praying.'[42]

This is the crucial point. Drumont's anti-Semitism belonged to the past because it conveyed the ancient beliefs in the maleficent power of money, possessed only by Jews because they made it their profession. Traditional anti-Semitism, the anti-Semitism which had been passed down unchanged through the ages, and which came to the surface in every latitude, in every society, was here simply brought to its high point. That new Shylock, Rothschild was king and, through his sbirri, the Master owned the state. It was on him that traditional nineteenth-century – but also twentieth century – anti-Semitism concentrated its fire. Drumont's work certainly established him in the public consciousness.[43] Economic anti-Semitism thus appeared as a sort of socialism.[44] The economic argument proved fundamental: Jewish high finance was all-powerful and it was engulfing the state. Influenced by Drumont, *La Croix* calculated that there were 'barely 70,000 Jews in France and they were represented in the ministry, the Senate, the Chamber. There are 40 of their race at the *École polytechnique*; they can be found in every public office.'[45]

Catholic anti-Semitism, for its part, has always made its own this theme of money associated with the absolute power of the Jews. It literally exploded in France at the turn of the century in the context of the Dreyfus Affair and in accordance with Drumont's ideas. Over two million copies of every issue of *La Croix*, with its regional editions in which anti-Semitism was omnipresent, were sold every week.[46] The link between Drumont and Catholic anti-Semitism was helped considerably by the crash of the *Union générale*, an important Catholic bank. Drumont and other contemporaries attributed its failure to the deliberate actions of the Rothschild bank.[47]

This economic anti-Semitism, shared by a considerable part of Catholic France at the time, implied as a consequence the total sovereignty of money and the non-existence of the state. These two dimensions are so closely linked that Drumont, drawing his inspiration from the situation which prevailed in the Middle Ages – that is, before the creation of the state – described how 'the feudal Jews on top of their piles of gold, lie in wait for every caravan that passes on the horizon carrying ideas or discoveries, like the lords on top of their donjons in former times. They bar the way to right and left by their press or their associates in the government, rob it, hold it to ransom.'[48] If, consequently, 'everything is in fief to the Jews', if 'the Jew has rebuilt the whole feudal system to his own advantage',[49] the explanation, according to this economic and mechanistic anti-Semitism (and, from this point of view, according to reductionist Marxism also), was that the very strong institutionalization of the state, with its ancient history as recounted by historians, had magically disappeared. Once again the people were left face to face with those new lords, the Jews.

To be fair, Drumont did sometimes hesitate and embark on a careful examination of 'the functioning of this state within a state that is Jewry'.[50] Naturally, he again found a formula, whose origins we have already traced when talking of Jacob Katz. He then slightly altered the international structure of his myth because, in these circumstances, the Jews dominated only one part of the state and not the entire state – and he continued to reiterate it at length in books and articles. It can be seen that the internal arrangement varied from one presentation to another. On other occasions, the Jews carefully kept their distance from a state bourgeoisie that they dominated and to which they owed the unlimited power they exercised over the people.

Such variations on the relationships between the rich, the bourgeoisie, the state and the people have come to the surface all through contemporary French history. Economic anti-Semitism simply introduced a particular group into this mechanism of ideas: the body which, it claimed, the Jews constituted. Nevertheless, it hesitated over the exact designation of the place that they occupied in it and the role which devolved on them.[51] The general perspective was none the less clearly drawn: the Jews were foreigners to the people of France who were impregnated with fervent Catholicism. They had come from far-off, exotic lands and could be identified by their physical appearance, the odour which generally accompanied them and a propensity to excessive sexuality. They were unsuited to any profession except usury and the speculative handling of money: in particular, they did not know the virtues of tilling the soil. They were strongly attached to ancestral traditions which strengthened their communal solidarity, transcending the frontiers of the country they were temporarily living in. To reinforce their world domination, they had no qualms about causing the disintegration of every society by means of an international revolutionary plot which would overturn the established order and the natural hierarchies. Nor were they reluctant to promote the spread of an equally cosmopolitan capitalism to aid the assertion, by one means or another, of their control of every state power. This definition of the Jews, in which each element was connected, led inexorably to the instrumentalist concept of a state that was fundamentally heterogeneous with regard to society. At the turn of the century, both the extreme Left and the extreme Right shared these views, for they were at the heart of traditional anti-Semitism. Gougenot des Mousseaux and Barrès on one hand, Toussenel and Chirac on the other, furnish the final proof.

From this point of view it is very instructive to re-read the champions of Catholic anti-Semitism. For Gougenot des Mousseaux, 'the Jew is or rather will be, our master'. In France, 'a state is taking shape within the state', that of the Jews, agents of the evil which wants to de-Christianize society. 'Do they not swarm in the administration, in the councils and in the high offices of state?'[52] Seeing himself as Toussenel's loyal heir, he could then conclude: 'The Jew has us in his grip, he is our master, not only because we no longer own the gold, but, let us never cease to repeat, because it is the gold which owns us. . . . he will only let go if confronted with the revival of Christian education.'[53] For him, as for Abbé Chabauty, the Jew was the Antichrist perverting Catholic France by virtue of his gold and the Third Republic which he had proclaimed.[54] Here is another explicit link between traditional anti-Semitism, both economic and Catholic – two dimensions which strengthen each other – and the instrumentalist interpretation of the role of the state in France.

Still on the extreme Right, Maurice Barrès, who was supported by Drumont and Rochefort in his electoral campaigns, denounced in his turn the high officials who 'come from the synagogue'. For the author of *Déracinés*, 'appointed prefects, judges, treasurers, officers because they have the money which corrupts', the Jews reign over the whole of France.[55] Adopting Drumont's socio-economic anti-Semitism for his own purposes, Barrès denounced 'Semitic high finance', which owned 'the public wealth' to such an extent that, according to him, 'most of the members of the government are Jews'.[56] Against the 'uprooted' of every ilk, he too preached respect for 'the land and the dead', excluding the Semites who corrupted French blood and vitality from the organically based national community. Barrès, the prince of literature on whom the young Léon Blum bestowed limitless admiration, interpreted the Dreyfus Affair as 'a war of races' and coined the inexorable, much-quoted phrase: 'From his race I deduce that Dreyfus is capable of treason.'[57] When Blum thought it natural to ask Barrès for his signature in support of Dreyfus, the refusal astonished him. It was a rude shock and, even if Blum forgave Barrès a great deal in view of the immense intellectual esteem he had for the writer, the break between the two men was complete. Blum had still been convinced of Barrès's 'true friendship' for him, his 'solicitude as for an older brother'. The cautious, negative reply was 'like a bereavement' to him. Something was broken, ended, 'one of the avenues of my youth was closed'.[58]

And it was Blum who condemned the pernicious influence of Drumont and Boulangism and denounced the editor of *La Libre Parole* which made no bones about its support for Barrès. He explicitly designated Drumont as the evil genius, Drumont who thought that the Jews were like 'a foreign body, a body impossible to assimilate'. This 'theoretical postulate', Blum emphasized, 'is precisely the one found again today in Hitlerian racism which has given it other forms and drawn all its consequences'.[59]

This was a poignant moment. Now the chips were down and everyone had taken up their final positions in perhaps the most harrowing and tragic Franco-French war which marked for all the protagonists the brittleness and limits of Franco-Judaism. From Drumont to Barrès and up to the completely Hitlerian delirium in its Vichyite manifestation, everything was done to eradicate 'the Jewish state within the French state', to adopt the phrase of the author of *Scènes et doctrines du nationalisme*, which followed the same path as traditional anti-Semitism. This therefore was at last the end of the 'religious marriage of Marianne and the wandering Jew'.[60] The Jews were 'barbarians': they must no longer be Frenchmen. The rejection of Léon Blum, Georges Mandel, Jules Moch and Pierre Mendès France was not far off.

Many historians have emphasized the emergence on the extreme Left in the second half of the nineteenth century of an identical, basically anticapitalist anti-Semitism, on which Drumont, Barrès and a number of champions of the radical Right never ceased to depend. For Toussenel, the Jews had every reason to proclaim aloud, 'The state belongs to us, its interests and its purse are ours.'[61] And it was this singer of socialism who oddly exclaimed: 'Our great sovereigns of France, Richelieu, Louis XIV, Napoleon, where are you now?'[62] Toussenel was a true precursor of the theory of monopolist state capitalism with which Drumont was equally obsessed. Toussenel thought that 'with the help of that parliamentary impotence, with the help of that inertia of power and torpor of spirits, mercantile feudalism is fast advancing into the heart of our institutions: the Jew rules and governs France.'[63]

Auguste Chirac's version of this theory is more reminiscent in its metaphorical style, disregarding its contents, of the revision that some authors have made to economic Marxism by introducing the distinction between a ruling group, a dominating political power, enjoying minimum autonomy, and a hegemonic group, owning the capital and remaining outside political power the better to control it.[64] For Chirac, in fact:

France considered itself free because it had guillotined a king but, by coupling itself to the Jews, it only succeeded in giving itself dozens of them, all the more formidable in that they work in the shadows and evade responsibilities.... legislators and governors have the security of France in their keeping.... above them hover those whom I have called the Kings of the Republic.[65]

Toussenel thought, on the contrary, that because the Jews owned the Bank of France's piles of gold, they controlled, openly and without middle-men the prefectoral corps, the Council of State, and so on. For the sake of brevity, it can be suggested that Toussenel regarded the Jews of France as court Jews and that he understood no more than Drumont or Barrès that, in the specific context of republican emancipation, they had in reality become essentially state Jews. Before Max Weber, Toussenel stated that patrimonialism – that is, the conception of power as a private realm – introduced private interests into public office and vitiated its universalist operation. He therefore wanted radically to separate public office from a political establishment which was not yet salaried and consequently subject to the world of money. This observation is intrinsically fair; and the social history of the political establishment at the end of the nineteenth century corroborated it, when differentiation of state from particularist interests was encouraged by paying salaries to members of parliament, thereby avoiding the necessity to depend upon the business world. But Toussenel drifted into demonology when he stated that the Jews who held the money were monopolizing access to public office:

Every administrative career is closed to those who do not provide proof of financial nobility... magistrature, prefecture, Council of State, consulates. Paid public office is the last means still open to the man of the people, a self-made man, who will one day succeed in exercising an influence on his co-citizens. Ability is the only legitimate privilege.[66]

Toussenel and Chirac, just like Gougenot des Mousseaux, Drumont and Barrès – and this is the essential point which makes their thought particularly anachronistic – still shared the presuppositions of traditional anti-Semitism. They proved incapable of assessing the significance of Franco-Judaism, defined by the opening up of the state to Jews on a solely meritocratic basis. What none of them saw, was that state Jews, as we have opted to call them here, were almost always what Barrès called 'scholarship boys' and not 'heirs'. On the contrary, it was their 'ability' which had opened to them the doors of public office, not the money that they were alleged to possess or some sort of purely imaginary relationship with the financial aristocracy. As a result, all these authors were blind to the great change which had taken place in modern emancipating France and which involved every citizen. Nevertheless, their traditional anti-Semitic vision was perpetuated despite the changing times, and large numbers of people on both sides still shared this nightmare during the period with which we are dealing, applying it most particularly to Léon Blum and Pierre Mendès France.

NOTES

1 *L'Univers israélite*, 8 May 1936.
2 *La Tribune juive Strasbourg–Paris*, 3 April 1936.
3 *L'Action française*, 21 April 1920.
4 See 'Antisémites d'hier et d'aujourd'hui', which satisfactorily analyses this continuity, in *Le Pays Libre*, 8 Feb. 1941.
5 Jacques Ploncard, 'La vie de Léon Blum', *La Lutte nationaliste*, no. 4.
6 Jacques Ploncard d'Assac, 'La politique', *Lectures françaises*, Sept. and Nov. 1984. Note that this author also published a laudatory article on Drumont, entitled 'Maître du nationalisme français', in *Lectures françaises*, March 1957.
7 See Frederick Busi, *The Pope of Antisemitism: The career and legacy of Edouard-Adolphe Drumont* (University Press of America, New York, 1986), pp. 153ff.
8 Jean Drault, 'Le cinquantenaire de *La France juive*', *La Libre Parole–le Porc Epic*, 15 May 1936.
9 Henry-Robert Petit, 'La trahison des chefs nationaux', ibid.
10 *Le cinquantenaire de la Libre Parole*, 20 April 1942.
11 Jean Drault, *Drumont, 'La France juive' et 'La Libre Parole'* (Société française d'éditions littéraires et techniques, Paris, 1935), p. 328.
12 Jean Drault, *Histoire d'antisémitisme* (Editions C.-L., Paris, 1942), p. 164.
13 *Je suis partout*, 21 May 1943.
14 Jean Drault, *Drumont* (Société française d'éditions littéraires et techniques, Paris, 1935), p. 52. For the *Cahiers juifs*, 'Today Hitler has power which Drumont never dreamed of. Hitler easily got the better of a republic ill-born of defeat. Poor Drumont, even with the support of the Jesuits and the racists of his day, broke his teeth, powerful though these were, on the foundations of French democracy' (*Cahiers juifs*, no. 19, 1936). For *Le Matin*, 'the disaster of

1940 made every Frenchman understand that Drumont was right' (*Le Matin*, 1 May 1944).
15 *Je suis partout*, 28 July 1944.
16 Henry Coston, *Les Financiers qui mènent le monde* (La Librairie française, Paris, 1957), pp. 132–47; and, also by Coston, *Le Retour des 200 familles* (La Librairie française, Paris, 1960).
17 See Joseph Billig, *L'Institut d'études des questions juives* (Centre de documentation juive contemporaine (CDJC), Paris, 1974).
18 *Service d'information de l'Institut d'études des questions juives*, 17 Oct. 1941.
19 Marc Knobel, 'Un événement bien parisien en 1941: Une cérémonie à la mémoire d'Édouard Drumont', *Yod*, no. 19.
20 *Aspects de la France*, 7 Jan. 1955.
21 Louis Ferdinand Céline, *L'École des cadavres* (Denoël, Paris, 1938), p. 35.
22 E. Beau de Loménie, *Édouard Drumont ou l'anticapitalisme national* (Pauvert, Paris, 1968). More generally, on the historiography of Beau de Loménie, see Jean-Noël Jeanneney, 'Un obsédé des "dynasties bourgeoises" ', *L'Histoire*, Oct. 1978, pp. 81–3.
23 *Le Monde*, 3 Aug. 1963. Note also that in 1984 *Chrétienté-Solidarité* published an article entitled 'Pauvre France', which ended as follows: 'Since Drumont, the clairvoyant, he [the Frenchman] is always enfeoffed, a yes-man, a contemptibly servile bitch, wanting the whip and the master who, by humiliating him, will again give him for a few lustra the illusion of being a man' (*Chrétienté-Solidarité*, June 1984, p. 13).
24 *Présent*, 17 Jan. 1986.
25 Ibid., 20 Oct. 1984.
26 See William Herzog, *From Dreyfus to Pétain* (Creative Age Press, New York, 1947), pp. 58 and 292; and Edward Tannenbaum, *The Action Française* (John Wiley, New York, 1962).
27 Michel Winock, 'Les Affaires Dreyfus', *Vingtième Siècle*, Jan.–March 1985, pp. 20, 35–6.
28 Ibid., p. 34. Lazare Landau also analyses the constant conflict between what he calls 'Jewish France' and 'Christian France' establishing a direct parallel between the Dreyfus Affair and the opposition to Léon Blum in the inter-war period (*De l'aversion à l'estime* (Le Centurion, Paris, 1980, p. 49). On this continuity, see also Pierre Pierrard, *Juifs et catholiques français* (Fayard, Paris, 1970), pp. 256ff.
29 Michel Winock, *Édouard Drumont et Cie: Antisémitisme et fascisme en France* (Le Seuil, Paris, 1982), p. 207; Robert Byrnes, *Antisemitism in Modern France* (Rutgers University Press, New Brunswick, N.J., 1950), pp. 320ff. See Jean Bastaire, 'Drumont et l'antisémitisme', *Espirit*, no. 325 (March 1964). There are also two theses of varying interest on Drumont: Norman James Clary, *French Antisemitism during the Years of Drumont and Dreyfus, 1886–1906* (Ohio State University Press, Columbus, Ohio, 1970). This author also thinks that Drumont's anti-Semitism was primarily economic, Catholicism being secondary, while it played a primordial role in Byrnes's schema (p. 80). See also the thesis by Jean Nelson Young, *Editorials of Édouard Drumont in 'La Libre Parole' 1892–1906* (Brigham Young University, Salt Lake City, Utah, 1980); and Thomas Anderson, 'Edouard Drumont and the origins of modern antisemitism', *Catholic Historical Review*, 53 (April 1967).
30 Zeev Sternhell, 'Roots of popular anti-Semitism in the Third Republic', in F. Malino and B. Wasserstein, *The Jews in Modern France* (Brandeis University Press, London, 1985), pp. 118 and 132. On Drumont and his school, see Zeev Sternhell, *La Droite révolutionnaire, 1885–1914* (Le Seuil, Paris, 1978).
31 Zeev Sternhell, *Ni droite ni gauche: L'idéologie fasciste en France* (Le Seuil, Paris, 1983; rev. and enl., Complexe, Brussels, 1987), pp. 28–9.
32 Sternhell, 'Roots of popular anti-Semitism in the Third Republic', p. 121.
33 Édouard Drumont, *La Fin d'un monde* (A. Savine, Paris, 1889), pp. 38–9.

34 Édouard Drumont, *La Dernière bataille* (E. Dentu, Paris, 1890), p. 80.
35 Ibid., p. 192.
36 Édouard Drumont, *La France juive* (Marpon & Flammarion, Paris, 1886), vol. 1, p. 16. For Drumont, 'Never has the domination of one race over another race been so brutally asserted . . . army, magistrature, republican institutions, discipline, private and public liberties, national honour . . . all have passed to them' (*La Libre Parole*, 15 May 1906).
37 Drumont's preface to August Rohling, *Le Juif selon le Talmud* (A. Savine, Paris, 1889), p. 2.
38 Édouard Drumont, *Le Secret de Fourmies* (A. Savine, Paris, 1892), pp. 6 and 90.
39 Quoted in Jean de Ligneau, *Juifs et antisémites en Europe* (Librairie Saint-Joseph, Paris, 1892), p. 85.
40 Drumont, *Le Secret de Fourmies*, pp. 86–90. On Fourmies, see the article by P. Pierrard, 'Le "complot juif" selon Drumont', *L'Histoire*, Dec. 1985, pp. 32–7.
41 Ibid., p. 106.
42 Édouard Drumont, *Le Testament d'un antisémite* (E. Dentu, Paris, 1891), p. 366.
43 There were countless publications on Rothschild at the time. Apart from Drumont's books, see Georges Dairnwaell (called Satan), *Histoire édifiante et curieuse de Rothschild 1er, Roi des Juifs* (Paris, 1846); Georges de Pascal, *La Juiverie* (Gautier, Paris 1887); Jacques de Biez, *Les Rothschild et le péril juif* (Paris, 1891); François Bournand, *Les Juifs, nos contemporains* (A. Pierret, Paris, 1898); Marquis de Morès and friends, *Rothschild, Ravachol et Cie* (Paris, 1892). See also the article by Jules Guesde, 'À mort, Rothschild', in Jules Guesde, *État, politique et morale de classe* (Giard, Paris, 1901), pp. 444–7. On this subject, see Jean Bouvier, *Les Rothschild* (Fayard, Paris, 1967); repr. Complexe, Brussels, 1980).
44 See Stephen Wilson, *Ideology and Experience: Antisemitism in France at the time of the Dreyfus Affair* (Associated University Press, London, 1982), chs 10 and 11.
45 Quoted in Pierre Sorlin, *'La Croix' et les Juifs* (Grasset, Paris, 1967), p. 83. For *La Croix*, 'It was known that the administration, the army, the magistrature, as well as finance, are overcrowded with international foreigners who hustle each other to take the Christian nations' (ibid., p. 110). Danielle Delmaire shows how *La Croix du Nord* denounced the Jews' ascendancy over the political life of Lille: *L'Antisémitisme de La Croix du Nord à l'époque de l'Affaire Dreyfus*, University of Lille III, 3rd cycle doctorate, 1980, p. 228. See also Pierrard, *Juifs et catholiques français*, ch. 2.
46 Byrnes, *Antisemitism in Modern France*, p. 196.
47 See Jeanne Verdès-Leroux, *Scandale financier et antisémitisme catholique: Le krach de l'Union générale* (Le Centurion, Paris, 1969). On this period, see also Jean-Baptiste Duroselle, 'L'antisémitisme en France de 1886 à 1914', in *Cahiers Paul Claudel* (Gallimard, Paris, 1968). One can also consult the small, now old, book by I. Levaillant, *La Genèse de l'antisémitisme sous la IIIe République* (Librairie Durlacher, Paris, 1907).
48 Édouard Drumont, *La France juive devant l'opinion* (Flammarion, Paris, 1886), p. 96.
49 Ibid., pp. 101 and 109.
50 Édouard Drumont, *Les Juifs contre la France: Une nouvelle Pologne* (Librairie antisémite, Paris, 1899), p. 85.
51 See Pierre Birnbaum, *Le Peuple et les gros: Histoire d'un mythe* (Grasset, Paris, 1979); and also 'Anti-Semitism and anticapitalism in modern France', in Malino and Wasserstein, *The Jews in Modern France*.
52 Gougenot des Mousseaux, *Le Juif, le judaïsme et la judaïsation des peuples chrétiens* (Plon, Paris, 1869), Introduction, pp. 9, 16, 19 and 23.
53 Ibid., pp. 354–5.
54 Abbé A. Chabauty, *Les Juifs, nos maîtres* (Société générale de librairie catholique, Paris, 1882), pp. 87, 181, 239, 241.

55 Quotations from Zeev Sternhell, *Maurice Barrès et le nationalisme français* (repr. Éditions Complexe, Brussels, 1985), pp. 228, 233.
56 Ibid., p. 233.
57 Maurice Barrès, *Scènes et doctrines du nationalisme* (Plon, Paris, 1925), vol. 1, p. 61. See the more-than-surprising and ambiguous interpretation by Yves Chiron, which puts the emphasis on the nuances in Barrès's anti-Semitism and thinks that he 'did not share Drumont's racial antisemitism' (*Maurice Barrès: Le prince de la jeunesse* (Perrin, Paris, 1986), pp. 133 and 212).
58 Léon Blum, *Souvenirs sur l'Affaire*, pp. 543–4.
59 Ibid., p. 535.
60 These two expressions are taken from Sternhell, *Maurice Barrès et le nationalisme français*, p. 236. In Barrès's mind it was, Raoul Girardet notes, as if it was 'the state, the institutional framework of the City, that had to be recast first and not the consciousness of its citizens' (*Le Nationalisme français* (Le Seuil, Paris, 1983), p. 217.
61 A. Toussenel, *Les Juifs, rois de l'époque: Histoire de la féodalité financière* (Librairie de l'École Sociétaire, Paris, 1845), p. 25. Left-wing economic anti-Semitism was much in favour in France in the nineteenth century and has been the subject of an exceptional amount of analysis. See, for example, Edmund Silberner, 'Charles Fourier on the Jewish question', *Jewish Social Studies*, 8 (1946); and 'French socialism and the Jewish question, 1865–1914', *Historia Judaica*, April 1954; 'Proudhon Judeophobia', *Historia Judaica*, 10 (1948); and 'Pierre Leroux's ideas on the Jewish people', *Jewish Social Studies*, 12 (1950); Zosa Szajkowski, 'The Jewish Saint-Simonians and socialist antisemites in France', *Jewish Social Studies*, 9 (1947); Verdès-Leroux, *Scandale financier et antisémitisme catholique*; Sternhell, *La Droite révolutionnaire*; Wilson, *Ideology and experience*.
62 Toussenel, *Les Juifs, rois de l'époque*, p. 39.
63 Ibid., p. 4. Jacques de Biez's writings are in the same vein. 'Drumont fired on the bastion of the Right', he said. 'I shall fire at the bastion of the Left. Apart from that, we are perfectly united against the Jew . . . Do not leave the Republic to the Jew. The Republic with the Jew is death to France. The Republic will not be Jewish or it will no longer be' (*La Question juive* (Flammarion, Paris, 1886), pp. 3 and 16).
64 See Nicos Poulantzas, *Pouvoir politique et classe sociale* (Maspero, Paris, 1968).
65 Auguste Chirac, *Les Rois de la République* (E. Dentu, Paris, 1888), vol. 1, p. 380, and vol. 2, p. 416.
66 Toussenel, *Les Juifs, rois de l'époque*, p. 114.

4
The Wandering Jew

Proof that Drumont's spirit still prowls is the sight of Léon Blum and Pierre Mendès France metamorphosed into modern versions of Ahasuerus, the Jew condemned by Christ to eternal wandering because he did not help Him on the road to the Cross. What emerges is a mythical image of the Jew tirelessly roving from country to country, restless, never at peace, always in flight. He is also the representation *par excellence* of rootlessness, of not belonging to any one homeland, one territory, one soil. Ahasuerus is a Christian invention, widespread in Europe from the first years of the seventeenth century. He bears on his own shoulders the whole weight of the collective punishment. He is the timeless witness to Christ's martyrdom and the Jews' guilt.[1] His wandering marks his fundamental maladjustment; even more, his neurosis, his perpetual disturbance further emphasizes his foreignness, his exotic character, his appearance as a nomad, forever on the move.

For Drumont, 'the Jewish race cannot live in any organized society; it is a race of nomads and Bedouins. When it has set up its encampment somewhere, it destroys everything around it ... and nothing but ashes are to be found in the places where they pitched their tents'.[2] His friend and contemporary Jacques de Biez was even more explicit when he warned the French people: 'to harbour the wandering Jew is to open up one's house to ruin, and allow death to enter. When, like Pharaoh's daughter saving Moses from the waters, the French Revolution tried to save the Jew from his fate as a slave, it was nourishing in its bosom the viper which is devouring it at the present time.'[3] The choice of quotations is unlimited: the French nation must watch out for the nomads who are invading it, the Jews, foreigners personified, making their way in ever-increasing numbers and choosing where to pitch their temporary tents.

Some 50 years later in 1941, Jules Blacas chastised Léon Blum in the same terms: 'Our masters ... sheenies such as Léon Blum, etc., all the tribes of Israel come to lay down the law in France and subject us to the yoke of international Yiddery ... Look out for yourself, Ahasuerus, wandering Jew, the people's awakening will be terrible ... For a long time, unsatiable vampire, you have feasted on the pure blood of Aryans.'[4] Blum–Ahasuerus was 'tall, thin, slightly bent, with sharp eyes which chose to look over the top of his eye-glasses, and with the hooked nose and cheek bones of his race'.[5] Similarly, in 1940 Laurent Viguier addressed Blum in the following terms in an amazing lampoon, *Les Juifs à travers Léon Blum: Leur incapacité historique à diriger un État*, which we will refer to frequently: 'Do you think we are going to put up with you any longer, wandering Jew, Jew who overthrew your own State, Jew who is already overthrowing ours?'[6] And Maurice Bedel gave his personal interpretation of the Popular Front in a book devoted almost entirely to Léon Blum, composed of articles first published in serial form in *Candide*: 'Mister President of the Council come from a wandering race, provisionally installed in Ile-de-France by chance which could just as well have taken him to New York, Cairo or Vilna, Mister President of the Council felt ill at ease being Leader of a nation foreign to his flesh.'[7] Expressing surprise at Léon Blum's election at Narbonne, he concluded: 'What those Languedocians would have denied to gipsies camping in an empty field, they have granted to nomads travelling in motor-cars with cockades flying.'[8]

The reason is obvious: the President of the Council, that distinguished member of the Council of State who had established himself as one of the outstanding literary critics of his day, praised for his elegance and manners which verged on dandyism, in reality concealed a vagabond with no ties, a predatory nomad for whom established Frenchmen, firmly rooted in their soil, were the predestined victims. How could one not see, exclaimed Pierre Gaxotte, that 'the man of the soil sacrifices to the nomad, and the Frenchman to the exile . . . It is the whole of the socialist experiment and it is profoundly immoral.'[9]

Although his ancestors had proved their unfailing devotion to the nation, the state Jew was in the last resort no more than a common wandering Jew. Pierre Mendès France shared this fate. 'He is the enemy', his bitter adversary Pierre Boutang forthrightly declared. 'We know where he comes from. We need to know where he is going and what he wants.'[10] For the moment, added *Aspects de la France*,

he, of all the Mendès, is the one provisionally settled between the Atlantic and the Pyrenees. He could equally well have been called Mendès Eure, his favourite domicile . . . The Mendès at present temporarily with us probably likes the constituency where he is registered. It is perhaps a sign of affection, if not of attachment, this place-name hooked on to his own . . . we would agree that 'France' here appears as the accessory and the temporary, and 'Mendès' as the main and permanent thing. But Mendès has, in addition, a slightly Iberian, even Portuguese, air for you; so much so that the specification 'France' is like a corrective.[11]

From the furthest depths of sweet Normandy during the campaign for the legislative elections of 1936, the mayor of Saint-Pierre-de-Vauvray also asked: 'Why France? The concept of homeland has always been unknown to the Jew.

The Jew settles well in a country for a time, but as he is of a nomadic race, he changes it easily. And M. Mendès France has come to Louviers for his personal gain. He will leave it as he came.'[12] And nearer our own time, we have 'the Fabius tribe' passing on its way.[13]

France was therefore nothing more than a land of wandering for the Old Testament tribes, come straight to the Hexagon from the desert in search of more clement skies. However, in the inter-war period, the Jews were not the only 'dagoes' or even the sole 'undesirables'. 'Macaronis', 'Polaks', 'Chinks' and 'Wogs' provoked just as much contempt and, frequently, violent racist and xenophobic reactions.[14] Hitler's advent to power caused the flight of the German Jews, who often sought refuge in France which had remained republican. There were already a good many East European Jews there escaping from pogroms which had broken out in countries which gained independence after the 1914–18 war and were subsequently wracked by brutal nationalist movements.[15] Paradoxically, the arrival of these Jews in France seemed a blessing to anti-Semites. In their caricatures and lampoons they deliberately identified them with the state Jews emancipated by the French Revolution.

Were they Frenchmen? Were they foreigners? And were not the ones who were legally French really closer to foreigners, even if they painted themselves as loyal and patriotic state Jews? These were the questions that the growing number of champions of anti-Semitic theories constantly hammered out. The xenophobes seized on this specific circumstance which the other immigrant groups did not share and tirelessly made it their stock argument against Léon Blum, Jules Moch, Georges Boris, Jean Zay and Pierre Mendès France. Labelled 'Dromedary' by Henri Béraud, 'Camel', by Charles Maurras,[16] Léon Blum had barely emerged from the most arid and distant desert, namely Palestine. 'The escapee from Palestine',[17] the modern reincarnation of the wandering Jew, received little sympathy from Marcel Jouhandeau who expressed more clearly than some where his preferences lay. 'Although I feel no personal sympathy for M. Hitler, M. Blum fills me with a deep and quite different repugnance ... the Führer is in his own country and master of his own country, while M. Blum and M. Benda are not of our country and, what is most significant, M. Blum is master of my country, and no European can ever know what an Asiatic is thinking.'[18]

At a time when the new European order was beginning to appear, when the West, threatened by barbarian hordes, had to close ranks, danger was coming from the East and Léon Blum best symbolized it. There was no shadow of doubt: 'M. Blum is Palestinian. This is the opposite of French simplicity and clarity.'[19] To Alfred Fabre-Luce, 'Blum was one of the family at Tel Aviv.'[20] As at the time of the Crusades, the Christian West had to save its soul, take up the challenge, fight these new orientals with their depraved customs, who were so good at dishing up Asiatic Bolshevism with a Jaurés-ian sauce. The Saint Louis of the 1930s, the distinguished historian Pierre Gaxotte enthusiastically plunged into the battle against these infidels from steppe and desert. His text-manifesto marks a milestone in virulence. Donning his coat of mail and lowering his helmet, he faced the 'accursed man', Léon Blum, spear in hand:

First of all, he is ugly. He wears the sad head of a Palestinian mare on the body of a disjointed puppet... How he hates us! He has it in for us for everything and for nothing: our sky which is blue, our air which is soft; he bears a grudge against our peasants for walking in sabots on French soil and for not having had ancestors who were camel-drivers wandering in the Syrian desert[with his] pals from Palestine... Socialism rules like these nomads, who used to sweep down on south Algerian oases, rob the settled population, gorge themselves and set off on other raids... A choice has to be made between France and the accursed man. He embodies everything which revolts our blood and our flesh. He is evil. He is death.[21]

'KARFUNKELSTEIN' AND 'MENDÈS PALESTINE'

Pierre Gaxotte was not alone in this Dant-esque fight to the death against the wandering Jew come from the East, brandishing the banner of socialism. His followers included Georges Suarez, who regarded Blum as 'a nomad who, being from nowhere, thinks himself at home everywhere... intellectual and historical vagrancy of which the Jewish fate consists'.[22] As well as Gaxotte there was Henri Béraud who, up to and during the Riom trial, dared to confront the 'Great Jew', 'the wandering tribune filled with fury' who was conducting this war, the deadly Karfunkelstein.[23] Léon Blum was now lumbered with this *nom de guerre*, terrifying in its foreign-ness, a barbarous patronym originating in the East. He thus acquired an almost monstrous dimension, sending a shiver through the sweet land of France. Like Mendès France and so many other state Jews, graduates of the *École normale* or the *Polytechnique*, such as Jules Moch, he too was given appalling surnames which during his whole life he could never cast off.

However, there was a degree of uncertainty. Henri Béraud wavered between Karfunkelstein, Finkelstein or even Karfurhelstein.[24] A speaker at a meeting at Puteaux, organized by Colonel de La Rocque's French Social Party, roared at the President of the Council: 'Blum, you came from Wisburg, in eastern Prussia, and your name is Karrefouceschtang. What are you and your apostles bringing in?... *Our* leader was born in the Auvergne.'[25] A few days later, a speaker at another meeting of the same party, held at the *Mutualité*, was more specific, the better to point to everything which set Colonel de La Rocque apart from the socialist party leader. 'You know that M. Blum is not a Norman.'[26]

The most fantastic myths die hard. *Petit Larousse illustré* is the working tool of a large part of the French population, who use it to check the state of their knowledge. The 1960 edition published a short biographical entry for the former President of the Council. Remember, this was no longer in the 1930s nor the Vichy period, yet his name again appeared as being the pseudonym of Karfunkelstein. The judgment of the Paris Appeal Court on 14 February 1962 was not without its basis in fact:

On the grounds that the reference attached to the name of Léon Blum was the partial and approximate reproduction of an imputation directed against this politician by polemicists who had exceeded the reasonable limits of political discussion.

That in 1936, when Léon Blum was President of the Council of Ministers, certain newspapers did in fact claim that he was of Bulgarian origin and concealed his name, which they said was Karfunkelstein, under an assumed identity.

On the grounds that this calumny was repeated between 1940 and 1944, when Léon Blum was hunted, and deported by the enemy then occupying French territory, no proof, not the slightest indication was offered by those who formulated it; that no refutation of the statement written by Léon Blum has been made or attempted.

On the grounds that the publishing company Éditions Larousse had thus failed in an elementary duty of prudence . . . [27]

The court found *Petit Larousse* guilty of an 'almost criminal error' and ordered it to omit the reference and pay a fine as compensation for the injury.

Pierre Mendès France was lumbered with an even greater variety of anti-Semitic surnames. In his capacity as President of the Council, he turned to René Coty, President of the Republic and also President of the Supreme Council of the Magistrature, to obtain redress for what he called 'the weak legal reaction' of the 17th December in its judgment of 18 January 1955 against abusive and defamatory articles in *Aspects de la France*.[28] 'Mendès in Hebrew means billy goat', *Aspects de la France* was constantly exclaiming. Pierre Gaxotte, the future Immortal of the *Académie française*, remained true to himself. He suggested a series of variations in the style of the inventive Charles Maurras, who had thought up the surname 'Camel' for Blum. 'Mendès France?, they said in the Latin Quarter', Gaxotte wrote. 'That's not a name, it's an address. The other Mendès are called Mendès Bessarabia, Mendès Bukovina or Mendès Poznania, depending on their second home.'[29] After that, imagination could run wild: 'Mendès Jerusalem', 'Mendès Egypt', 'Mendès (known as) France', 'Mendès Anti-France', 'Mendès Palestine'.[30] *Rivarol* even endowed it with solid sociological backing when it gravely thought that 'Durkheim's works on the persistence of primitive totemism' in a few backward regions should be consulted in order to understand the origin of the first name of Pierre Mendès France's father, Cerf-David, Cerf might perhaps be 'a totem, who knows?'[31]

ORIENTAL ORIGINS

These nomads may have begun their long periplus in the East, but their exact point of departure was unknown. Asia was a very long way from Prussia or even Frankfurt. On 7 June 1936 a Bulgarian newspaper, *Zora*, launched the insane rumour that Léon Blum was born at Vidine. The story did the rounds of the editorial offices and was later revived by countless political commentators who all came close to believing this enormous hoax. The serious *Nouvelles économiques et financières*, for example, in October 1937 emphasized afresh:

> It is good to recall – since people forget – that our ex-premier, still a minister, is called Karfunkelstein . . . ; Leon Karfunkelstein known as Blum was born at Vidine, in 1872. He came to Paris with his parents in 1874 . . . Karfunkelstein calls himself Blum; Rothschild calls himself Mandel. Left-wing Frenchmen acclaim the first; right-wing Frenchmen place their hopes in the second. Poor fools![32]

For years on end Blum vainly denied all this and proved that he was really born in Paris of a father who was himself born in the Lower Rhine. In vain did *Le Populaire*, like *L'Univers israélite* or *Tribune juive Strasbourg–Paris*,[33] strive to refute such assertions. Nothing worked. Other people preferred to see Blum as a German. For example, Urbain Gohier, Drumont's old collaborator, suggested sending this wandering Jew back to his Frankfurt ghetto.[34] Charles Maurras unflaggingly translated 'Blum' as 'flower'. 'M. Blum, whose name means flower in German, does not forget that his Yeddish [sic] blood is not without some good Germanic globules.'[35] Still others, as we have seen, saw Blum as basically 'a Palestinian'. 'Léon of Judaea and his court',[36] after long wandering, truly ruled a France transformed, according to Marcel Jouhandeau, into the 'land of Canaan'.[37]

The surnames ascribed to Pierre Mendès France, mentioned above, show that he was endowed with the same places of origin, apart from Bulgaria: Germany, Palestine, Egypt and – this is specific to him – Spain. However little the idea of classing Germany as one of the countries haunted by barbarians was accepted . . . and this was fairly common at that ferociously nationalistic period – it was from the Orient that the wandering Jews came, even if they sometimes, like the Arab invaders, made a detour via the Iberian peninsula to reach the Hexagon. In short, Léon Blum and Pierre Mendès France, were depicted, in turn and despite themselves, as orientals.[38]

In 1937 Jean Renoir made the film *La grande illusion*. The heroes were Frenchmen from all backgrounds taken prisoner by the Germans during the First World War. A great deal of attention was paid to the fact that the role of Rosenthal, an assimilated, good-humoured Jew, was taken by a Jewish actor, Dalio, who delighted in emphasizing the features and manners which are assumed to be those of an oriental Levantine Jew.[39] In the same year, *Gringoire*, for example, never stopped attacking Léon Blum and Jean Zay, denouncing them as so many 'oriental invaders'.[40] The 'provokingly Asiatic' leader of the band, the new President of the Council, could not but arouse the 'old French tradition' against himself.[41] To Hubert Bourgin, a graduate of the *École normale* and an old schoolmate of Blum's, the latter appeared as a 'mixture of messianism and Jewish prophetism adapted to modern circumstances, of oriental passion, Asiatic frenzy, and European or French intelligence, of refined aestheticism'.[42] The thing was that Léon Blum did not hide his natural liking for 'oriental comfort: music, perfumes, carpets . . . a European could only fault

[him] for being too steeped in pommade'.[43] What could he and his ilk, coming as they did from such distant lands, know of the French soul? Towards this soul he shamelessly employed – as Laurent Fabius himself did more recently – 'seduction with a velvety, oriental gaze',[44] not unreminiscent of the 'too-sweet gaze of an oriental charmer' which, according to Henri Béraud, Léon Blum possessed.[45] To complete this exotic panoply, Laurent Fabius, in the wake of Léon Blum and Pierre Mendès France,[46] was also designated 'a parvenu and wily carpet dealer', the better to emphasize these oriental origins.[47]

For Bertrand de Jouvenel, Blum had 'Turkified' France.[48] 'M. Blum does not feel France, he conceives it', thought Pierre Gaxotte. And he suddenly turned lyrical, adding, 'To commune with the soul of the nation, to hang one's childhood memories on the chestnut tree in the courtyard or the church bell-tower, does not require reasoning. The instinct for the soil is the best, the most upright of the intelligences.'[49] Less grandiloquently, at a meeting held by Pierre Mendès France at La Haye-Malherbe, in the heart of Normandy, an old peasant suddenly eyed him from head to toe and exclaimed: 'You don't come from our part of the world then? So shit off old man.'[50] This was certainly not much different from Drumont's day, when the *Nouvelle complainte des Juifs-Errants*, set to a tune by Wagner, had widespread currency as a warning:[51]

Is anything anywhere
More disgusting
Than the sham despair
Of the Jews in their wandering
How tiresomely sad
Is their fate which is bad.

Don't waste your pity –
Here's a fine wheeze:
My friends in our city,
Take up your tweezers, given them a squeeze
Throw the Yids in the main
As a whole down the drain.

They will be brokers, given their luck
Usurers, bankers, they've gone up a rung
But they come from the muck
And they still stink of dung
This will not stop that
They grow rich and fat

Until France takes a stand –
And I wait for a sign –
Gets sick of this band
[*censor cuts line*]
It is thus that will die
Judas's race if we try.

NOTES

1 Galit Hasan-Rokem and Alan Dundes, *The Wandering Jew: Essays in the interpretation of a Christian legend* (Indiana University Press, Bloomington, Ind., 1986).
2 Édouard Drumont, *La Dernière Bataille* (E. Dentu, Paris, 1890), p. 16. See also his preface to Raphael Viau, *Ces bons Juifs*! (Librairie Pierrel, Paris, 1898), where he describes those 'razzia-rousing Bedouins' (p. 11). According to Drumont, 'Outside Jerusalem, every country, whether it be France, Germany or England, is merely a stopping-place for the Jew, any old place, a social agglomeration, amidst which he can be comfortable, which it can even be profitable for him temporarily to serve its interests, but which he only forms part of as a free partner, a temporary member' (*La France juive* (Marpon & Flammarion, Paris, 1886), vol. 1, p. 59).
3 Jacques de Biez, *La Question juive* (Flammarion, Paris, 1886), p. 165.
4 Jules Blacas, *Sous l'étreinte juive* (Centre de documentation et de propagande, Paris, 1941), p. 48.
5 Louis de Launay, *Les Entretiens d'Ahasuerus* (Édition du Courrier politique, littéraire et social, Paris, 1938), p. 16. For René Saint-Serge, 'The international is the wandering Jew' (*L'Invasion juive* (Rassemblement Anti-Juif de France, Paris, 1939), p. 7. After attacking the Jew Blum, and the Jew Mendès 'who adds the name of France to his own name', *Le Grand Occident* can conclude: 'The Jew Gamberlé, known as Gambetta, a well-known metic whose nomad parents ended up by stopping at Cahors, founded a so-called republic which, logically, sooner or later had to culminate in Blum. Foreigners are the masters there' (April–May 1938).
6 Laurent Viguier, *Les Juifs à travers Léon Blum: Leur incapacité historique à diriger un État* (Éditions Baudinière, Paris, 1940), p. 27.
7 Maurice Bedel, *Bengali* (Oeuvres françaises, Paris, 1937), p. 108.
8 Ibid., p. 138.
9 *Candide*, 8 Oct. 1936.
10 *Aspects de la France*, 2 July 1954. And Boutang added: 'Son of a reader of *La Libre Parole*, the Jewish fact, in his case, seems to us to be in no way negligible.'
11 Ibid., 18 June 1954.
12 *L'Industriel de Louviers*, 14 March 1936.
13 *Rivarol*, 24 Aug. 1984. Note that contrary to Blum or Mendès France, Laurent Fabius belonged to a family of Jewish origin but which had converted. Note, moreover, that anti-Semitic attacks were directed more against Jews or even people who were converted but of Jewish origin, who were members of left- rather than right-wing parties. In the other camp, a more systematic analysis would be required of the anti-Semitic reactions provoked by the presence in power of Georges Mandel, René Mayer and Michel Debré, who was in a similar situation to Laurent Fabius. We shall return to these comparisons.
14 See Ralph Schor, *L'Opinion française et les étrangers, 1919–1939* (Publications de la Sorbonne, Paris, 1985), pp. 125–6 and 176–89; Nancy Green, *Les Travailleurs immigrés juifs à la Belle Époque: Le 'Pletzel' de Paris* (Fayard, Paris, 1985).
15 For E. Beau de Loménie, Blum and his colleagues 'committed the imprudence of establishing all sorts of Jews around themselves in their ministerial cabinet, some of whom were newly arrived from central Europe under the immediate influence of the Nazis' anti-Semitic violence, and they arrived in our country, inspired by anti-Hitler and anti-fascist passions' (*La mort de la Troisième République*, Édition du Conquistador, Paris, 1951), p. 39.

16 *L'Action française*, 11 Sept. 1936. See also the articles by Pellisson in ibid., 18 Jan. and 2 March 1937, on the 'Jewish camel'.
17 Ibid., 22 Jan. 1937.
18 Marcel Jouhandeau, *Le Péril juif* (Fernand Sorlot, Paris, 1936), p. 12.
19 *Je suis partout*, 12 Sept. 1936.
20 Alfred Fabre-Luce, *Vingt-cinq années de liberté* (Julliard, Paris, 1962), pp. 205–6.
21 *Candide*, 7 April 1938.
22 *Aujourd'hui*, 13 March 1942.
23 *Gringoire*, 23 Jan. 1941.
24 Ibid., 7 April 1938.
25 *Archives nationales*, F.7 12966.
26 Ibid.
27 *Fonds Léon Blum*, Fondation nationale des sciences politiques, 5BL2, Dr1.
28 See Pierre Mendès France, *Oeuvres complètes*, vol. 3 (Gallimard, Paris, 1986), pp. 740–1.
29 *Je suis partout*, 18 March 1938.
30 See, for example, *La France enchaînée*, 26 March and 12 April 1938, and *Aspects de la France*, 25 June 1954. On this point see Pierre Birnbaum, 'Attaques antisémites contre Pierre Mendès France', in François Bédarida and Jean-Pierre Rioux (eds), *Pierre Mendès France et le mendésisme* (Fayard, Paris, 1985), pp. 176–7.
31 *Rivarol*, 29 July 1954.
32 *Les Nouvelles économiques et financières*, 22 Oct. 1937. *Le Charivari* undertook to demonstrate Blum's birth at Vidine since 'the archives of the Israelite community there are very well kept and, if necessary, could be consulted to find the exact date of the circumcision of little Léon, born of a German Jew and a Bulgarian Jewess' (*Le Charivari*, 20 June 1936). In the same vein, but with more caution, see Jacques Ploncard, 'La vie de Léon Blum', *La Lutte nationaliste*, no. 4, pp. 4–6. Henri Béraud also called Blum 'the Bulgar with a monocle' (*Gringoire*, 23 Jan. 1941). For *La France enchaînée*, 'Rothschild–Mandel, right-wing Jew, is going to continue the work of Blum–Karfunkelstein, left-wing Jew, with the continued and necessary help of the good, fat, foolish Frenchmen in their respective parties' (22 April 1938).
33 See again, *Tribune juive Strasbourg–Paris*, 1 April 1938.
34 *La Vieille France*, 25 Jan. 1923. Drumont himself declared: 'On every tribune, I see people who were naturalized yesterday, German Jews, foreigners, nomads from every corner of the world' (in *À bas les Juifs!*, lampoon, Bibliothèque nationale, Lb57 10678, p. 7).
35 See *L'Action française*, 11 May 1936 and 7 Jan. 1937.
36 *Tracts antisémites*, Bibliothèque nationale, 4o Ld 18346, 8 Jan. 1945.
37 *Je suis partout*, 30 July 1937.
38 In Germany the same type of accusation was made against the Jews. Thus Sombart thinks that 'arid' bourgeois civilization was created by Jews from the Orient who had preserved their 'desert' mentality (Werner Sombart, *The Jews and Modern Capitalism* (Collier Books, New York, 1962), pp. 299–323). On the image of the Jews as 'orientals' in Germany, see Paul Mendès-Flohr, 'Fin-de-siècle orientalism, the Ostjuden and the aesthetics of Jewish self-affirmation', in J. Frankel (ed.), *Studies in Contemporary Jewry* (Indiana University Press, Bloomington, Ind., 1984), vol. 1, pp. 96–139.
39 See Lilly Scherr, 'Le personnage du Juif dans "La grande illusion" ', in *Communautés juives (1880–1978)*, Actes de Colloque International (INALCO, Paris, 1982), p. 442.
40 See, for example, *Gringoire*, 5 Nov. 1937.
41 *Choc*, 24 Dec. 1936.

108 Drumont's Legacy

42 Hubert Bourgin, *De Jaurès à Léon Blum* (Fayard, Paris, 1938), pp.508–9.
43 Fayolle-Lefort, *Le Juif, cet inconnu* (Édition de France, Paris, 1941), p. 64.
44 *Rivarol*, 27 July 1984.
45 *Gringoire*, 5 June 1936.
46 See, for example, *Crapouillot*, Jan. 1959.
47 *Présent*, 28 Oct. 1985.
48 *L'Émancipation nationale*, 5 Dec. 1936.
49 *Candide*, 24 June 1937. For the *Revue littéraire juive*, on the contrary, 'the Jew of France is a Western man . . . He has not suffered persecutions like the eastern Jew' (2.(1928)).
50 *L'Industriel de Louviers*, 14 April 1936.
51 'Arrivée du choléra et des futurs barons crasseux à Paris: Nouvelle complainte des Juifs-Errants', Bibliothèque Nationale, 1892, Fol. Wz 714.

5
The Land and the Dead

Being in transit does not inculcate loyalty. Perpetual wandering is an incentive to flight, not sacrifice, in time of danger. Whatever their military achievements in the service of the homeland and despite their enthusiastic enlistment in the nation's armies whenever an enemy threatened the land of modern France, the Jews, whatever they did to prove their deep-seated patriotism, were labelled incorrigible cowards, potential traitors. Again it was Drumont who set the tone. In his eyes, 'the Semite is instinctively a merchant; he has an aptitude for commerce, a bent for everything that can be traded, for anything which offers an opportunity to get the better of his fellow-men. The Aryan is a farmer, poet, monk and, above all, soldier; war is his true element, he goes gladly to meet danger, he defies death.'[1]

In short, Jews did not physically feel the significance of rootedness in a land that men defended simply because they were born there and not by invoking the great principles of the rights of man or even justice. Barrès, close to Drumont, waged war on all the 'rootless' ones, all 'barbarians', who lacked that instinct of inalienably belonging to a soil where the national identity was fashioned. According to him, this was the reason why 'foreigners do not have brains made in the same way as ours'.[2] As a result, their possible naturalization looked like a 'legal fiction . . . which could not succeed in making the blood of a Levantine take on the qualities of the blood of a French peasant, a Parisian worker'.[3]

When Barrès created that image of 'the land and the dead', destined to become almost mythological, he went on to make more specific criticisms of the idea of homeland suggested by Léon Blum. According to Barrès, 'the Jews have no homeland in our sense of the term. For us, the homeland is land and ancestors, that is to say the land and the dead. For them, it is the place where they find the greatest benefit; homeland is a concept. But what concept? The one which is most useful to them, the concept for example, that all men are brothers, that nationality is a prejudice.'[4]

After formulating this emblematic definition of nationalism embodying its own substance rooted in the soil, Barrès attacked Blum's concept of homeland on the grounds that it was too normative. Claiming kinship with Charles Maurras, Barrès thought that Blum, in his *Nouvelles Conversations de Goethe avec Eckermann*, had not understood that the ideas developed in *Le Culte du moi* were compatible with acceptance of a deep-seated determinism which emerged in *Les Déracinés*.[5] Léon Blum–Goethe 'asks himself whether Barrès, like Taine, has not placed too much importance on the effect of environment, whether he has not been too quick to believe in the spirit of races and countries'. Léon Blum the state Jew, added, 'It is in a centralized and levelled nation that individuals are truly free.'[6] Blum unconsciously linked up with the ideas that Durkheim, another Alsatian Jew, expressed at the same period. According to Durkheim, the state was 'a reflection unit', a 'clear awareness' which 'liberates' individuals from local 'prejudices' which surrounded them.[7] Blum – like Mendès France later – claimed more kinship with the logic of the state than with the determinism of territories.

> I do not know that family piety which attaches so many men to one land or one house; it is a cause of weakness for all mankind; it is the greatest obstacle to the changes necessary to mankind. No, I cannot attach myself to the worn-out and mortal forms of life. That is not what I want to have in common with my fathers. What I want to share with them is love of Life, Truth and Reason . . . sincere love of Justice and Reason is the true bond, the only legitimate link between the generations.[8]

This purely rationalist interpretation of the homeland understandably brought down the thunderbolts of the nationalist Right. From Barrès to Vichy, it was indefatigably contrasted with the virtues of rootedness in the soil, which in itself was hardly an incentive to an outpouring of humanitarianism. This was where the real split occurred between the champions of Franco-Judaism, who did not hesitate to die on the battlefield to defend republican, emancipating France, and those who were prepared to make the same sacrifice only for 'the land and the dead'. This is a crucial point; and the good Émile Faguet, French professor and critic, also rebelled against the way in which Léon Blum unhesitatingly stigmatized Maurice Barrès in his writings. To this master of literary criticism it was obvious that Blum 'detests the ideas of homeland and patriotism, he is a socialist . . . A man who cannot understand that one loves one's country, that one can be attached to the soil, that one can love one's ancestors, is someone who does not exist. What is left? Ideas, general systems of sensibility.'[9] As can be seen, Émile Faguet inflexibly adopted Barrès's argument against Léon Blum, though he still behaved with the utmost courtesy and sent Blum a very friendly personal letter a year later.[10] These criticisms are all of a kind and as a whole remained, strictly speaking, unchanged from one generation to the next.[11] A single example, taken from an article by another literary figure, illustrates this. According to Henry Bordeaux, Léon Blum did not have the slightest idea of respect for race, or the sacred character of marriage. Joseph de Maistre's famous definition, 'the homeland is an association on the same soil of the living with the dead and those still to be born', could not speak to his brain or his heart which is foreign to our past and, more seriously, indifferent to our future, since he despises or mocks the strength that endures.[12]

THE BLOOD QUESTION: FROM RITUAL MURDER TO THE JEWISH WARS

Traditional anti-Semitic rhetoric is constantly finding fresh proof to strengthen the image of the Jew disloyal to his homeland. To support their theories, xenophobic lampooners, never lacking in imagination, invented the most macabre mathematics, consisting of meticulous comparisons of the respective proportions of Aryan and Jewish dead in the French population. The 1914–18 war provided choice material for such calculations which unflaggingly fed a whole anti-Semitic tradition. Apart from temporary lulls, this has been an unfaltering tradition in contemporary France. A similar accusation was made in the wake of the 1940 defeat when the macabre book-keeping flowered afresh. It appeared again at the time of the bloody decolonization battles. On each occasion, the Jews, quintessential patriots, protested in the name of the many of their number who had died on the battlefields and tried to annihilate this calumny which they found deeply wounding. It struck at the idea of the equality of all citizens to which they were particularly attached since it alone could guarantee their emancipation in perpetuity.

In this anti-Semitic perspective, the bloody wars that France had to face were seen as the ultimate expression – the most nightmarish – of the traditional myth of the ritual murders which Jews, thirsting for Christian blood, were said to have committed since time began. This lunatic accusation, peddled by every anti-Semitic agitator, purveyed in France by *La Libre parole* and in the world at large by the *Protocols of the Elders of Zion*, ceaselessly republished in all latitudes up to the present day, reached its climax precisely at the turn of the century. You find it, of course, in the writings of Gougenot des Mousseaux,[13] but also, and most particularly, in those of Drumont, who gave detailed descriptions of the Tisza Eszlar affair, the Damascus affair and many others, to prove 'Jewish persecution' of Christian peoples.[14] It was spread amongst the public at large by the paper *La Croix* and confirmed with ample detail by Drumont's friends who tried to demonstrate that 'the Jew has always taken insatiable delight in blood'.[15] To them it was confirmation of the Jews' responsibility for Christ's crucifixion. The ritual murders were always a live issue for Albert Monniot, Drumont's close collaborator, who carried on his anti-Semitic struggle far into the twentieth century.[16] He cited the famous example, utilized by very many European anti-Semites, of the Jew Beilis at Kiev in 1911, and that of Finkelstein, said to have taken place slightly earlier at Bucharest. Devotees of a particularly savage anti-Semitism then prevalent referred very frequently to this latter case, with its unwilling hero who – can it be pure chance? – had one of the surnames most often bestowed on Léon Blum.[17]

This frenzied cosmology depicted the Jews as responsible for the French Revolution, provoked to weaken a Christian nation. Above all, it was they who anticipated and organized to their greatest advantage the scenario of the wars which France was forced to wage. From the war of 1870 to the conflicts surrounding the decolonization of Indo-China and North Africa, the terms of the accusation showed little variation. For Drumont, 'cosmopolitan Jewry had inspired, financed, waged and prolonged the war' of 1870 to ensure its victory and the establishment of a 'Jewish Republic'.[18] This ritual murder on a national scale was reproduced, according to his heirs, in 1914–18, in 1940, and later, under the Fourth Republic; Léon Blum and Pierre Mendès France were held to be the guilty parties.

A controversy broke out between Edmond Bloch, president of the *Union patriotique des Français israélites*, one of 'the minute Jewish minority who shared the fate of the majority of Frenchmen old enough to bear arms on the battlefield', and Charles Trochu, president of the *Association nationale des officiers combattants* which was very influential in the inter-war period. Trochu exploded in anger at Jews like Léon Blum, whom he specifically named: 'And what Jews! The worst type, that scum from the Orient recently camped on our land, soaked with the blood of those who achieved that magnificent moral unity which is the homeland.'[19] In many respects this totally Barrèsian definition of the homeland is a model because it was propounded by a very influential personality. It openly linked oriental origin with the propensity to flee from the supreme sacrifice. Léon Daudet, ever-faithful to Drumont, gave a concise summary of this point of view: 'His innermost nature forces Blum to want war.... He is very highly strung and this makes him both bloodthirsty and cowardly.'[20] Away from Paris, in his constituency of Narbonne, his opponents did not mince their words. He always seemed like a 'wandering Jew ... ', they claimed, 'sticky, misshapen, nauseating, a long, engorged leech resting in the social "sunspot" after his latest suckings'.[21]

According to this perspective, Mendès France could not be other than cowardly and bloodthirsty. At an election meeting in the small Norman village of Quatermore during the 1936 legislative elections, one worthy voter stood up and asked: 'Where would you go if there was a war?'[22] Less than 20 years later Jacques Duclos had no hesitation in publicly declaring that Pierre Mendès France was 'a little scared Jew'. Others, taking the analogy to its logical conclusion, were not afraid to state that 'what claims to be the government of France has lived by trading in French blood (and I do not exclude Mendès France from this)'.[23] Charles Luca, editor of *Fidélité*, the battle-sheet of the French Phalange, 1950s version, wrote: 'We Phalangists are in the habit of calling a spade a spade and Mendès a rogue ... we refuse to mingle our blood with that of another colour.'[24] Times had barely changed.

The Land and the Dead 113

Here again, abundant quotations are available. 'No, citizen Blum', declaimed *Le Franciste*, 'you are not, you have never been and you can never become one of our fellow citizens. Because there is something you lack. The blood of a French soldier . . . and more besides.'[25] What an elegant, concise way they have of saying these things! Listen to Pierre Taittinger: 'the blood that M. Léon Blum has not shed on the battlefield, that blood which he is jealously saving to mount an attack on republican legality',[26] set him apart from the national community. For Dorsay writing in *Je suis partout*, all is clear: 'Since he does not feel bound to any homeland, M. Léon Blum does not know the honour of blood that has been shed.'[27] But the very large-circulation satirical weekly, *Charivari*, takes the prize. Wary of French military involvement in the Ethiopian affair, Jean-Pierre Maxence was carried away:

From August 1914 to November 1918, fifteen hundred thousand men died for France. . . . We have never heard tell that M. Léon Blum was amongst those who exposed themselves to danger. Not only did this anarchizing aesthete not pay his tribute of blood like so many young men, but he was never to be seen where bullets were flying. . . . M. Blum took the profits. He preaches the crusade of the democracies. He gets drunk on blood and death. He instigates the assassination of the new Reich chancellor. What does he care! If a million young Frenchmen pay with their fine blood for the fatal effects of his Semitic rage . . . as in 1914, he will not be there. . . . Too old a crow to batten on corpses again, he takes delight in sniffing innocent blood. The old crow has breathed the scent of blood so much that he would be happy to die of it. . . . The hyena is quivering: a distant odour of blood is rising from Ethiopia.[28]

IS A JEW WORTH A BRETON?

On 5 April 1938 an unusually violent incident broke out in the Chamber of Deputies during a debate on the financial policy of the second Blum government. Pierre Mendès France held the crucial office of Under-Secretary of State to the Treasury. This time our two state Jews faced the anti-Semitic press in full cry at the same moment, and the press, of course, associated their names closely. It happened suddenly during a very technical debate on capital tax, and very quickly, by a particularly obvious association of ideas, the issue once again was blood and war. The discussion began on the financial impact of the fight against unemployment. Insults spread rapidly and tension mounted between deputies of opposing parties. A tremendous uproar broke out and Ihuel, closely connected with the agrarian group, and Marx Dormoy, Minister of the Interior, rose to their feet, made threatening gestures and almost came to blows. The tumult reached a climax. President Herriot was forced to suspend the sitting. It was then that socialist and right-wing deputies turned on one another and a general free-for-all seemed about to break out. Léon Blum tried to intercede. The shouts which rose from the benches were those heard so often on the streets of Paris. 'Down with the Jews', 'France for the French', 'Blum is no real Frenchman'. Marx Dormoy roared at M. Ihuel: 'Herd of swine! A Jew is certainly worth a Breton.'[29] *L'Action française* did not miss the chance of denouncing the presence of 'Mendès (Jerusalem)' on the government benches.[30]

To dare to compare a Jew with a Breton was the supreme sacrilege; even old proverbs and popular wisdom bore witness to this. Brittany was a Christian nation of peasants and warriors who remain to this day the incarnation of purity, courage and attachment to the land in current National Front campaigns. Such blasphemy roused a storm throughout the land. It mixed the pure and the impure with impunity, the virtues of the land of France with the turpitude of the cosmopolitan Jews, the sacrifice of the Bretons during the First World War with the alleged cowardice of the Jews. It concentrated all the ingredients of the most virulent anti-Semitism, and this very dramatic confrontation, rarely mentioned by historians, immediately placed Blum and Mendès France in the front line. For some years after that, the Vichy period included, this intolerable comparison followed them to Paris as well as to Narbonne and Louviers.

In the corridors of the Chamber, a Breton deputy burst out, 'Fewer than 2,000 French Jews were killed in the war (1,689 to be exact). But 400,000 Bretons fell on the battlefield. The ratio is 1 to 236. Therefore, one Breton is worth 236 Jews to France.'[31] Soupault replied to Marx Dormoy through clenched teeth: 'A Jew will be worth a Breton... the day when the Jews give France a Duguesclin, a Duguay-Trouin, a Surcouf or a Jacques Cartier... peasants labouring to enrich its soil; obscure heroes to save souls in peril, and 400,000 of their own people to defend the homeland.' Many leaflets circulated in the streets of Paris, including the following:

These are the neo-Breton Jews: Karfunkelstein, a Jew from Germany, father of the hateful and obscene cynic, Léon Blum; wife Aric, Jewess from Bulgaria, mother of the aforesaid 'Dog–Camel–Jackal'. A Jew is worth a Breton, then here is a Breton: Karfunkelstein Léon who hides under the name of Blum.... Money and institutions (that is to say, the Republic) have today allowed this foreign Jew, who does not have a single drop of French blood in his veins, to misgovern and ruin France.

And later on, Pierre Mendès France, Jean Zay and Jules Moch were cited amongst other Bretons.[32] Now the press moved in for the kill. For *L'Action française*, 'at least there is this difference: in France, a Breton is in his own country. The Jew is only a leech from the Dead Sea.'[33] For *Le Nouveau Cri*, 'Bretons and Corsicans alike hate the Jews. There is not a single Jew in these two races and they would be sufficient to clean out judaized France as easy as winking.'[34] The prize goes, as so often, to *Pilori*: 'When it comes to fiddles and to filling pockets, a Jew is not worth one Breton, he is worth a thousand of them. But when it comes to picking up a rifle and going out to get a bullet in the gut, they're no match, the Yids and the Bretons.'[35]

The Land and the Dead 115

On the day after this confrontation in Parliament the walls of the Stock Exchange were covered with caricatures of Léon Blum dressed as a Breton. Inside the building, the 'new Hebrew hymn: the Paimpolaise' was sung, and numerous drawings showed 'Leonec Blum' suggesting a visit to the rocks of 'Blumanach'.[36] Robert Brasillach, incensed by Marx Dormoy's rash phrase, compared the new anti-Semitic movement against Léon Blum with the Dreyfus Affair.[37] The last word belongs to Jean-Charles Legrand, one of the most consistent anti-Semitic propagandists up to the Vichy period. Speaking to poor Marx Dormoy, who was not Jewish himself, but who had committed the sin of being a socialist minister and a friend of Léon Blum, he declared:

You do not know Brittany, land of the druids, you are for the land of Judas. You prefer the International to the land of the Celts, our ancestors. The underworld of Jews camping on usurped soil, that is your family. You understand the oriental sonorousness of their vocabulary; but you do not know how to speak Breton; you stammer out French but you love Yiddish. The Breton is a Frenchman, Dormoy: your Jews are not of our blood. They are not of our race. The Bretons are called Yves, Jean, Pierre or François; these are the forenames of our country. You, yours is Marx. And if 'a Jew is certainly worth a Breton', Dormoy, go and tell that to the people of Dixmude and Yser. If they could still speak, the poor lads with red pompoms would tell you just how much the Jews stood by them in 1914 when they halted the invasion with their hairless breasts. . . . Go and look at their wooden crosses, bend over the soil they saved. . . . And you will hear our lads' reply rising up towards you, like a slap in the face: Swine.[38]

The sacrilegious comparison, 'a Jew is certainly worth a Breton', cleared the way for the expression of all the nightmares of traditional anti-Semitism: blood, the Jewish war, the Frenchness of the race and the soil, the cowardly and cosmopolitan preoccupation with business. Even Colonel de La Rocque who, unlike his troops, took most care not to drift into summary anti-Semitism, said, 'what does it mean coming from the mouth of a Minister of the Interior, this comparison between a religion, worthy of respect like any belief, and a glorious province?'[39] The answer was, decisively, 'no': a Jew could not be worth a Breton. For this equation to be imaginable, the state Jews would need to have fulfilled their obligations as citizens by making the supreme sacrifice without hesitation. This the anti-Semites did their utmost to refute by means of macabre calculations.

The communal institutions now tried to end such anti-Semitic insinuations which presupposed an inequality of deaths – unacceptable in view of the deep-seated patriotism of the Jews of France – by a scientific balance-sheet of Jewish and non-Jewish deaths. A few months after the outbreak of this controversy, in which Blum and the Jewish members of the second 1938 government, like Pierre Mendès France, involuntarily played an important role, the communal institutions published a scholarly comparative study which proved that the ratios given in *L'Action française* were incorrect. Out of a total population of 190,000 Jews, 32,000 soldiers were mobilized and 6,500 died on the battlefield, including 7 military chaplains out of the 31 rabbis mobilized. In addition, 12,000 foreign Jews volunteered, at least 2,000 of whom died on the battlefield. Out of 148 former Jewish students at the *École polytechnique* (classes of 1895–1914), 24 were killed, or 15.4 per cent (against an overall average of 14.3 per cent); out of 49 former Jewish students at the *École normale supérieure* (classes of 1895–1914), 11 were killed, or 22.5 per cent (the same as the average total percentage).[40] Chief Rabbi Liber, Maître Edmond Bloch and Georges Rivollet, secretary general of the *Confédération nationale des anciens combattants*, were officially commissioned at a meeting at the Salle Wagram, to collect more statistics to belie the anti-Semitic accusations.[41] Overall, it can be shown that the proportion of Jewish soldiers who died was 3.5 per cent while the total proportion of all soldiers who died was 3.4 per cent.[42] The patriotism of the Jews of France, assimilated Israelites or recent immigrants, could not be doubted and all the evidence showed that the anti-Semitic propaganda was incorrect. The Jews had participated massively in the war effort, with enthusiasm and bravery. The many citations and military medals attested to it.

The Great War was experienced as a sort of new exodus from Egypt, capable of offering certain equality to Jewish citizens. Numerous letters sent by Jewish officers to Maurice Barrès attempted to convince him of their deep-seated patriotism. Others were sent to *L'Univers israélite* by Jewish soldiers proclaiming their love for the homeland, and all declaring that they were thus entitled to their title of citizen.[43] Some of these letters later became famous, for example the one Sergeant Pierre David, a member of *Action française*, wrote from the trenches to Charles Maurras on 26 October 1915. On 28 October 1918 *L'Action française* published the very respectful letter written by this royalist Jew:

I was born of a Jewish family but completely separated myself from the Jewish tradition. It was enough for me to be a good Frenchman and to be true to myself in order to adopt the doctrines of *L'Action française* with all their consequences. When you read these lines, which will reach you only if I die, I shall conclusively have acquired the nationality I claim by mingling my blood with that of the most ancient families of France.

One of the most significant deaths was that of the military chaplain Abraham Bloch. He was killed by a shell when, in extremely dangerous circumstances under enemy fire, he unhesitatingly broke cover to give a crucifix to a mortally wounded soldier. Maurice Barrès waxed enthusiastic about this episode and it became a positive standard example testifying to the absolute patriotism of French Jews. The famous Captain Dreyfus voluntarily went back into service, joining a particularly large number of Jewish officers of all ranks, including generals. (The Jews' identification with the state had already been translated into army careers for several generations.)

For a very short period, anti-Semitism diminished in the wake of this national unity, to reappear very rapidly in the immediate post-war period. This fact, well known in itself, takes on a quite different meaning when account is taken of the place already held by Léon Blum in post-war anti-Semitic writings.

We know that in *La Vieille France* in 1920, Urbain Gohier published the complete version of the *Protocols of the Elders of Zion*, which was then very widely circulated and reprinted – by Monsignor Jouin in the *Revue internationale des sociétés secrètes*, for example.[44] From now on, the prelate also explicitly attacked Léon Blum. But, in the same way as this review attacked him untiringly in the inter-war period as well as during Vichy, so *La Vieille France*, via Urbain Gohier, wrote in August 1920:

> The Jew Blum allows a deferment for the Jew Rouff, by order of the Jew Ignace, despite the military authorities' refusal: this is a summary of the war contrived by Jewry. The extermination of 1,700,000 Frenchmen was desired and perpetrated by the *Alliance israélite universelle*, in order to settle a million Hebrews in their place in France.[45]

On 10 December 1919, not long after the end of the war, the following solemn declaration appeared on a full page of *La Vieille France*:

> The men who have saved France bear the names of Foch, Castelnau, Pétain, Mangin, Gouraud. The men who are going to make the laws for France are called Rothschild, Mandel, Blum, Israel, Bokanowski. By the will of the sovereign people, Rothschild, Mandel, Blum, Israel, Bokanowski are going to command Foch, Castelnau, Pétain, Mangin, Gouraud, who will obey like soldiers.

The anti-Semitic truce was short-lived, and right away Léon Blum, like Georges Mandel, faced the first assaults. Very soon *L'Action française*, and Léon Daudet in particular, broke the national consensus. Together with all the nationalist movements, they relaunched the turn-of-the-century anti-Semitic agitation, concentrating their attacks on Léon Blum. Georges Mandel, a right-wing Jew who made no secret of royalist sympathies which bound him to Bainville, Daudet and Barrès, escaped similar anti-Semitic attacks until 1934. Even in 1933, Pierre Gaxotte, Blum's bitter enemy, described Mandel as a 'high class Israelite'.[46] The following year, when Mandel drew closer to the radicals and appointed Léon Blum to the governing board of Radiodiffusion, he became the target for Gaxotte's anti-Semitic fury. Now, any restraint was out of place: 'Blum and Mandel, it's all the same.'[47] Henceforth, they were both traitors to the nation, and denials of their activity during the war made no difference.

Blum was too old to bear arms, but in 1914 he became principal private secretary to Marcel Sembat, Minister of Public Works, in order to play a part in the national effort. Georges Mandel was Clemenceau's assistant in internal affairs where he proved very active and nationalistic. But fact carried little weight in the face of the anti-Semitic frenzy, which grew and was incessant up to the Vichy period, when Mandel, Blum and Mendès France, regardless of their political affiliations, were imprisoned. Mandel, like Jean Zay, was assassinated by the Militia; Blum was deported to Germany and threatened repeatedly with the same tragic end; Mendès France succeeded in escaping from his prison. He reached London to enlist in the air-force and carried out several bombing missions over France.

THE *MASSILIA* AFFAIR

The German army's advance in June 1940 was so crushing that the situation soon seemed hopeless. Resistance in France appeared to be impossible. A strategic withdrawal to North Africa would enable the fight against the invader to be continued with undamaged military forces. They alone were capable of upholding national sovereignty, averting the making of a separate humiliating peace which would cut France off from her allies.

President Reynaud was in favour of this. The government at that point had withdrawn to Bordeaux. As Minister of the Interior, Georges Mandel showed unfailing resolve, to such an extent that the English saw in him the spirit of the resistance, capable of galvanizing the nation in that tragic situation and of carrying those armed forces which were still undamaged into future battles against the Nazis. However on 16 June a new government was formed under the leadership of Marshal Pétain who, as early as 17 June thought that 'the struggle must cease'. Georges Mandel, on the contrary, persisted in wishing to continue it.

In the face of German demands, the government envisaged a withdrawal to North Africa and made arrangements for this on board the *Massilia*. On 19 June F. Darlan gave the order to set sail the next day as the ship had to take the politicians and senators who had taken refuge in Bordeaux. As their military position was in order and covered by the military authorities, Jean Zay, Pierre Mendès France, Georges Mandel, Yvon Delbos, Le Troquer, Daladier and many others, 27 politicians in all, left France and sailed to North Africa, in the belief that they would re-form the government there and carry on the fight. Léon Blum hesitated. Édouard Herriot, as he himself says, begged him to leave with Mandel: 'You two leave in any case, whatever happens. Don't stay in the hands of our present masters. I know their hatred of you all too well.'[48] This was a terrible plot by the new authorities who were determined to pursue negotiations for surrender with the Germans. By facilitating this departure they would remove the opponents of their compromise policy.

The die was cast: by a strange combination of circumstances and a whole series of lies by their opponents who were in favour of a separate peace with the Germans, these politicians were none the less cast as traitors. They became criminals in the eyes of future Vichyist propaganda, and every effort was made to stir up public opinion against them. This was too good an opportunity to miss: Go for the Jews who desert in face of the enemy; denounce the Jews who, as is typical of their cowardly, timid character, flee and leave the national soil. By twisting the truth, by systematically mutilating the facts, the supporters of the new collaborationist Vichy regime tried to make public opinion believe that the men most firmly resolved to resist were traitors.[49] Herriot and Jeanneney vainly strove to re-establish the truth by bringing out the facts about the departure of the politicians on board the *Massilia*, which had taken place with the agreement of the public authorities. To no avail. The affair took a symbolic turn. For the unleashed press, the cause was obvious: once again, the Jews, after having provoked a war in which so many true Frenchmen were giving their blood, had abandoned the national soil. For Louis-Charles Lecoc, 'Mandel is Shylock personified, the man who exacts the debt of a pound of flesh promised to Lord Samuel and Churchill, who wants the last soldier in France to shed the last drop of his blood.'[50]

On board ship, violent incidents broke out with the crew who had been worked up by the propaganda. As soon as they arrived at Casablanca, Georges Mandel was arrested, carrying his bust of Clemenceau from which he was never parted. Scuffles broke out on the quays. A demonstrator slapped Jean Zay's face. The PPF demonstrated. Insults flew.[51] The anti-Semitic press passionately denounced the passengers of the *Massilia* which *Candide* renamed 'Jitter-city'. This paper, no stranger to vehement anti-Semitism, reported that 'the Bretons' (Mendès France and Jean Zay) aroused 'the disgust of the young lads' (the sailors). They would give the boat a thorough cleaning before it set sail again, to 'remove the last traces of contamination'.[52] *Gringoire* published several portraits of Mendès France, 'the officer–deserter'. It was not averse to employing the most astonishing biblical comparisons: 'Israel, who borrowed a boat for its migration this time – the ocean not having the slightest desire to imitate the Dead Sea to let it pass – was well represented' on the ship. Were not Georges Mandel, Jean Zay, Georges Boris on board, along with Henri de Kerilis, de Delbos and Daladier, all uniformly described as 'fleeing warmongers'?[53] And in 1964 Saint-Paulien added his own subtle comments: 'They were probably warmongers, not warlike.'[54]

RIOM AND CLERMONT-FERRAND

Pierre Mendès France was brought back to France forcibly, like Georges Mandel. He was incarcerated in Clermont-Ferrand prison, while Jean Zay was transferred to the prison at Marseilles, then to Riom. Here, he met Léon Blum, also arrested by the Vichy regime. The idea was to make an example of them, to construct spectacular show trials in which the Third Republic would be attacked and finally desacralized. In the process, the Jews would be in the position of defendants, blamed for the misfortunes of the homeland, when they had actually been its loyal defenders. Vichy was really the anti-Dreyfusards' revenge. They were finally triumphant and, under the eyes of the occupying power, even with its help, could settle their scores. The trials of Riom and

Clermont-Ferrand, put together out of anything that came to hand, specifically against the two famous state Jews, Léon Blum and Pierre Mendès France, in this sense revealed a challenge to the institutionalization and strength of the state identified with the emancipating Republic. It was the Republic which was the target via the state Jews. Charles Maurras's 'divine surprise' was tantamount to the possibility now offered of challenging the process of differentiation of the state, and its claim to independence which alone allowed it to impose universally egalitarian norms on all citizens. The expulsion of the Jews from the state was in itself evidence of the ending of a certain type of state, dreamed of by champions of an old inegalitarian order since time began.[55] The expulsion had been loudly demanded by anti-Semites in the inter-war period. It was achieved at one stroke by Vichy legislation, acting with full discretion on its own convictions and in the occupied zone in the image of the Nazi occupier, who had already brought the Prussian state to an end in Germany. At Vichy the state Jews faced a crucial moment in their history since it was their emancipation itself which was challenged. Access to the state was henceforth forbidden them. At one blow, the very heart of Franco-Judaism was under attack. Some were at that time tempted to return to particularism. This withdrawal, this abdication by the state, deviating from its own logic by betraying some of its citizens, drove certain Jews to turn back to society to protect the conditions necessary to maintain their own particularism.

Without turning their backs on their Jewish origins and their own social attachments, Léon Blum and Pierre Mendès France intended to remain faithful to the model of Franco-Judaism at the particularly dramatic moment when they appeared together before the law. Blum himself tells us that his friends advised him to seek safety quickly while it was still possible to leave the country, when the physical threat was becoming more specific: 'They will degrade Jews; and you are both a socialist and a Jew, and yourself, on top of everything else!'[56] He replied: 'Absence would become desertion. Therefore, I will be there and I will fulfil my duty as a socialist, a republican, a Frenchman, albeit silently.'[57] Imprisoned in the fortress of Portalet and at Bourassol, he faced his judges, preparing his defence and his plea in a particularly hostile climate. But it was quite clear: 'The Republic had disappeared; it was replaced by the French state',[58] which was its antithesis from all points of view. Pierre Mendès France was also conscious of the significance of this crucial change which transformed the nature of citizenship. His letter to Marshal Pétain of 21 June 1941, at the time of his escape from Clermont-Ferrand prison, went straight to the point. 'No one can be mistaken', he wrote to the head of this French state. 'They did not want to punish the officer. The target was the politician, the left-wing deputy, the Jew. And the newspapers which have reported the trial have emphasized this quite clearly.'[59]

The national and regional press restrained its anti-Semitic hatred no longer. On this occasion, it flowed out in great waves and swelled in the face of the talent with which the accused defended themselves. In such a hopeless situation, they themselves became the pitiless accusers of the new collaborationist regime.[60] While Léon Blum in prison had no qualms about putting portraits of Marx Dormoy and Roger Salengro on the walls of his cell while he carefully prepared his defence,[61] general intelligence informs us that 'on the occasion of the Riom trial, certain papers like *Je suis partout* or *Au Pilori* received instructions from the German authorities to carry on an active campaign against the men of the former régime'.[62] 'We demand heads. All the heads', insisted *Au Pilori*, in response to the audacity of the 'Jew Léon Blum–Suss' in wishing to defend himself.[63] *Je suis partout*, not to be left behind, exclaimed: 'How can we demand the noose for hoarders if pacts are made with traitors? Mendès France has not been deprived of French nationality, no one has even dared ask him to stop attaching the name of France to that of Jew.'[64] At the same time, Marshal Pétain later confided to Maurice Martin du Gard that he had received a large number of letters demanding that Léon Blum and Paul Reynaud be put to death. 'Every Frenchman', he said, 'pressed me to shoot them.'[65] On 26 April 1942 Doriot, before a large crowd gathered at Bordeaux, also demanded that Blum and Mandel be shot.[66]

In an exceptionally violent book written in 1942, entitled *À la barre de Riom*, Hector Ghilini denounced 'Léon Blum's racial hatred'. He concluded: 'He claimed to be assimilated. . . . he remained a Karfunkelstein whose ancestors, in Henri Béraud's earthy phrase, scratched their fleas in the shadow of the Carpathians.'[67] Lucien Rebatet's frenzy reached unsuspected heights in *Les Décombres*, which also appeared in 1942:

This is a total and resplendent Jewish takeover, all the Aryans in khaki and all the Jews seated at table; things were a little hard but now it's going well. Blum? That was a timid attempt. It is now the masterpiece of Israel's great phoney conversion. . . . I have never touched the FM24. Hardly is the marvellous little weapon against my shoulder than I feel like a new man, invincible. Oh my machine gun, so often caressed in my dreams, facing the despised gangs of the Popular Front, the platforms of Blum and Thorez, Daladier, La Rocque, the gilded ghettos and the Sodoms of the well-known Parisian festivities! A hundred well-aimed machine-gunners. . . . I shoot like a god, greedily, passionately, in small steady bursts.[68]

In his diary of the occupation, Robert Brasillach thought on several occasions in 1942, at the time of the trials, that the deaths of Blum and Mandel, who were not 'French', would be desirable.[69] More examples of this literature can be found in the voluminous file on the Riom trial in the *Archives nationales*. They lack all restraint and appear demented by contrast with Léon Blum's dignity and strength of conviction. Vichy was consequently forced to shorten this trial abruptly because it had become more like a plea in favour of the Republic and particularly of the much-detested Popular Front experiment which had gone on to rearm France in the face of rising danger.[70]

Réagir, a Marseilles paper, had no hesitation: 'Are we to let the tribe spewed up by the ghetto, the race of Karfunkelsteins, Rothschild known as Mandel, still use our skins after the collapse they have led us into.... No, the victor of Verdun, having seen his glorious work submerged by the Jewish vermin',[71] would at last bring them to their senses and impose exemplary punishment by shaking up a too-scrupulous justice. The press protested at the slowness of the law which was taking too long to pronounce the death sentence. When Léon Blum confronted his judges, *Le Petit Parisien* thought that 'he still wants to raise his Jewish fist at France',[72] while *Le Cri du peuple* spitefully thought that at Riom, 'The Jew will have seized everything! Blum is taking over Joan of Arc.'[73] In such a hopeless situation, *Je suis partout* considered that the former leader of the Popular Front retained 'the thoughtlessness and impudence of the sheeny'.[74] Alone against the world, threatened on all sides, he still remained, according to *L'Émancipation nationale*, 'the insolent, arch-millionaire Jew.... the Jewish master'.[75] *Jeunesse* formed quite a different opinion: 'Jew, he has the reactions of a Jew, that is to say of a coward, without shame or modesty.'[76]

Despite his 'oriental magnetism',[77] which *L'Avenir du Plateau Central* found frightening, nothing could save him, particularly not the unforeseen interruption of the trial which succeeded in exasperating the whole extreme Right, shocked by Vichy's sudden caution. 'Twelve bullets in his skin', that ought to be Léon Blum's fate, in *Pilori*'s unqualified view.[78] No, the national revolution was certainly not radical enough. It was the spineless who triumphed and who bridled the ardour of the true supporters of a new order. And the birth of this order implied the elimination of the Jewish symbols of the Republic and, as a top priority, Léon Blum whom Vichy justice was taking too long to punish. Jean Boissel, who edited the paper *Le Réveil du peuple*, known for its vehement anti-capitalism, doggedly returned to the charge against 'the Bulgarian Jew Léon Blum.... Frenchmen, see things straight', he implored. 'The Jew has led you into a foolish war. But watch out: the Jew is still there, always amongst us as he was at the time of the Dreyfus Affair. The 200 families, 150 of them Jewish, remain the masters of France.' He saw only one solution that would genuinely change the course of history: 'The Riom defendants must be shot.'[79]

Pierre Mendès France also faced the mob and with an equal sense of honour. Preparing his defence, he made a firm resolve: 'As far as I am concerned, I will not allow an anti-Semitic allusion at the hearing to pass unanswered.'[80] In the event, the whole trial was awash with anti-Semitism. The same patterns of exclusion operated. We will give a few brief examples. General d'Astier de La Vigerie was very quickly nicknamed 'General d'Astier de La Juiverie' when he vouched for the military position of the former mayor of Louviers, thus giving an official denial to the accusations of desertion made by the Vichyist and collaborationist press, still pursuing the idea of the wandering Jew. In this context where everyone constantly appealed to 'the land and the dead', where purity of blood was the sole guarantee of citizenship, Pierre Mendès France's lawyer was also forced to employ a similar vocabulary to defend his client. He affirmed:

The Land and the Dead 123

I know his compatriots in Alsace. . . . I was on the general staff, in the secret *deuxième bureau*. I was associated with quite a few operations. I know the incomparable services that our brothers in Alsace, and particularly those amongst us who are of the same religious faith as he, rendered during the 1914–1918 war. Because, gentlemen, I do not have a drop of blood in my veins that is not Christian, I can do it. I can render that homage with respect, and I can say that they have been the best defenders of our French traditions on the banks of the Rhine, despite the imperfections that we know they have.[81]

The demands of patriotism and of the dead on the battlefields of the Great War degraded to the very prosaic idea of 'services' performed; the secrets of the general staff as in Dreyfus's time when treason was never far away; the purity of Christian blood, guaranteeing the opinion formed of Pierre Mendès France; and finally, that terrible phrase in the mouth of a courageous defender strengthening his advocacy with a flourish: 'despite the imperfections that we know they have': here we have the best of intentions perverted by the atmosphere of the time. The collaborationist reporters, for their part, were fully aware of the meaning of the metaphors he was employing. It is enough to look at *Gringoire*. That paper declared:

We have never ceased to demand the indictment of the Jew Mendès France, known as Mendès-Egypt, erstwhile associate of Blum . . . Like the deserting Jew, Zay, another passenger in the *Massilia*, the deserting Jew, Mendès France, is condemned. . . . Where were you, Mendès France, when our brothers were being killed, when France was being defeated? On the road. . . . That says it all! And this man, with his wrinkled eyelids, with the eyes of a hunted animal, who is trembling for his life, was a minister, able to dictate governmental instructions to Frenchmen![82]

The wandering Jew, the deserter, the traitor, the coward . . . In these circumstances, it is possible to understand that Pierre Mendès France, champion of a proud Franco-Judaism, product of a long line of ancestors who fought in the ranks of the French army, had no place in a France which was temporarily turning its back on the universalist ideal to adhere wholly to the reactionary tradition of 'the land and the dead'. Now there was only one possible outcome: the escape which stupefied the Vichy press.[83] Mendès France successfully brought it off in perilous conditions and, after several months, succeeded in reaching London. He enlisted in the air-force and faced the enemy, as he had always wanted.

However, even London was not completely free of anti-Semitism: 'General De Gaulle's army not excepted', Pierre Mendès France noted.[84] When the question of reshuffling the national committee came up, his appointment was envisaged: 'I would be mentioned', he said, 'and de Gaulle would be in favour'; but he added: 'The difficulty is that he is a Jew and there is already René Mayer. The question of counterbalancing Mayer would be raised.'[85] The old rivalry which broke out later, when the Mendès France government fell, thus appeared in absurd circumstances. Still in London, in between two missions, he noted again, this time on the subject of the leaders of the internal resistance, 'their manoeuvres and their actions when the Jewish question is involved . . . basically show considerable fear of appearing to be men of the Popular Front, the Judeo-Masonry and the Third Republic (even the left-wing ones)'.[86]

In this Gaullist France, Georges Boris, life-long friend of Léon Blum and Pierre Mendès France, heard an officer rallying the General's troops with him, say: 'Hum, a lot of Jewish names here.' Boris answered: 'I'm sorry this offends you because I am a Jew myself.' When the officer replied, 'What I don't like are Jews like Léon Blum, those revolutionaries who don't have a homeland', Boris put an end to this strange conversation held in the heart of London: 'I am even more sorry: I was Léon Blum's colleague and he is my dearest friend.'[87] This exchange says a great deal about the insidious influence of Drumont's legacy, even in the ranks of the supporters of Free France: very obviously it was incomparably weaker there. In July 1944 Pierre Mendès France accompanied de Gaulle to New York. De Gaulle turned and surveyed the cheering crowd. 'On the whole my supporters are negroes and Puerto Ricans, cripples and cuckolds, emigrants and Jews', he said.[88]

The broad outlines of the history of Vichy and the Jews, which has taken so long to become a legitimate academic subject, is beginning to be known.[89] From now on people will no longer be completely ignorant of the legislative bills which planned to exclude Jews from public life, of the coercive measures, often decided autonomously in conjunction with the occupying power, of the violence, the deportations; but also of the unexpected help the population sometimes gave Jews, which compensated to a small extent for the state's betrayal of its own citizens. The picture of this exceptional society still needs to be filled out to make it come alive at the level of everyday life, by discarding the declarations made by the stars of the collaboration and echoed by a servile press. What has still to be done is to collect the millions of small dramas, in countryside and town, in the offices and in the army, as well as in the networks of the resistance, which made up the fabric of life of all the actors. Because it is through them that the significance of Drumont's legacy, in this short period of his triumph, took on its full meaning. For whom, in short, was a Jew worth a Breton?

NOTES

1 Édouard Drumont, *La France juive* (Marpon & Flammarion, Paris, 1886), p. 251.
2 Quoted in Z. Sternhell, *Maurice Barrès et le nationalisme français* (repr. Éditions Complexe, Brussels, 1985), p. 251.
3 Ibid.
4 Maurice Barrès, *Scènes et doctrines du nationalisme* (Plon, Paris, 1925), vol. 1, p. 68.
5 Ibid., p. 93, n. 1.

The Land and the Dead 125

6 Léon Blum, *Nouvelles Conversations de Goethe avec Eckermann*, in *L'Oeuvre de Léon Blum, 1891–1905* (Paris, 1954), p. 220.
7 See Pierre Birnbaum, *Dimensions du pouvoir* (PUF, Paris, 1984), pp. 39ff.
8 Blum, *Nouvelles Conversations de Goethe avec Eckermann*, pp. 223–4.
9 Émile Faguet, 'M. Léon Blum', *Revue latine*, 25 Feb. 1907, pp. 66 and 72.
10 Letter from Émile Faguet to Léon Blum, 10 Sept. 1908, Bibliothèque nationale, *Manuscript*, NAF. 16: 'I was infinitely touched by the sollicitude you so kindly expressed and I can not tell you how grateful I am for your kind words.'
11 See, for example, *L'Action française*, 16 May 1937, where Pellisson sets out consecutively Barrès's and Faguet's arguments against Blum.
12 *Écho de Paris*, 11 Dec. 1937.
13 Gougenot des Mousseaux, *Le Juif, le judaïsme et la judaïsation des peuples chrétiens*, pp. 226ff.
14 See, for example, Drumont, *La France juive*, vol. 2, ch. 3.
15 An example of this is the thesis by Dr Martinez which was explicitly inspired by Drumont's viewpoint, in *Le Juif, voilà l'ennemi* (A. Savine, Paris, 1890), p. 143. See also, Henri Desportes, *Le Mystère du sang chez les juifs de tous les temps* (A. Savine, Paris, 1889), pp. 54 and 251; Preface by E. Drumont.
16 Albert Moniot, *Le Crime rituel chez les juifs* (Pierre Tequi, Paris, 1914), pp. 290 and 297. See also, G. de Lafon de Savines, 'Le quadrilatère de l'antisémitisme. 2: Le meutre rituel', *Revue catholique et royaliste*, July 1991, BAIU. In 1931 A. Rosambert very optimistically thought that in France 'a benevolent and balanced country... people prove resolutely hostile to superstition and prejudice'; whence, according to him, the decline of those fables in 'Crimes rituels?', *Revue Lorraine d'Anthropologie*, 1931–2, p. 29, BAIU.
17 Léon Blum was sometimes regarded as a prince of the Kahal responsible for its ritual crimes: Henry Robert Petit, *Les Juifs au pouvoir* (Centre de documentation et de propagande, Paris, 1943).
18 Drumont, *La France juive*, vol. 1, pp. 394 and 430.
19 *L'Action française*, 12 May 1937. In the same spirit, in an anti-Semitic leaflet distributed in May 1935, there is a letter from a Dr Tournay which declares, 'We must not confuse the old French Jewish families, rooted in our soil for generations and who have proved their attachment to the national community in so many ways, with the Jewish metics who have arrived from Poland and Rumania since the war, with their accents, their mentality, their total shamelessness. There is no common ground between a Lautman, a Jean Meyer who did their duty magnificently during the war, and the immigrant German Jews who formerly fought against us' (Bibliothèque nationale, *Tracts antisémites*, 4 Ld 183.46).
20 *L'Action française*, 14 March 1938. Already in 1920 Léon Daudet upbraided the French peasant in the following terms: 'Peasant, who carried the weight of the war and whom Miss Yid–Blum wants to deprive of your fields and your house, in the name of high international fraud, are you going to hide in your barn?' (*L'Action française*, 5 May 1920).
21 *Courrier de Narbonne*, 7 Nov. 1936.
22 *L'Industriel de Louviers*, 21 March 1936.
23 André Figueras, 'Objectif France', *Cahiers de la France*, no. 1 (1956), p. 18.
24 *Fidélité*, March 1956.
25 *Le Franciste*, 26 July 1936.
26 *L'Ami du peuple*, 11 Feb. 1936. According to this paper, 'Léon Blum will fool no one. In 1915 he was in Bordeaux or somewhere, in the process of treating his rheumatics and his vapours like an old tart. At the same time, millions of Italians were being killed in the trenches of the Argonne to help us save civilization and liberate the land of France. The workers, peasants, soldiers have

not forgotten this, but Léon Blum cannot understand it. He is not one of us' (22 April 1936).
27 *Je suis partout*, 9 Jan. 1937.
28 *Le Charivari*, 14 Sept. 1935. According to Charles Maurras, 'every globule hostile to the native land is circulating in the fine anti-French blood of the new master of France' (*L'Action française*, 28 May 1936).
29 *Le Temps*, 7 April 1938.
30 *L'Action française*, 6 April 1938.
31 *La France enchaînée*, 12 and 19 April 1938.
32 *Archives nationales*, F7 14781.
33 *L'Action française*, 6 April 1938.
34 *Le Nouveau Cri*, 9 April 1938.
35 *Au Pilori*, 13 Dec. 1940.
36 *Je suis partout*, 8 April 1938; *L'Action française*, 7 April 1938.
37 *L'Action française*, 15 April 1938.
38 Jean-Charles Legrand, *Paroles vivantes* (Édition Baudinière, Paris, 1941), pp. 196–8.
39 *Le Petit Journal*, 7 April 1938.
40 Comité de vigilance, 23 Nov. 1938.
41 Ibid., 12 May 1938.
42 See Philippe Landeau, *Les Juifs de France et la Grande Guerre*, thesis for a master's degree in history, University of Paris VII, 1984, p. 140.
43 A large number of these astonishing letters are analysed by P. Landeau, ibid.
44 For example, Mgr Jouin, 'Le péril judéo-maçonnique', *Revue internationale des sociétés secrètes*, 5 (1925), pp. 9–10.
45 *La Vieille France*, 12–19 Aug. 1920.
46 *Je suis partout*, 30 Sept. 1933.
47 *Je suis partout*, 13 April 1935. See John Sherwood, *Georges Mandel and the Third Republic* (Stanford University Press, Stanford, Conn., 1970), pp. 82ff.
48 *L'Oeuvre de Léon Blum, 1940–1945*, p. 60. See p. 67 for Blum's comments on the way Mendès France, Jean Zay and Georges Mandel were treated when the ship arrived at Morocco.
49 See Christiane Rimbaud, *L'Affaire du 'Massilia'* (Le Seuil, Paris, 1984), pp. 166–7.
50 Louis-Charles Lecoc, *L'Enjeu de la guerre: Les Juifs* (Sorlot, Paris, 1941), p. 11.
51 Rimbaud, *L'Affaire du 'Massilia'*, pp. 167–8. The author does not present the outbursts of the anti-Semitic press.
52 *Candide*, 31 July 1940.
53 *Gringoire*, 1 and 8 Aug. 1940. On 29 Aug. and 5 Sept. *Gringoire* demanded that Pierre Mendès France be tried immediately. On 13 Sept., after asking that Léon Blum be tried, that paper, which was never short of historical comparisons, added: 'One man betrayed Algeria to the Jews. It was a Jew by the name of Adolphe Crémieux ... a Jew to the tips of his crooked nails, he cunningly made the coup ... In 1870 Crémieux gave Algeria to the Jews. In 1940 the Jews of the *Massilia* turned back to their empire.' On 26 Sept. and 19 Dec. *Gringoire* returned to Pierre Mendès France's presence on board the *Massilia*. See also *Je suis partout*, 7 March 1941, which maintained that Mendès France was fleeing France on board the *Massilia*.
54 Saint-Paulien (joint pseudonym of Maurice Yvan Sicard and others); he was chief editor of *L'Émancipation nationale*, the weekly in German France of Doriot's PPF (*Histoire de la collaboration* (L'Ésprit nouveau, Paris, 1964), p. 105).
55 Birnbaum, *Dimensions du pouvoir*, ch. 9.
56 *L'Oeuvre de Léon Blum, 1940–1945*, p. 61.

57 Ibid., p. 70.
58 Ibid., p. 99.
59 Pierre Mendès France, *Oeuvres complètes*, vol. 1 (Gallimard, Paris, 1984), pp. 334–5.
60 On these trials in general, see Pierre Béteille and Christiane Rimbaud, *Le Procès de Riom* (Plon, Paris, 1973); Henri Michel, *Le Procès de Riom* (A. Michel, Paris, 1979); Christiane Rimbaud, *Le Procès Mendès France* (Perrin, Paris, 1986).
61 See Archives nationales, *Procès de Riom*, F7 15288. This very full, rarely opened, file also contains copies of letters sent by Blum and his friends.
62 Ibid.
63 *Au Pilori*, 5 Feb. and 19 March 1942.
64 *Je suis partout*, 30 June 1942.
65 Quoted by Michel, *Le Procès de Riom*, p. 22.
66 See Sherwood, *Georges Mandel and the Third Republic*, p. 272. On the increasingly violent anti-Semitism of Doriot, who was particularly attacking Blum, see Philippe Burin, *La Dérive fasciste: Doriot, Déat, Bergery, 1933–1945* (Le Seuil, Paris, 1986), pp. 295–6.
67 Hector Ghilini, *À la barre de Riom* (Jan Renard, Paris, 1942), pp. 103 and 125.
68 Lucien Rebatet, *Les Décombres* (Pauvert, Paris, 1976), pp. 276 and 311.
69 See Géraldi Leroy and Anne Roche, *Les Écrivains et le Front populaire* (Presses de la Fondation nationale des sciences politiques, Paris, 1986), p. 37.
70 See Robert Frank, *Le Prix du désarmement français, 1935–1939* (Publications de la Sorbonne, Paris, 1982).
71 *Réagir*, no. 1 (1942). According to *Le Matin*, 11 Feb. 1942, 'Blum was the man who prepared the way to defeat, the man who inoculated the virus of idleness into the blood of a nation'. In this spirit, see Paul Allard, *Les Responsables de la défaite* (Éditions de France, Paris, 1941), 2nd part.
72 *Le Petit Parisien*, 12 March 1942.
73 *Le Cri du Peuple*, 12 March 1942. According to *Le Petit Parisien* too, 'Blum identifies himself with Joan of Arc' (12 March 1942). On Vichy's celebration of Joan of Arc, see Gabriel Jacobs, 'The role of Joan of Arc on the stage of occupied Paris', in R. Kedward and R. Austin (eds), *Vichy France and the Resistance* (Croom Helm, London, 1985).
74 *Je suis partout*, 21 March 1942.
75 *L'Émancipation nationale*, 28 Feb. and 21 March 1942.
76 *Jeunesse*, 8 March 1942.
77 *L'Avenir du Plateau Central*, 14 Feb. 1942.
78 *Au Pilori*, 13 March 1942. *Le Cri du peuple*, founded by Doriot, also demanded Blum's and Mandel's deaths. See the issues of 6, 25 and 27 June 1942.
79 *Le Réveil du peuple*, 2, 14 and 21 Feb. 1942.
80 P. Mendès France, *Oeuvres complètes*, vol. 1, pp. 323–4.
81 Quoted in Rimbaud, *Le Procès Mendès France*, p. 166.
82 *Gringoire*, 9 and 23 May 1941.
83 See, for example, *Je suis partout*, 30 June 1941. *L'Action française*, strangely enough, was more cautious in its comments on the escape; see the issue of 11–12 May 1941.
84 Mendès France, *Oeuvres complètes*, vol. 11, p. 688.
85 Ibid., p. 739.
86 Ibid., p. 714.
87 See A. Weil-Curiel, *Le Temps de la honte* (Édition du Myrte, Paris, 1944), vol. 1, p. 270. On this point, see the thesis by Marie-France Toinet, 'Georges Boris (1888–1960)', thesis for the Fondation nationale des sciences politiques, Paris, 1969, p. 270.

88 Quoted by Jean Lacouture, *Pierre Mendès France* (Le Seuil, Paris, 1981), p. 160.
89 See, for example, Michael Marrus and Robert Paxton, *Vichy France and the Jews* (Basic Books, New York, 1981); Serge Klarsfeld, *Vichy–Auschwitz* (Fayard, Paris, 1985); *Vichy, 1940–1944: Archives du guerre d'Angelo Tasca*, ed. Denis Peschanski (Éditions du CNRS-Feltrinelli, Paris, 1986); John Sweets, *Choices in Vichy France* (Oxford University Press, Oxford, 1986); Marc Ferro, *Pétain* (Fayard, Paris, 1987).

6
Wine, Water and Milk

If our state Jews sometimes lacked 'French guts', as Pierre Poujade charmingly put it, it was because, despite their emancipation, they remained in his eyes – as in the eyes of all champions of anti-Semitism – strangers to the customs of the nation, its ways of speaking, acting, thinking, and above all, feeling. Their citizenship was entirely superficial: Jews they were, Jews they remained. They could not integrate into the national body, share its pleasures and its sufferings, quite simply be French, as all the sons of the native land were by nature. What they lacked was rootedness in the land: France's identity was its countryside, its valleys and its hills, its gentle rivers and its peaceful villages nestling between two water courses as if sheltered by their church. If the Jews could not comprehend the mystique of 'the land and the dead', it was because, although they had been a presence on the national soil for many generations, they still continued to be wandering Jews at heart, open to the world, eager for ideologies, indifferent to the soil. Drumont summed up the terms of the accusations in one sentence: if only to speak French, it was 'necessary to have sucked the native wine at birth, really to be sprung from the soil... only then does your language have a tang of the land drawn from a common fund of feelings and ideas'.[1] It can be understood *a fortiori* why Barrès considered that the purity and meaning of *Bérénice* must inevitably remain inaccessible to the Jews.

FROM NARBONNE TO LOUVIERS: LANDLESS JEWS

The paradox of a representative régime is that one deputy, elected in one constituency, none the less represents national sovereignty. He is welfare officer to his electors but, in good republican theory, he should be deaf to the interests of his region in order to devote himself entirely to the national interests. Logically, deputies should not try to put down roots in any one area which would encroach on their national responsibilities. The reality, however, is quite different. The deputies stand in close relationship to their electors who must be able to see themselves in the deputies. Particularly in the period leading up to the constituency poll, deputies immerse themselves in local affairs. This mimesis, far removed from Rousseau's ideas, identifies the deputy with a specific area in which he himself puts down roots. In these circumstances, how can someone be both Jew and deputy when the prevailing ideology denies to the Jew any quasi-earthy connections with the soil?

Take Blum, for example. For *Je suis partout* it was simple. The journal found it highly incongruous that he could be a deputy:

That M. Léon Blum can be deputy for Narbonne and that in this capacity, he is allowed to play a part – and what a part! – in the French Parliament, indicates the extent of the absurd and tragic in the electoral world. M. Léon Blum is neither from the North, nor the Centre, nor the East, nor the West, nor the South of France. What family does he claim to be descended from? What soil is he attached to? Where is his native patch? What stock does he come from?[2]

This says it all: as a Jew by definition must always wander, he cannot hope to become a deputy. Joseph Caillaux clearly expressed this in a conclusive sentence, destined to become famous, when he reflected quite bluntly that Blum, unlike Jean Jaurès, did not have 'enough French soil on the sole of his shoes' to claim to represent his constituency, still less France. This was such an unmistakable statement in the eyes of many of his contemporaries that it has been in constant use from Maurras up to the present day.[3]

Of course, there have been several variations on the formula, but the central idea has never been shaken: Blum had no connection with the rural world, with the peasant communities where, far from abstract ideas and humanitarian daydreams, the character of the nation was really forged. France, on this basis, was conceived as a rural society, its innate qualities differing from the ideologies which were newly formed in the towns. The artificial nature of these towns increasingly drew the Jews towards them and this was where most of them lived. This organicist and xenophobic perspective, similar to de Bonald's, or Tönnies's at the turn of the century, depicted France as a 'community' tightly united by its ancient traditions, and not as a 'society'.

We shall briefly illustrate some of the variations on Caillaux's theme. Henri Béraud, who used Léon Blum as his whipping boy for a number of years, had lost none of his imagination. He drew the enduring portrait of Blum in his own particular style: 'Look at the master of the hour', he advised. 'There he stands, pale, nervous, letting his gentle, too gentle, gaze of an oriental charmer wander over the benches. Strange man. He holds the destiny of our old nation in his thin fingers. . . . Oh yes, my dear Léon, it is indeed an ancient land, an ancient land of honest soil, where it is true to say grandfather Blum never coarsened his hands by pushing the plough.'[4]

Soil on the soles of shoes, and coarsened hands: such were the symbols of the Frenchness which was beyond Blum's aspirations. When a certain L. O.

Frossard, who had Jewish connections, acknowledged this and preached return to the land, *Le Nouveau Cri* was horrified by such heresy and exclaimed: 'This sermon hardly becomes a representative of the race of Léon Blum', for Blum, like Jules Moch, and so on, 'do not have the coarsened hands and the mud of France on their shoes.... inseparable from the life of a true peasant. Who if not the real peasants fight for them in wartime?'[5]

The most apocalyptic text conceived by an imagination prey to absolute frenzy was unquestionably penned by Maurice Bedel. It must be quoted at some length here. He gave what he considered an edifying history of Bengali, a Jewish immigrant from Smyrna who, after many adventures, succeeded in hoisting himself on to the highest rungs of political power. He became a deputy, even had a seat in the government, and then went off with Léon Blum on a tour of the provinces to sound out opinion in deepest France. To bring this astonishing scene to life, Maurice Bedel carefully sketched an image that would symbolize the incongruity of the presence of a Jew on French soil:

Once there, M. Blum was shown an isolated farm about two hundred metres away, where he would be able to converse with local people.... The day was grey and cool: the air smelt of damp earth. Mr President slid on this clay-like mud, which the finely shod feet of the workers' leader were in no way made for. And, as he straddled a puddle of water, he lost his balance and fell. 'What curious stuff we are walking on!' he said. 'This,' said Bengali, 'is what they call the earth of the fields.' 'I would not have believed,' said M. Blum, 'that it could cause a Prime Minister to fall.' M. Blum did not know where to put those feet of the leader of the French section of the Workers' International. It is all very well being the guide and support of the workers, but a long apprenticeship is needed to learn how to walk on soil worn by the tramping feet, the comings and goings of twenty generations of labourers, shepherds and poultry hands. Mr President was horrified to hear the liquid manure from the dung squelch under his feet. The dogs began barking furiously when they saw him, something they usually reserved for chair-menders, hawkers selling rabbit skins and tramps who roamed the countryside.... It is a curious feature of this leader of the Workers' International that he seems afraid of contact with the land. He does not walk shod in stout boots along the field paths where he might meet men whom the poverty of life affects just as much as others.... he has never shivered when the smell of the furrow opened by the iron plough reached his nostrils. He is foreign to everything which is sap, humus, mossy springs, paths between hedges, nuts that one shells with one's heels, dreaded nettles, mint trampled along the river banks, pebbles rolled in torrents, bushes with wrens, breezes which dance on the thatch, puddles after showers, soil, clay, rich earth, the earth of good friendship. Oh! this man is not one of us.... This is when the kitchen garden gave the first signs of revolt. The lilac was first to attack: several bees were seen to abandon the perfumed panicles whence they drew honey, hurling themselves as if by command at the nose, cheeks and ears of Mr President of the Council.... M. Moch found this surprising. One might have said that the earth of this small garden of France was rejecting him. The attack began when a mole dug away the soil under one of the legs of the chair on which Mr Secretary was sitting, and Mr Secretary clumsily tumbled right into the tank where the proprietor put his stock of snails to purge.... The shrew-mice joined in.... Let us adjourn the sitting, says Mr President of the Council, waving his handkerchief.... The land had refused M. Moch its vote. But a few days later, men gave him theirs.[6]

This inspired, enlightened text, a tiny jewel of anti-Semitic literature, says it all. Rarely has love of the land of France and hatred of the Jews, bucolic poetry and rejection of the outsider, of the man who does not have his feet firmly planted in the land, nor his rootedness in the soil, been carried so far. Expressed with such calm and simple faith, this mystical devotion makes one shudder: it marks the limits of republican consensus, of the superficial equality of all citizens. Foreign even to fascism and the ideologies of the radical right, it shows that well into the twentieth century there still persisted organicist thought opposed to an abstract republic which legalized the presence of Jews, no matter that they had been elected by their fellow citizens. The conclusion was simple and terrifying: France could not be represented by elected Jews, even on the basis of universal suffrage. Such elections, in the secrecy of the polling booth, would be a betrayal of the land which violently rejected them. What men, wrongly convinced that these were the virtues of the representative parliamentary system, failed to do, the land undertook.

This is a long way from the extremist political ideologies which flourished in the 1930s: this radical rejection carried all the more weight because it claimed to be based on the nature of a France which had remained unchanged over the centuries. In terms of this argument the 'legal country' – the electorate – appeared astonishingly fictitious because it was at the opposite pole from the 'real country'. France, in this sense, had no use for a Republic which betrayed the virtues of the soil, since it allowed the unnatural election of Jews. In short, what could Franco-Judaism do in face of the clay, the rich earth, the moles and the shrew-mice? What was its legitimacy if the land and those who lived on it shuddered and bristled at contact with the most assimilated Jew, steeped in French culture, product of the *École normale supérieure* or even the *École polytechnique*, resplendent with diplomas and completely devoted to the national interest? Forget its rejection of the immigrant Jews straight from Russia or Poland, but Blum, Moch, Mandel, Mendès France? There was now no hope at all for a recently immigrant Jew, whatever his sense of sacrifice to his new homeland.

This unexpected deadlock seemed all the more tragic at local level, far from Paris where the Republic and the universalizing ideologies prevailed. At Narbonne, Blum 'who only drinks water, has not a word to say about viticulture.... He knows as little of the problem of defending viticulture as of the flora of the high plateaux of Abyssinia.... It is necessary to belong to a peasant family to understand this difficult period when the wine-growing environment is threatened with a plunge into the most abysmal distress tomorrow!'[7] And the local journalist added in a tone at once premonitory and long-suffering: 'He has strong fears of the concentration camp for himself in the near future, which would still be the least which could befall him.'[8] *L'Indépendant de l'Aube* could only go one better, with the anguished question: 'When will the Yid finally decide to leave the seat of Narbonne to a local militant?'[9]

At Louviers, Pierre Mendès France fared scarcely any better. He faced Alexandre Duval in the 1932 elections. *L'Industriel de Louviers*, an important local paper which did not conceal its sympathy for the right-wing parties, regarded Duval as a 'child of the country who has remained loyal to it and served it well.... Scion of an old family of distinguished farmers who have worked the same farm from father to son for two hundred years', he temporarily moved away, but very soon 'ancestral attachments brought him back to the land'.[10] A little later, in 1936 Mendès France's electoral opponent was Modeste Legouez. He again described himself as the 'son, grandson and great-grandson of farmers who had worked a small farm at Epreville since 1600. After leaving school at thirteen with the usual stock of elementary knowledge, he went to work in the fields.'[11] An official election poster pasted on all the hoardings went straight to the point: 'Jews do not cultivate the land. The outgoing deputy criticizes Legouez for agitating on behalf of the French peasants. No one will criticize the lawyer Mendès for this.... Out with the lawyer who has betrayed the peasants.'[12] Some 30 years later, Pierre Poujade formulated the same idea and drew similar conclusions: 'No! Mendèses, sub-Mendèses or potential Mendèses, when one is the son of an old land like France, one is not made for slavery, of any sort.... The people of France did not ask you to come.... They will not retain you.'[13] The land and the wandering Jew. At Louviers as at Narbonne, age-old rootedness in a piece of land appeared as a *sine qua non* for any hope of election. In this system of logic, peasants could only be represented by other peasants and not by rootless intellectuals: by what obscure route, what ineradicable lunacy, did Blum and Mendès France none the less succeed in being elected to rural constituencies where neither of them had ancient roots in the land?

TO DRINK OR NOT TO DRINK: THE MYTHOLOGY OF WINE

By a strange coincidence, Léon Blum and Pierre Mendès France represented constituencies where alcohol was even more important a factor in sociability than in the rest of France. To drink wine in the Aube or calvados in the Eure was the usual practice which structured social networks, strengthened local identity and ensured the homogeneity of the community. To drink was a normal action which marked the rhythm of local life, which tended to ensure, through various ceremonies, the transmission of the culture from generation to generation. As Roland Barthes noted,

the French nation feels that wine is peculiarly its own possession.... It is a totem-drink, corresponding to Dutch cows' milk or the ceremonial drinking of tea by the English royal family.... In its red form, its old hypostasis is blood, the thick, vital liquid.... believing in wine is a compulsive collective action: the Frenchman who stood aloof from the myth would expose himself to minor but specific problems of integration – in the first place, just having to explain himself.[14]

Léon Blum drank mainly water, although he did not scorn a good Burgundy now and then.[15] Pierre Mendès France launched a veritable crusade in favour of milk, going so far as to brandish a symbolic glass of milk in the precincts of Parliament (the right-wing press also made fun of the fact that Léon Blum had water brought to him there). Thus they were both permanently obliged to 'explain themselves'. So was Jules Moch, deputy for Sète. Laurent Fabius, also elected for western France, barely touched cider and most frequently asked a friend to drink in his place, as did Léon Blum to whom he explicitly referred.[16] As cider was the totem-drink of Brittany, the sentence which had resulted in so many repercussions, 'a Jew is not worth a Breton', was immediately recalled, and people are still debating it today.[17]

A sort of terrible correlation emerged which inevitably implied exclusion: Jews did not tolerate wine, calvados, cider; they preferred water or milk; they did not have the same blood as Bretons or the peasants of the France of the winelands. Because they were not at one with the soil, of which wine was the soul and which conferred strength on those who feasted on it, they had no place in the national community, rejecting as they did one of its most vital symbols. Not to drink was tantamount to fleeing before the enemy and refusing to shed one's blood, as so many Bretons – and Narbonnais – had courageously done. To illustrate such logic, *Je suis partout* imagined the following sketch in which an inhabitant of Narbonne spoke to Léon Blum:

I fought in the war. I was at Verdun. Where were you? Oh, I don't blame you. You weren't there. If I could have done what you did, I would have stayed at Narbonne to tend my vine . . . drink! It's the ration of the trenches. Let me tell you about an idea I had down there, citizen Blum, one evening, under the stars. The social question would be solved if everyone drank wine from his vine and ate chickens from his hen-house. Come on, drink up! What do you think of this plonk? It's warm, stimulating, syrupy! Are you pulling a face? Do you despise your elector's wine?[18]

Integrated into the national community, here and there sharing in all its unifying myths, certain Jews also went so far themselves as to equate wine and blood. They were anxious to proclaim their patriotism loud and clear, particularly during the First World War when, as has been seen, they gave their lives for France equally with the Bretons. On 8 October 1915, for example, *L'Univers israélite* published the following poem by Joseph Cahn, a testimony to the Jewish soldier's patriotism:

> My country is the blood which flows in my veins,
>   The clear air that I breathe and the wine that I drink,
> It is the infinite extension of my self, I think,
>   The soft speech which tells of my love and my pains.[19]

Under Vichy, the solidarity of the trenches was no longer fashionable. Inspired by Céline's prose, *Au Pilori* had it wrong when it indicted 'the impotent, drunken, thieving Society Blum and Co.', which set out to 'transform France into a bistro'.[20] The Jews could hardly be held responsible if France were covered with cafés, bistros and bars – and historians have traced their emergence, emphasizing their indispensable function to sociability in a rapidly changing France.[21] In actual fact, our state Jews, who hardly enjoyed patriotic allegories phrased in terms of blood and wine, did not seem to frequent them much, and thus excluded themselves from those networks of social relationships where convivial friendships were forged. For Roland Barthes, 'society calls anyone who does not believe in wine, sick, infirm or vicious: it does not understand him'.[22] In order to separate the wheat from the chaff, as Darquier de Pellepoix plainly stated in front of 600 people who had come to a meeting organized by the *Rassemblement antijuif de France* on 16 February 1938, the solution was simple and radical: 'One should neither shake a Jew by the hand nor even drink with him.'[23]

Léon Blum and Pierre Mendès France soon experienced this ostracism. At Narbonne, Émile Sabatier was one of the most violent anti-Semitic critics of the local deputy Léon Blum: 'To think that the lucid and sensitive men of Narbonne', he exclaimed, 'have entrusted the defence of their most basic interests as vine growers to that puppet who is both sybarite and satrap, makes one shudder with incomprehension.... Blum might manage to tell the difference between a white wine and a red by its colour not its taste.'[24] Léon Daudet posed the same question: 'I ask myself what the stout vine growers of Narbonne can think about that clown who has about as much affinity with them as a Baltic herring has with our local cocks.'[25] The *Journal des débats* jeered at the efforts of 'the apprentice boozer': 'The citizens of the Aude agree with the proverb that all the wicked are water-drinkers – well proved by the Flood – and subject the unfortunate Blum to trials which he puts up with heroically. Despite everything, M. Blum still does not drink. He would die of it.'[26]

Pierre Mendès France who dared to attack the privileges of the home distillers – 'the superman of milk', as *Rivarol* baptized him[27] – was pilloried no less. For *Fraternité française*, 'Wine, even the most lowly plonk, is an excellent thing, it is an exclusively French beverage. Unless you are called Pierre Mendès France, try doing without the precious red when staying abroad'. Certainly the symbol of treachery was the 'milk of that man who tried to drive us crazy, that fellow who is always curdled, who liquidates France by drinking whey, that Mendes who loves milk [Fr. = *lait*] because he himself is ugly [Fr. = *laid*]'.[28] From one period to the next, in 1929–36, 1954–7 and even in 1985, there was no getting away from the argument. For *Minute*, calvados had not been drunk at the Matignon since Laurent Fabius was master there: 'A product which does not seem to have seduced the master of the place, although pure Norman.'[29] To conclude this sample of everyday anti-Semitism, here is the portrait of Léon Blum that *Le Rire* drew for its large popular public. It needs no comment.

136 Drumont's Legacy

> My glory, my pride is my love for wine,
> Pour, drink up,
> Wine is pure, wine is fine!
> Pass the cup!
> My horror for water will always last;
> You men of the vine lend your ears,
> That at my baptism in times that are past
> 'Twas not water I chose, but the shears.
> Let's lay no stress on the minor bit,
> Pour, drink up,
> For after all I abandoned it,
> Pass the cup.
>
> They're telling you lies, good people, you know
> When they say that I always have had
> A taste for the castle, for pomp and for show
> And a hate for our wines good or bad.
> If you believe this quite sanely,
> Pass the glass!
> We answer equally plainly,
> Poor ass!
>
> Thinking about that 'something'
> which the rabbi cut as a sign,
> as a child, I looked reproving
> When my parents lopped my vine.
> What say you to this version?
> Pour, drink up!
> Constituents, note my assertion,
> Pass the cup![30]

LOCAL ANTI-SEMITISM

According to police reports, *L'Action française* was firmly entrenched in the 1930s in the Aude, particularly at Narbonne, and in the Eure.[31] Philippe Henriot, Xavier Vallat and Taittinger held many meetings in the large towns of the Aude in 1936–7.[32] Roland Dorgères, future head of the Green Shirts, was himself very active in the Eure. His paper, *Paysan*, zealously supported the candidature of Modeste Legouez against the 'Jew Mendès France'. Legouez, rival to the mayor of Louviers, later became departmental delegate to the *Corporation paysanne* in 1941.[33] That two Jews could be elected in peasant constituencies was a scandal which the extreme Right found intolerable and against which the leaders of the local moderate Right also rebelled. None the less, the population loyally persisted in voting for them in one election after another, and it was not until Vichy that so shocking an anomaly came to an end.

On 5 October 1940 portraits of Pétain finally replaced those of Léon Blum in the offices of the Narbonne town hall.[34] As the report by the prefect of the Aude noted in September 1940, Léon Blum's internment 'has been favourably received by our Narbonne population'. Elsewhere he noted a heavy increase in requests for shooting licences, which seemed to him a 'healthy distraction'. Furthermore, he added 'Marshal Pétain knows the vine growers of the Midi very well, he is one of their own by adoption.' For the representative of the new French state there was no question about it, 'the French soul is awakening'[35] in that region which formerly looked steadfastly to the Republic. In his report of November 1941, the prefect of the Aude noted that Blum 'is almost totally forgotten by the large majority of his former friends'; and in June 1942 he emphasized with satisfaction that 'the Aude has given Marshal Pétain an enthusiastic welcome'.[36] According to the *Courrier de Narbonne*, the assembled crowd roared a powerful 'Long live the Marshal', and the journal added: 'In 1936, the Jew Blum came to visit his "good town of Narbonne". Léon peddled his moonshine while keeping his distance. . . . none the less something has changed.'[37]

In this town, which had so long stayed loyal to Léon Blum, Philippe Henriot had several thousand Narbonnais hanging on his words in October 1943 and, shortly after his assassination, a solemn mass was said with great ceremony at the basilica of Saint-Just and Saint-Pasteur de Narbonne in memory of 'the great patriot' who had passed away.[38] The socialist leader was in fact truly forgotten. 'Léon Blum? Don't know him', was *Candide*'s simple comment, noting that if Narbonne 'did have its brainstorms, the people pull themselves together. . . . the sweet wine' now flowed once again.[39]

The change took time to register in the Eure, traditionally looking towards Great Britain, now the sworn enemy of Vichy. In his reports of January and May 1941, the prefect thought that 'the idea of collaboration has made little progress'. Even in February 1942, according to him, the population still remained anglophile, even if it was attached to Marshal Pétain.[40] The prefect was forced to wait gloomily until March 1942 to have good news to report: 'The arrival in London of the former deputy mayor of Louviers, Mendès France [sic] has caused a sensation in the Eure and given rise to a certain disappointment in some circles which retain an anglophile tendency and which think that this event is not of the sort to enhance ex-General de Gaulle's credit in the department.'[41] If on several occasions he consoled himself by noting that the local population was primarily 'materialistic', solely preoccupied with 'good living and good eating', 'indifferent' to the trials being held at Riom and Clermont-Ferrand, he was forced to admit throughout 1943 that it vowed 'vindictive hatred' both to the occupying power and the French authorities.[42]

This, then, was the picture in the Eure, Pierre Mendès France's influence and prestige seemed to have gone for ever. *L'Industriel de Louviers*, his bitter enemy, congratulated itself on the fact; the 'adventure' which Louviers had lived since 1932 'will have been the saddest and most deplorable in our history.

It is over, let us turn the page with the desire to work together to forget it.'[43] For the *Journal de Rouen* it was 'the end of the petty Jewish lawyer who managed, no one knows how, to get himself elected deputy for one of the pleasantest districts of Normandy, against a local "lad", a man from a peasant family, Modeste Legouez, who was as a matter of fact Dorgères's comrade and lieutenant.'[44] At Narbonne, the wind finally changed in the same direction: the majority of socialists there, like those in the Midi, approved of the Vichy régime, and many were the friends of Léon Blum who abandoned him.[45]

As deputies for rural constituencies, Léon Blum and Pierre Mendès France spared no effort to fulfil their function as representatives. Léon Blum never really became a southerner, and his visits to his constituency were only fleeting. He really remained more a national political personality than a public figure immersed in local affairs. None the less he took pains to defend viticultural interests when they were threatened by a slump in wine or even by serious flooding; he strove to obtain compensation, intervened with the Minister of the Interior, acted with other deputies for viticultural areas to improve the quality of wine,[46] thus giving the lie to Colonel de La Rocque who publicly accused him of not knowing his electors in Narbonne.[47] Pierre Mendès France, for a long time deputy for the Eure, cut more of a figure as a local dignitary watching over his electors' interests. Familiar with the department, he knew its diversity, appreciated its richness, the beauty of its landscapes and its rivers; in short, he had an unswerving love for 'this land of the sweetness of living amidst the harshness of toil – this beautiful countryside of the Eure – the epitome of France'.[48] He too gave of himself unstintingly to defend farmers who had fallen into debt as a result of the terrible agricultural situation.[49]

Both, to the great chagrin of their often anti-Semitic opponents, were constantly re-elected by those two rural constituencies, who chose them as deputies for the ideas they defended and the concrete actions they undertook and not on the traditionalist image of rootedness in a specific piece of land, whereby Normans only recognized themselves in a Norman of ancient stock and the people of Narbonne in a long-standing heir of Occitania.

The *Courrier de Narbonne* was truly appalled by 'the grotesque representation of our Languedoc Midi. . . . It must be supposed that our population, however much Latin commonsense it has inherited, has gone mad.'[50] For the *Journal des débats*, 'this "outsider", this northerner, this water-drinker, is not at Languedoc's temperature'.[51] In these circumstances, Léon Blum's victory both at the local level and in the national elections could only be explained by madness or a successful infamous conspiracy. Charles Maurras literally fulminated against 'the vagabond, the wanderer, the stateless man . . . asked to sit in the legislative seat for Narbonne, although the whole Midi, from the Médoc to the Var, had expressed its horror of this water-drinker [who] forced his way in with every secret support, Masonry, money, over which he had gained supreme power'.[52] Maurras, so sensitive to the charms of the language of Oc (the dialect of southern France), of the Félibrige (the Provençal literary brotherhood) and of

Provence, was dismayed to see the formation of a 'Palestine of the Aude' in that southern land to which he was so attached.

Blum's election goes beyond the boundaries of one district or one area. It affects all France. This Jew has a specific role. The strange coalition of the most diverse organizations in his favour shows what influence gold and, without a shadow of a doubt, foreign gold, has exercised in his campaign. In Parliament, Blum will set little store by local demands. . . . His activity will be brought to bear on foreign policy.[53]

In short, Maurras thought, together with Léon Daudet, that 'the Republic of the Aude is Germany. Blum will represent the interests of German capitalism in the French Parliament.'[54]

This was the key to the whole affair: the Latin commonsense of the French population counted for nothing because the culprit was again, as always, foreign gold seeking to strengthen its control over French policy by buying French electoral constituencies one by one. No greater misfortune could be imagined. From now on, according to Laurent Viguier – author of *Les Juifs à travers Léon Blum: Leur incapacité à diriger un État*, a book which is crucial to our thesis – Blum rules over the 'southern capital of old Gaul . . . electorally, this constituency represents the homeland of Clovis and Joan of Arc'.[55] 'Is the town of Narbonne still in France?', asked his local opponent, Émile Sabatier. For him, 'Red Narbonne has become a corner transplanted from Palestine where the merchants have again invaded the Temple. . . . Citizens of Narbonne, how can you tolerate the tyranny of this man of another race?'[56] What evil spell so blinded them that they voted for Blum and scorned the candidature of people like Sabatier who were not 'indifferent to viticultural matters'?

Despite all its efforts, *L'Indépendant de l'Aude*, official organ of the Republican Union of the Aude, in which Louis Marin himself published numerous articles, did not manage to throw any light on this mystery. In 1936, for example, the paper appealed to people to 'Vote French', that is to say, for Henry Leroy-Beaulieu, grandson of Paul Leroy-Beaulieu who had been president of the *Societé de Viticulteurs de France*; or for Robert Albouy, Republican candidate of *Action sociale et viticole* who, according to this paper, could claim to his credit that he was 'a true viticulturist who worked with his hands'.[57] To no avail: the vine-growers remained deaf and persisted in their choice. Nevertheless, *Le Courrier de Narbonne* urged them ceaselessly to reverse it: 'Viticulturists, merchants who live off the fruit of the vine, put your trust in the candidate who best knows your needs . . . Blum doesn't give a damn for viticulture. Vote French'.[58] In article after article in this local paper, Laurent Viguier allowed his vengeful fury to break out. He was joined by Hubert Bourgin, Léon Blum's fellow-student at the *École normale supérieure* and author of the book *De Jaurès à Léon Blum*, who also used the paper to attack his old school-mate's 'biased dictatorship marked with Hebraic messianism'.[59]

One can see from this that a certain number of national figures were strengthening the hand of the local anti-Semitic press which, as already noted, was also receiving support from leaders of right- and extreme right-wing parties, who travelled down to hold meetings in the Aude. The whole conservative press was unleashed and hurled anathema upon anathema against Blum and his deputy; the latter's name was Lacroix, which, by association, lent itself to the most anti-Semitic play on words and caricatures. However, the local SFIO united behind its candidate and defended him tooth and nail, not hesitating in its turn to use the weapon of the language of Oc, this time in Blum's favour. This fine song, written in that language, bears witness to this:

> Here we have the great Blum
> Poking fun at this critic.
> Here we have the great Blum
> Who can't face up to this insult.[60]

In November 1935 Dorgères was the star speaker at a large meeting which took place at Montpellier on the occasion of a gathering of viticulturists, and *Le Courrier de Narbonne* invited the inhabitants to participate.[61] Now Dorgères, as already noted, also supported Modeste Legouez in his contest against Pierre Mendès France in the Eure. Moreover, identical arguments were used. What strange cabal could lead true Normans into error, what sinister plot drove the electors to throw themselves into the arms of a Parisian lawyer 'who mixes up the different sorts of beetroot',[62] a mirror image of Blum who was incapable of telling a white wine from a red? In the Eure, as in the Aude, for Dorgères, as for Maurras, only money could explain such suicidal behaviour. According to the agitator of the peasant world and supporter of fascist ideas, the surprising election of Pierre Mendès France, 'the man with the large flour-mill', was incontrovertible proof that 'gold flows in waves' in this constituency.[63] For *L'Industriel de Louviers*, there could be no doubt that 'Jewish solidarity' was on the march:

If the Jew Mendès thinks he has the right to criticize the Norman Legouez for being at the mercy of counts and marquises, generals and industrialists, may it not be thought that he himself, because of Jewish solidarity, owes something to his Jewish co-religionists? The Rothschilds, Louis Dreyfuses, Kaufmans are no longer yokels in clogs with five sous in their pockets. Can they be taking an interest in the Jew Mendès's political career? This seems very natural. Legouez must be helped. He will be helped. Who will help him? Everybody ... the workers who put in their forty sous as well as the bourgeois ... they all come from our part of the world, they are clubbing together as best they can for a man from our part of the world who represents the interests of our part of the world. There will be no King of Finance nor Corn King amongst them, no Persian or Oriental Carpet King no Coffee King. There will be no Worms, Stam or Cahen amongst his electors. ... Who will pay for Mendès? Jewish solidarity.[64]

In the Aude, as in the Eure, in the very depths of the French countryside, without a shadow of a doubt Vichy came well before Vichy, and apocalyptic theories sprung straight from Drumont obsessed local consciousness. Current anti-Semitic propaganda now aimed to stir up this consciousness against the cosmopolitan plot. In the peaceful French countryside as in Paris, the nation as a whole, regardless of class, had to unite against the bloated rich, identified here solely with Jewish capitalists hailing from a distant, unclean Orient. The myth of the bloated rich – foreign to the good people of France who comprised all social classes and served as a standard for the Popular Front – was dragged out once more, transformed into a weapon against the Jews who alone were not always 'from our part of the world'. Against such devilish power with its international influence, 'the small farmer' Modeste Legouez, who 'is from our part of the world and has not just come there', appealed at one electoral meeting after another for a revolt against the Jews.[65] He even managed to convince left-wing electors, such as the small merchant who explained his conversion in the following terms: 'I have always voted for left-wing candidates. Till now it was easy. They were called Baudehan, Delamare, Ernest Thorel. Last Sunday I voted "white". The reason why is simple. L'Eliacin of the Radical Party is a Jew.'[66] In the small market towns and the countryside, anti-Semitism showed itself to be a social habit and not pure ideology without concrete consequences. During his electoral campaign in 1934, at Gaillon and elsewhere, Pierre Mendès France saw the farmers forming ranks against him; incidents, often violent, broke out here and there, and for many there was no doubt that 'Mendès's nose will grow longer' if despite this he persevered in his struggle.[67]

As in the Aude, where Léon Blum's enemies exploited their role as vine-growers, Modeste Legouez sought to confront Pierre Mendès France as a pure peasant. 'Son, grandson, great-grandson of farmers', Legouez belonged to none 'of the two hundred families' and could not call on the support of 'Isaac's gangsters' to fight his battles.[68] On 22 April 1936 at Louviers, before 3,000 people, the worthy Modeste Legouez thundered: 'There is not one single Jew amongst the Norman farmers. Why should they choose one to represent them? It is not a question of religion but of inclination: the Jews are lawyers and financiers; they have nothing in common with the Norman population.'[69]

Legouez simply contented himself with repeating in his turn the reasoning common to all the 'heirs' since Barrès, in order to construct a theory of national representation which ignored the French Revolution. He also adopted the reactionary tirades which the editor of *L'Industriel de Louviers* had employed in favour of Alexandre Duval, his predecessor, defeated by Pierre Mendès France in 1932. Addressing Mendès France, he had already declared:

You do not know, Sir, the state of mind of the Normans whose votes you are canvassing. They do not like to give their votes to people they do not know. When someone claims the honour of being chosen as representative of the people, he must first introduce himself if he is not known, particularly if he is facing a man like M. Alexandre Duval whose family cultivated the same farm in Neubourg for 200 years and who really is a 'local lad'. If your family history during the same period of 200 years were known, rest assured no doubts would remain. It is true to say that the fact that you are a Jew is held against you. You must understand that this objection comes spontaneously to the lips of many electors. But make no mistake. This is not a question of the religion you practise. It is the question of race which is involved. The Jewish race, whose purity has been maintained despite its dispersion, has virtues and failings . . . which cannot be compared to those of landowners such as us. The great majority of the electors of this region are countryfolk attached to the soil. The Jews are a race, you will agree, that is inclined to wander and seldom stays still. I do not believe it includes farmers, in any case, none are known in our part of the world. And that, you see, again creates a spontaneous distrust of men who do not attach themselves anywhere. . . . When the inhabitants of this region hear you vituperate against the great trusts, big banking, the large flour mills, international high finance, the thought quite naturally comes into their minds that there are more Jews than Normans to be found in those circles. For my part, it matters little to me that you are called Mendès France and that you are a Jew. You yourself have raised the question; I wished to clear it up objectively.[70]

Fortunately, at both Louviers and Narbonne, republican France still abided by a different 'objective' conception of French society. In its eyes, citizenship and eligibility did not involve working the same piece of land since 1736 (Duval) or 1600 (Legouez), and the peasants of Languedoc and Normandy, those lands which, with Brittany and Alsace-Lorraine, symbolized national identity, 'spontaneously' retained their confidence in the republican contract. In both areas, they rejected a return to pre-emancipation organicist and reactionary theories which could only be put into practice with the defeat of the Republic and with the corporatist French state of Vichy.

Contrary to the wishes of the editor of *L'Industriel de Louviers*, 'the vast majority of rural electors attached to their piece of land' continued to identify with the radical deputy and his socialist colleague, despite their shared Jewish origin. Ideas prevailed, not the ineffable bonds with the soil. The fact that the editor of a locally important paper in the Eure, which represented the ideas of moderate France, advertised his deep-seated anti-Semitism so openly; that in the Aude the republican right wing was not afraid to echo such sentiments, revealed that ordinary anti-Semitism went way beyond the revolutionary radical and Axis-orientated right wing alone. The fact that numerous local anti-Semitic demonstrations broke out in the uttermost depths of the countryside, as they had at the time of the Dreyfus Affair, also implied that even at this period anti-Semitism in France took the form of a social fact and not a simple ideology professed only by solitary, fanatical intellectuals.

That Léon Blum and Pierre Mendès France, Jews who were not 'local lads' but had used the customary method of 'parachuting' which had initiated so many parliamentary political careers, should nevertheless have had little trouble in being constantly re-elected in those rural constituencies (even though neither of them seemed fully to appreciate the virtues of wine and alcohol which were rooted in the very depths of local culture) finally marked the limits of those ideas and their patterns of exclusion. For all that, they did not disappear, so persistent was the symbolism of shared wine, for example, the source of a healthy conviviality in which those who did not drink could not participate. Just think of Poujadist prose which had its hour of glory and which always contrived to link wine to war and spilt blood. In the 1950s, this type of pronouncement could still be heard: 'Our fathers, who went to bistros, were at Verdun, and Mendès was not there.'[71] 'Admit', added Pierre Poujade, 'that you don't care a damn about the health or the blood of our people.... If you had a drop of Gallic blood in your veins, you who represent our France, world producer of wines and champagnes, you would never have dared to have a glass of milk served to you in an international situation! On that day, Monsieur Mendès, you dealt every Frenchman a smack in the face.'[72] In 1955 anti-Semitic remarks directed at Pierre Mendès France resounded loudest in towns in the vine-growing regions: at Mâcon, Béziers and Montpellier there were meetings where the insults which were commonplace at times of crisis such as the Dreyfus Affair or during the thirties were heard again – 'Mendès the Yid!', 'Dirty Jew!'[73] It was as if the symbolic association of wine and Jews could cross the ages unchanged, each time provoking their rejection.[74]

NOTES

1 Édouard Drumont, *La France juive* (Marpon & Flammarion, Paris, 1886), vol. 1, p. 30.
2 *Je suis partout*, 27 Oct. 1934.
3 See, for example, articles by Charles Maurras in *L'Action française*, 19 July 1936, and Pierre Taittinger in *L'Ami du peuple*, 19 June 1936. In the opinion of Louis Guitard, even in 1983, 'nothing is further removed from Blum than the physical, carnal patriotism of men like Clemenceau or Caillaux, both passionately enamoured of a plot of land, with the land which their ancestors fashioned and which must be delivered up, ever more glowing, to future generations.' This author then explicitly adopts Caillaux's terms vis-à-vis Blum (*Mon Léon Blum, ou Les défauts de la statue* (Regirex-France, Paris, 1983), pp. 204–5).
4 *Gringoire*, 5 June 1936.
5 *Le Nouveau Cri*, 9 April 1938. See also, Jean Renaud, *La Solidarité française attaque* (Oeuvres françaises, Paris, 1935), p. 122. In the same spirit, according to *L'Alerte*, 'Blum did not have a clod of French earth on the soles of his shoes'. That was why he bought 'a plot of land to get himself elected at Narbonne' (*L'Alerte*, 31 Oct. 1942).
6 Maurice Bedel, *Bengali* (Oeuvres françaises, Paris, 1935). The quotations are taken from pp. 116–47.
7 *Le Courrier de Narbonne*, 3 Oct. 1936.
8 Ibid., 12 Sept. 1935.
9 *L'Indépendant de l'Aube*, 7 March 1936.
10 *L'Industriel de Louviers*, 16 April 1932.
11 Ibid., 4 April 1936.
12 Quoted by Françoise Chapron, *Pierre Mendès France dans l'Eure: Trente années de vie politique (1932–1962)*, 3rd cycle doctorate, University of Rouen, 1984, p. 100.

13 Pierre Poujade, *J'ai choisi le combat*, (Société générale des Éditions et des Publications, St Céré, 1955), p. 116.
14 Roland Barthes, *Mythologies* (Le Seuil, Paris, 1981), pp. 74–5.
15 According to a militant socialist in Narbonne, Blum, contrary to the myth which makes him a water-drinker, 'drank in moderation . . . but as an amateur' (see Jean Lacouture, *Léon Blum* (Le Seuil, Paris, 1977), p. 222.
16 Broadcast, 'L'Oreille en coin', France Inter., 15 Feb. 1987.
17 Thus Jean-Marie Le Pen stated on 13 Feb. 1984: 'I regard the Jews as citizens like the rest . . . they are no more citizens than the Bretons or the rest. I do not feel obliged to love the Old Testament, to admire Chagall's painting or to approve of Mendès France's policy' (quoted by Alain Rollat, *Les Hommes de l'extrême droite* (Calmann-Lévy, Paris, 1985)).
18 *Je suis partout*, 12 Jan. 1935.
19 Quoted by Philippe Landeau, *Les Juifs de France et la Grande Guerre*; thesis for a master's degree in history, University of Paris VII, 1984, p. 49. On p. 50, Landeau points to another poem by Joseph Cahn, 'For our damaged fields, our wretched roads. For our vines, our woods, our roofs dressed with ivy', and so on.
20 *Au Pilori*, 29 Jan. 1942.
21 See, for example, Priscilla Clark, *The Battle of the Bourgeois* (Didier, Paris, 1973); Jean-Pierre Panouille, 'Et les Français prirent goût à l'absinthe', *L'Histoire*, no. 52 (Jan. 1983). Social salons and circles fulfilled the same function: see Maurice Agulhon, *Le Cercle dans la France bourgeoise, 1810–1848: Étude d'une mutation de sociabilité* (A. Colin, Paris, 1977).
22 Barthes, *Mythologies*, p. 75.
23 *Bulletin* of the *Centre de documentation et de vigilance*, no. 59 (Feb. 1938).
24 *L'Insurgé*, 13 April 1936. On 17 May 1936 a meeting was held at the Club du Faubourg in Paris, specifically on the bistros and wines of France. Pierre Andreu introduced his book, *Sachons boire*, by stressing the strength and the health that wine gives; then Mlle Chanel took over and declared that she had just taken part in the electoral campaign against Blum at Narbonne and that she, for her part, 'likes tasting good wines' (*Archives nationales*, F7 13986). After citing the 'revolutionaries' Marx and Blum, Henri Béraud asked himself: 'Anti-Semite? No . . . Is it inhospitable to want to gather in one's harvest, drink the wine from one's vine and protect the house of one's fathers?' (*Popu-Roi* (Éditions de France, Paris, 1938), p. 158).
25 *L'Action française*, 11 April 1929.
26 *Le Journal des débats*, 11 April 1929.
27 *Rivarol*, 3 Feb. 1955.
28 *Fraternité française*, 19 May 1956 and 2 March 1957. On this point, see Dominique Borne, *Petits-bourgeois en révolte?: Le mouvement Poujade* (Flammarion, Paris, 1977), p. 231.
29 *Minute*, 16 Nov. 1985.
30 *Le Rire*, 27 April 1929.
31 *Archives nationales*, F7 13202.
32 See *L'Indépendant de l'Aude*, 11 and 21 Jan. 1936; 27 Feb. 1937.
33 See Chapron, *Pierre Mendès France dans l'Eure*, pp. 91, 92, 178.
34 *L'Indépendant de l'Aube*, 5 Oct. 1940.
35 *Archives nationales*, F 1CIII 1141. In this context, it should be recalled that Pétain had ordered the suppression of a scene from a war film shot in 1917: a scene in which he pulled a wry face after tasting a soldier's ration of wine (Marc Ferro, *Pétain* (Fayard, Paris, 1987), p. 679).
36 Ibid.
37 *Le Courrier de Narbonne*, 18 June 1942.

38 Ibid., 28 Oct. 1943 and 3 Aug. 1944.
39 *Candide*, 18 Sept. 1940.
40 *Archives nationales*, F 1CIII 1152.
41 Ibid.
42 Ibid.
43 *L'Industriel de Louviers*, 17 May 1941.
44 *Journal de Rouen*, 8 May 1941. Quoted by Chapron, *Pierre Mendès France dans l'Eure*, pp. 178–9.
45 Henri Lerner, 'Léon Blum à Narbonne', *Nouvelle Revue socialiste*, nos 10–11, p. 63.
46 See Anne-Lise Massa, 'Léon Blum, deputé de Narbonne', dissertation for a master's degree from the *Institut d'études politiques d'Aix-en-Provence*, 1979, pp. 23–32.
47 On 20 Feb. 1937, during a political meeting organized by the *Parti social français* in the Salle Magic City, Colonel de La Rocque stated: 'No, M. Blum, the people will not rise in revolt, not even your electors in Narbonne whom you barely know' (*Archives nationales*, F7 12966).
48 Pierre Mendès France, *Oeuvres complètes*, vol. 1 (Gallimard, Paris, 1984), p. 202.
49 Pierre Mendès France, interview with Chapron, in *Pierre Mendès France dans l'Eure*, p. 91.
50 *Le Courrier de Narbonne*, 21 March 1935.
51 *Le Journal des débats*, 11 April 1929. On 8 April 1929 *L'Ami du peuple* revealed that 'Léon Blum and his friends are worried: things are not going well at Narbonne. What does most damage to this pale candidate is his horror of wine. He cannot see a glass full of this generous liquid without fainting away. The vine-growers of Narbonne shrug their shoulders in pity' (*L'Ami du peuple*, 8 April 1929). See also the issue of 10 April 1929.
52 Charles Maurras, *Dictionnaire politique et critique* (Fayard, Paris, 1931), vol. 1, p. 199.
53 *L'Action française*, 16 April 1929. From 1929 to 1942 there are many diatribes by Maurras against the scandal which Blum's election at Narbonne represented for him. See, for example, *L'Action française*, 26 Oct. 1942. The *Cahiers jaunes* was no longer surprised at anything: 'when the red-wine drinkers of Narbonne can be seen electing this miscarriage of a water-drinker' (*Cahiers jaunes, Institut d'études des questions juives*, Oct. 1943). And *Candide* made fun of the 'red workers of Narbonne who fall on their knees when they see Blum and say: Here is the new Messiah' (*Candide*, 2 Dec. 1935). For Georges Saint-Bonnet, 'in three months, when he had to, this water-drinker became the most learned vine-grower in the Palais-Bourbon' (*Le Juif ou l'internationale du parasitisme* (Éditions Vita, Paris, 1932), p. 196.
54 Léon Daudet, 'Le décharonné narbonne', *L'Action française*, 20 April 1929. For Léon Daudet, 'a few weeks ago, the indescribable androgynous Blum declared his readiness to go to war to avenge the German brethren. We understand by that that he would have had the vine-growing electorate of Narbonne massacred to the last man for such a worthy cause. But 24 hours later, after the Bank Benard or other bank feeding his "un-Compere-Morel-ised" caboodle had spoken to him, the *précieux ridicule* of Karl Marx declared that he had only meant to talk about a completely theoretical and verbal war, a *guéguerre* of the drawing room or the barrel. The oenophobic circumcised Bacchus had only danced his Pyrrhic for peace' (*L'Action française*, 7 Oct. 1933). Here, Drumont's admirer has combined all the ingredients of anti-Semitism.
55 Viguier, *Les Juifs à travers Léon Blum*, p. 17.
56 *Le Courrier de Narbonne*, 1 Aug. 1935.
57 *L'Indépendant de l'Aube*, 25 Feb. and 28 March 1936. *Candide* emphasized that 'the local and true vine-growing candidate had a serious advantage in the neighbourhood of Narbonne over the gentleman from Paris, who was more familiar with dress rehearsals than with wine harvests' (*Candide*, 22 Oct. 1931). Conversely, Arthur Conte noted that 'the strangest thing is that this tribune–poet, so highly intellectualized ... more a silhouette of the drawing-room than the

representative of the people, should have been able to appear so much at ease, from the human point of view, with the rough vine-growers of Gruisson or the sardine fishermen of Leucate' (*Le 1er Janvier* (Plon, Paris, 1977)), p. 222.
58 *Le Courrier de Narbonne*, 23 April 1936.
59 Ibid. A very large number of anti-Semitic articles by Laurent Viguier were published in the Jan. and Feb. 1936 issues. See also the article by Hubert Bourgin on 25 June 1936.
60 *La République sociale*, 19 March 1936.
61 *Le Courrier de Narbonne*, 21 Nov. 1935.
62 *L'Industriel de Louviers*, 30 April 1932. In the same spirit, see the issue of 22 April 1932 where it is emphasized that 'Mendès does not know how to tell sugar beet from mangolds'.
63 *Le Progrès Agricole de l'Ouest*, 18 Oct. 1932.
64 *L'Industriel de Louviers*, 21 March 1936.
65 *L'Industriel de Louviers* gives a faithful account of it, for example, in various issues in Feb. and March 1936.
66 *L'Industriel de Louviers*, 7 May 1932.
67 See the information given by *L'Industriel de Louviers* and *La Dépêche de Louviers* between March and May 1934.
68 *L'Industriel de Louviers*, 21 and 28 March and 4 April 1936. Modeste Legouez received the support of *Candide* which compared P. Mendès France, that 'newly fledged Norman', to that young farmer with his smallholding (*Candide*, 16 April 1936).
69 Ibid., 22 April 1936. See Pierre Birnbaum, 'Attaques antisémites contre Pierre Mendès France', in François Bédarida and Jean-Pierre Rioux (eds), *Pierre Mendès France et la mendésisme* (Fayard, Paris, 1985), p. 176.
70 *L'Industriel de Louviers*, 16 April 1932.
71 Quoted in Stanley Hoffman, *Le Mouvement Poujade* (Cahiers de la Fondation nationale des sciences politiques, Paris, 1958), p. 227.
72 Poujade, *J'ai choisi le combat*, p. 114. For *Aux Écoutes*, 'This is a terrible man, say his opponents; he does not drink, eat, smoke. And abstinence is irritating' (*Aux Écoutes*, 16 Oct. 1956). In *Rivarol*, A. Paraz published a derisive article entitled 'J'irai revoir ma Normandie' in which he made fun of the Normans who 'adore to vote for a mayor who above all else must not practise the religion of his fathers'. And he added: 'on the streets of Louviers young Norman women can be seen offering flowers to the gracious Lily Cicurel [P. Mendès France's wife]. She at least acknowledges her Arabo–Asiatic origins' (*Rivarol*, 21 Oct. 1954).
73 See *Le Droit de vivre*, Feb. 1956.
74 Although it does not seem that the association was taken as far as seeing wine as the blood of Christ, killed by the deicidal Jewish people.

7
Hermaphroditism and Sexual Perversion

> Léon Blum appeared in the guise of a prophetess, somewhat like Deborah or the Witch of Endor mentioned in the Bible. He also has something of a Judith in him since on 11 May 1924, he could be seen penetrating the republican camp covered all over in aromatics, making love with the radical Holophernes, then, having made his lover drunk, cutting off his head once the night had ended.
>
> Pierre Dominique, *Le Rappel*, 3 March 1927

JOAN OF ARC, MARIANNE AND JUDITH

Unnatural beings *par excellence*, so fundamental was their bisexuality considered to be, that Jews were often identified with women. In anti-Semitic discourse, they certainly had nothing in common with Joan of Arc or even with Marianne or Madelon, all strong, virtuous heroines. They were so depraved that they were, rather, incarnations of Judith, Rebecca or Deborah. The better to cheat their opponents and establish their power ever more firmly, they used tricks and seduction, not shrinking from any stratagem to exploit the sexual weaknesses of their Christian enemies. From this point of view, the Jews were depicted as hermaphrodites, sometimes men, sometimes women, possessing a disturbing sexual nature with which they deluded their naïve Christian enemies all the more easily. Judith stands at the opposite pole to Joan of Arc, the virgin who devoted herself body and soul to her king and people; the tragic heroine who rose up, weapon in hand, to confront the invader; the instrument of good who never forsook her vision of King Charles VII being finally anointed in Rheims cathedral and who stayed valiantly at his side during the ceremony, brandishing her oriflamme near the altar.[1]

Judith was a prostitute, the image of evil, who acted treacherously to save her people. She was the femme fatale who, despite her courage and her sacrifice, was always portrayed in the sculpture and painting of the Middle Ages, the Renaissance and even in contemporary iconography and literary representations as a monster of perversion. She was the personification of the dangers of seduction by Jewish femmes fatales to which so many aristocrats succumbed, falling into the snares of dangerous Judiths and Rebeccas.[2]

Joan, the peasant maid, the Christian, the virgin, the Celt, has carried all the hopes of the nationalist and anti-Semitic Right from the end of the nineteenth century to the present day. During Vichy, 'with Pétain as with Joan, the battle remains the same':[3] against the Jewish Republic that Judith symbolized. For Robert Brasillach and many others, 'the Republic is a woman of the streets' as was Judith,[4] analogous, according to Bucard, head of the Francist movement, to 'France–Madelon, whom anyone can accost and tap on the buttocks, and who will agree to prostitute herself to the red beast'.[5] In this sense, even if the character of Joan of Arc expressed a whole group of symbols far removed from those conveyed by the image of Marianne,[6] both seem far removed from Judith – even though anti-Semites often looked for the presence of Judith the Jewess within the features of Marianne the republican. When Marianne left for battle,[7] often with the cap of liberty on her head, calm or violent, sovereign and courageous, sometimes brandishing lance or sword, the feminine allegory which obsessed republican-inspired poetry, sculpture and painting, that superwoman also became a saint, even a proud and benevolent virgin. Like the Virgin Mary, Mary-Anne's austere bared breast recalled in simple fashion that she was also the nation's foster-mother. On postage stamps and coins, she was a symbol of courage and abundance; on the 'Ceres stamps', for example, she had corn, grapes and laurels on her head. There was nothing here that could be compared with the nudity and amorality of Judith or Rebecca, femmes fatales, greedy, bringers of desolation.

Unfortunately, there is not enough material available to extend this comparison between Joan and Marianne on the one hand, and Judith on the other. The first were pure heroines with whom the nationalist Right and the republican Left in particular identified, but who despite their differences, none the less eventually became an integral part of the national culture. From this culture Judith remained excluded, so great was her depravity and the strangeness of the supposedly disloyal Jews whom she personified. In anti-Semitic nightmares, Jews were women like Judith, with obscure, excessive and bewildering sexuality. They were in consequence utterly and entirely different from Joan of Arc or Marianne who were female allegories devoid of sexual desire, pure and innocent warriors, in the likeness of the young virgin maids of France.[8] In the innermost depths of Western Christian consciousness, Jews, like women, were carnal beings, privileged agents of Satan, the masters of darkness, the inspiration behind all witchcraft, which aroused fear and terror and heralded the end of the world.[9]

JEWS, WOMEN AND MADNESS

Even during the Enlightenment, when fear of Satan was much diminished, the identification of Jews with women remained widespread. Moreover, the question of Jewish emancipation was being debated at the same time as the question of women's admission to citizenship. Identical arguments for and against were brought up in both cases, relating to their essential nature, their sexuality, their capacity as a result of education to commit themselves to the paths of progress. In addition, Jews, like women, sometimes faced common and declared opponents, like the champions of anti-Semitism who saw them, according to the famous formula, as 'a state within the state'. They also had the same supporters.[10]

This common fate was accompanied by exclusion from public affairs where only the male sex of the Christian religion had legitimate scope for action. The triumph of rationalism during the Enlightenment did not necessarily change this perception. As Jews were constantly compared with women, they appeared to be fundamentally bisexual beings, with scarcely any role in a male-dominated society that was steeped in virility and valued physical effort, the use of force, bloodshed and the consumption of alcohol.[11] In anti-Semitic representations, they even ended up becoming mankind's only bisexual individuals, thus freeing other men from such indignity. This has been a matter of great interest to psychoanalysis, which has sometimes been tempted to see repression solely as the suppression of the bisexuality which is common to all men.

Before applying these ideas to the anti-Semitic critics of our state Jews, remember that the great quarrel between Fliess and Freud turned precisely on this essential point. Freud ended up rejecting it, because it implied that it was only their homosexuality that men repressed, their passive and, to put it briefly, their feminine dimension. This debate was crucial because in anti-Semitic discourse only Jews retained this bisexual nature. It was even more interesting because it was carried on between Freud, Fliess and Weininger, three assimilated, and even, in the case of the latter two, converted Jews. Now the hypothesis that Fliess formulated and which Freud dismissed was at the heart of Weininger's misfortune. He expressed his self-hatred by rejecting both the Jewish and the female elements of his being. As with many Austrian and German Jews ravaged by *Selbsthass*, self-hatred, suicide was the only way open to him, because it allowed him literally to kill the feminized Jew in himself.[12]

We could prolong this digression into the quarrels of psychoanalysis, so varied and antithetical were the interpretations of the Jews' bisexuality, such as those suggested by Groddeck, for example.[13] It does not take us away from our subject since, in response to Hitler who was aware of Weininger's theses and agreed with them right down to their logical conclusion, the French champions of anti-Semitic theories shared this fantasy, using Édouard Drumont as their base.

In France, one of Weininger's most severe critics, horrified by this self-hatred, was none other than André Spire, Léon Blum's colleague on the Council of State, devotee of that Franco-Judaism which extended into a commitment to Zionism. Now Spire, anxious to understand the reasons for Weininger's repudiation, in his book examined the case of Proust as well.[14] Proust was another converted Jew; he was fascinated by homosexuality. In *À la recherche du temps perdu* he might, for example, have found his inspiration for the character of Bloch, the sensitive intellectual, the Jewish dandy, assimilated but still exotic, in Léon Blum. (Blum's most bitter enemy, Léon Daudet, was Proust's close friend.[15]) It was as though a chain stretched from Freud to Weininger, Proust and Léon Blum, but also, as we shall see, to Georges Mandel and even Pierre Mendès France, in which were intertwined bisexuality, Judaism, homosexuality and, lastly, anti-Semitism and its ravings about the Jews' alleged perversions.

In many ways, Drumont and Hitler, and Barrès and Maurras as well, shared the same repulsion for the many features heralding a modernity which they identified with the decadence largely caused by egalitarianism. Egalitarianism, in their eyes, promoted the unlimited influence of Jews, who lacked the attributes of healthy, male virility. Their influence was as a result of the fact that the coherence of the family unit had almost disappeared and that there had been a marked decline in the traditional division of sexual roles. This was eminently favourable to their Judaic bisexuality because it encouraged transvestism and forms of homosexuality. In this sense, defending the race or nation meant trying to preserve the energy of society. It had been undermined by luxury, pleasure and the ever-more-varied vices which, in this *fin de siècle* mood, stimulated appetites, spread moral anarchy and perverted societies. It led inexorably to the abandonment of all discipline and all morality, leaving the door open to every disease and infection.[16] In anti-Semitic imagery, the Jews were the incarnation of these dangers which threatened the hitherto undamaged structure of Christian societies. Some commentators diagnosed the hatred which Christian champions of anti-Semitism seemed to vow to the Jews as stemming from an Oedipus complex, the sexual rivalry which pits the sons against the father whom they paranoically reject.[17]

From this standpoint, Jews, like women, had a biological predisposition to the madness which conduced unfailingly to every perversion. In this *fin de siècle* period, science entered the fray to justify the dread that they inspired. In psychiatric experiments during his famous *Leçons du mardi à la Salpêtrière* in 1888, Charcot thought that Jews were subject to neurasthenia and hysteria, an illness to which women had always been susceptible.[18] Shortly afterwards, other doctors, some Jewish themselves, like Rafael Becker, investigated this relationship between Jews and madness. Their aim was to explain the appearance of psychopathological symptoms, particularly Jews' surprisingly nervous predisposition, not by biological reasons but by social causes resulting from difficulties in assimilation that invariably aroused self-hatred. A quasi-medical justification was thus provided for the Zionist argument . . .

The precise content of these debates on the nature and reality of mental illnesses peculiar to Jews, which troubled the psychiatrists and psychoanalysts of the day, are not very important here.[19] What should be remembered primarily is that Drumont himself was aware of Charcot's experiments. He often referred to them specifically,[20] before concluding that 'leprosy has mounted to the brains of many Semites. Formerly, they were content to scratch themselves, now they feel the need to excite themselves.'[21]

Charcot's verdict, adopted by European psychiatry, coincided with the views of August Rohling, whose book, *The Talmud Jew* (1871), was widely known in France at that period. It fitted into the more general framework drawn by Drumont and so many other polemicists of his day, who depicted Jews in the most varied forms of animal life (hyena, jackal, vulture, crow, octopus, monkey, pig, mole, serpent, grasshopper, and so on). A little later, Blum was portrayed as a camel, a weasel, a mare and a dog; Mandel as a serpent, for example, or a spider;[22] Pierre Mendès France as an owl; and Daniel Mayer as a 'black, wriggling, viscous tadpole'.[23] Laurent Fabius was likened to a monkey with prehensile feet,[24] one of many features which put him in the same category as Mandel, already described as 'an insolent baboon' by *Humanité*,[25] which ironically and knowledgeably added: 'The subtle Jeroboam is the living demonstration of Darwin's theory that man is descended from the apes.'[26] Note that curious parallels were now drawn by both extremes of the political spectrum. For Léon Daudet, Blum 'the little girly citizen suddenly releases the odious serpent hissing under those pink satin cushions'.[27] According to Florimont Bonte, a leader of the Communist Party, when 'that little darling of the bourgeoisie'[28] is in 'a paroxysm of anger, his feverishness is extreme. He is like a serpent trampled by the hunter's feet. The reptile raises its angry head and spits venom.'[29]

The extreme Right in particular had also emphasized since the end of the nineteenth century the tendency to madness of these 'Bohemians' which reached its peak in the Jewish woman.[30] For Drumont, 'Jewish neurosis is the implacable disease of the Jews'.[31] The unhealthy and manipulative sexuality of Jewish women had done nothing but corrupt the aristocrats and bourgeois who thereby forfeited their national stamina,[32] spreading an uncontrollable fear of the most unnatural perversions in what were still in many ways peasant societies.[33] This fear was all the more justified in that, according to Drumont, the Jews wanted 'to circumcise every Frenchman'.[34] Paul Lapeyre revived this idea a few years later in his book *La Sociologie catholique*, where he denounced the 'demons of the Talmud with their secateurs',[35] obsessed by their own castration complex.[36] Looked at in this delirious way, the danger was doubly urgent. Jewish women – amongst the most famous of them at that period were Rachel and Sarah Bernhardt – did not resort only to seduction and prostitution in order to pervert the French soul. Hence the many Jewish beauties in contemporary novels (by Balzac, Zola, Maupassant, Alphonse Daudet) who did not hesitate to prostitute themselves to slake their hatred and satisfy their own interests. They reappeared later in works by Drieu La Rochelle and Céline. The Jews with their disturbing sexual nature also set out to emasculate the French in order to make them like themselves.[37] Anti-Semitic imagery reached a state of perfect coherence when, in the wake of Leo Taxil's article 'La France chrétienne', Drumont violently denounced the scandal to beat all scandals, namely that a Jewish actress, Sarah Bernhardt, could with impunity play the hallowed character of Joan of Arc on the stage, as if evil could claim to represent good, or the impure the pure.[38]

A few years later, the anti-Semites' target was no longer the famous actress. It was Léon Blum, another feminine character who also had the cheek to 'play the virgin', as Charles Maurras charmingly expressed it,[39] rather as Laurent Fabius was 'made virginal by his white shirt' in the 1980s.[40] By so doing, the leader of the Popular Front dared to appropriate this symbol of staunch and healthy purity. This explains the violent indignation of the *Cri du peuple* at the time of the Riom trials: 'The Jew will have seized everything! Blum is taking over Joan of Arc',[41] an unthinkable crime at a time when Vichy was burning incense before the Virgin, currently immensely popular even in the cinema.[42] How in fact was it conceivable that Blum–Judith could slip without warning into the garments of Blum–Joan of Arc? 'Little girly Blum', as Léon Daudet called him, appeared in the many anti-Semitic lampoons Daudet wrote as a 'mademoiselle', 'Miss funky weasel', whose fundamentally 'hybrid' nature conclusively made him a 'hermaphrodite'.[43] Georges Mandel, Clemenceau's colleague, who later became Minister of the Interior, was according to Georges Suarez, certainly 'sexless, his illness is that he has no sex, he has been forced to borrow from male and female',[44] like Jules Moch who has 'no stomach, chest or buttocks'.[45]

The heirs of Drumont and Maurras had no doubts: unnatural Léon Blum and Pierre Mendès France indisputably were. According to them, Blum, 'Beelzebub let loose'[46] and 'socialist Satan'[47] was in many respects close to 'Mendès, the Lucifer, the Tempter, the mad gambler'.[48] To the MRP, he was the incarnation of 'the devil, the accursed one who deserves nothing but the sword of the angel of death'.[49] It was a punishment that Christians had long reserved for Jews and, in general, for Luciferian foreigners, with sexual norms orientated towards an unacceptable enjoyment, similar, in that respect, to women, who were by nature hysterical.[50] Their unnaturalness also showed in their repulsive physical appearance: thus Georges Mandel was 'hideous ... a calamity for pregnant women who saw him'.[51] Also attacked was Pierre Mendès France whose 'crazed ugliness'[52] was so satanic that in 1958 it aroused 'patriotic and almost physical repulsion' on the part of Jean-Marie Le Pen.[53] Paradoxically, as will be seen later, this physical infirmity did not prevent them appearing, like Léon Blum or Laurent Fabius, as captivating dandies, dangerous seducers of the innocent women of France. With its roots plunged deep into the Middle Ages,[54] the demoniacal figure of the wandering Jew from the Orient, the fearful wizard threatening the Christian West with his witchcraft and poisons, the carrier of venereal diseases and microbes, spreading plague, typhus and cholera, was constantly applied as much to Léon Blum as to Jules Moch, Jean Zay, Georges Mandel or Pierre Mendès France, whose names are very often associated from this point of view.[55]

Their enemies, such as Charles Maurras, unflaggingly associated the 'Jewish fever' which gripped the Jews, particularly Léon Blum,[56] and the madness of the Jews with the madness of Freud himself, another Jew who shook the foundations of Western civilization[57] by departing from Charcot's standpoint.[58] An unconscious connivance between Blum and Freud seemed to be established in the eyes of supporters of militant anti-Semitism, based on a common obsession with sexuality which turned these two Jews into positive monsters close to the animal world.[59] At the other extreme of the political spectrum, *L'Humanité* wrote: 'Blum is struck with Freudian wrigglings . . . Shylock Blum in jovial mood claps his hands.'[60] Running like a leitmotif through almost all anti-Semitic lampoons was the implication that Léon Blum and Pierre Mendès France should be taken for dangerous lunatics, obsessed with a murky sexuality – in the likeness of Catulle Mendès, the poet who to many symbolized the idea of decadence resulting from the most morbid type of eroticism[61] and whose writings the future socialist President of the Council favourably reviewed.

Blum was a 'great hysteric, a great maniac, already ripe for a padded cell and strait jacket',[62] 'a Jewish neuropath',[63] a hysteric who took after camels or serpents,[64] an individual struck with 'delirium tremens',[65] who expressed his sadism by constant use of the whip. Doriot saw him as an 'intellectual sadist',[66] and in the Salle Wagram, before 10,000 people and in the presence of François Coty, Jean Renaud, head of *Solidarité française*, described him as 'Valentine the acrobat of danses macabres brandishing the whip' in order to conquer power.[67] The radicals themselves attacked the 'Great Lama, the superlative thinker in the tradition of Spinoza' who thought he could tame them by using the whip, an expression of his sadistic madness[68] which, according to *Candide*, was shared by Jules Moch, Georges Boris and 'Mendès (called France)', who formed 'a small group of sadistic illuminati'.[69]

Later, Pierre Dominique, one of Léon Blum's regular bullies, maintained that Pierre Mendès France's case was equally 'known to psychiatry. This great neuropath, cyclothymic like many others, alternates between attacks of euphoria and depression.' Directly echoing Drumont's style, he saw Mendès France as 'a poisonous flower' stretched out over 'a rotting world, a stinking world, a world which needs to be swept clean'.[70]

DANDIES AND BOHEMIANS

In the nineteenth century, dandyism could still sometimes be found both on the Right and on the Left: Barbey d'Aurevilly was on one side, Eugène Sue on the other. At the period which concerns us, this had changed little since Drieu La Rochelle, probably with his old friend Aragon in mind, thought that his 'enemies sensed very well the inverted feminine nature of my love of strength. It was quite visible. But you find the same thing in some communist intellectuals, as well as in some fascists.'[71] Earlier, at the turn of the century, decadent Paris was 'the Mecca of dandyism',[72] the home of Mallarmé, André Gide, Pierre Louÿs, Oscar Wilde, Maurice Barrès but also of Daniel Halévy, Marcel Proust and Léon Blum. Now it so happened that Drieu, as well as Gide, Pierre Louÿs and Barrès, voiced anti-Semitic opinions of Léon Blum. It is therefore important to take a closer look here at this connection between dandyism and the rejection of the Jews – who nevertheless sometimes gave the impression of being dandies themselves.

In the decadent Paris of the turn of the century, in the review journal *La Conque* with André Gide and Pierre Louÿs, and the *Revue Blanche*, which he did much to enliven, Blum joined forces with dandyism triumphant. Concerned to make a show, careful about their clothes, as elegant as their idols Max Beerbohm and Brummel, with feminine and openly androgynous profiles, affected in their gestures and manners, the dandies were born seducers whom women found attractive. None the less, the dandies most frequently distrusted women, despised the marriage bond, mocked at the family structure and more or less openly flaunted their homosexuality which negated the bourgeois order. Their wish to poke fun at conformism, to reject the burden of the moral order, drew some from the radical Right, like Léon Daudet, Maurice Barrès, Paul Morand and Jacques Chardonne, to militant anti-Semitism. The Parisian Bohemian thus ended up by rejecting the Jews who remained almost the only genuine Bohemians, supposedly originating in the distant and exotic Orient. Drumont was not wrong to fight the adherents of Bohemianism in the very name of anti-Semitism, rejecting out of hand both dandyism and 'women-Jews', alien to the solid traditions of the nation.[73] In the case of a few of these former dandies who were happy to be part of this reactionary and anti-capitalist trend, the cult of self, from the beginning showing the characteristics of dandyism, changed its meaning and became exaltation of the collective self, denial of the Republic, virulent anti-Semitism and later, under Vichy, sometimes even led to collaboration. The friendship between Barrès and Blum and then their break, in many ways epitomized the historical evolution of dandyism, finally rejected by the radical Right when it turned towards an all-out anti-Semitism.

On the right in particular, but often on the left too, France now wanted to be virile, strong and healthy. It tracked down signs of decadence, resignation, femininity, evidence of a bygone era. The effeminate dandies, who had come from outside the Hexagon, were Jews, real Bohemians, marked – as we have seen – by their origin, despite the fact that their arrival on the national soil was lost in the mists of time or their more recent naturalization. The anti-Semites invariably located these origins, as in the example of Blum and many other state Jews, in Eastern Europe, around Rumania, Bulgaria, the far-off forests of Transylvania or the banks of the Vistula. Some of them – for example, the Tharaud brothers – took the trouble to visit these exotic countries so that they could give their numerous readers first-hand evidence of the squalid poverty and disease which prevailed there. Therefore, if Jews pretended to be dandies, it was only the better to mask their real nature as miserable Bohemians.[74]

Blum was a dandy in the style of Disraeli, with whom he was often compared.[75] His contemporaries found him an extremely sensitive young man and this sensitivity predisposed him to adopt manners furthest removed from tough virility. In sympathy with the *fin-de-siècle* atmosphere which prevailed in Parisian literary circles at that time, he admitted to a propensity for introspection and refined elegance.[76] We have the biased and treacherous evidence on this score provided by Gustave Téry, an old school-fellow at the *École normale supérieure*. Like Hubert Bourgin, Téry became his political enemy, never rejecting the worst anti-Semitic insinuations which were constantly exploited by the extreme Right. In a savage portrait which *La Libre Parole*, *L'Action française* and *Je suis partout* avidly seized on, Téry maintained that Blum 'had left scarcely anything in the rue d'Ulm, except the memory of an over-graceful ephebe with wavy hair and waving hips'.[77] According to him, 'in the rue d'Ulm he was in the habit of dressing up as a mad virgin in a low-cut, sleeveless gown, his lips painted, carefully plucked, made-up and perfumed. The Israelite ephebe liked sitting on his comrades' knees and being embraced for the love of grecian things.'[78]

That the 'fop of Israel', as Téry elegantly called him, always took care to avoid any resort to violence, preferring seduction to the use of force, that the heroes in his youthful writings had feminine features,[79] was a godsend, conducive to the most imaginative ravings. Even Pierre Mendès France, friend and loyal colleague, himself a favourite target of the champions of anti-Semitism, agreed in a little-known interview that Blum exercised 'an almost feminine seduction'.[80] In this perspective, Léon Blum, the 'Jewish Barrès', became the dandy *par excellence*,[81] living proof of the decadence of France, the man who was always 'strutting around' during his trial at Riom.[82]

This was a foretaste of the future socialist Prime Minister of France, Laurent Fabius, also described as an unrepentant 'dandy'.[83] Blum, that 'faded rose', that 'slightly decadent aesthete', goes off, 'handkerchief in hand', 'the oriental eye',[84] 'hoisted up on his sepoy's legs with long, flat feet... struts, crop swelling, into the drawing-rooms of Oustric or even Stavisky'.[85] Everything seemed to associate him with Marcel Proust to whom he was close through the *Revue blanche*, the amoralist personifying the decomposition of French society, mocked by Henri Massis in 1941 who preferred fascist involvement.[86] In 1962 Alfred Fabre-Luce compared the 'courtesan'-like Léon Blum, with Marcel Proust, 'another Jew', both of whom always expressed themselves in 'wheedling ways'.[87]

In this spirit, the Third Republic became the scene of 'feminine squabbles' in which the 'eunuchs of the harem', Léon Blum and Georges Mandel, enthusiastically joined.[88] In short, Blum was a woman, Léon Daudet's 'little girlie', the 'Hebrew Adonis who wets his bench in the Chamber'.[89] Daudet described him publicly, in that solemn precinct, as 'entranced with admiring ecstasy'.[90]

Charles Maurras[91] considered him 'a complete sexual pervert'.[92] He also stirred Jean-Pierre Maxence's imagination:

There is nothing virile about that narrow shadow. His voice is feminine, his gestures are feminine; his twitchings, his emotional anger, his imprecations, his rages are feminine; feminine is that style which gives way, backs out, flees; feminine are his thoughts, steeped in passion through and through; feminine are those sudden enthusiasms, that taste for detailed discussion, the physical shudder – attraction, repulsion? what does it matter – before the reality of strength. See him in front of a session of Congress . . . here is a *femme savante* who is sparkling before her dazzled salon. See him in the heat of a meeting: here is a female who sometimes prowls around the male, sniffs him, flatters him, and sometimes threatens him with her groans.[93]

The anti-Semitic right went to unimaginable lengths to expose Blum's feminine nature which made him unsuitable to lead a country like France. With admirable consistency, Henri Béraud made fun of 'his old Blumiche – an old woman out for a scratch', of that 'boudoir Septembriseur' whom he, like Maurras and so many other polemicists called 'Blum-Flower, baptized with the secateurs', like Moch, Wurmser and Mandel.[94] For Léon Daudet, the former dandy, Blum 'is actually the poisonous flower of the golden ghetto, the flower which benumbs and which kills over-trusting French trade unionism'.

At a time when the radical right was being re-formed, Daudet linked Drumont's national–populism with Proudhon's anti-Semitic socialist discourse. 'Ah! Proudhon, revolutionary of the blood of France', he exclaimed. 'Were you living now, what would you, great man, say about this new breed of women and these swine, powdered red.'[95] The French, stout fellows, had nothing in common with such Jew-women, 'with sinuous body, well turned out in a grey suit of English cut',[96] or with the man whom Léon Daudet, in a phrase destined to become famous, described as a revolutionary 'in pearl grey gloves'. All these accoutrements symbolized the English dandies who now led the workers' movement from which the radical right strove to detach the French. They linked up directly with Proudhon in order to lead the people back into a virile Frenchness which later triumphed under Vichy. Does this populist dimension, which extreme right-wing anti-Semitism could assume, explain why *L'Humanité* regularly described Léon Blum as a 'great coquette',[97] 'an old servant of the bourgeoisie, an old seducer of the radicals', even though it refrained from specifying his Jewish origin?[98]

One of the most astonishing texts remains that of Pierre Gaxotte, who has already been mentioned. For this distinguished historian 'the Palestinian mare . . . whines all the time, groans, snivels, wails. He twists his handkerchief, he wriggles, he grows weak, he is exhausted, he is dying! Monsieur le President has the vapours! Let someone bring him his salts and vinegar.'[99] This theme of the vapours strengthened the identification of Jews with women, supposedly weak beings *par excellence*, unpredictable and irritable, doomed to the most extreme nerviness which, even the rationalist philosophers of the Enlightenment thought, engulfed them in hysterical passions. Gaxotte unwittingly revived the great tradition of the doctors – such as the famous Dr Pomme – or the various authors of the *Encyclopédie*, who defined woman as a fundamentally sick and pathological being, and, particularly in the eighteenth century, studied the significance of the vapours in the feminine condition by connecting the hysteria peculiar to women to their sex and the expression of their madness.[100] Gaxotte, like so many others, gave this an anti-Semitic dimension by transforming the Jews into weak and raving women. *L'Humanité-Dimanche* provided a variation on the same theme, though without explicit anti-Semitic intent: there was nothing of the old woman about Pierre Mendès France, it concluded, for 'he broke all the records set by Marilyn Monroe and Jane Russell'.[101]

Blum, 'the SFIO-ist' became the incarnation of the androgyne, with his effeminate gestures.[102] His white handkerchief became the delight of innumerable extreme right-wing caricaturists, as also of *L'Humanité*, who saw it as incontrovertible proof of his murky and decadent dandyism.[103] And when the socialist leader for the first time in French political history also appointed three women to his Popular Front government, his enemies regarded this innovation as concrete and irrefutable evidence that he belonged to the weaker sex.[104]

'DON JUAN OF THE SYNAGOGUE'

Jews might have been particularly effeminate, the most devilish hermaphrodites. They were none the less perceived as formidable 'Don Juans of the synagogue'. This nickname was specially invented for Léon Blum by the Comte de Puységur in a little-known book, which deserves to be a landmark in the annals of contemporary anti-Semitism: *Les Maquereaux légitimes: Du coursier des croisades au bidet de Rebecca*.[105] This text illustrated both the fear and the contempt that Jews sometimes still aroused in contemporary France. Drumont had taken the precaution of warning his contemporaries as early as 1905: 'France', he maintained, 'is a female nation: it is accessible and penetrable. As soon as the door was opened to the Jew, he therefore found a nation ready to yield to his influence.'[106]

Unfortunately, in the 1930s, the early warning was not always heeded. Behind the leader of the socialist movement there not only lurked a formidable Don Juan[107] who could easily conquer the naïveté of the unsuspecting women of France, but also 'a conquistadore of decadent society ladies and haughty literary ladies in jabots'.[108] He was not alone in this, since the anti-Semitic imagination apparently endowed all state Jews with an incalculable capacity for overcoming the resistance of French beauties. Georges Mandel had innumerable mistresses.[109] The same applied to Pierre Mendès France, 'the Sephardic Jew, who allied Latin seduction to Talmudic decline',[110] who could never have won over the radical party without the help of 'a band of Amazons',[111] and did not hesitate to seduce his 'pretty typist' to execute his strategy.[112] However, some people thought that although 'his campaign of charm', once he was leading the government, was indisputably successful,[113] the conditions for it were hardly favourable because of 'the circles round his eyes, an ancient beard . . . and an arrogant profile designed for contempt'.[114] The portrait by his friend, Henri Caillavet, expressed the cultural contrast between the *bon vivant* who knew how to handle his fork and who unfailingly evoked tenderness, and the thin man orientated towards the intellect who won hardly any sympathy.[115] Caillavet amicably explained that Mendès France, who, it will be recalled, drank little wine and was not interested in putting on weight,

> wanted to be loved, he thirsted for love. . . . Herriot was loved by the militants, Pierre Mendès France was respected, he appealed to reason . . . he addressed the intelligence . . . he could not seduce . . . it was not in his nature nor in his physique . . . he had 'an impossible mug', larded hair, a sky-coloured complexion . . . he was not attractive . . . Neither was Herriot, you will say, but Herriot overflowed, even his stomach was exciting, while Pierre Mendès France's features were not, except when they were tragic.[116]

Seductive the former President of the Council was, despite a physique which some found unpromising. He was just as seductive as Léon Blum, Georges Mandel and, more recently, Laurent Fabius, whom many on the extreme Right and several on the extreme Left considered dandies. In his youth 'Little Bob', that is to say, Léon Blum, found pleasure in organizing balls, leading the cotillion,[117] proving himself a fine dancer, and playing at being a playboy.[118]

In 1984 'Lolo's charm' was in operation, 'with his slightly sad, mocking smile. So as not to look too much like the loukoum seller, he knows how to veil a beautiful langorous look when he has to.'[119] Without doubt, here 'with his dandyism and his diplomas, is a Blum arrived young', parading 'in the hall of the rue Saint-Guillaume, to Sciences Po, in a blue velvet dinner-jacket, on the arm of Elizabeth Huppert, in long fur coat and mini-skirt'.[120] At this time, we find him 'very smart at the wheel of his Aston Martin, nothing could resist him, particularly not, it was said, pretty girls'.[121] The 'sexual bombshell' with 'a mouth drawn like the mouths of the fat odalisks in the Sublime Porte's harem',[122] wrought such havoc that the new socialist Prime Minister, like the former leader of the Popular Front, appeared 'cool, an ex-skirt-chaser, but always amusing with women, a sort of new Mandel in the with-it urchin style'.[123] It was like being back in the thirties, so impressive was the consensus achieved in both camps, on the seductive powers of the 'Judas Cherubin',[124] which was how many people saw 'Prime Minister Dandy',[125] carefully preparing his files 'at the Pantheon, near the ghosts of Blum and Mendès'.[126] We have come full circle, through Mendès France and George Mandel and inexorably back to Léon Blum.

The fact remains that these 'Don Juans of the synagogue', whether they were from the Left (Blum, Mendès, Fabius) or the Right (Mandel) were perceived as essentially subversive beings whose words were considered misleading because they were seductive. In this sense they remained consistent with the myth of Don Juan, himself committed to challenging the social and political norms imposed by societies whose values, on the whole, were Christian. To attach this label to these state Jews who were in fact completely committed to the strength of the emancipating state and to egalitarian public service, was to transform them into modern dandy-faced Satans. This meant, in other words, that they had become present-day Don Juans who had come to take over the role of the Don Juan of the librettist Da Ponte, son of a Jewish shoemaker, who converted in order to marry a young Christian girl and confronted perhaps with the fate of the marranos, as our state Jews may have been in the minds of contemporary anti-Semitic lampooners.[127]

They were primarily subversive in the manner of Alfred Naquet, the first in anti-Semitic tradition to attack the French family by introducing divorce into legislation in 1884. Together with Crémieux, Alfred Naquet was the *bête noire* of all who explained the misfortunes affecting French society by the deliberate, underhand activity of Jews intent on destroying its coherence by attacking its basic traditions. This evil activity would prove propitious to their seizure of power. Drumont relentlessly exposed the disintegrating character of Naquet's initiative – divorce being, in his eyes, 'an absolutely Jewish idea'.[128] This demonological interpretation of the Jews as being set on destroying the Christian character of French society, which Drumont had launched, gladly took Léon Blum as its target in later years. It did so by associating the consequences of divorce, conceived by Naquet, with the advice given by Léon Blum in his work, *Du Mariage*, in 1907. Following Fourier,[129] he recommended the early sexual liberation of young girls on emancipatory and egalitarian grounds, to encourage their full development, as well as to encourage more mature reflection at the time of their marriage. The '*mariage de raison*', source of their full development, consequently had the effect of averting shabby and degrading adultery.[130]

Drumont's *La Libre Parole* immediately seized on this text which seemed to confirm his predictions, and published large extracts from it. The storm that this text aroused grew visibly up to the Vichy period, the anti-Semitic Right referring to it again and again, feeding its fears of the turpitude it attributed to the Jews. As early as 1907 *La Croix des Alpes-Maritimes* put to its readers the following question: 'Who more than the hideous Naquet has contributed to the destruction of the French family?' The answer was obvious 'Léon Blum, criminal of the pen . . . who sows corruption and death. The breakdown of the family and of society is worsening. The Jew can be content with his work . . . as an eternal outlaw.'[131] The hatred unleashed at the turn of the century, well before Pierre Gaxotte, Charles Maurras and Henri Béraud, cannot fail to be striking, though attention has rarely been drawn to it. For *Jaune*, for example,

the senior Jewish civil servant who has written and published this 'filth' should have his bottom spanked before the assembled populace, like Thalamas. What else is there? I personally find that this man is Hebrew in his rhythm, in his mode of being and that he strikingly synthesises the effrontery, the absence of shame, of modesty, as Drumont says, of his race. Why should the joyous Blum not go to the synagogue in the rue de la Victoire, for example, on the Sabbath day, after service, and expound on the precepts we have just been studying with the help of lantern slides to the young folk of the aristocracy and Israelite high finance?[132]

There are innumerable examples of this sort, which Léon Blum's biographers have strangely ignored. They plunge us into the very heart of anti-Semitic nightmares rooted in sexuality, which also surfaced in respect of other minorities in France at this time.[133] Numerous virulent libels, little-known today, bear witness to the symbolic character that Léon Blum's book assumed for the fierce upholders of traditional sexual and family norms. Take for example, *Léon Blum: 'L'homme qui se trompe toujours et qui trompe les autres* (Léon Blum: The man who always deceives himself and deceives others) by his 'licentious, corrupting and destructive'[134] writings; and do not forget that Goebbels and German propaganda denounced the effects of Jewish influence in France and, specifically, *Du mariage* where 'the intellectual–Bolshevik anarcho-sexual lucubration of the Jew Léon Blum' was given free rein.[135]

Like their German masters, French collaborators displayed incredible zeal in their loud and clear denunciation of this book, which by then was already very old. An example is the nauseous prose of one of occupied France's prolific authors, Jean-Charles Legrand. For him, in *Du mariage*, Blum, 'spiteful as a eunuch and tenacious as a crab', set out 'to teach our wives and daughters complacence at the rutting of his friends, shirking in the rear'.[136] It is true that here too collaborationist literature was only following the line of thought outlined by Léon Daudet and *Action française* in the inter-war period. When *Du mariage* was republished right in the middle of the Popular Front period, papers such as *Gringoire* and the *Nouvelle Voix d'Alsace et de Lorraine*, already noted for the strength of their anti-Semitism, published long extracts from it, following the earlier example of *La Libre Parole*. For Léon Daudet, still as virulent and imaginative as when he supported Drumont in his struggle, Léon Blum's essay was the work of an 'immoralist, a complete stranger to our mores, customs, habits, commonsense, as Westerners understand it'.[137] In short, this was a book describing customs practised by 'Turks or Persians'.[138]

Daudet, brilliant polemicist, friend of Barrès and familiar figure at every elegant literary circle, was skilled in the use of an obscene style. It was similar to that used by Céline at the same period in *Bagatelles pour un massacre*, to denounce the prostitution of women in which, so it was said, monied Jews eagerly engaged. It was not a question, Daudet argued,

of a medical student's joke but of a destructive form of perversion, related to ethnic origin, which raises defilement to the level of a principle. To put it plainly, the Blum tribe, in the person of its leader, has come amongst us to satisfy its natural needs, in the manner of burglars who come to plunder a private dwelling.[139]

In these circumstances, one can understand how Gide, author of the *Caves du Vatican*, 'secretly supporting – satanically – Céline's anti-Semitic entertainment',[140] in his turn went so far as to consider *Du mariage* a 'dangerous' book. It proved that 'the Jews are pastmasters in the art of breaking up our most respected, most venerable institutions, those that are the foundation and support of our Western civilization, to further I know not what licence and relaxation of morals, which our commonsense and our Latin instinct for sociability fortunately find loathsome'.[141] Even more surprising than this unexpected judgement by André Gide is its repetition in almost identical terms by Romain Rolland, despite the fact that he signed numerous manifestos against anti-Semitism and was quintessentially a man of peace.

Lucien Lévy-Coeur, with Sylvain Kohn one of the two most important Jewish characters in *Jean-Christophe*, was said to have been directly inspired by Léon Blum's behaviour. However, Romain Rolland subsequently drew still closer to Blum, to the extent of writing to him in February 1936: 'the more you are threatened, the more I sense your value, and the more I have for a long time wanted to extend my hand to you'.[142] Nevertheless, if this hypothesis is to be believed, Romain Rolland at one time saw Léon Blum as comparable to Lévy-Coeur, a great Jewish bourgeois who, although a socialist, was none the less susceptible to pornography: 'He represented the spirit of irony and decomposition which attacked softly, politely . . . everything which was great in the old dying society: family, marriage, religion, homeland; everything in art which was virile, pure, healthy, popular'[143] – all criticisms which were commonly made of Léon Blum himself.

Being such seductive dandies, the Jews devised sophisticated and allegedly liberating theories to promote their purpose – the enslavement of 'the white woman'. For example, to Hector Ghilini, another successful author of the 1940s, *Du mariage* constituted 'an apology for rape, for outrage to modesty and for the abduction of minors. Not only did Blum want to hand us over to Stalin but he also had erotic dreams of transforming the whole of France into a vast brothel where virginities would be reserved for obscene old men.'[144] The example was in fact a warning, since 'this depraved moralist would like French women to follow in the lewd tradition of the daughters of Lot, Ruth, Judith, Delilah and Esther, in short, the biblical heroines whose exploits seduced his early youth'.[145]

Don Juan, fine and elegant in a suit of English flannel, at last clearly confessed the hidden springs of a seduction of which the sweet women of France would otherwise have remained unaware. The androgyne with the white handkerchief, unmasked, proved to be no more than an unscrupulous pimp, bent on making Joan suffer the dark fate of Judith. From age to age, the Jews – dandies and seducers all – were in fact vulgar pimps from the Orient.

HOMOSEXUALS

To be complete, this list of perversions requires a section on homosexuality. It was implied in the preceding paragraphs. It is also explicit in a very large number of often surprising texts, about which historians of contemporary France seem to have an agreement to keep quiet. Drumont's sexual obsessions appear to be overtaken in this respect because he does not make much of homosexuality. For once, he leaves the field to a contemporary author, Charles Castellani.

Castellani denounced Moloch, the Hebrews' demon, 'the emblem of all foreign lewdness: filthy, sensual, patron of pederasts: a black and viscous reptile'.[146] The obsessive frenzy constantly broke new ground, since homosexuality seemed to be a characteristic of androgynous Jews, from Blum to Fabius, well before the discovery of AIDS which encourages so many flights of moralizing oratory by the extreme Right today. Charles Maurras, a future member of the *Académie française* and a very eminent author, had no doubt about it: 'Basically sadistic and perverted',[147] Léon Blum was notoriously an inveterate pederast[148] since, 'hugging an obese admirer, for example, he cannot meet a friend without putting his arm round his waist, fondling him, stroking him, turning him to and fro in every direction'.[149] What was more, as *Au Pilori* gravely revealed, 'one evening in June 1936, Blum was walking along the banks of the Seine, carefully holding two ecstatic adolescents by the neck; two inspectors of the so-called *Sûreté nationale* followed ten metres behind them; professionally blasé, they watched the equivocal love affairs of the putrid aesthete, in love with profitable corpses.'[150]

These Jewish dandies and seducers with their formidable charm who, according to the terms of this mad logic, collected mistresses, were truly demoniacal individuals. Not only did they appear to be common pimps but also they did not neglect the pleasures of pederasty to satisfy an uncommon and oriental sexuality at will. Seen from this point of view, Georges Mandel, a methodical man and an austere nationalist, was none the less Mephistophelian, a formidable homosexual.[151] Jean Zay had 'a flag stuck between his buttocks'.[152] Later, when Pierre Mendès France seized the Radical Party, surrounded by 'a tumultuous band of ephebes',[153] did he not agree 'to couple for pleasure with François Mauriac',[154] and was he not seen 'falling into Maurice Thorez's arms'?[155] Finally, no one was unaware that, after 1984 and the second government appointed by President François Mitterrand, 'the socialist state finances homos and reds',[156] and everyone knew that 'the perverted couple Fabius–Jospin' were at its head.[157]

It is true that, irrespective of period or personality, Léon Blum, like Walter Rathenau in Germany at more or less the same time,[158] attracted the greatest proportion of sarcastic comments and caricatures and was the victim of a dungcart of predominantly homosexual insults. Homosexuality was still

Hermaphroditism and Sexual Perversion 163

fashionable at the turn of the century[159] in avant-garde circles that rejected social conventions in displaying deviant practices regarded as depraved. It was always latent in the circle of dandies attracted by decadence, flaunting their contempt for bourgeois conventions. Now at a time when the spirit of nationalism was advocating virility, it was the embodiment of the supreme shame. Like dandies, pederasts were no longer in season. Rejected by the national ideology on grounds of unhealthy femininity, their eccentricity was no longer attractive at a time when strength was the dominant virtue.

This logic of exclusion was applied equally to Jews, most particularly to Léon Blum, the former dandy who, according to his enemies, seemed to delight in seductive attitudes no longer acceptable in a Europe where the new man was being created in terms of ideologies that were certainly antagonistic to them. In these circumstances and at a time when no law really penalized the abuse expressed in the most obsessive ravings, everything about the former Jewish dandy, fierce enemy of fascism but also former opponent of the Congress of Tours, played into his enemies' hands. Little did it matter that the accusation was totally untrue,[160] the case had been prejudged, with André Gide as a false witness.

Gide made fun of Léon Blum's 'specifically Jewish faults', in his *Journal* at different times between 1907 and 1914. It was, he wrote, hardly surprising that 'the qualities of the Jewish race should not be French qualities'.[161] *Du mariage*, he thought, was only 'the skilful prelude to all today's Jewish drama',[162] an assessment which the enemies of the leader of the Popular Front relentlessly employed.[163] Like Romain Rolland, André Gide later came round to expressing more favourable opinions. At the time of the Popular Front, he declared that 'a great need for truth and justice animates the best representatives of Israel, animates Blum in particular . . . with the triumph of the Popular Front, I am pleased to see France animated by this concern for justice.'[164]

The 'particular friendships'[165] attributed to Blum had a certain piquancy, and it is absolutely essential to pause and consider the broad effect of Proustian symbolism at that time. Homosexuality occupied a central, latent place in this, when a Dreyfusard Jew, Swann, stood side by side with Bloch, a Jewish writer in the process of assimilation, sentimental and oriental who, as we have said, could have been inspired by certain characteristics of Blum himself.[166] At the time of the *Cartel des Gauches*, according to Pierre Dominique, 'his lips damp from the kisses that Herriot and Painlevé daily gave him', he seemed incapable of governing France.[167] Pierre Dominique showed the measure of his talent on this theme: 'Herriot is already being subjected to the pernicious blandishments of M. L. Blum, the most disturbing evil flower of the SFIO. Blum! Blumchen! Flower! Flowerlet! M. Herriot goes away picking the petals off radicalism, and the first outlines of the romance between "My pipe" and "My flower" appear.'[168]

Léon Daudet showed no surprise at the revelations of the behaviour of the SFIO's leader, he 'could still hear Poincaré billing and cooing to him in public in the Chamber, while our androgyne listened, wriggling his buttocks and shoulders'.[169] Somewhat later, in 1938, after many vicissitudes in 'Herriot's unhappy love for Blum',[170] 'Paul Reynaud opened his arms to him'.[171]

In this perspective, which raised the anti-Semitism in France at this time to a level rarely seen, the socialist leader seemed to sail imperturbably from one party leader to another. As the inevitable Léon Daudet again noted, Marcel Sembat made no secret of his 'perverted liking for Blum', who was, however, already 'involved in a deep intrigue with Jouhaux'.[172] And, as *L'Humanité* observed, 'this sensualist'[173] had been seen 'lying indolently in M. Lasteyrie's bed'.[174] To be fair, this was hardly surprising since he had also 'lain in Pierre Laval's bed without even bothering to change the sheets'![175] Better still, Léon Blum, who seemed hardly consistent in his choices, 'is making the Führer's bed'.[176] At Vichy, Blum put his arms round Louis Marin's neck, 'according to his deplorable habits of the Palais-Bourbon'.[177] There are endless comments of this nature, each more ribald than the last.[178]

The theme of homosexuality gave birth to what are perhaps the most unimaginable excesses. Intellectuals such as Drieu La Rochelle, who were fascinated by the Jews, projected on to them, as did Hitler,[179] their own desires and perversions, anxious to affirm their virility. They themselves were obsessed with an unadmitted homosexuality and portrayed Jews – in *Gilles*, for example – in a way which even present-day readers find embarrassing, even if these intellectuals did refrain from openly using explicit obscenity when such writings had literary pretensions.[180] Crudity and ignominy knew no bounds in leaflets and polemical articles in the journals most frequently connected with the radical Right, and also particularly in the widely read satiric press that we largely refer to here. The modern historian is justified in hesitating to resurrect such abominations from their well-deserved oblivion.[181] Far removed from the usual study of the great declarations and works of famous intellectuals (whose deep-seated motives could only be unmasked by meticulous psychoanalytical biographies, if they were at all practicable),[182] these writings none the less bear witness to the banality of anti-Semitism. This defamatory 'poetry' is a good example:

> Don Quixote, without being rude,
> This Don also plays the prude,
> Blum is the Flower, that we know,
> That is why he tricks you so
> Blum is always lying low
> in order to play the ...
> Rear end game.
>
> When Blum was at *Normale*, abnormal, you might say,
> just like impalement, anyway,
> what started well, ended ill. As a student his first stance
> was nosing out the debutantes.

He played every game you know
He played violin, he played spinet,
He played every game you know
Particularly the . . .
Rear end game.

Blum is very fond of fairies,
Ratatas, and all that's airy,
Trumpets and the rest, you know,
Everything that makes a show . . .
Briand in guttural voice, says all,
'this would be better at a ball',
Blum answers with conviction,
A cannon ball's better, still more clean,
I know what I'm doing, that's a cinch, A long time's passed since I have seen
the . . . Rear end game.[183]

'SEMITIC SWORDSMANSHIP'

Faced with so much infamy besmirching their dignity, the only resort left to the Jews in France, as in Germany, was to demonstrate their strength. In the 1880s bloody duels took place between Jews and anti-Semites in Austria and Germany, particularly in the student fraternities.[184] It was accusations of degeneracy that caused Max Nordau to intervene at the Second Zionist Congress held in Germany in 1898, to appeal for the creation of 'muscular Jews', with the hope that pale, thin intellectual 'café Jews' would disappear.[185] A year later in France, when Jews who had been attacked made known their willingness to fight back, Drumont mocked the advent of 'Semitic swordsmanship'.[186] At the height of the Dreyfus Affair, duels with sabres, swords and pistols took place more and more frequently, very often between Jews and anti-Semitic opponents of Captain Dreyfus. Drumont himself, an incomparable fighter, always on the go, confronted Bernard Lazare, one of Dreyfus's very active supporters, in the presence of witnesses. He also met Meyer, in a fierce battle which turned out badly and caused a public scandal, because Meyer, a right-wing nationalist Jew, unwittingly seized Drumont's sword with his left hand during the fight, proof to the anti-Semites of Jews' duplicity.[187] Drumont's follower Raphael Viau did battle with Camille Dreyfus, Maxime Dreyfus, F. Bloch and G. Mayer, one after another.[188]

Jean Drault, loyalest of the loyal, who was still just as enthusiastic under Vichy, kept a sort of balance-sheet of these violent encounters. He carefully recounted the events of the duels between Drumont and Camille Dreyfus, editor of *La Nation*, in 1893; between Drumont and Bertrand Lazare in 1896;

and between Drumont and Clemenceau in 1898; those between Viau and Maurice Schwob, editor of *Phare de la Loire* in 1894; Viau against F. Bloch and then Germain Mayer, both managers of a state factory, in 1896; and lastly, in 1898 the indefatigable Viau against Anspach, a Jewish friend of Dreyfus. He also noted the fight between André Spire, state Jew and Léon Blum's colleague on the Council of State, and Albert Monniot, an anti-Semitic author who later published a number of texts between the two wars.[189] Raphael Viau's book, *Vingt Ans d'antisémitisme*, describing the circumstances and events of these duels, probably gives the best indication of their importance.[190]

The most tragic series followed one another in 1892: between Drumont and Captain Crémieux-Foa; M. de Lamase and the same Captain; then between Morès, Drumont's equal in anti-Semitism, and Armand Meyer, an officer in the Engineers. Meyer was killed in this last fight and the army paid homage to him. The whole affair began with an article by Drumont in *La Libre Parole* on 23 May 1892, which attacked Jews commissioned as officers in the army, specifically naming them, as was done again in the inter-war period. For him, 'the day they command the army, Rothschild will have the mobilization plans passed to him, and we all know for what purpose'. Captain Crémieux-Foa challenged Drumont to a duel following this explicit accusation of treason, which was even more intolerable in that it was made in the context of the loss of Alsace-Lorraine from where so many Jews, who had opted to remain loyal to France, had come. Then came the fight between Crémieux-Foa and M. de Lamase, author of anti-Semitic articles in *La Libre Parole*; and lastly the one between Armand Meyer, wrongly accused of having made public the proceedings of the previous duel, and Morès, who would normally have faced Captain Crémieux-Foa in his turn, had not the military authorities prevented the Captain's appearance.[191] There were a large number of Jews in the army, and they were now rising to the ranks of general, colonel and captain. They diligently proclaimed their patriotism, even if many officers, hostile to the Republic, were still dreaming of 'a St Bartholomew's Day of the Jews'.[192]

This was the age of duelling when the code of honour was scrupulously respected. In December 1904, for example, Jaurès faced Déroulède with pistols. The Jews responded bravely to the virulent anti-Semitism of the day. Catulle Mendès met Paul Foucher and then Georges Vanor; Camille Dreyfus also fought Henri Rochefort; Reinach confronted Paul Déroulède; and Henry Bernstein, Léon Daudet. Witnesses noted that these duels were almost always extremely violent. Camille Dreyfus charged 'like a buffalo', and Bernstein, the dramatist so often attacked by the extreme Right even in the inter-war period, fought like a lion against Daudet.[193] That Jews were able to face their enemies in duels – in a society where this had long symbolized the Frenchman's 'ardour', his 'Gallic humour', explicable by the fact that he was 'full of blood'[194] – that they were also able to prove their courage and fight bravely, testified to their integration into a society whose modes of defending honour they now shared. Paradoxically, the anti-Semites who laid bets on the Jews' cowardice, their feminine character and their homosexuality, did so to their own cost, in so far as they involuntarily contributed to proving their statements false.

It was not only Jewish professional soldiers who engaged in these trials of strength at the turn of the century, but also Jews from the world of arts and letters. The narrator in the *Recherche du temps perdu*, never tires of recalling the duels at the time of the Dreyfus Affair. Proust himself did not tolerate insulting remarks aimed at him, most frequently connected with femininity or homosexuality. He once sent his seconds to the Marquis de Lagrenée, who retracted.[195] When Jean Lorrain, poet and homosexual, made unequivocal remarks on the nature of his friendship with Léon Daudet, Proust demanded redress: a duel with pistols took place at which Proust gave full proof of his courage. Later, when he published *Sodome et Gomorrhe*, Paul Souday, critic of *Le Temps*, described him as 'a nervous aesthete, slightly morbid, almost feminine'. Proust hastened to reply: 'Feminine is only one step away from effeminate. The men who have acted as my seconds in duels will tell you if I have the flabbiness of the effeminate.'[196]

In October 1912 a violent altercation at the Théâtre des Arts was followed by an exchange of blows between Léon Blum and Pierre Veber. A duel was inevitable. It took place at 11 o'clock on the morning of the 12th, in the Parc des Princes. Once again, all the spectators emphasized the violence of the fight and Blum's courage. This 'serious duel which almost ended in tragedy' was 'a fierce fight'. 'M. Blum charged vigorously. And here is the upshot: M. Blum was suddenly able to take his opponent's sword, execute a double seconde and lunge. The blow struck like an arrow. To the right of the sternum, the sword entered at the level of the bottom rib which fortunately stopped it.' Another journalist noted, 'Blum enthusiastically charged his opponent and executed a series of parries with his sword which kept the onlookers in constant suspense.' Léon Blum had attacked with 'force', yet he was still described as 'nervous'.[197] Once again, he was no less a man for being Jewish and nervous. The anti-Semites of the inter-war period maintained a prudent silence about this little-known episode because it ran counter to their argument. The socialist leader's supporters, on the other hand, hastened to stress the many factors which spoke of his strength. For example, during the 1934 election campaign at Laon, Léon Blum, 'commanded general silence despite his thin voice'. In the same spirit, during the 1936 election campaign, Léon Blum, when he had to, 'dropped his jacket and went on in shirt sleeves.'[198]

Four years later, in 1940 at Rabat, an altercation took place in the Balima restaurant between Pierre Mendès France and an officer in the colonial infantry. In the words of the radical deputy,

he challenged me to come back and dine in the same restaurant the next day; I accepted his rendezvous, determined not to let myself be humiliated by that sort of fanatic, even though he might have a stripe more than me . . . If things had taken their course, it would have been a fine scrap. But General François, commander in chief of the troops in Morocco, was terrified and immediately silenced Captain Dujonchay by ordering him to leave for Fez that evening.[199]

At a time when man-to-man combat by sword, pistol or fist was still a method of defending one's honour in the public arena by demonstrating a virility which guaranteed both social integration and political citizenship, Jews took it on themselves to prove, as they had done on a massive scale during the First World War, that they too had 'blood' and that it was as 'hot' as that of their fellow citizens. They thereby vainly hoped to put paid to a mythology of exclusion which was largely sexual in its inspiration. But demonology was indifferent to facts, and even today follows a different logic.

Pierre Mendès France's physical courage was irrefutable. On 16 December 1943 he was awarded the *Croix de Guerre* with bar, with the following citation:

High-class observer, volunteer serving in a fighting unit immediately after his eventful escape from Vichy prisons, just participated in several difficult missions with the 'Lorraine' group, especially on 3 October 1943, when, in the capacity of chief observer, he brilliantly directed the low-flying bombardment of an important objective in the Parisian region. Despite very heavy anti-aircraft fire, his magnificent precision made it possible to annihilate the objective while averting loss of life to the inhabitants of the district.[200]

In the same spirit, General de Gaulle signed the following statement at the end of the war on 1 September 1945:

Responding to the call of France in peril of death, you rallied the Free French forces. You belonged to the voluntary team of good comrades who kept our country in the war and preserved its honour. You have been one of those in the front line who made it possible to achieve Victory! At this moment, when the end has been achieved, I want to thank you as a friend simply in the name of France.[201]

Pierre Mendès France retained this determined, pugnacious attitude throughout his life and did not withdraw when faced with aggression from time to time in daily life. For example, he was dining at a restaurant in Les Halles with Marie-Claire Mendès France shortly after 1960 when a man at the next table said in German to the person sitting opposite him: 'That is the Jew Mendès.' Marie-Claire Mendès France got up and slapped him. Then the former President of the Council rushed at the man who had insulted him and hit him. His companion quickly joined him, and amidst the general silence, a skirmish broke out. At the same period, when they were both at a cinema in the Champs-Elysées, a young man noticed Pierre Mendès France and in a loud voice asked his companion mockingly: 'You saw him down there. . . . What, I ask myself, was he doing during the war.' Immediately Pierre Mendès France retorted: 'Come here and repeat what you said. Come and say it to me!' The young man preferred to beat a retreat.[202]

To conclude with an amazing anecdote: We know that Charles Maurras, Léon Blum's bitter enemy, cried out: 'This is revenge for Dreyfus!' when he was condemned at the end of the Second World War. It was also a revenge for Léon Blum, who had been very active in the Dreyfusard camp, as has been

Hermaphroditism and Sexual Perversion 169

seen. Now, during the war Pierre Mendès France met Captain Dreyfus's son abroad and at once invited him to join the Free French Forces, which were fighting the Vichy régime and its supporters, the survivors of the anti-Dreyfus camp.[203] It was as if, in that instant, the protagonists in that prolonged struggle, when the Republic faced the same enemies, joined hands through them in that brief unforeseen encounter.

NOTES

1 See Jacques Le Goff, 'Reims, ville du sacre', in Pierre Nora (ed.), *Les Lieux de mémoire, La Nation*, vol. 1, pp. 140–2.
2 On the difference between Joan of Arc and Judith, see Hans Mayer, *Outsiders* (MIT Press, Cambridge, Mass., 1984), chs. 2 and 3.
3 Quoted by Michel Winock, *Édouard Drumont et Cie: Antisémitisme et fascisme en France* (Le Seuil, Paris, 1982), p. 72. See his analysis of the connections between Joan of Arc and the Jews when he describes the different themes which contrast them.
4 *Je suis partout*, 7 Feb. 1942.
5 *Archives nationales*, F7 12 964. Bucard's speech in the Salle Wagram on 13 March 1936.
6 See Maurice Agulhon, 'Politics, images and symbols in post-Revolutionary France', in Sean Wilentz (ed.), *Rites of Power: Symbolism, ritual and politics since the Middle Ages* (University of Pennsylvania Press, Philadelphia, Pa, 1984), p. 186. The author still approaches this point cautiously.
7 Maurice Agulhon, *Marianne au combat: L'imagerie et la symbolique républicaines de 1789 à 1880* (Flammarion, Paris, 1979).
8 Yvonne Knibiehler, Marcel Bernos, Élisabeth Ravoux-Rallo and Éliane Richard, *De la pucelle à la minette: Les jeunes filles de l'âge classique à nos jours* (Temps actuels, Paris, 1983).
9 See Jean Delumeau, *La Peur en Occident* (Fayard, Paris, 1978), chs. 9 and 10. There is a vast amount of literature on the body and social and political representations; see Bryan Turner, *The Body and Society* (Basil Blackwell, Oxford, 1984).
10 Julius Carlebach, 'The forgotten connection: women and Jews in the conflict between enlightenment and romanticism', *Leo Baeck Year Book*, no. 24, 1979.
11 In reality this relationship proved more complex, since at the end of the nineteenth century numerous authors, such as Le Bon, Taine and Tarde, associated the crowds of women and alcoholics, whose irrationality and decadent character would inevitably lead to the destruction of France (Susanna Barrows, *Distorting Mirrors: Visions of the crowd in the late nineteenth century* (Yale University Press, New Haven, Conn., 1981)), p. 72.
12 On the whole debate, see Peter Heller, 'A quarrel over bisexuality', in Gerald Chapple and Hans Schulte (eds), *The Turn of the Century: German literature and arts* (Bouvier-Verlag, Bonn, 1981); and Jacques Le Rider, *Le Cas Weininger: Racines de l'antiféminisme et de l'antisémitisme* (PUF, Paris, 1985), chs 4 and 8.
13 See Roger Lewinter, 'Groddeck: (anti) judaïsme et bisexualité', in *Bisexualité et différence des sexes, Nouvelle Revue de psychanalyse*, no. 7 (Spring 1973).
14 André Spire, *Quelques juifs et demi-juifs* (Grasset, Paris, 1928).
15 See the articles by Juliette Hassine, 'Le personnage juif proustien face à la critique des années 1970–1980', and Judith Camy-Darmon, 'Bloch, personnage proustien', in *Yod*, vol. 17.
16 See, *inter alia*, Colette Capitant-Peter, 'Maurrassisme, sadisme et nazisme', *Esprit*, Feb. 1972; George Mosse, *Towards the Final Solution: A history of European racism* (J. M. Dent, London,

1978); George Mosse, *Nationalism and Sexuality: Respectability and abnormal sexuality in modern Europe* (Howard Fertig, New York, 1985); Eugen Weber, *Fin de siècle: La France à la fin du XIXe siècle* (Fayard, Paris, 1986).

17 See the classic works by Rudolph Loewenstein, *Christians and Jews: A psychoanalytic study* (International Universities Press, New York, 1951); and Morton Seiden, *The Paradox of Hate* (South Brunswick, New York, 1967).

18 Sander Gilman, 'Jews and mental illness: medical metaphors, antisemitism and the Jewish response', *Journal of the History of the Behavioural Sciences*, 20 (April 1984).

19 See Sander Gilman, *Jewish Self-hatred* (Johns Hopkins University Press, Baltimore, Md, 1986), pp. 286ff.

20 É. Drumont, *La France juive* (Marpon & Flammarion, Paris, 1886), vol. 1, pp. 106 and 561.

21 É. Drumont, *Le Fin d'un monde*, Introduction, p. 18.

22 Pierre Dominique, *Monsieur le Parlement* (Éditions Baudinière, Paris, 1928), p. 44.

23 André Figueras, *Zoologie du Palais-Bourbon* (Éditions Georges Burnier, Paris, 1932), p. 129.

24 *Minute*, 14 Dec. 1984.

25 *L'Humanité*, 17 March 1921.

26 Ibid., 11 March 1922.

27 Léon Daudet, 'La fifille savante et le chat Bossu', *L'Action française*, 2 Jan. 1920.

28 *L'Humanité*, 15 Feb. 1930.

29 Ibid., 6 March 1931.

30 See Jeanne Verdès-Leroux, *Scandale financier et antisémitisme catholique: Le krach de l'Union générale* (Le Centurion, Paris, 1969), pp. 122ff. In the same spirit, see the astonishing book by Ruth Malhotra, *Horror Galerie* (Dortmund, Harenberg, 1955), which analyses several caricatures of Dreyfus, Reinach, Sazoc-Kahn, Rothschild, etc., depicted in the form of the most diverse animals.

31 Drumont, *La France juive*, vol. 1, p. 105.

32 Ibid., p. 16.

33 See the analysis by Lionel Rothkrug, 'Peasant and Jew: fear of pollution and German perceptions', *Historical Reflections*, no. 3 (1983). These comments can easily be applied to the case of France.

34 É. Drumont, *La Dernière Bataille* (E. Dentu, Paris, 1890), pp. 130 and 133.

35 Quoted by Pierre Pierrard, *Juifs et catholiques français* (Fayard, Paris, 1970), p. 117.

36 A. Adler explains the Jews' castration complex by their circumcision: *Le Tempérament nerveux* (Paris, 1926), p. 125.

37 See the superb chapter by Stephen Wilson, 'Sexual antisemitism: "Horribly Sensual" ', in *Ideology and Experience: Antisemitism in France at the time of the Dreyfus Affair*, ch. 15.

38 Ibid., p. 593. See for the same period, Abbé Lémann, *Jeanne d'Arc et les héroïnes juives* (Paris, 1873).

39 *L'Action française*, 4 July 1936. See also *Choc*, 13 May 1937, which denounces the confusion between Léon Blum and Joan of Arc, 'the purest figure'. Léon Daudet, on the contrary, entitled his article in *L'Action française*, 8 May 1937, 'Léon Blum contre Jeanne d'Arc'. In Jan. 1984, *Écrits de Paris* was still describing Léon Blum as a 'frightened virgin'.

40 *National-Hebdo*, 7 Sept. 1984.

41 *Le Cri du peuple*, 12 March 1942. On 12 March 1942, at the time of the Riom trial, *Le Petit Matin* also made fun of Blum who 'wanted to be identified with Joan of Arc'. See, in the same spirit, the file 'Procès de Riom' in the *Archives nationales*, F7 15288.

42 François Garçon, *De Blum à Pétain* (Éditions du Cerf, Paris, 1984), pp. 111ff.

43 Léon Daudet, *Termites parlementaires* (Éditions de Capitole, Paris, 1930), pp. 174ff.

44 *Gringoire*, 8 Feb. 1929.
45 Ibid., 30 April 1937.
46 Georges Suarez, *Nos seigneurs et maîtres* (Éditions de France, Paris, 1937), p. 11. *Aujourd'hui* also describes Léon Blum as 'Beelzebub', 13 March 1942.
47 *Le Rappel*, 12 Aug. 1926. *Candide* frequently attacked 'the satanic irony' or the 'satanic calculations' of Léon Blum. For example, *Candide*, 24 April 1930 and 1 Jan. 1931.
48 *Rivarol*, 8 March 1956.
49 Pierre Olivier Lapie, *De Léon Blum à de Gaulle* (Fayard, Paris, 1971), p. 579.
50 Marc Lévy, 'Chez Dupont tout est bon, interdit aux juifs et aux chiens', in 'L'Étranger: Crise-Réprésentation', *Collectif Événement Psychanalyse* (Paris, 1983), p. 235.
51 Dominique, *Monsieur le Parlement*, p. 44.
52 Figueras, *Zoologie du Palais-Bourbon*, p. 129. Similarly, Daniel Mayer was 'the ugliest' (p. 125).
53 Quoted by Allain Rollat, *Les Hommes de l'extrême droite* (Calmann-Lévy, Paris, 1985), p. 32.
54 See the great book by Joshua Trachtenberg, *The Devil and the Jews* (Meridian Books, Cleveland, Ohio, 1961); first published 1943.
55 Paul Ferdonnet, *La Guerre juive* (Éditions Baudinière, Paris, 1940), pp. 220 and 252; XXX, *Est-ce que je deviens antisémite?* (Éditions de France, Paris, 1938), pp. 105–6, an amazing work which contains an improbable imaginary dialogue with Léon Blum when he is supposed to explain his strategy for establishing his power over 'France, a Jewish colony'. G. Welter, 'Le poison juif', *Mercure de France*, 190 (1926). *L'Antijuif* (the editor was Darquier de Pellepoix), no. 1 (3 June 1937). See also Darquier's articles in the paper he founded in 1938, *La France enchaînée*; relentlessly attacking Blum, Jules Moch, Jean Zay, Georges Mandel and Pierre Mendès France, he maintained that France was 'a Jewish plutocracy', and added: 'One does not cure syphilis by painting the ulcer with orange blossom ... the microbe has to be destroyed. The limb has to be amputated' (*La France enchaînée*, Dec. 1938, pp. 15–31). In *L'Action française*, Blum is described as 'a mushroom which proliferates', for example, on 17 March 1942. More generally, see 'La peste et le typhus', *La Vieille France*, 7 Oct. 1920. This extremely anti-Semitic paper also printed the following: 'It is not rats, it is Jews imported en masse by the *Alliance française* which are infecting Paris with bubonic plague, typhus, cholera, as they have already infected it with leprosy, elephantiasis, and granulous and purulent conjunctivitis' (*La Vieille France*, 26 Aug. 1920). Later, a leaflet distributed by the Poujadist movement stated: 'Pierre Poujade holds out his hand to honest folk. Pierrot is here ... the trash has gone' (*Bibliothèque nationale*, Tracts politiques, 4° Lb 465). On these depictions of the Jews as carriers of the most varied diseases, see Alex Bein, 'The Jewish parasite: Notes on the semantics of the Jewish problem with special reference to Germany', *Leo Baeck Year Book*, no. 9, 1964.
56 Maurras on a number of occasions describes 'the Jewish fever which must devour Blum' (*Dictionnaire politique et critique*, vol. 1, p. 189).
57 See, for example, Jean Jacoby, *1940* (Les Libertés françaises, Paris, 1941), p. 139. In the same spirit, *Choc*, 18 June 1936. This journal entitled its article on Blum, 'Un cas de freudisme'.
58 On the connections between Freud and Charcot, on the one hand, and between Freud and Judaism, on the other, see Peter Gay, *Freud, Jews and other Germans* (Oxford University Press, Oxford, 1976).
59 L. Viguier, *Les Juifs à travers Léon Blum: Leurs incapacité historique à diriger un état* (Éditions Baudinière, 1940), p. 100.
60 *L'Humanité*, 14 Feb. 1928.
61 Alice Kaminsky, 'The literary concept of decadence', *Nineteenth-Century French Studies* 4, 3 (Spring 1976).

62 *Le Réveil du peuple*, 1 March 1936.
63 *L'Action française*, 6 Nov. 1936.
64 Ibid., 14 June 1937.
65 *L'Ami du peuple*, 21 July 1933.
66 *L'Émancipation nationale*, 20 Jan. 1939.
67 *Archives nationales*, F7 13238. This meeting took place on 29 June 1933.
68 See, for example, *L'Ère nouvelle*, 24 March 1924.
69 *Candide*, 7 April 1938.
70 Pierre Dominique, *Sous le règne des Bouffons* (Nouvelles Éditions Latines, Paris, 1957), pp. 29, 30 and 100.
71 Quoted by Marylène Delbourg-Delphis, *Masculin singulier: Le dandyisme et son histoire* (Hachette, Paris, 1985), p. 205. This author describes the parallel drawn between Barbey and Sue. See also Pierre Andreu and Frederic Grover, *Drieu La Rochelle* (Hachette, Paris, 1979).
72 Ibid., p. 47.
73 Jerrold Seigel, *Bohemian Paris: Culture, politics, and the boundaries of bourgeois life, 1830–1930* (Viking Press, New York, 1986).
74 See, for example, Henri Béraud, 'Et les juifs', *Gringoire*, 23 Jan. 1941. In this article, Béraud calls Blum 'the Bulgarian with the pince-nez . . . the Bohemian'.
75 See, for example, Fayolle-Lefort, *Le Juif, cet inconnu* (Éditions de France, Paris, 1941), p. 64.
76 See Geoffrey Fraser and Thadée Natanson, *Léon Blum: Man and statesman* (J. B. Lippincott, Philadelphia, Pa, 1938), pp. 14–18 and ch. 4; Louise Elliot Dalby, *Léon Blum* (Thomas Yoseloff, New York, 1963), p. 111.
77 *L'Oeuvre*, 29 Sept. 1910.
78 *L'Oeuvre*, 16 Feb. 1911. See also, by the same author, 'Vie de monsieur Léon Blum. Suivi d'un Portrait du président du Conseil', *L'Action publique*, no. 2 (1936).
79 Marcel Thiébaut, 'En lisant M. Léon Blum', *Revue de Paris*, May and June 1937. This anti-Semitic analysis of Blum's youthful work enjoyed a similar success to Téry's articles and was referred to time and again in the press and in lampoons. See Robert Brasillach's comments on it in *Je suis partout*, 22 May 1937. Reading Thiébaut's articles, the academician André Bellessort confessed to the 'repulsion' he felt in respect of Léon Blum (*Je suis partout*, 10 Sept. 1937).
80 This interview is described in Marie-France Toinet's thesis '*Georges Boris, 1888–1960: Un socialiste humaniste*', thesis for the Fondation nationale des sciences politiques (Paris, 1969), p. 234.
81 Elliot Dalby, *Léon Blum*, p. 24. See, for example, *Revue de Paris* which in 1937 presented him as 'the dandy, the modern nabi of Israel' (p. 901).
82 *L'Émancipation nationale*, 21 March 1942.
83 *Rivarol*, 20 July 1984.
84 Pierre Dominique, *Monsieur le Parlement* (Éditions Baudinière, Paris, 1928), pp. 84–5.
85 Jean-Renaud, 'Léon Blum au pilori', *La Solidarité française*, 26 May 1934.
86 Henri Massis, *Les Idées restent* (H. Lardanchet, Lyons, 1941), p. 155. There is nothing on this point in Michel Toda's speech for the defence: *Henri Massis: Un temoin de la droite intellectuelle* (La Table ronde, Paris, 1982).
87 Alfred Fabre-Luce, *Vingt-cinq années de liberté* (Julliard, Paris, 1962), pp. 113–114. On Blum and Proust, see *Candide*, 12 Dec. 1935.
88 Paul Allard, *Les Favorites de la Troisième République* (Éditions de France, Paris, 1942), pp. 71 and 114. Blum was very often caricatured as a eunuch. See, for example, *Je suis partout*, 11 July 1936. *Candide* also saw him as a 'physiological impotent' individual (*Candide*, 21 April 1938).

Georges Mandel was also described as a eunuch on numerous occasions. See Dominique, *Monsieur le Parlement*, p.45.
89 *L'Action française*, 18 Aug. 1925.
90 *L'Action française*, 7 and 24 Feb., 1 April 1920. On 16 April 1920 Daudet denounced 'his little girlie face, hardened and tense in the need for levelling, in the judicial hatred of the invader for the invaded. Because he is the consummate type of Hebrew who says "you others" when talking to Frenchmen.'
91 *L'Action française*, 12 April 1929, 24 May 1936.
92 Ibid., 2 July 1936.
93 Jean-Pierre Maxence, *Histoire de dix ans* (Gallimard, Paris, 1936), p. 361.
94 Henri Béraud, *Popu-Roi* (Éditions de France, Paris, 1938), pp. 13–115 and 238.
95 *L'Action française*, 13 June 1920. Even as late as 1987, a nostalgic article in *Action française* made fun of 'Blum's dainty cynicism, his girlish nervous, burping temper-tantrums ... of his high waist on his little tootsies' (Pierre Monnier, *À l'ombre des grandes têtes molles* (La Table ronde, Paris, 1987), p. 54).
96 *Candide*, 11 June 1936.
97 *L'Humanité*, 17 Oct. 1930.
98 Ibid., 26 Oct. 1932.
99 Pierre Gaxotte, 'L'homme maudit', *Candide*, 7 April 1938. On 25 April 1936, Gaxotte was already describing Léon Blum in *Je suis partout* as a man troubled by 'rumblings, hiccups, moanings, tremblings, with absolutely irresistible wheedling and simpering recoveries'.
100 On this point, see, for example, Paul Hoffmann, *La Femme dans la pensée des Lumières* (Ophrys, Strasbourg, 1976); and Yvonne Knibiehler, *La Femme et les médecins* (Hachette, Paris, 1983). On women, Jews and diseases at the turn of the century, see Jacques Le Rider, 'Misères de la virilité à la belle époque', *Le Genre Humain*, no. 10.
101 *L'Humanité-Dimanche*, 5 May 1954.
102 See, for example, *Charivari*, 26 July 1930 or 5 Sept. 1931.
103 There are countless verbal and pictorial references on this point. See *Je suis partout*, 18 Sept. 1931, 24 Sept. 1937. In *L'Action française*, 27 March 1938, the inimitable Léon Daudet called him 'the neuropath with the white handkerchief'. For the communist editor Pierre Vaillant-Couturier, 'yesterday, Léon Blum threw a small nervous breakdown after gnawing his inseparable little handkerchief ... the symptom of intellectual degeneracy' (*L'Humanité*, 8 Dec. 1928).
104 *Candide*, 14 and 15 April 1937.
105 Comte A. de Puységur, *Les Maquereaux légitimes: du coursier des croisades au bidet de Rebecca* (La Technique du Livre, Paris, 1938), pp. 141–2.
106 *Almanach de La Libre Parole* (Paris, 1894), p. 76. See also the *Almanach* of 1905, p. 9.
107 See, for example, *Le Rire*, 18 Nov. 1933.
108 Louis-Charles Lecoc, *L'Enjeu de la guerre: les juifs* (Sorlot, Paris, 1941), p. 13. In the same spirit, see *Le Réveil du peuple*, 29 Nov. 1940, which claimed that 'Léon Blum's success in the most titled drawing-rooms of fashionable Paris is explained by the fact that our nobility is stuffed with Jews'.
109 Lecoc, *L'Enjeu de la guerre*, p. 11.
110 *France réelle*, 16 July 1954.
111 René Saive, *Mendès France* (Éditions Journal du Parlement, Paris, 1954), p. 137.
112 *D'Artagnan*, 7 July 1934.
113 *Paris Match*, 22–29 Jan. 1955.
114 *Paris Match*, 5–12 and 12–19 Feb. 1955.

115 On this subject, see Jean-Paul Aron, *Le Mangeur du XIXe siècle* (Laffont, Paris, 1973).
116 Henri Caillavet, interview, IHTP, 1983, 65ff.
117 Geoffrey Fraser and Thadée Natanson, *Léon Blum, Man and Statesman* (J. B. Lippincott, Philadelphia, Pa, 1938), pp. 51–3.
118 Louise Elliot Dalby, *Léon Blum* (Thomas Yoseloff, New York, 1963), p. 24.
119 *Minute*, 1 Oct. 1984.
120 *Libération*, 31 July 1984.
121 *Rivarol*, 27 July 1984.
122 *Présent*, 4 Sept. 1985 and 21 Feb. 1986. *Minute* also describes L. Fabius as a 'sexual bombshell' (17 Aug. 1985). For *Rivarol*, Laurent Fabius had 'a velvet, oriental seductive gaze' (27 July 1984).
123 *Minute*, 2 Nov. 1985.
124 *Figaro-Magazine*, 15 Sept. 1984.
125 *National-Hebdo*, 14 Sept. 1984.
126 *Figaro-Magazine*, 26 Oct. 1985.
127 Jean-Pierre Winter, 'L'hystérie masculine', *Carnets de psychanalyse*, no. 5 (1983).
128 É. Drumont, *La France juive* (Marpon & Flammarion, Paris, 1886), vol. 1, p. 114. To associate Naquet with Blum became almost commonplace in anti-Semitic literature. For Henri Faugeras, 'the whole demolition process of the family, from Naquet to Blum and Zay, from divorce to sexual education, is Jewish' (*Les Juifs, peuple de proie* (Documents contemporains, Paris, 1943), p. 61). See also, for example, *Le Temps*, 1 June 1906, Fondation nationale des sciences politiques (hereafter FNSP), Fonds L. Blum; *L'Appel*, 13 Nov. 1941; Gérard, *Le Juif*, Union nationale pour la défense de la race, 1943, Bibliothèque du Centre de documentation juif contemporain. On the destruction of French customs by Crémieux, Naquet and the Jews, see Robert Launay, *Figures juives* (Nouvelle Librairie nationale, Paris, 1921).
129 For an analysis of *Du mariage*, see William Logue, *Léon Blum: The formative years, 1872–1914* (Northern Illinois University Press, De Kalb, Ill., 1973), pp. 200ff.
130 See also, anon., 'Bolchevisme de salon et Faisandisme juif', in *Les Cahiers de l'Anti-France* (Éditions Bossard, Paris, 1922), pp. 498–503, BAIU. The author denounces Blum's 'cloacal declarations' in *Du mariage* which made 'this Jew from Lorraine an infinitely dangerous serpent'.
131 *La Croix des Alpes-Maritimes*, 7 July 1907, Fonds L. Blum, FNSP.
132 'Pour les vierges de Sion', *Jaune*, 24 Feb. 1909, Fonds L. Blum FNSP. (The Thalamas of the quotation was a professor of history who was prevented from giving his course at the Sorbonne in 1908 by the young royalists of *Action française* who blamed him for having spoken of 'auditory hallucinations' in respect of Joan of Arc (Jean-François Sirinelli, 'Action française: main basse sur le Quartier latin!', *L'Histoire*, Dec. 1982, pp. 6–15). See also, in the Fonds Blum, the articles in *Je dis tout*, Jan. 1916, which steadily attacked Léon Blum, 'that senior civil servant who wants to undermine one of the most robust supports of French thought... in order to erect I know not what sort of cosmopolitan Golden Calf on this disaster of French hearts and brains'.
133 For example, during a debate organized by the Forum, on 22 Feb. 1934 about the role of the men in the Stavisky affair, M. de Goldenbach declared: 'The Jews and the negroes have a taste for bestiality that you gentlemen have not, and which women find attractive' (*Archives de la préfecture de Police*, BA 1855).
134 Léon Blum, *L'Homme qui se trompe toujours et qui trompe les autres* (CDJC, Paris, n.d., anon.).
135 Hitler, Rosenberg, Goebbels, Streicher, *Guerre aux Juifs* (Centre de documentation et de

propagande, Paris, 1939), BAIU.
136 Jean-Charles Legrand, *Paroles vivantes* (Éditions Baudinière, Paris, 1941), pp. 184–5. See also Raymond Recouly, *Les Causes de notre effondremont* (Éditions de France, Paris, 1941).
137 *L'Action française*, 19 April 1937.
138 *Au Pilori*, 4 Oct. 1940.
139 *L'Action française*, 11 May 1937. See also the review of Blum's book, *La réforme gouvernementale*, by *Je suis partout*, which stated 'the author of the essay on *Le mariage* is visibly pleased with those constitutional miscarriages. He lovingly collects the foetuses' (*Je suis partout*, 18 July 1936).
140 Jeffrey Mehlman, *Legs de l'antisémitisme en France* (Denöel, Paris, 1984), p. 136.
141 André Gide, *Corydon* (Gallimard, Paris, 1925), p. 115.
142 See A. Spire, *Souvenirs à bâtons rompus* (A. Michel, Paris, 1962), p. 201. On the similarity between Lévy-Coeur and Blum, see Spire's book, and also Bertrand Barrière, *Romain Rolland, l'âme et l'art* (A. Michel, Paris, 1966), p. 211; Lazare Landau, *De l'aversion a l'estime: Juifs et catholiques en France de 1919 à 1939* (Édition le Centurion, Paris, 1980), pp. 109ff.; E. Spatz, *Les Juifs dans l'oeuvre des principaux romanciers français de la génération de l'affaire Dreyfus*, thesis, Paris, EHESS, BAIU, p. 168. More recently, see Pierre Citti, *Contre la décadence. Histoire de l'impureté française dans le roman, 1890–1914* (PUF, Paris, 1987), p. 157.
143 Romain Rolland, *Jean-Christophe: La foire sur la place* (Livre de poche – Gallimard, Paris, 1957), p. 746.
144 Hector Ghilini, *À la barre de Riom* (Jean Renard, Paris, 1942), p. 128. In the same spirit, but in a more elaborate style, see *La Revue de Paris*, 1937, p. 901.
145 *Gringoire*, 2 July 1937.
146 Charles Castellani, *Entre Moloch et Satan* (Paris, 1901), p. 6.
147 *L'Action française*, 18 Sept. 1936.
148 *L'Action française*, 9 Oct. 1936.
149 *Gringoire*, 3 Jan. 1936.
150 *Au Pilori*, 18 Oct. 1940.
151 See, for example, *L'Atelier*, 7 Dec. 1942. See also John Sherwood, *Georges Mandel and the Third Republic* (Stanford University Press, Stanford, Conn., 1970), p. 266.
152 *Je suis partout*, 22 Aug. 1936.
153 Saive, *Mendès France*, p. 137.
154 *Journal du Parlement*, 3 Nov. 1955.
155 Ibid., 17 Oct. 1956.
156 *Présent*, 10 Nov. 1984.
157 *Écrits de Paris*, 16 Nov. 1984.
158 Mosse, *Nationalism and Sexuality*, pp. 141–2. See his chapter 'Manliness and Homosexuality'.
159 Weber, *Fin de siècle*, pp. 56ff.
160 Dalby, for example, makes a point of demonstrating this in *Léon Blum*, p. 29.
161 André Gide, *Journal, 1889–1939* (Gallimard, Paris, 1951), p. 397. On Blum, Gide, the Jews and pederasty, see Mehlman, *Legs de l'antisémitisme en France*, ch. 4.
162 Ibid., p. 250.
163 On Gide's attitude to Blum, see the little-known article by Rabi, in *La Terre retrouvée*, 15 April 1950, which states: 'it would not be difficult to pick out the "specifically" Jewish defects in Gide's work for which he criticizes the Jews in general: his ambiguity, a way of cultivating his dualism with love, that fear of action and above all that lack of modesty (that indecency) in displaying his private life in public and notably his homosexual life'. In 1936, when Gide's

portrait of Blum was reprinted, Henri Massis added: 'This portrait succeeds so well in capturing the general, the essential, the race itself, that it can never become out of date' (*Revue universelle*, 15 May 1936).

164 Quoted by Géraldi Leroy and Anne Roche, *Les Écrivains et le Front populaire* (Presses de la Fondation nationale de sciences politiques, Paris, 1986), p. 109.

165 *Candide*, 12 June 1932.

166 See the articles by Judith Camy-Darmon and Juliette Hassine already cited, as well as Spatz's thesis, *Les Juifs dans l'oeuvre des principaux romanciers*. Likewise, Mayer, *Outsiders*, pp. 345–50.

167 Pierre Dominique, *Monsieur le Parlement* (Éditions Baudinière, Paris, 1928), p. 83. *L'Action française*, 7 June 1924, did not hesitate to resort to poetry to illustrate this interpretation:

> 'Ah!' said Herriot gaily!
> 'Kiss me Blum! Kiss me Blum!'
> 'Ah!' said Herriot gaily!
> 'Kiss me Blum, my child.'

168 *Le Rappel*, 25 July 1927.

169 Léon Daudet, 'Un juif qui sème l'antisémitisme', *L'Action française*, 11 Oct. 1933.

170 *Revue universelle*, 15 Jan. 1936.

171 *Revue universelle*, 13 March 1938.

172 *L'Action française*, 17 June 1920.

173 *L'Humanité*, 26 July 1925.

174 *L'Humanité*, 16 July 1925. It should not be forgotten either that L. Blum had 'tender connections with the Finaly group' (*L'Humanité*, 14 Feb. 1928). Even today, however, the radical Right maintains that Blum 'was kicked in the arse by the communists' during the Popular Front (Monnier, *À l'ombre des grandes têtes molles*, p. 53).

175 Rhillon, 'Léon Blum: Lavaillon de Genève', *Documents et Témoignages*, Aug. 1936, p. 3.

176 *Revue universelle*, 1 Oct. 1938.

177 *France: Revue de l'État nouveau*, no. 19 (March 1944).

178 A very large number of articles and books describe how Blum 'put his hand on the shoulders' of his colleagues (see, for example, Louis Guitard, *Mon Blum, ou les défauts de la statue* (Regirex-France, Paris, 1983), p. 208), how he wrapped 'a fraternal arm' round them (see, for example, *Choc*, 31 Dec. 1936). For Laurent Viguier, 'Legally speaking, the law of Moses is no longer valid; pederasts and people who commit incest are no longer put to death; they display and teach their ignominy; they express it, like the Jew Léon Blum in his book on marriage. And the synagogue remains open to them': *Les juifs à travers Léon Blum: Leur incapacité historique à diriger un état* (Éditions Baudinière, Paris, 1940), p. 59.

179 Saul Friedländer, *L'Antisémitisme nazi: Histoire d'une psychose collective* (Le Seuil, Paris, 1971), pp. 133ff.

180 See Robert Soucy, *Fascist Intellectual: Drieu La Rochelle* (University of California Press, Berkeley, Cal., 1979), ch. 10.

181 On this point, *Le Chat Rit* can be counsulted; for example, 5 Dec. 1936.

182 Saul Friedländer, *Histoire et Psychanalyse* (Le Seuil, Paris, 1975).

183 *Charivari*, 22 Nov. 1930.

184 P. G. Pulzer, *The Rise of Political Anti-Semitism in Germany and Austria* (John Wiley, London, 1964), pp. 253ff.

185 Mosse, *Nationalism and Sexuality*, p. 42.

186 *Almanach de La Libre Parole, 1899*, p. 61.

187 Édouard Drumont, *La France juive devant l'opinion* (Flammarion, Paris, 1886), ch. 6: 'L'escrime sémitique'. On the meeting between Drumont and Meyer, see Léonce Reynaud, *Les Juifs français devant l'opinion* (A. Lahure, Paris, 1887), ch. 6, where the author demonstrates that Meyer in no way acted disloyally.
188 *Almanach de La Libre Parole, 1897*.
189 Jean Drault, *Drumont, 'La France Juive' et 'La Libre Parole'* (Société française d'éditions littéraire et techniques, 1935), pp. 191, 223, 248, etc.
190 Raphael Viau, *Vingt ans d'antisémitisme* (Eugène Fasquelle, Paris, 1910).
191 This famous series of duels is described by Ernest Crémieux-Foa, *La Campagne antisémite: Les duels. Les responsabilités* (Alcan-Lévy, Paris, 1892).
192 William Serman, *Les Officiers français dans la nation, 1848–1914* (Aubier, Paris, 1982), p. 105.
193 Simon Arbellot, *La Fin du boulevard* (Flammarion, Paris, 1965).
194 François Billacois, *Le Duel dans la société française des XVIe et XVIIe siècles* (Éditions de l'EHESS, Paris, 1986), p. 82.
195 Arbellot, *La Fin du boulevard*, p. 117.
196 On this incident, see Jean Recanati, *Profils juifs de Marcel Proust* (Buchet-Chastel, Paris, 1979), pp. 118–119.
197 On this fight, see the file 'Duel' in the Fonds Blum, Fondation nationale des sciences politiques.
198 Pierre-Bloch, *Jusqu'au dernier jour* (A. Michel, Paris, 1983), pp. 59 and 66.
199 Pierre Mendès France, *Oeuvres complètes*, vol. 1 (Gallimard, Paris, 1984), pp. 393–4.
200 *Archives privées Marie-Claire Mendès France*, E.1.
201 *Archives privées Marie-Claire Mendès France*.
202 Private interview with Marie-Claire Mendès France.
203 Private interview with Marie-Claire Mendès France.

8
The Antichrist

Catholic anti-Semitism has always formed one of the traditional foundations of hatred of the Jews. It sees them as the deicide people, veritable Satans responsible for the death of Christ, rejecting both his law and his love, resolutely turning its back on the teachings of the Church on which the Western world is based. Traditional anti-Semitism continues to this day to regard them as the devil's handymen and to blame them for all the perversions just described. In the direct line of Saint Paul, Christian tradition in France, from Bossuet to de Bonald, Gougenot des Mousseaux, Léon Bloy and Bernanos, in the past as in the present, has never ceased to disseminate a virulent anti-Semitism, penetrating popular consciousness, holding up to public obloquy those sinners responsible, through their ignorance of the Holy Spirit, for the misfortunes of Christian France.[1]

At the turn of the century Drumont's theses were particularly favourably received by the minor clergy who publicized them tirelessly. For Drumont, 'it was the Jews who organized the pillage of the churches, the destruction of masterpieces inspired by faith.... What more magnificent opportunity to satisfy their hatred and their greed and at the same time, to insult Christ and make money!'[2] Many parish priests became Drumont's most zealous propagandists. The *Revue du monde catholique*, edited by Eugène Veuillot, opened wide its doors to them, and many priests jostled to enter a competition organized by *La Libre Parole* to find the best solution to 'bring about the annihilation of Jewish power in France, the Jewish danger being considered from the point of view of race and not religion'. Song-writing abbots had the time of their lives denouncing the 'jackal stinking of filth and tainted blood', and the anti-Semitic hatred of the prelates themselves knew no bounds.[3]

Drumont owed much to the constant help of *La Bonne Presse* which, in particular, distributed *La Croix*. In August 1890 this paper proudly proclaimed that it was 'the most anti-Jewish paper in France', and solemnly stated: 'the Jew is the enemy, this is the Christian cry from Golgotha to the present day'.[4] *La Croix* and its many provincial editions covering the whole of France devoted all its energies to this anti-Jewish struggle. It reinforced the efforts of *Le Pèlerin*, a popular weekly, which dealt primarily with the rural world, constantly voiced anti-Semitic theses and had at the time a particularly large circulation. In fact, the whole Catholic press participated to a greater or lesser extent in this unceasing struggle against the Jews, whether it belonged to the Christian-Democrat wing (*Le Peuple français, La Voix de la France, La Terre de France*, and so on) or whether it was, like *La Croix*, very far removed from it (*Le Monde, L'Univers*, and the rest).[5]

Georges Bernanos, in an immensely successful book, *La Grande Peur des bien-pensants*, set the seal of respectability on this trend. He saw Drumont's *La France juive* as 'a magic book', written by a 'visionary historian', and denounced 'those strange fellows who talk like monkeys with their hands . . . with their black hair, their features chiselled by centuries-old anguish, the savage pruritus of bone-marrow worn out since the reign of Solomon, wasted in all the beds of lascivious Asia'.[6] The great Catholic writer was thus Drumont's equal in his denunciation of the 'Jewish race' which, he claimed, had secured control of Christian France. He thereby contributed to legitimizing the anti-Semitism that abounded in the heart of the Catholic world.

CATHOLICISM AND ANTI-SEMITISM IN THE 1930s

In the thirties, what became of this virulent struggle that Catholic France waged against 'Jewish France'? Did the fact that the Church rallied to the support of the Republic at the turn of the century result in a decrease in its anti-Semitic discourse?[7] Did the Pope's condemnation of the doctrine of *L'Action française*, which had a wide influence on the Catholic world, also involve a decline in Catholic anti-Semitism? In the thirties integralism had far from disappeared even though a Christian democracy was unfolding, concerned with the social question and also acknowledging the legitimacy of the Republic. A greater diversity of political trends was now expressed, marked by the creation of *L'Aube, Sillon* and *Témoignage chrétien*.[8] After 1926, even *La Croix*, under the influence of Abbé Merklen, underwent a profound change of direction which seemed to distance it from its earlier standpoints.[9]

In that period when political and socio-economic dogma in general were being challenged, French Catholicism exploded into very diverse currents of thought. Witness the rapid strengthening of social Catholicism, as expressed in the *L'Aube, Sept, Esprit* and *Temps présent*, hostile to anti-Semitism and racism. Note too the very effective action taken by the pioneers of Judeo–Christian friendship under the influence of Père Bonsirven and the tireless Oscar de Férenzy who founded *La Juste Parole* in October 1936. This journal devoted itself in the main to fighting anti-Semitism, which brought down upon its head the thunderbolts of traditional Catholicism and the extreme Right. The enemy camp unceasingly sharpened its arguments. Alongside *L'Action française* and a host of other papers, particular mention must be made of the *Revue internationale des sociétés secrètes* which, under the editorship of Monsignor Jouin, unflaggingly helped to exacerbate the anti-Semitic struggle. We shall refer to it on a number of occasions.

The Popular Front brought these internal schisms in the Catholic world clearly to the fore.[10] As early as July 1935, *La Jeune République*, an off-shoot of *Sillon*, joined the *Rassemblement populaire* under the impetus of Marc Sangnier and Maurice Lacroix. After the famous speech when Maurice Thorez held out a hand to the Catholics, came the Pierre-Henri Simon affair, of more direct interest here. In his book, *Les Catholiques, la politique et l'argent*, he suggested a line of conduct for future legislative elections on the basis of several stated options. Now the second option was absolutely crucial since it envisaged the presence of both a declared anti-clerical and a clerical nationalist. His advice on how to vote caused a scandal:

We have no reason to choose one in preference to the other. We will abstain, or else we will vote for one of them on grounds of political expediency which will have nothing to do with our religious duty. Suppose that this wonderful symbolic duel was between M. de Kerilis and M. Léon Blum! That would mean stating a preference on an emotional basis.[11]

That an eminent Catholic, a close friend of Monsignor Chollet, Archbishop of Cambrai, could envisage preferring a socialist and anti-clerical Jew to a leader of the nationalist Right proved that certain members of the hierarchy had genuine misgivings. Nevertheless, many people found this intolerable and a large number of Catholic groups reacted strongly, calling for sanctions. On 2 October *La Croix*, which did not acknowledge such points of conscience, appealed for a massive vote, whatever the stated option, against the Popular Front. As Henri Noguères noted, 'the Church has chosen its camp. The Left is not mistaken':[12] the majority of Catholics voted for the Right.[13]

We have still to investigate how far the specific presence of Léon Blum at the head of the Popular Front caused the old anti-Semitism, which had never disappeared, to re-emerge stronger than ever in certain sections of the Catholic world. If *La France catholique* and General de Castelnau hastened to reject any suggestion of Catholic collaboration with the Blum government, an equal number of Catholic leaders none the less registered their distance in respect of the Leagues.[14]

The positions *La Croix* took up deserve particular examination because of its ominous past. Even in 1920, commenting on a statement by Léon Blum on the subject of the tax on capital, *La Croix* stated that it reflected the position 'of a Jew whom one is not surprised to find in this work of social disintegration'.[15] Later, in 1927, its Avignon regional edition, after quoting Drumont's warnings of the Jewish peril, as had long been its custom, attacked Léon Blum, 'son of Israel'. 'Everyone knows he is a Jew', it added; 'everyone knows he is a multi-millionaire; the two things go perfectly together.'[16] In 1936 *La Croix* never attacked Léon Blum as a Jew, even though it was hostile to the Popular Front and would shortly be opposing its educational policy. It generally preferred the precepts specific 'to Christian charity' to those of socialism which, it claimed, led to 'a totalitarian régime'.[17] Contrary to the type of discourse which was very widespread on the Right at that time, *La Croix* observed an extreme caution and refrained from making any connection between the Popular Front and the Jews whom, contrary to its long-standing custom, it quite simply did not mention. Moreover, its criticism was balanced: for example, it acknowledged that Léon Blum acted 'wisely', that he 'continues the tradition of heads of French governments for over fifteen years. And when he appeals for confidence, he expresses himself as did M. Poincaré himself ten years ago.'[18]

Times really did seem to have changed and Drumont would no longer have recognized himself. It was true that many of his heirs relentlessly attacked Léon Blum at this period, while *La Libre Parole* was reborn from its ashes in 1930 to confront the Jewish peril. It was also true that Bernanos brought out *La Grande Peur des bien-pensants* in 1931 in homage to Drumont; and the militant Catholic Right, in the wake of Charles Maurras and Léon Daudet, declared war on the Jew, Léon Blum. In journals and at public meetings Henri Massis, Henry Bordeaux, Marcel Jouhandeau and Xavier Vallat, of the *Fédération nationale catholique*, and also Darquier de Pellepoix, appeared and proclaimed their Catholic faith loud and clear. But *La Croix*, suspicious of the Popular Front experiment, avoided getting mixed up with the violent anti-Semitic struggle that the Right and part of the Catholic world were prepared to wage. On 22 September 1938 *La Croix* even went as far as to identify anti-Semitism with paganism, and on 31 August in the same year, definitively broke with its past, when it declared: 'With the Pope, let us recognize that the Jews are our brethren, men as we are, chosen by God as much and, in certain respects, more than we are.'[19] It could not be counted on to lead the anti-Semitic attack on Blum.

Études prophetically thought that '*Le Populaire* is edited by M. Blum, the future leader of the government. This is hardly reassuring for religious peace.'[20] *L'Aube*, on the other hand, published favourable comments on Blum's ministerial declaration under the signature of Georges Bidault,[21] while Emmanuel Mounier and the revue *Esprit* also reacted enthusiastically to Blum.[22]

On the Catholic Right, anti-Semitic clamour grew louder and louder. Following Léon Daudet, who urged 'Catholic France' to rise up against 'Blum's ambition, oriental at source',[23] a Jean-Charles Legrand bluntly declared: 'It is intolerable that our country should be represented by a Jew. We speak French, not Yiddish. The soil of France is made to bear steeples not synagogues.'[24] He foreshadowed the forthright comment by *Cahier jaune* in January 1943, when it waxed indignant at 'the insult shown to Notre-Dame de Paris on the day that Blum entered its sanctuary, as successor to Clovis, Saint Louis, Richelieu, Napoleon'.[25] In the same vein, Georges Suarez openly feared that Léon Blum would deliberately persecute the Catholics,[26] so 'great is his devotion to the synagogue'.[27] Addressing 'Minister Blum's Jews', *Conquête de la France* exclaimed: 'France, Catholic in spirit despite appearances, has nothing to do with that Russia of the Czars and the Schism', and the paper declared itself ready to confront 'his satanic power'.[28] *Contre-Révolution*, which openly claimed affiliation with this trend, declared war on 'Blum – Jew and freemason'.[29] During a meeting organized by *Jeunesse patriotique* in the Salle des Centraux in Paris, Charles des Isnards, Paris deputy and municipal councillor, proclaimed: 'a foreigner is going to lead a fundamentally Catholic country for the first time since France became France. What will he do about that international finance, whose foremost leaders are his co-religionists and friends?'[30] Even song-writers echoed this sometimes indignant reaction from certain sectors of the Catholic world. The following imaginary epitaph for Blum's grave by one of them was heard on the famous stage of the Théâtre des Deux Ânes on 7 February 1936:

> May He perish,
> the true good Lord,
> who failed to punish
> God's imposter and fraud.[31]

Such sketches are much more revealing of the extent of anti-Semitism than are the writings and speeches of political leaders or even those of major authors. Although they were not actual public meetings, they took place in popular places where a lively atmosphere conducive to the propagation of the worst type of hatred blossomed.[32]

MAURIAC AND MOUNIER: AMBIGUOUS PHILO-SEMITISM

We could continue to criticize the press and the various writings of Catholic inspiration or which defended its cause by showing open hostility to Léon Blum. It is more useful, however, to examine the ambiguities which came to the surface in declarations by important personalities in the Catholic world, who were, on the contrary, explicitly favourable to Blum. Consider, for example, the virtually unknown positions taken by François Mauriac, Emmanuel Mounier and Stanislas Fumet. These Catholic personalities were opposed to anti-Semitism but none the less used terms that were more than equivocal in respect of the experiment Léon Blum was conducting.

François Mauriac, beyond all doubt, approved of the Popular Front experiment, including its policy towards Catholic Spain which aroused so much criticism in France. In April 1937 he joined *La Juste Parole*, edited by Oscar de Férenzy, which was specifically devoted to fighting anti-Semitism in the name of Catholicism. This episode has remained so little-known that it seems indispensable to quote at length François Mauriac's letter on joining the journal:

The Antichrist 183

For a Catholic, anti-Semitism is not only an offence against charity. We are bound to Israel, we are tied to it, whether or not we wish it. I believe, however, that Israel is sometimes partly responsible for the defensive instinct that it arouses in certain nations. . . . Jews cannot perpetuate themselves, marry amongst themselves, jealously isolate themselves from Christians, without creating a state of defence and hostility. They cannot corner international finance without giving people the feeling of being dominated by them. They cannot swarm everywhere into a place where one of them has insinuated himself (the Blum Ministry), without arousing hatred, because they themselves indulge in reprisals. Some German Jews acknowledged in my presence that there existed in Germany a Jewish problem which had to be resolved. I am afraid that in the end one will also exist in France.[33]

This text is surprising because it seems such a pale copy of the virulent anti-Semitic lampoons of the period directed at Léon Blum as the head of the government. It in fact adopts accusations most frequently purveyed by the integralist Catholic press, and it is astonishing to find the usual myths of the Jews' international economic domination coming from the pen of François Mauriac. As for the verb 'swarm', applied here to the Jews who were said to be invading the Blum government, after he himself had 'insinuated' himself illegally, as if housebreaking, into the Presidency of the Council, it belongs more to the vocabulary of Drumont, or Bernanos, the other great Catholic writer, although it is even more frequently found in the writings of Céline, Maurras or Darquier de Pellepoix. In addition, the claim that there were too many Jews in the entourage of Léon Blum and Pierre Mendès France appears to be a real litany, the extent and consequences of which will be assessed later.

The Centre de documentation et de vigilance sent the following reply to François Mauriac in the name of the Jewish community:

It is with deep gratitude that French Jewry learned that that eminent writer, that zealous Christian, had joined the committee of patrons of *La Juste Parole* which aims to fight the prejudices and base instincts which engender anti-Semitism. Nevertheless, the terms on which M. Mauriac has joined have aroused some emotion amongst our co-religionists . . . First of all, a human collectivity, though it be exclusively religious, cannot legitimately be criticized for perpetuating itself . . . What, therefore, can the criticism formulated by M. Mauriac mean, if not the demand for Israel's total disappearance as the sole remedy for anti-Semitism? . . . The second series of complaints lacks – which seems more serious – the religious basis which excused the first. It is true that M. Mauriac makes no claim to competence in financial matters. The surprising complaint that the Jews 'corner international finance' must probably be attributed to his naïveté in this area. . . . Judaism is reluctant to discuss the swarming of Jews 'into a place where one of them has insinuated himself (the Blum Ministry)', because this again concerns a purely political polemic which is doubly surprising coming from M. Mauriac's pen. On the one hand, in the issue of *La Juste Parole* which contains his declaration of support, he will find very useful information on the real number and careers of the present ministry's members of Israelite origin. On the other hand, has M. Mauriac already forgotten what he wrote in *Le Figaro* on 19 March 1937 about 'the most intelligent of the men on the extreme Left' whom 'the popular wave carried to the Presidency of the Council'? It seems that M. Mauriac at that time considered M. Blum as head of the socialist party, which he actually is, while now suddenly he no longer remembers anything but his Jewish origin. Finally, M. Mauriac's letter contains a sibylline phrase saying that the Jews indulged in reprisals . . . we would like to know what reprisals can really be involved here.[34]

Later, in February 1938, François Mauriac published an article entitled 'Pour Israël' in *Temps présent*, where he bluntly maintained that 'we must start with a public act of opposition to anti-Semitism'.[35] His letter of support was for that reason all the more disturbing in that it revealed – down to its vocabulary – how pervasive anti-Semitic mythology was, when its insidious nature could even influence such exceptional personalities as François Mauriac. This text, which historians of Catholicism never quote, seems even more revealing of the frightening ambiguities of that period which was to founder in tragedy.

In addition it should be noted that, at the same time as François Mauriac was unhesitatingly making a sort of act of contrition, his son Claude Mauriac published in Gaston Bergery's paper, *La Flèche*, a defence of the Frontist position on anti-Semitism, utilizing arguments which, however, could only strengthen it.[36] Although he began by acknowledging that Jews were Frenchmen 'like the rest', he in his turn blamed them for being too concentrated in certain sectors and added: 'The interests of the Jews and the French converge here. It is most undesirable, moreover, that "saturation point" be determined by a statutary order (numerus clausus): it is a question of tact, of sensitivity.'[37]

We now need to examine an article by Emmanuel Mounier published in *Le Voltigeur*, which seems to be as little-known as François Mauriac's. To mention Mounier's name inevitably implies an approach to the more general debate on the political ideas of the editor of *Esprit*, particularly his assessment of fascism. Zeev Sternhell maintains that 'Mounier, like the great majority of contestants, has a certain indulgence, a certain understanding in respect of Fascism, often even a certain admiration, which basically originates from their common perception of the weakness and inadequacies of liberal democracy'.[38] This thesis has surprised historians because at first glance it appears to take little account of the entirely moral figure of the theorist of personalism, who resurrected *Esprit* during the first year of Vichy, and was then arrested and imprisoned, after which his name was associated with the Resistance. It provoked a lively controversy which need not be examined in detail.[39] Let us rather emphasize, as the Introduction to this book has already done, that the question of anti-Semitism forms a specific subject in its own right which needs to be distinguished from attitudes to fascism. Let us also note that Mounier's position in respect of Jews and anti-Semitism is nearly always absent from the lively discussion which has broken out in recent years.

Now, from this point of view, the article published in *Le Voltigeur* on 1 March 1939 deserves very careful examination because it indicates Mounier's position on this question, and also sheds new light on the debate on the more general understanding of fascism. This text is not utilized in the general controversy and deserves to be quoted at length. It is crucial, even if it too belongs to the history of ideas – which contemporary historians have, often rightly, denounced. They deny the possibility of assimilating this perspective into the analysis of facts and attitudes in an area as charged with significance as the study of the reality of fascism in France. However, it is one of Mounier's rare writings concerning Jews at a time when, by definition, facts – for example, the concrete assistance numerous Catholics were giving Jews during Vichy – could not be used when the need arose to correct the implications of everyday statements. For him, this issue of *Voltigeur*, put together in response to the publication of *Je suis partout* on 17 February and entitled 'Les Juifs et la France',

is not a plea for the Jews. If it is defending anything, it is the health of the French national organism against an illness which is endemic but today of foreign origins: anti-Semitism. To defend the Jews, to draw up a balance-sheet of their services, corresponding to the balance-sheet of their misdeeds, is to accept the central postulate of anti-Semitism: that the Jews, in France, constitute a special case, so manifest that there are grounds for making anti-Semitism one of the axes of French reconstruction. It is clumsy and ineffectual to reply to this claim that there are no Jewish problems in France. There are; in so far as the Federation of French communities is diversified and the Jewish community there remains differentiated. But these problems exist for the same reasons as specifically Alsatian, Bordelais, Catholic, Protestant, worker or peasant problems exist. There are other Jewish problems in as much as Jews here and there tend to cluster together here and there, and within the national community form hard incrustations, if they do not secede from it. It is a fact that the cinema is invaded by a particular category of maggotty Jews. Before the war, higher education experienced a certain monopoly by that specific category of Jews – the rational and sociological Jews. M. Léon Blum unwisely multiplied in his entourage that sub-set of politicos who are Jewish socialist politicos. It is the same way in which the guild of coal-merchants is flooded with Auvergnats, faculties of law with reactionary professors, primary schools with pacifist teachers, the customs service by moustachioed Corsicans, the Chamber with southern deputies, and governmental circles with the radical-socialist party. If the 'numerus clausus' is demanded for Frenchman of Jewish blood, we are requiring it for Auvergnats in trade, for Corsicans in the excise business, for lawyers in Parliament. . . . We are also demanding it for financial power in the control of newspapers and for their envoys in ministerial antechambers. If the 'numerus clausus' is required for the rabble, we require it for all the rabble. . . . French anti-Semitism has no content. It is only a pretext and a sham. It is not as a doctrine but as a pretext and sham that it must be exposed. It is no accident that it emanates from circles which want the synchronization of France and national-socialist Germany in a peace of shared guilt. It is, and it is nothing more than, a symptom of the slow nazification of the bourgeoisie. You do not cure the plague with cholera.[40]

In many respects this text is comparable to François Mauriac's. Like the latter, it is surprising in its blunders, here again made by an important personality in the Catholic world, of high moral stature and openly favourable to the Popular Front. The arguments are almost identical and the vocabulary used to plead whole-heartedly the cause of anti-Semitism is all the more surprising because of the strange connotations it reveals. Note first the constant resort to medical metaphors peculiar to the most reactionary organicist thought used primarily in the anti-Semitic discussions of the period. France is considered as 'an organism', the 'health' of which is 'endemically attacked'; the 'incrustation' of the Jews which almost medically forms them into a separate group; the 'Frenchmen of Jewish blood' who must be strongly defended; the 'maggotty' and consequently sick Jews, gnawed by worms, who have 'invaded' the cinema, and so on. These expressions are all closely related to the idea of the 'swarm' of Jews utilized by Mauriac to emphasize their precipitate haste when one of them has 'insinuated' himself into a certain sector. What we have here is pure Bernanos, this time used to serve thought which is democratic, anti-racist, respecting particularisms.

Next, let us emphasize that Mounier and Mauriac readily accepted, without taking the trouble to verify, the statements of the anti-Semitic press which unflaggingly denounced the dominant presence of Jews in the cinema and around Léon Blum. This is a crucial element: both Mauriac and Mounier took as gospel truth the anti-Semitic lucubrations uttered against Léon Blum, portraying him as the Jew who surrounded himself with a large number of co-religionists and not merely socialist leaders.[41]

In the same spirit, a man like Stanislas Fumet, who opposed anti-Semitism in the name of Catholicism, and took part in the resistance alongside none other than Mounier, nevertheless wrote a bewildering text barely distinguishable from the worst anti-Semitic prose of the period. He called for exclusion measures to be taken against the Jews, reminiscent of those applied shortly after 1940. In the bosom of this benevolent Catholic world, Vichy took place well before Vichy. In *Temps présent*, Stanislas Fumet thus condemned

> racism in the name of Catholicism . . . But the nations are justified in defending themselves from the excessive percentage of Israelites in the highest positions in the country. National susceptibilities, for example, are rightly alarmed when a Léon Blum calls on disproportionate participation by the Jewish element to form his ministry. It is this lack of discretion, this lack of tact, peculiar to a certain type of Judaism. . . . It is possible that the numerus clausus is not an arrangement to be rejected.[42]

This text is surprising on more than one count. If Mounier also emphasized the presence of Jews around Léon Blum and in the cinema – in his eyes far too large a number – he none the less at an early stage opposed the numerus clausus which Stanislas Fumet very surprisingly seemed to accept at the outset. But in his article Mounier made the following strange reservation, which we have already indicated: 'If the numerus clausus is demanded for the rabble, we demand it for all the rabble', a comment which can only leave the best-disposed reader perplexed. In addition, the parallel that Mounier drew between the Jews' 'incrustation' in the cinema and around Léon Blum and that of Auvergnats as coal-merchants or Corsicans as customs officers – or even . . . of reactionary professors in faculties of law – is no less disconcerting. If it seemed proven that, at that period at least, this type of situation had been created amongst coal-merchants or in the law faculties, nothing, outside anti-Semitic lucubrations, proved that this was the case as far as Blum's entourage was concerned. Lastly, this analogy is all the more inappropriate in that in France in the 1930s it was only Jews, and not Auvergnats, Corsicans and, even less, law professors, that *Je suis partout, Gringoire, Candide* and *L'Action française*, to mention only these journals, took as their daily target.

André Siegfried, founder of French political science and a declared adherent of the Christian movement, shared this view even after the Second World War, at a time when it was applied to Pierre Mendès France and frequently found in the writings of the worst anti-Semitic authors. For the famous author of *De la IIIe à la IVe République*, 'Jewish international and communizing influences are too easy' to discern in Pierre Mendès France's entourage.[43] Stanislas Fumet made his own the comments that are found in Gide's *Journal*, for example, about the alleged lack of tact or discretion of the Jewish 'race' and of Blum in particular.[44]

Emmanuel Mounier was careful to indicate in both the first and last sentence of his article, that he thought that anti-Semitism was entirely foreign in its origin[45] and affected a specific class rather than the nation as a whole. Is this not another way of reducing its significance in French society, at a time when passions were inflamed and when exclusion measures were already being carefully prepared which others would soon set in motion?

There remains the famous interview granted by Léon Blum in February 1937 to *Sept*, the Catholic weekly which appealed to the working-class world and was hostile to the Leagues. Blum declared: 'You ask me if I believe collaboration between the Catholics and the government of the Popular Front is possible? Certainly, I think it is possible. . . . And from the moment it becomes possible, would the Catholics not agree that it is desirable?'[46] The same issue of the Catholic paper made the following comments on this reply: 'If the interests of certain Popular Front initiatives and the reforms demanded by the Catholic social school actually do coincide, we see no reason not to give them our loyal support.' This interview had considerable repercussions: if the bishops did not condemn this reply – and some of them, like Cardinal Liénhart, even approved of it – the response from the Catholic Right was not long in coming. Philippe Henriot attacked this 'kiss of Judas'[47] and *France réelle* declared: 'Never yet has France been governed by a Judeo-masonic camarilla, allied with and the accomplice of revolutionaries, an anti-religious rabble if ever there was one. And that is what *Sept* takes account of, hears and endorses! Christian democracy has never before fallen into such base degradation.'[48]

THE NEW ALSACE-LORRAINE QUESTION

The incident which led to an explosion of anti-Semitic hatred in the heart of the Catholic world also dated from this period. It was learned that the Popular Front government was thinking of changing the educational system in Alsace-Lorraine by extending the school-leaving age to fourteen or fifteen, and imposing syllabuses identical to those in the rest of France, whilst retaining the bi-lingualism and religious education that these regions had preserved since the First World War.[49] Immediately the decks were cleared for action in departments where a certain anti-Semitic tradition persisted. On 12 March 1937

Canon Hincky, director-general of works in the diocese of Strasburg, wrote to *Tribune juive*: 'Catholics are not anti-Semites . . . but we note with indignation that every time since 1918 that our religious status has been attacked, an atheist Jew like Georges Weil, Grumbach, etc., is in the wings. Today, it is MM. Blum and Zay, Blumel and Moch. We will never bow down to dictatorship by a minority, that of atheist Jews.'[50] Things very rapidly worsened: for *Les Jeunes d'Alsace*, 'it was left to the first Jewish atheist President of the Council of the French Republic to offer Alsace a foul-smelling Jewish product. This nation of believers will fiercely and with all its strength prevent the hands of an atheist Jew removing the crucifix from our schools.'[51]

Although Léon Blum had written a letter to Monsignor Ruch confirming that he had no wish to impose secularism, anti-Semitic demonstrations broke out at Mulhouse and throughout Alsace-Lorraine.[52] Moreover, the ground had been prepared for them since 1936 by the wide distribution of anti-Jewish leaflets throughout eastern France, appealing for 'Catholic France to be saved from the domination of verminous and rapacious Jews'.[53] When visiting Strasburg to give a lecture, Madame Léon Brunschwicg, Under-Secretary of State for Education, met anti-Semitic students and could not make herself heard above their shouts of 'France for the French!', 'Down with Blum!'[54] For *Le Messin*, 'if an anti-Semitic wave swamps the country tomorrow, the instigator, Léon Blum, will be to blame'.[55]

The *Mulhouser Volksblatt*, very widely read by Alsace Catholics, gave vent to unbridled rage against the Jews, Blum and Moch;[56] while *La Rafale anti-juive* of Metz did not mince its words: 'No, Léon, old man, not this time. You make us sick, you are hated, you are asked to clear off. . . . Go away, dirty Jew, leave our land and go and find your brethren in Palestine.'[57] This same sheet, having changed its name and now called *La Tempête*, concluded: 'France is too good and too blind, the Jew wants to foist himself on it in order to suck its blood, paralyse it, destroy it. . . . France is not a Jew-Park nor a rubbish dump. . . . *La Tempête* is raging; it will see to that. . . . We wish M. Léon Blum a national or even international funeral, on condition that the obsequies take place as soon as possible.'[58]

The anti-Semitic statements which *La Nouvelle Voix d'Alsace et de Lorraine*, 'organ of militant Christians', had directed against Blum in particular since the turn of the century have already been quoted on several occasions. It had not lost its touch. As one of the main papers of the region – which testifies to the spread of anti-Semitism in certain provinces – it was the real leader of the struggle. It printed countless anti-Semitic pieces against Léon Blum. As early as April 1937, it had a headline 'France! Here is your master', and added: 'This is the Talmud in its worst applications. . . . The Blum government has shown its Jewish hand.'[59] This time, Catholics of all opinions seemed to reject the educational policy proposed by the Popular Front for those regions – using different arguments, of course. For example, *La Juste Parole*, which continued to lead a crusade against anti-Semitism, always bringing the thunderbolts of the extreme Right down on its head, also declared:

> We have been fully objective about M. Léon Blum's government. We have not hesitated to emphasize the good citizenship of the former President of the Council; we have corrected the fantastic figures released to the public of the Israelite colleagues he surrounded himself with; we have demonstrated the falsity of the ridiculous statements alleging his foreign origins – but we have also protested against the blunder he has committed in connection with the educational question in Alsace-Lorraine.[60]

Its editor, Oscar de Férenzy, who had been at the head of the struggle against anti-Semitism since the creation of this Catholic paper, suggested a subtle distinction, which he often made, between believing Jews, with whom Catholics of good will could get on, and atheist Jews, whom they could only reject, in the same way as they opposed all forms of atheism. For the philo-semitic editor of *La Juste Parole*, 'the common enemy of believing Christians and Jews is the militant atheist whether he be of Christian or Jewish origin'.[61] Since Léon Blum, an atheist Jew, seemed to be preparing to challenge the religious status of Alsace-Lorraine, *La Juste Parole* on this basis joined the Catholic groups and journals which, sometimes with anti-Semitic arguments, rebuffed his policy. It did not fall back on the most absurd of the anti-Semitic ravings, which had even been entertained by important personalities in the Catholic world, like François Mauriac, Emmanuel Mounier and Stanislas Fumet, however worthy and informed they were. Instead, *La Juste Parole*, unflagging advocate of the Jewish cause in the Catholic world, attacked the hydra which secularism always represented, and abandoned the defence of Léon Blum on this point, though without making use of anti-Semitic arguments.

In the crusade against the head of the Popular Front government, integralist Catholics readily appealed for help to Alsatian Jews who were also concerned at the changes in educational policy envisaged by the Popular Front government. *La Nouvelle voix d'Alsace et de Lorraine* generously commented: 'We are well aware that the old Jews of Alsace are trembling at this time. They know Blum's plans, they fear lest the blame rebound on them should they fail. But they are powerless to save either themselves or us.'[62] This is tantamount to saying that any means were acceptable to fight the plans of Léon Blum, submissive to 'enraged women, to fantastic Jewesses'.[63] Even Chief Rabbi Schwartz supported Monsignor Ruch in defence of the specific nature of Catholic education in Alsace-Lorraine, a guarantee that the teaching of Judaism would be maintained in the same conditions.[64] The Catholic paper, *Le Lorrain*, thanked M. Edmond Bloch, the nationalist Jewish leader, as well as the *consistoires* and rabbis of Alsace and Lorraine, for wanting to participate in the struggle to preserve the educational and religious status peculiar to the regions.[65]

Finally, we need to look at the visit Léon Blum paid to the nuncio's residence in February 1937 with his wife, François de Tessan and André Blumel, head of the President of the Council's private office. Blumel recalled that it 'had a bombshell effect. Three Jews and a heretic!'[66] As against this rapprochement, which caused a sensation, and also in spite of the many declarations by Church leaders in favour of the Popular Front's social laws, we should recall the absence, even at the end of 1938, of categorical condemnation of the persecution of the Jews in Germany.[67] Recall too that the Church rallied to the Vichy régime, and that the archbishops in the free zone declared on 5 September 1940: 'Without surrender, we want complete and sincere loyalty to be shown to the established power. We revere the head of state, etc.' Equally, it should not be forgotten that its declared hostility to racism did not prevent the Vatican from making known, through the intermediary of the French ambassador to the Holy See, Léon Bérard, that 'it will not seek a quarrel' with France over the statute on the Jews which had just come into force in Vichy France. Lastly, we must always remember the admirable courage of the Archbishop of Toulouse, Jules-Géraud Saliège, and the Bishop of Montauban, Pierre-Marie Théas, who openly protested against the persecution of Jews; and also the courage of hundreds of parish priests who took immense risks to save them. But we must not forget 'the almost absolute silence of the Catholic hierarchy in the face of Vichy's anti-Jewish legislation';[68] Philippe Henriot's funeral on 1 July 1944 at Notre-Dame when Cardinal Suhard gave absolution; and lastly, amongst so many contradictory actions, Cardinal Gerlier's declaration when he received representatives from the Lyons Jewish community in 1941: he reminded them of Léon Blum's activities, which he considered evil, and talked about 'expiation', even if he then in his turn raged at the crimes committed against the Jews.[69] These are all pointers which confirm the earlier analysis and highlight the ambiguities in the relationship between the Catholic world and Judaism, still in existence in the inter-war period and during Vichy – far from the crisis period when Drumont, *La Croix* and a large part of the clergy declaimed their hatred of the Jews. And these ambiguities had long crystallized around the personality of Léon Blum.

THE 'BLACK INTERNATIONAL' VERSUS PIERRE MENDÈS FRANCE

In actual fact, the head of the socialist government was not the only target of the varying degrees of hostility of part of the Catholic world. For example, when the possibility that Georges Mandel might accede to the Presidency of the Council was mooted, Aristide Briand said to one of his friends: 'France is a Catholic country . . . It would not accept an Israelite at the head of the government.'[70] In 1954, however, a similar situation again occurred when Pierre Mendès France came to power. As in the days of the Popular Front, the most contradictory reactions came to the surface in the Catholic world – but on a lesser scale: there had been the Nazi genocide in between.

The first serious incident soon broke out. An editorial in *L'Actualité religieuse dans le monde* openly lamented: 'How short a time it takes to change everything! M. de Gaspéri, champion of European unity, has just died suddenly. Neither M. Robert Schuman nor M. Georges Bidault any longer direct France's Foreign Affairs. What is more, they have been replaced in that crucial position by a Jewish freemason.'[71] That a quasi-official journal of the Catholic world should resurrect that old traditional anti-Semitic refrain nearly 60 years after Drumont and so soon after the end of the Second World War and the defeat of Vichy, provoked a violent reaction from *Esprit*. For Jean-Marie Domenach,

what is worrying about Mendès right from the start are his 'neutralist' arguments.... He will thus be a 'Jew', a 'freemason' and an 'enemy of the Church'. Another and much more serious problem lies behind these excesses, which are infrequent on the whole: that of the place of Catholics in the State ... the mass of French Catholics have not entirely acknowledged that theirs is a secular State.[72]

Embarrassed at having laid bare his most intimate convictions, the author of the editorial in *L'Actualité religieuse dans le monde* claimed in the following issue that his text had been erroneously cut, that 'this little incident' must not make us forget that 'anti-Semitism is to be banished from our thoughts'.[73]

But it did not stop there. *Le Pèlerin*, which printed 600,000 copies a day, acted very cautiously until the fall of the Mendès France government, though it opposed his policies, particularly on Indochina and the Algerian question. However, things changed rapidly. Suddenly, *Esprit*, always anxious to denouce the strong stench of anti-Semitism, sprang into action, reporting that *Le Pèlerin* 'distils malice in a glib and insinuating tone reminiscent of the scurrilous pamphlets of the religious party in the last century'.[74] On 13 February 1955 there was no longer room for doubt when *Le Pèlerin* insidiously noted that 'the blow has been struck by M. René Mayer who does not only have radicalism in common with M. Mendès France'.[75]

But times had changed and the anti-Jewish hatred, which was expressed so freely in Catholic circles at the time of the Dreyfus Affair, or to a lesser degree during the inter-war period, was no longer acceptable. Most of the large Catholic papers took care to dissociate themselves from it. *La Vie catholique illustrée*, 'whether its leader is called Mendès France or Durand, every Frenchman not blinded by partisan spirit will always approve the placing of bets which will benefit our country'.[76] In *Témoignage chrétien*, Antoine Goléa said he was 'staggered' when someone commented apropos Mendès France: 'He is a Jew, he has the head of a Yid.'[77]

La Croix welcomed Pierre Mendès France as favourably as it had Blum. On 16 June 1954 it thought that the new head of government 'spoke like a statesman.... As for his national sense, he has proved it in battle.'[78] A character sketch of Pierre Mendès France in the same issue made no mention of his Jewish origins. Again and again, it emphasized 'the courage' of the new

President of the Council,[79] most frequently approving of his policies, including that towards Indochina. A few discordant notes still remained, which a careful reader cannot fail to pick up. On 1 September 1954, for example, Pierre Limagne wrote: 'That man has confidence in the future of our country. I am convinced of that.... But the motives on which his hopes are founded include almost none of those which primarily inspire my own Christian optimism.'[80] Another portrait of the President of the Council at the end of 1954 contained the following phrases: 'He is an Israelite... his wife owned considerable interests in several bazaars in Cairo and Alexandria... courageous during the war... he has restored the sense of State... M. Mendès France is surrounded by advisers almost all of whom belong to circles of high finance and heavy industry... dynamic and tentacular capitalism.'[81] Here, once again, were the spectres of yore unexpectedly resurrected, the hidden vocabulary reappearing, surprisingly reminiscent of Drumont's legacy or the strange phrases of irreproachable Catholic personalities like Mounier or Mauriac, quoted above.

Truth to tell, something fishy was always going on behind the outwardly proclaimed good intentions. As already mentioned, the MRP was engaged in a real undermining process,[82] especially Pierre Henri Teitgen in his speeches to the MRP's XIIth national congress at Montrouge: 'At the time every observer noted the anti-Mendès frenzy, in short, the anti-Semitic frenzy which stirred the audience.'[83] The whole 'Black International'[84] seemed almost 'pathologically'[85] to be declaring what François Mauriac called 'the lowest form of religious war'.[86] The singer René Paul echoed this at the Théâtre des Deux Ânes:

> The street girls of the MRP
> Who do not like his virile way,
> Would like his skin, but dare not say,
> *He* can kick their arses any day!
> *He* is the Man!
>
> Bidault swills the Beaujolais,
> A magnum is nothing in a day.
> *He* chooses milk to fill his flask;
> It's the baby's bottle against the cask!
> But the eunuchs who sit in the House,
> Who clearly predominate, man or mouse,
> Will know how to act when the right times come,
> And who will then fall down on his bum?
> *He* is the man!
>
> One evening, you'll see, he'll catch his heel
> On the statutory banana peel,
> Édouard Herriot will sound the knell,
> And Schuman himself will ring the bell!

He will be buried and join his peers,
With everyone weeping crocodile tears,
The deputies will breath again
Because the greatest fear for them
Is the Man![87]

Had the song-writer been blessed with foresight, he might have made some reference to the debate, very largely concerned with North African policy, which preceded the vote of confidence on 5 February 1955, at the end of which the Mendès France government fell. M. Henri Bouret, an unaffiliated ex-MRP deputy, interrupted the head of government to express the hope that France would regain its true tradition, 'that of Christianity'. After the crucial vote which marked the government's defeat, and an unusual debate provoked by Pierre Mendès France who wanted to speak again amidst violent protests, a socialist deputy faced the opposition and shouted out: 'Down with the skull cap!'[88]

La Croix itself, which thus seemed to be taking up fluctuating standpoints, reported such goings on and unreservedly condemned them. As Émile Gabel pointed out, 'a deputy who is a Catholic should not be asked, as a Catholic, to leave a ministry dealing with contentious questions like the freeing of currency transactions, the Atlantic pact, the transfer of M. Bourguiba. Questions of pure policy, questions of the temporal city should not be turned into questions of faith.'[89] The actual pressure that certain Catholic circles constantly brought to bear on the Mendès France government from a purely religious point of view, could not be more explicit. *Esprit* showed particular awareness of this when it wrote as early as October 1954: 'Certain ecclesiastical circles have put strong pressure on "Christian" ministers to make them leave the government. Unofficial approaches, discreet advice, allusions dropped from the pulpit or in parish bulletins have awakened an old clamour reminiscent of the intrigue mounted against Léon Blum in 1936 and even of the anti-Semitic voice of Vichy anti-Semitism.'[90]

Had the old demons returned, once again, as at the worst moments in the recent history of French society, driving certain sectors of Catholicism towards more or less acknowledged anti-Semitism, true to Drumont, Daudet and all the Vichy regime's virtuous collaborators? This would appear to be so from even the most cursory glance at the Catholic-inspired, extreme right-wing press which expressed a theologically based Christian anti-Semitism in France at the end of the 1950s as vigorously as ever.[91] The imaginary dialogue between the Pope and Pierre Mendès France conceived by the still very active Xavier Vallat is convincing enough,[92] and so are the frequent allusions in *Rivarol* which explained Pierre Mendès France's foreign policy by the fact that 'there is not a single Catholic amongst his advisers'.[93] This weekly journal protested strongly against what it called 'the abandonment' of the Catholics of Vietnam: 'They are only Catholics, that is to say obscurantists. Ah! if they were Israelites, we would soon see the Joint Committee, the Great Orient, the PC, the MRPs,

Sartrécamus, *L'Étang modern*, Mauriac, signing petitions with both hands for them to be respected.... But Catholics... let them die.'[94]

Pierre Boutang rediscovered the zest of the extreme right-wing polemicists and did not mince his words. For him 'the office of Vergennes where Mendès has parked himself? It is a carpet dealer's counting house. The dream of taking hold of the eldest daughter of the Church, cherished a thousand times in centuries-old ghettos, is realized for the third time: Mendès after Blum and Rothschild–Mayer.'[95] And it added slightly later, in the same glib tone: 'Why is this dictatorship Jewish, I am asked? Because neither Mendès, nor Schreiber, nor Nora, nor Boris, nor Waiskopf-Gombault won first prize in catechism at church. They all have exotic expressions.'[96] This trend continued undisguised: closer to the present day, *Présent* raged in like manner against Laurent Fabius, 'the little monster, cold and icy... a monstrous stranger to the anguish of France... to the national and religious identity of France'.[97]

NOTES

1 There is an immense amount of literature on Christian anti-Semitism. See, for example, Rudolph Loewenstein, *Christians and Jews: A psychoanalytic study* (International Universities Press, New York, 1951); Jules Isaac, *Genèse de l'antisémitisme: Essai historique* (Calmann-Lévy, Paris, 1956); Léon Poliakov, *Les Juifs et notre histoire* (Flammarion, Paris, 1973); F. Lovsky, *L'Antisémitisme chrétien* (Editions Cerf, Paris, 1970); Freddy Raphael, 'Le Juif et le Diable dans la civilisation occidentale', *Social Compass*, 4 (1972).

2 É. Drumont, *La France juive* (Marpon & Flammarion, Paris, 1986), vol. 1, p. 298.

3 See Pierre Pierrard, *Juifs et catholiques français* (Fayard, Paris, 1970), pp. 61ff.

4 Pierre Sorlin, *'La Croix' et les Juifs* (Grasset, Paris, 1967), pp. 79 and 95.

5 Maurice Montuclard, *Conscience religieuse et démocratie: La démocratie chrétienne en France, 1891–1902* (Éditions Ouvrières, Paris, 1965), p. 137; Stephen Wilson, *Ideology and Experience: Anti-Semitism in France at the time of the Dreyfus Affair* (Associated University Press, London, 1982), ch. 14.

6 Georges Bernanos, *La Grande Peur des bien-pensants* (Le Livre de Poche, Paris, 1969), pp. 163 and 381. See Lazare Landau, *De l'aversion à l'estime: Juifs et catholiques en France de 1919 à 1939* (Edition Le Centurion, Paris, 1980), pp. 216ff.

7 A. Sidgwick, *The Ralliement in French Politics, 1890–1898* (Cambridge University Press, Cambridge 1965). Philippe Levillain, *Albert de Mun: Catholicisme français et catholicisme romain du syllabus au ralliement* (École français de Rome, Rome and Paris, 1983).

8 Émile Poulat, *Intégrisme et catholicisme intégral* (Casterman, Paris, 1969); Jean-Marie Mayeur, 'Catholicisme intransigeant, catholicisme social, démocratie chrétienne', *Annales*, March–April 1972.

9 André Metzger, *'La Croix' et la vie politique française, 1927–1939*, memoir of the Institut d'études politiques, Paris, 1970.

10 Pierrard, *Juifs et catholiques français*, ch. 5; Paul Christophe, *1936: Les catholiques et le Front populaire* (Éditions ouvrières, Paris, 1986).

11 Quoted by Christophe, *1936*, p. 50.

12 Henri Noguères, *La Vie quotidienne en France au temps du Front populaire, 1935–1938* (Hachette, Paris, 1977).

13 Aline Coutrot and François Dreyfus, *Les Forces religieuses dans la société française* (A. Colin, Paris, 1966), p. 191.
14 René Rémond, *Les Catholiques, le communisme et les crises, 1929–1939* (A. Colin, Paris, 1960), pp. 137–42, 149–55.
15 Quoted by René Rémond, 'L'évolution du journal "La Croix" et son rôle auprès de l'opinion catholique, 1919–1939', *Bulletin de la Société d'histoire Moderne*, 12th series, 7.
16 *La Croix*, Avignon, 2 Oct. 1927, Fond Léon Blum, FNSP.
17 *La Croix*, 18 June and 3 Aug. 1936.
18 Ibid., 10 and 12 May 1936.
19 Ibid., 22 Sept. and 31 Aug. 1938.
20 *Études*, 5 June 1936.
21 *L'Aube*, 16 May and 7 June 1936. In *L'Aube* of 14 May 1936, Georges Hourdin none the less declared: 'I am not unaware of the virtues of the socialist leader, shrewd amongst the shrewd ... but he has not got a strong enough voice ... he lacks power.' On *L'Aube* in general, see Françoise Mayeur, *L'Aube: Étude d'un journal d'opinion, 1932–1940* (A. Colin, Paris, 1966).
22 *Esprit*, 1 June 1936.
23 *L'Action française*, 9 March 1926.
24 *Le Défi*, 20 March 1938. In Feb. 1944, *Cahier Jaune-Revivre* was continually worried about the desire shown by the Jews, including Léon Blum, to 'transform destroyed cathedrals into synagogues'.
25 *Cahier jaune*, Jan. 1943.
26 *L'Ami du peuple*, 1 June 1937.
27 *Charivari*, 12 April 1935.
28 *Conquête de la France*, Nov.–Dec. 1936.
29 *Contre-Révolution*, July 1938.
30 *Archives nationales*, F7 13983.
31 *Archives nationales*, F7 12961.
32 On 21 Feb. 1937, for example, after a ball at the Moulin de la Galette, organized by the PSF, the following scene was performed: 'Blum is dead. He introduces himself to St Peter in heaven and is sent to hell; the devil refuses to let him in, saying: "You have created a Soviet hell in France, go back to it." Blum goes away looking embarrassed; he meets a young PSF who takes him back to the devil. He asks him where Karl Marx is. The devil shows him and he asks Marx the following question: "Was it you who wrote 'Capital'?" "Yes", answers Karl Marx. "All right, then, here's the interest on it," says the young PSF, pointing to Léon Blum' (*Archives nationales*, F7 12966).
33 Letter reprinted in *Bulletin du Centre de documentation et de vigilance*, no. 28 (8 April 1937), and also by *L'Univers israélite*, 23 April 1937.
34 Letter reprinted in *Bulletin du Centre de documentation et de vigilance*, no. 28 (8 April 1937), and also by *L'Univers israélite*, 23 April 1937. See also *La Juste Parole*, 20 April 1937.
35 *Temps présent*, 11 Feb. 1938.
36 See the analysis by Philippe Burin, *La dérive fasciste: Doriot, Déat, Bergery, 1933–1945* (Le Seuil, Paris, 1986), p. 238.
37 Claude Mauriac, 'Réponse à B. Lecache', *La Flèche*, 28 Oct. 1938.
38 Zeev Sternhell, *Ni droite ni gauche: L'idéologie fasciste en France* (Le Seuil, Paris, 1983), p. 301.
39 On this discussion, see ibid.; Michel Winock, *Histoire politique de la revue 'Esprit'* (Le Seuil, Paris, 1975); John Hellmann, *Emmanuel Mounier and the New Catholic Left, 1932–1950* (University of Toronto Press, Toronto, 1981); Zeev Sternhell, 'Emmanuel Mounier et la contestation de la démocratie libérale dans la France des années trente', *Revue française du*

science politique, Dec. 1984; for him too, 'in this way Mounier is disseminating certain ideas, and he has political reflexes common to both fascists and non-fascists, like himself, who regard the fascist struggle against the established order with varying degrees of sympathy' (p. 1144). See also the revised edition of *Ni droite ni gauche* (Complexe, Brussels, 1987); Étienne Borne, 'Un Mounier hypothétique', *Revue française de science politique*, Oct. 1985; and for a general presentation of the arguments of both sides, but which still runs counter to the views of Sternhell and Hellmann, see John Wright, 'Emmanuel Mounier, *Esprit* and Vichy, 1940–1944: ideology and anti-ideology', in Roderick Kedward and Roger Austin (eds), *Vichy France and the Resistance: Culture and ideology* (Croom Helm, London, 1985).

40 *Le Voltigeur français*, 1 March 1939.

41 This was also the case with *La Juste Parole* which warmly defended the Jews, and Léon Blum in particular, but still stated: 'Today we will make one criticism of M. Léon Blum: that he has surrounded himself with a general staff which includes so many of his co-religionists that many far-sighted Israelites are the first to regret it. If the indications of the antisemitic press are correct . . .' (*La Juste Parole*, 20 Jan. 1937).

42 *Temps présent*, 9 Sept. 1938. In its issue of 22 April 1938, the same paper condemned the special issue of *Je suis partout*.

43 André Siegfried, *De la IIIe a la IVe République* (Grasset, Paris, 1956), p. 172.

44 In April 1938, André Gide reported on a lecture by Maritain on the Jews and anti-Semitism, and concluded: 'The question is not religious but racial. Nothing can be done about that. . . . The Jews contribute a feeling for justice. . . . I would like to see Maritain concerning himself more with this positive side of the contribution of the Jewish race' (*Nouvelle revue française*, 1 April 1938).

45 In the same spirit, in *L'Aube*, 1 March 1939, Georges Bidault, who courageously fought anti-Semitism, congratulated E. Mounier on his article, without pointing out its ambiguities, and in *L'Europe nouvelle* attacked *Je suis partout* very harshly, stating that '*Je suis partout* thinks and feels like Hitler. . . . Hitler's propaganda is impotent when it appears without a mask. But under the mask of French nationalism, it can still do damage. That is why we have torn off the mask' (*L'Europe nouvelle*, 19 Aug. 1939).

46 *Sept*, 19 Feb. 1937.

47 *Renaissance 37*, 1 March 1937. Quoted by Aline Coutrot, *Un courant de la pensée catholique, l'hebdomadaire 'Sept' (March 1934–August, 1937)* (Cerf, Paris, 1961), p. 279. Aline Coutrot analyses all the reactions aroused by Blum's interview.

48 *France réelle*, 24 Feb. 1937. Quoted by Rémond, *Les Catholiques, le communisme et les crises, 1929–1939*, p. 234. The author presents a large number of articles both in favour and against *Sept*'s initiative (pp. 230–52).

49 Jean-Marie Mayeur, 'Une bataille scolaire: les catholiques alsaciens et la politique scolaire du gouvernement du Front Populaire', *Cahiers de l'Association inter-universitaire de l'Est*, 1962, pp. 85–101.

50 *Centre de documentation et de vigilance*, BAIU, Bulletin no. 24. *Tribune juive's* response is clear: 'As soon as civil equality is recognized, it is also illogical to investigate a politician's social and religious origins. Politically, there are only fellow citizens'. On this affair, see Christophe, *1936*, pp. 174–80.

51 *Les Jeunes d'Alsace*, 7 Feb. 1937, quoted in *Centre de documentation et de vigilance*, Feb. 1937, nos 22 and 23. The national press also joined in: for *Choc*, 'it is hard to suppose that M. Léon Blum, whose family crossed Alsace during its migration, should know nothing about the history and the men of Alsace and Lorraine. The idiocy of his attitude to the recovered provinces must therefore be ascribed to hatred – which has been of the strongest – to ethnic fanaticism and

also, it must be said, to a neuraesthenia growing stronger by the day' (18 Feb. 1937).
52 *Centre de documentation et de vigilance*, no. 25 (11 March 1937).
53 Ibid., no. 51.
54 Ibid., 4 March 1937.
55 *Le Messin*, 2 Feb. 1936; quoted in *Centre de documentation et de vigilance*, 4 March 1937.
56 Quoted by *Centre de documentation et de vigilance*, 4 Feb. 1937.
57 *La Rafale anti-juive*, 10 Dec. 1938.
58 *La Tempête*, organ of the anti-Jewish Front, 8 Jan. 1938.
59 *La Nouvelle Voix d'Alsace et de Lorraine*, 17 April 1937.
60 *La Juste Parole*, 20 April 1939.
61 *La Juste Parole*, 5 Feb. 1937. In its issue of 20 Jan. 1937, this journal considered that the leader of the Popular Front, 'should have foreseen the attacks that this would provoke and which are affecting all the Jews of France to a greater or lesser degree, even those furthest away from M. Blum's political ideas'.
62 *La Nouvelle Voix d'Alsace et de Lorraine*, 2 April 1938. See also the issues of 4 and 11 June 1938.
63 In its issue of 4 June 1938, this journal wrote: 'Léon Blum has always been manipulated by excited women, fanatical Jewesses. There is something of the female, the hysteric, about Blum, a sort of rottenness and breakdown.'
64 *Centre de documentation et de vigilance*, 27 Feb. 1937.
65 Quoted by ibid., 4 March 1937.
66 Pierre Renouvin and René Rémond (eds), *Léon Blum, chef de gouvernement* (Presses de la Fondation national des sciences politiques, Paris, 1981), p. 166.
67 Alain Fleury, *'La Croix' et l'Allemagne, 1930–1940* (Cerf, Paris, 1986), pp. 132ff.
68 Pierrard, *Juifs et catholiques français*, p. 297. See Louis Allen, 'Jews and Catholics', and Bill Halls, 'Catholicism under Vichy: A study in diversity and ambiguity', both in Kedward and Austin (eds), *Vichy France and the Resistance*. And above all, *La France et la question juive, 1940–1944: La politique de Vichy, l'attitude des Églises et des mouvements de Résistance*, a collective work published under the aegis of the *Centre de documentation juive contemporaine* (Sylvie Messinger, Paris, 1981).
69 See Jacques Duquesne, *Les Catholiques français sous l'occupation*, new edn (Grasset, Paris, 1986), pp. 54, 244, 252, 257 and 352.
70 Quoted in John Sherwood, *Georges Mandel and the Third Republic* (Stanford University Press, Stanford, Conn., 1970), p. 174.
71 *L'Actualité religieuse dans le monde*, 1 Sept. 1954.
72 Jean-Marie Domenach, 'Mendès, les catholiques et la politique', *Esprit*, Oct. 1954.
73 *L'Actualité religieuse dans le monde*, 15 Sept. 1954.
74 *Esprit*, Sept. 1954.
75 *Le Pèlerin*, 13 Feb. 1955.
76 *La Vie catholique illustrée*, 1 Aug. 1954.
77 *Témoignage chrétien*, 25 June 1954.
78 *La Croix*, 16 June 1954.
79 See, for example, *La Croix*, 24 June 1954 and 18 June 1955, in which it defends Mendès France against an attack by *Pravda*, considering that Mendès France was, on the contrary, continuing the work of Maurice Schumann.
80 *La Croix*, 1 Sept. 1954.
81 *La Croix*, 30 Dec. 1954.
82 See Robert Buron, *Les Dernières Années de la IVe République* (Plon, Paris, 1968).
83 Michel Launay, 'La renaissance de l'antisémitisme sous Mendès France', unpublished article,

p. 26. See the file made by PMF, 'Réfutations, insultes Teitgen', *Archives privées Marie-Claire Mendès France*. On Pierre Henri Teitgen's anti-Semitism, real or otherwise, with regard to Pierre Mendès France, see *Le Monde*, 29 Oct. 1982, and P. H. Teitgen's reply, *Le Monde*, 24 Nov. 1982. René Rémond considered that the animosity to Mendès France in Catholic circles was aimed 'less at the Jew than at the former freemason' (interview IHTP). See also, Georges Gombault, 'La haine déferle: Mendès France comme Léon Blum et Combes', *Le Droit de vivre*, 30 Sept. 1954, which describes what it calls the hatred of the 'Vatican party'.

84 *Aux Écoutes du Monde*, 26 Nov. 1954.
85 Alexander Werth, *La France depuis la guerre, 1944–1957* (Gallimard, Paris, 1957), p. 561. See also, Pierre Olivier Lapie, *De Léon Blum à de Gaulle* (Fayard, Paris, 1971), p. 579. In *Témoignage chrétien*, Edmond Michelet asks: 'Is it an exaggeration to claim that some people who say they are good Christians not so long ago cunningly exploited this diffuse anti-Semitism (Poujade's), appealing to the most confused popular instincts, against Mendès France?' (*Témoignage chrétien*, 16 Jan. 1956).
86 Quoted by the *Bulletin de nos communautés*, 14 Jan. 1955.
87 Quoted by *Combat*, 18 Nov. 1954.
88 Pierre Mendès France, *Oeuvres complètes*, vol. 3 (Gallimard, Paris, 1986), pp. 726 and 731.
89 *La Croix*, 15 Sept. 1954. See also the article by Émile Gabel, 28 Oct. 1954.
90 *Esprit*, Oct. 1954, p. 496.
91 See 'Racisme, antisémitisme et xénophobie en France', *Après-demain*, no. 8 (Sept. 1958).
92 *Aspects de la France*, 21 Jan. 1955.
93 *Rivarol*, 23 Sept. 1954. See also, for example, the issue of 23 Feb. 1956.
94 Ibid., 25 Dec. 1954.
95 *Aspects de la France*, 25 June 1956.
96 Ibid., 1 Oct. 1954.
97 *Présent*, 6 Sept. 1985.

9
Bloated Capitalist and Little Revolutionary

The conflict between the bloated rich and the little man runs right through the history of contemporary France, more or less unchanged, irrespective of the nature of the social actors involved. This myth has proved so powerful that it shapes the most varied ideologies and, in one form or another, always cements the unity of the people. Its function, both on the extreme Right and the extreme Left, remains constant: to mobilize the little man dominated by the Wall of Money, big capital, the 200 families and stateless capitalism, thought to be so powerful as to spread like an octopus over the whole land. The people – innocent of all sin – appear as the eternal victims of the bloated rich, who are veritable demons, greedy, parasitic and depraved beings whose power is all the greater because it remains concealed, distant and impalpable. In this sense, the myth of the bloated rich is one of the most reliable ferments of chauvinistic and xenophobic nationalism.

Although its more general version does not necessarily imply anti-Semitism, it is never very far away since the almost inevitable slide into anti-Semitism has the virtue of allowing only native bloated rich to be reintegrated, conferring on them, despite everything and *in extremis*, the natural innocence of the little man. Every meeting, every national union, every reconciliation policy, between classes or between believers and atheists, potentially runs the risk of ending in anti-Semitism, so greatly does rejection of the Jews facilitate embraces and reconciliation all round between Frenchmen sprung from a common soil, united by a similar cult of the land and the dead, rejecting with one voice the Antichrist, bearer of all perversions.[1]

If the Jews did not exist they would have to be invented. Moreover, it is well known that hatred of Jews can be transmitted from generation to generation in societies from which they have been excluded for several centuries. This means that a unifying anti-Semitism very often hides behind the myth of the bloated rich. None the less, though there is everything to be gained on either side of the political chessboard from collective mobilization against the bloated rich, often identified with the Jews the better to mark their position external to the nation, the resemblance between Right and Left seems to break down when the contrary and complementary myth is considered, that of the revolutionary little man. This time, the various right-wing groups have the almost exclusive privilege of identifying the revolutionaries with Jews casting about for upheavals likely to increase their power. Formidable demons with the most macchiavellian strategy, the Jews are not then depicted as bloated capitalists exploiting the naïveté and productive power of the kindly little men of France – a theme on which supporters of the most contradictory ideologies often agree – they are also depicted as revolutionary little men, just as internationalist as the bloated capitalist, skilled in the most radical subversions carried out in the name of socialist ideologies, of which every Frenchman, bloated rich or little man, suffers the consequences. They are capitalists in the eyes of both the extreme Right and the extreme Left, but it is only supporters of the established order who view them as dangerous, Marxist-inspired revolutionaries, whereas the Left often sees them as false revolutionaries in the service of Jewish international capital.

One might smile and treat lightly such absurdities which have no historical or sociological basis, and discount the extreme social diversity of the Jews attached to the synthesis of Franco-Judaism. In reality, it mattered little that French Jews only exceptionally had access to big capital and that the majority of them had long been wary of revolutionary doctrines which ran the risk of damaging their status as state Jews, emancipated and equal before the law. From Drumont till today, it is self-evident that they alternately donned the garb of bloated capitalist and little revolutionary, so greatly do these myths manipulate class relationships and facilitate the resort to strategies of union and togetherness.

That the Jews appear as bloated holders of parasitic capital *par excellence*, sharing none of the virtues of the working class, is one of the best-established myths of traditional anti-Semitism. Economic anti-Semitism and its worn-out nightmares are lost in the mists of time. They have the advantage of proclaiming in advance the innocence of the real holders of economic power, who do in fact form part of every social system and whose role is legitimized by the system of values which ensures social control. In France in the modern period, the myth came to the surface, as has already been noted, in the writings of socialist-inspired authors, such as Proudhon, Leroux, Fourier and Toussenel, as well as in those of reactionary or radically right-wing conservative theorists, such as Drumont or Barrès. It is also found in the writing of enlightened Catholic authors, such as Léon Bloy and Georges Bernanos, activated by an obscene and unnatural anti-Semitism which no theological dialectic, however subtle, can render legitimate in any degree whatsoever.

Supported by such a long and constant tradition, fed by strongly contrasting ideological sources, it is hardly surprising that the golden age of economic anti-Semitism comes at times of crisis because it serves to diminish the internal logic of the crisis. In the 1930s, when national unity was threatened by social confrontation – diverse economic and cultural conflicts provoked street demonstrations in Paris and the large provincial towns to such an extent that they seemed uncontrollable[2] – the anti-Semitic myths of bloated capitalists and little revolutionaries provided an extremely useful vent for insatiable internal hatreds.

FROM THE RIGHT WING

While all the left-wing factions joined in a relentless attack on the 200 families, those new feudal lords who had to be conquered and hurled down from their new Bastille, the Right, once the Popular Front's victory had been announced, used the same metaphor and concentrated its fire on Léon Blum. Everything was now clear: the bloated capitalist and (or) the little revolutionary was the new head of government: Jew, bourgeois and revolutionary, all in one. Moreover, it had long held this key to every mystery since, as early as 1920, the inevitable Léon Daudet argued that:

Léon Blum's role consists of serving as a link between the international of the rich, between anonymous, roving wealth and the workers' international. Those of his race have always known how to put the proletariat's demands into revolutionary shares and long-term debentures.... Israel, in the person of Blum, proposes to liquidate the land of France, to throw it into the hooked claws of the bankers of New York, Berlin and Frankfurt.[3]

The socialist leaders of the time were proposing to institute a tax on capital. By contrast, frenzied rumours were already circulating about Léon Blum's supposedly prodigious private wealth, the unparalleled luxury of his famous silver plate, mentioned so frequently, even after Vichy. Nevertheless, it was Léon Daudet, whose name recurs so often in this anthology of historic anti-Semitic idiocy, who helped a great deal to launch this accusation before it went the rounds of the drawing-rooms and thatched cottages.

Blum, speaking against capital, 'Das Kapital' of his master Karl Marx, is probably regaling himself with thoughts of his silver plate.... I ask myself: will Blum melt it down when his tax on capital has been voted through, in order to distribute it to the poor? Because it is not possible to be both Plutus and Savonarola at the same time; a choice has to be made ... it is important to establish a counter-plan, French this time, not Hebrew, which will aim exclusively at the concentrations of capital used for speculation, nomad money.[4]

As early as 1920, the essential elements of the anti-Semitic version of the myth were thus already in place. Native capital was exonerated and the need stressed for the union of all Frenchmen from all classes of society who were anxious to establish a healthy system of production in accordance with the national norms that had been ruined both by stateless capital and by its chosen instrument, the workers' international. 'Little Blum, Jew of silver plate and the Council of State',[5] in reality never gave up trying 'to crush the little man and bring about the union of the bloated rich'.[6]

This model would never change. In 1938, when the second Blum government embarked on a reform of public finance again involving a levy on capital and a general increase in income tax (this was the task of the Under-Secretary of State at the Treasury, Pierre Mendès France, and also of Georges Boris who was later close to Mendès France when he came to power), the anti-Semitic press exploded. An example of its work was an extraordinary strip cartoon drawn by Ralph Soupault, published by *Gringoire* and inspired by Pieds Nickelés: 'Croquignol [i.e., Blum] disguises himself as a "great Frenchman" and helps himself to the safe. Finding this inadequately stocked and afraid that he will not be able to have another go at "National Defence", he goes back to the old dodge of the "ceiling breaker", and co-opts a magnificent assistant pompously named Mendès France.'[7] Historians, it seems, have never shown any interest in this strip cartoon. Yet it is one of the very rare drawings in which Léon Blum and Pierre Mendès France are associated in the same anti-Semitic caricature, depicting them both as fearsome robbers of French wealth. However, there is one other which, strangely enough, appears to be equally unknown; this shows Pierre Mendès France literally picking the pockets of an innocent little Frenchman, while Léon Blum, still motivated by war-like enthusiasm, delicately places an infantry-man's helmet on his head.[8]

It would not be practicable to quote all the material at our disposal to illustrate this myth of the Jew as a bloated capitalist. There are too many texts, speeches and even commonplace, everyday comments, picked up and referred to by police reports at one time or another in the political life of contemporary France. For Hector Ghilini, 'the attraction of the golden calf explains Blum's slide towards the Wall of Money ... communism was achieved by Jewish banking',[9] consequently running the risk of unleashing an anti-Semitic movement feared by 'certain bloated Jews'.[10] Enamoured of contradiction, Pierre Gaxotte exclaimed: M. Blum is rich ... he is the damned of the earth ... he is a contradiction made into a man';[11] a contradiction so sharp that 'he represents both the workers' international and the financial international, the latter employing the former as an instrument to serve its designs for world domination. And that is why M. Blum has so strong a hatred of good Frenchmen!'[12] *Candide* gave another version of this contradiction: 'In the Chamber, M. Léon Blum says to the bourgeois: "I hate you!" In the Palais, he says to capital: "Be off with you, I don't hate you at all." '[13] As we know, these pleasant little jokes ended in tragedy, when an unsustainable version appeared at the time when collaboration, ardently desired by so many, was finally established. Witness the following dialogue published by *La Vie nationale*, a new paper, as early as 3 July 1940. A character named Blumenfeld is talking to

Karfunkelstein, a pseudonym created, it will be recalled, by anti-Semites to illustrate Blum's supposed name: 'But there'll be a boom, a bick boom, Karfunkelstein! You'll see, vun can schtill make money, a lot of money vith dese gut little Chermans.'[14]

These stereotyped representations – typical of specifically French economic antisemitism – were unflaggingly reproduced, time after time whenever a Jew, or a person with Jewish connections, however tenuous, and claiming kinship with left-wing ideals, undertook national responsibilities at the head of the state. In 1955, according to Henry Coston whose vision of the world had hardly changed since the inter-war period and Vichy, 'the Lazare Frères bank which defends the permanent interests of Judeo-Britannic high finance in Paris, London and New York... supports M. Pierre Mendès France's political activity'.[15] A leaflet aimed at small tradesmen and distributed in Normandy at the time of the 1956 legislative elections, declared that 'you know the man who is most determined to ruin you, he is the millionaire Pierre Isaac Mendès France, General Agent of International High Finance.... We have had quite enough of being governed by a cohort of foreigners.... A vote against Mendès, the tool of High Banking, is a vote for France.'[16] In 1958 this 'son of wealth'[17] appeared as the natural ally of 'big capital which is subsidizing Anti-France',[18] according to Georges Virebeau, another astonishingly long-lived anti-Semite. (He had already written under the Blum government that 'the 200 families, whom we don't mention, or the 200 tribes'[19] dominated France.) In fact, such associations were legion. For example, a lampoon, unfortunately completely forgotten, by the philosopher Pierre Boutang, who expounded the most violent anti-Semitism, compared Joinovici, a formidable smuggler who swam from one social milieu to another, to Léon Blum and Pierre Mendès France.[20]

Fraternité française saw Mendès France as a pillar of the 'stateless capitalism threatening France', 'bastion of Christianity'.[21] The Poujadist movement proved particularly quick to adopt a vicious economic anti-Semitism. A few years after the end of the war, it distributed a leaflet in the streets of Paris, reading as follows:

> Honest Frenchmen! Frenchmen of old stock.
> Reach for your torches.... Set fire to
> Jewish money, it means poverty for everyone else.
> Don't buy anything from Jews any more.
> Track down their rackets, Build up your files.
> Know that Mendès (called France) has just sold Paris
> To international Jewry.[22]

Soon afterwards, Laurent Fabius who, according to the amiable report in *Figaro-Magazine*, 'stinks of gracious living',[23] was shown 'involved in big deals... and will soon experience the martyrdom of the fat cats'.[24] Described as a 'socialist in silk pyjamas and alpaca suits... Rolls at hand',[25] he was none the less alleged to 'know how to make people forget he was a great bourgeois'.

The press had no hesitation in publishing a photograph showing the new socialist Prime Minister sitting negligently at table in state dress, before a plate that looked very much as if it were made of silver.[26] Since he also put into operation an important fiscal reform affecting great wealth, he aroused the anger of the well-off bourgeoisie at the very time when, as *Minute* again pointed out, 'so many rich men had not been seen in the seat of power since Blum'.[27] We have come full circle.

For the Right wing, these bloated Jewish owners of capital also slipped into the garb of little prophetic revolutionaries in order to preserve their power in perpetuity by any means available. Naturally, on the model of Crémieux,[28] both Léon Blum and Pierre Mendès France were likened to Moses, the prophet of the Jewish people. For *L'Émancipation nationale*, the head of the Popular Front, a new 'Marxist Jehovah', was taking up the torch of 'Moses, his illustrious ancestor'.[29] Henry Coston later repeated this idea, this time in respect of Pierre Mendès France, 'the Moses of the French Left',[30] many of whose actions Laurent Fabius, the 'demiurge messiah', imitated in his turn ... [31]

Since he openly claimed allegiance to humanist socialism in this period of harsh confrontations, it was primarily Léon Blum whom his anti-Semitic opponents ceaselessly associated with Moses in order to discredit his tactics, which they regarded as alien to French traditions. At a meeting organized by the Comité antijuif de France in the Salle Wagram on 4 June 1937, Bietrix, deputy for the Doubs, let his imagination run wild. According to him 'the seven plagues of Egypt are as nothing beside this régime. . . . Léon Blum thinks he is the Messiah and advances towards the clouds of Sinai surrounded by his 35 acolytes'. Inspired by so beautiful a flight of oratory, the excited audience shouted, 'France for the French! Long live Maurras!'[32] *Paris-Social*, equally enamoured of biblical history, ironically asked whether 'M. Blum can make messianic manna fall from the sky and immediately fill the ecstatic beaks of the new crusaders of the Popular Front'.[33] As Léon Guerden again notes, 'we see the vengeful flame of biblical prophets light his eyes. If he possessed Moses's supernatural power, the waters of the Seine would immediately divide to swallow up the elegant Marquet and little Déat.'[34]

The many lampooners, who wrote anonymously or under pseudonyms, also quite naturally drew their inspiration from this parallel when they pretended to address Léon Blum as co-religionists. We shall quote two of them here. In 1938 G. de La Fouchardière recounted the fable of the Jew who came from afar, attracted by the power which, it was said, Léon Blum had managed to seize in France. He left Palestine, crossed Germany, then Bolshevik Russia and finally arrived without mishap in the land of the 'new prophets: he is called Léon Blum ... from the heights of the mountain of the Law, he curses the Golden Calf and casts anathema on the Rich'.[35] In the same vein an anti-Semitic author produced a piece in the name of Jacob Nathan Hourwitz of such menacing frenzy that even today it leaves the reader speechless. This imaginary Hourwitz was supposed to have sent a long letter from the USSR to his 'dear Léon Blum' giving him some practical advice on consolidating his power in France. The effectiveness of this advice was well-guaranteed in that it had already been put into practice in the USSR a long time ago. He should, for example, conduct 'experiments in vivisection on the most inveterate reactionaries, a source of marvellous progress. . . . Does this idea not bear the grandiose mark of our Israelite and socialist spirit, both practical and mystical at the same time?'[36] The author even strongly advised experiments in cannibalism; and the institution of 'proletarian butchers' shops' producing 'corned man' where 'tanned bourgeois skin' could be carefully cured for fancy leather goods; and utilizing burnt bones for the manufacture of beetroot juice and the viscera for animal feed.[37] That it was possible to give vent to such ravings and to find a publisher for them in France in the 1920s says much about the hatred of Jews which was already concentrated on the person of Léon Blum. Eichmann's elder brothers were now in place – well before his time and in republican France – inventing the recipes of a nightmare which, with the help of the dignitaries of the Nazi regime, he alone would have the privilege of transforming into reality.[38]

That the workers' movement should recognize itself in Léon Blum revolted the propagandists of anti-Semitic theses. They saw him as a Kerensky[39] or associated his name, and sometimes Pierre Mendès France's too, with the names of other Jewish leaders of the working-class world: Marx, Trotsky, Rosa Luxemburg and Bela Kun.[40] In their eyes, these people formed less a workers' international than an 'international of blood',[41] exploiting the body of workers. In short, Blum was 'greedy for workers' blood'.[42] To put an end to the anomaly of the working class rallying to Blum, which they found shocking, they did everything possible to detach the workers from him so that the workers would cleave to their nationalist vision, as at the time of the 'yellow movement' in the past when some workers sympathized with the employers' ideas. The star performers of anti-Semitism hoped to demonstrate that the working class was radically different from a man like Léon Blum whom they ceaselessly depicted as a false prophet acting in the name of Jewish capital, and in reality scorning the interests of the sincere, naïve, little French workers. As *Gringoire* forcibly put it, 'if the sound and healthy people of France knew the perversion of that woolly mind, with which they have nothing in common, neither blood nor class, nor history, if the worker in the suburbs knew M. Léon Blum, he would understand the mistake he is making today and realize that he has been wounded to the quick.'[43]

The masses could do nothing except turn away from the man who despised them so much,[44] the man who, as Bucard publicly howled in front of his militia men at a meeting at the Vel' d'Hiv, 'pretends to personify their working class aspirations while really serving the interests of his race'.[45] Here again, the extempore poet does not hesitate to join in the fun, denouncing the Popular Front government's fiscal policy, allegedly conducted exclusively in the Jews' interest:

> I have again forgotten to tell
> That this super-tax, so brilliant and fine
> The need for which we knew full well
> Was not an ordinary tax off the line.
> To our squirming Blum, it brings joy I fear,
> It is the tax of the Popular Front,
> It's supposed to make life a bit more ... dear.
> And the 200 families bear the brunt.
> You can't understand, for Heaven's sake,
> The policy of these half-witted kids,
> What they primarily seek to take
> Is bread from the French to feed the Yids.[46]

Whatever the argument employed, horror was never far away, and the historian can only pause each time before setting such infamies down on paper. The prize undeniably belongs to Henry Robert Petit and Jules Blacas. For the one, 'the deceived worker watches all Blum Léon's circumcised co-religionists, placed in the most fruitful and profitable positions of command, pass by in sumptuous limousines with lackeys in livery'.[47] For the other,

> Léon Blum, called Judas, native of Palestine ... is the complete traitor who turns your skin into money and gambles on your failure or your blood in the cesspool of shit of the international banks, enemies of your country.... French workers, prove your commonsense, understand that you are in the hands of cynical profiteers whose victim or dupe you are ... shake off all the Blums hooked to your shoulders, who are sucking your blood like a tic or a flea. He is not French! He stinks of the ghetto and he hates you.[48]

As has been seen, this theme of blood constantly reappears in anti-Semitic ravings, whether they are concerned with sexuality, war, the connection with the soil or with the working class. It is the crucial element in an anti-Semitism with a radical or religious (the blood of Christ) base, which in the last resort misrepresents the Jews precisely by excluding them from that community of blood which they want to appropriate so that they may integrate into it or destroy it in the name of universalist ideologies. From Blum to the present day, it is therefore no surprise to find it repeated so often in the writings of those inspired by the traditions of the radical Right, which Barrès himself employed in his myth of 'the land and the dead'. Even today the extreme Right in contemporary France still harks back to this theme in, for example, its polemic with Laurent Fabius's government.[49]

FROM THE LEFT WING

The anti-Semitic tradition in France, as elsewhere, was also built on a galaxy of socialist-inspired authors. From Proudhon to Fourier, Toussenel and Benoît

Malon, anti-Semitism spread insidiously in the ranks of the working-class Left in the nineteenth century, as has been seen. We also know that, in the name of anti-capitalism and the struggle against the bourgeoisie, the leaders, like the Guesdist or Blanquist militants, sometimes joined the most militant anti-Dreyfusards in denouncing the bourgeois order which, to them, the Jew Dreyfus embodied.

But although both Right and Left supported fascist ideology beyond the turn of the century, from the inter-war period to the present day anti-Semitism seems to be the almost exclusive domain of the champions of radical or reactionary right-wing ideas. Apart from a few aberrations, which historians regard as rare and incongruous incidents, this xenophobic reaction for the most part only came to the surface amongst the communist leadership, who sometimes succumbed to it, or in the writings of non-conformists.[50]

There seems to be nothing more to add, except a few details: in this perspective, the Left was on its guard against the excesses which were so familiar to the various right-wing sectors. The formula 'neither Right, nor Left' – which can still form the subject of a debate on the intellectual origins of Fascism – would be almost meaningless in relation to the anti-Semitism which has been expressed so openly in France at certain periods since the end of the First World War. However, we need to look more carefully at this too superficial assessment. The discussion proves tricky because on the Left, the anti-Semitism contained in certain writings often remains allusive and emerges primarily through the vocabulary employed, which was common to the various right-wing groups. As for the anti-Semitism openly expressed in oral statements, it occurred less frequently, even though traces can be found in certain archives.

As heir to the rationalist tradition oriented towards universalist or egalitarian struggles, the ideology which underlies the Communist Party's activities is poles apart from anti-Semitism and racism. It is dedicated to the class struggle and rejects exclusion in terms of race or ethnic group. There is obviously no question here of examining the interpretation of the Jewish destiny in Marx or his epigones in France, Germany or Austro-Hungary. It did in fact often verge on anti-Semitism, justifying it by the struggle against international capitalism with which, from Marx to Stalin, Judaism was often identified. From the self-hatred into which Marx himself at times sank, to Stalin's ravings about Jewish doctors, through the incessant speeches by the leaders of the Third International abusing the militants of the *Bund*, traditionalist Jews and, *a fortiori*, those enthusiastically involved in the Zionist movement, anti-Semitism has without doubt rarely been absent from the practical activities of the international communist movement. As such, it has often been accompanied by the use of violence and discriminatory measures which belie the universalist perspective of its general vision of the world. None the less, the Communist Party in its speeches and the positions it adopted under the Third and Fourth Republics, always joined the ranks of those fighting racism and anti-Semitism, and relentlessly battled against the radical right-wing parties which proclaimed their racism. Officially, everything seems clear; the Communist Party, like the Left as a whole, had nothing but contempt for anti-Semitism.

Is this because of the influence of the theoretical interpretation of Judaism that Marx put forward? Is it due to the fact that the man who largely contributed to the breakdown of the Congress of Tours and still managed to become the subsequent leader of the Popular Front was a bourgeois Jew? Again, was it the result of the direct influence which the Comintern strongly exerted at that time?

Despite everything, anti-Semitic outbreaks against Léon Blum became almost commonplace events, reminiscent of the worst actions of the various right-wing parties. To begin with the most famous – which are not necessarily the most shocking. On 7 October 1939 an 'Open Letter to M. Léon Blum' appeared in Brussels in the paper *Le Monde*. It was written by André Marty who was then a member of the secretariat of the executive committee of the Communist International at Moscow. It ended with this much quoted passage: 'You, Blum, close friend of the greatest cosmopolitan financiers – decorated for their pillage or for their thefts – like your friend Oustric'.[51] This important communist leader therefore saw Léon Blum as a bloated cosmopolitan capitalist, a vocabulary more fashionable with the other end of the political spectrum.

Things got even worse. The words of Maurice Thorez marked the transition from a class judgement phrased in a suspect vocabulary to the foulest abuse formulated by the former ally of the Popular Front. In 1940 Thorez published an article entitled 'Renégats et policiers d'Union sacrée. Léon Blum tel qu'il est', in *Die Welt* and then in *L'Internationale communiste*, in which the communist leader phrased an internationalist analysis in the vocabulary of Drumont or Maurras. The political perspectives were different, but the terms used were common to both. They were those regularly employed by the editors of *Gringoire* or *Je suis partout*. 'Blum', declared the general secretary of the Communist Party, 'must, like Lady Macbeth, be haunted by the ghosts of his innumerable victims; he must see with terror the innocent blood which forever stains the long, hooked fingers of his hands.'[52] This time there is no possible room for doubt: by his use of such terms to attack the 'jackal Blum ... with the stinking hypocrisy ... with the contortions and hissing of a repugnant reptile', Maurice Thorez was directly linking up with the most obscene anti-Semitism. The International itself seemed to approve of this line of thought, since the new edition of the *Soviet Encyclopedia* in September 1950 still regarded Blum as 'closely connected with monopolistic capitalism ... an agent of American imperialism ... a fierce propagandist of the out-of-date ideology of cosmopolitanism', a 'moral and political monster', settled 'in comfortable conditions' at the time of his imprisonment in Germany; a man 'the working class can only nail to the pillory'.[53]

These texts are relatively well known and reveal to what extent the communist leaders took turns to descend into the most shameful anti-

Semitism. But it is necessary to go beyond these few famous declarations and examine the more everyday anti-Semitism appearing in the press, in writings and in various spoken remarks, traces of which can still be found. The previous chapter on sexual perversions already noted *L'Humanité*'s constant use of a sexual type of vocabulary, identical with that of the extreme Right, to attack Shylock–Blum, 'the great coquette' seized 'with Freudian wrigglings', the man whom Florimond Bonte called 'the little darling of the bourgeoisie ... the reptile [which] raises its angry head, and spits its venom'.[54] It is unfortunately all too easy to prolong this anthology. Léon Blum never ceased to assume the features of a wealthy and depraved bourgeois. As early as 1925 he was described as a 'multi-millionaire', 'sensualist', a 'dancer' whose daring manoeuvres aroused 'the admiration of the highest bourgeois politicians'.[55] There were constant allusions to sexual ambiguity, similar to those made by Léon Daudet. Recall, for example, that Paul Vaillant-Couturier himself calmly wrote in *L'Humanité*: 'Yesterday Léon Blum suffered a small nervous breakdown and, after having chewed his inseparable little handkerchief he made a terrible scene from the back page of his *Populaire* ... I think it should be seen as nothing but a symptom of intellectual degeneracy. ... Ah! Never hit a man when he is down! Is that not so, Blum?'[56] Although these varied texts never specifically mentioned Léon Blum's Jewish origin, judged by their vocabulary and images they might still have come straight from *Gringoire* or *L'Action française*. *L'Humanité* had no hesitation in publishing the following passage on 14 April 1928:

M. Léon Blum, drawing-room socialist, business lawyer and valiant defender of the bourgeois Republic, supported by the Minister of the Interior. It is like a picture of the fundamental contrast which exists between our party, robust, bold, combative, riddled with blows from the enemy, and old social democracy, degenerate, elegant and sceptical, constantly flirting with the regime which overwhelms it with sinecures.[57]

No greater contrast is imaginable than between the virility which the Communist Party claimed and the entirely feminine degeneracy it attributed to the socialism embodied in Léon Blum. The Party liked to think of itself as strong, healthy, hard, hostile to 'decadent' cosmopolitanism. This attitude was shared by a number of radical right-wing movements, tempted by strength and scornful of the 'flabbiness' of the bourgeois democracies which, they claimed, had fallen into the hands of Jews from the Orient. This parallel did not escape Charles Maurras, Léon Blum's bitter enemy. He tossed a 'My good Thorez' at the secretary-general of the Party to convince him that he had nothing in common with 'the boorish sensitivity of the camel Blum'.[58] *L'Action française* also emphasized the difference between Blum, who 'would delight in seeing the entrails of the French trickle into the mire', and Cachin or Vaillant-Couturier who were not, like him, warmongers.[59]

Finally, like the radical right-wing parties, the Communist Party disinterred the hatchet of war against 'Blum the Oustricard'. Florimond Bonte was one of the first to voice accusations about Léon Blum's alleged connections with speculative financial capitalism. According to him, 'the banker Oustric, king of the swindlers, whom the editor of the *Populaire* meets in the drawing-rooms of the widow Abel Fery, secured for him a supplementary monthly allowance of 3,000 francs'.[60] This sort of accusation would be made a thousand times. Without respite, *L'Humanité* impeached 'Léon Blum, the social-Oustricard who maintains shameful relations with the enemies of the working class'.[61] It demanded an investigation of 'his bizarre, suspicious and equivocal personality' which led him to 'live the life of a capitalist businessman'[62] and to establish 'loving links'[63] with the Finaly bank, the Jewish origin of which was left to the reader's imagination.

At the time of the Popular Front, the Communist Party certainly muted its attacks, which were comparable in many respects with those by the radical right-wing parties, the one great difference being that Léon Blum was never described as a Jew from this side of the political chess board. During the few months of unity in 1936, Maurice Thorez even used the formula 'My dear Blum' on one occasion, and relations became undeniably more cordial. The customary imprecations were no longer in use.[64]

But the calm did not last long, and ambiguous, if not explicit, abuse soon burst out again, as is seen from the texts quoted above. This time the change was definitive and on 5 February 1940, for example, *L'Humanité* wrote: 'Don't say: citizen Blum. Say: City-man Blum'.[65]

The extent of the anti-Semitic outbreaks, too numerous to be passed over in silence, can be better measured if we add that *L'Humanité*, like the radical right-wing parties, often made fun of Léon Blum, 'the water-drinker who has become a vine-grower', while keeping on his 'sumptuous Parisian dwelling';[66] and that in January 1948, a few years after the Liberation, the provincial communist press, to emphasize even more the absurdity of the election of Jewish deputies for the districts of deepest France, pointed out that the names Léon Blum, Jules Moch and René Mayer 'smelt neither of Beauce nor Berry'. Arthur Ramette, communist deputy, made a point of stressing that 'we communists have only real French names'.[67] *L'Humanité* (6 February 1934) called on page 1 for 'demonstrations', and Marcel Cachin hoped to see the nation rise up against 'the advocates of a wait-and-see policy and their accomplices, like Blum and Zyromski'; and on the very same day a leaflet from *Solidarité française* also called for demonstrations against 'Blum, Kaiserstein and other Zyromskis, whose genuinely French names are a programme in themselves'.[68]

But it is still difficult to give a really satisfactory interpretation because, particularly in the 1930s, the communists had joined in the battle against this sort of racialism. The Communist Party's ideology and practices were in no way comparable with those of extreme right-wing organizations, as some people have been too quick to argue.[69] But it is just as inaccurate to maintain, with others, that the Jewish question had only minimal importance in Communist

Party discourse.[70] Whether through the language unfailingly used to denounce Léon Blum's policy or, even more, through the power of the capital whose loyal servant he was said to be, and which was symbolized by Rothschild (or the Finaly bank), the Communist Party, in its struggle against capitalism and its alleged servants, showed that it was receptive to the forms of anti-Semitic rhetoric more often found amongst the radical right-wing parties. Although they were not explicitly designated as Jews, Rothschild and Léon Blum appeared to the Communist Party to be bloated capitalists and not dangerous revolutionaries, a title which Communist Party leaders reserved for themselves. They were not particularly anxious to publicize the growing number of Jews in their own organization during the inter-war period.

Consciously or unconsciously, Jews were therefore far from absent from communist discourse. This was proved by new outbreaks, identical in many respects to those just examined, that took place during the Mendès France experiment. It was as though the presence of Jews on two occasions at the head of political affairs awakened the old demons which had so often appeared in the socialist movement in the nineteenth century. We must start with a brief reminder of the best-known anti-Semitic outbursts by communist leaders, which everyone at the time found shocking. The most famous is certainly the one we have already quoted by Jacques Duclos. When he heard of Pierre Mendès France's refusal to count the Communist Party's votes in his majority in Parliament, he exclaimed: 'He is a coward, a little scared Jew who chatters away and is afraid to act! He is a shit but without the silk stockings.'[71] In the same circumstances, Waldeck-Rochet's reaction was to compare Mendès France's attitude with 'the MacCarthyism which led to the Rosenbergs' assassination', an elegant formula which observers thought was meant to draw attention to the Jewish origins of the new President of the Council.[72] One of the most noteworthy outbursts by a prestigious communist leader followed a speech by Pierre Mendès France. Laurent Casanova made himself famous with his clear statement: 'In spite of everything, France is not this little Jewish carpet dealer.' Jean Recanati, who tells this anecdote, adds: 'I am told that Casanova made the word "France" ring out in a Barrèsian, almost royal, tone, whereas his features were distorted, miming horror and disgust at the words "little Jewish" and "carpet dealer".'[73]

These remarks, which one would rather expect to find in the mouths of radical right-wing leaders, are too well known to delay us further. There is no need to say more: popular anti-Semitism sometimes impregnated the response of the communist leaders who lost their sang-froid when faced with the personality of Pierre Mendès France.[74] Most significant is what gradually emerges from a close reading of the communist press. The political bureau incessantly presented Pierre Mendès France, like Blum, as 'the servant of big capital',[75] acting, according to Maurice Thorez, as a servant of the 'great monopolies',[76] a formula that Jeanette Vermeersch transformed into 'bloated capitalists'.[77] The most experienced theorists, like Marcel Prenant, themselves emphasized that the President of the Council 'in actual fact is in no way qualified to lead a Jacobin government'[78] – not to say a French government – because he was in reality in the power of American and German trusts. This was confirmed by several of the most authoritative Party spokesmen, pontificating this time in the theoretical revue of the Communist organization, *La Nouvelle Critique*.[79]

There was no room for doubt: Mendès France was the tool of the 'big trusts'. That was why he entrusted industrial reconstruction 'to F. Bloch-Lainé, the son of a director of the Lazard bank'.[80] Some Jewish-sounding names, very pointed metaphors, a few images, suddenly introduced another dimension into the denunciation of Mendès France, relentlessly pursued as the tool of big capitalism. It was evident in a large number of caricatures devoid of the slightest anti-Semitic nuance: they always depicted the President of the Council with a remarkably straight nose.

None the less, 'the prophecy of the magus Mendès France'[81] caught the attention of Foster Dulles, the very anti-communist American leader. When the President of the Council came to America, Foster Dulles was represented in a caricature as a great Indian chief, addressing him in the following terms: 'Golden Suckling Calf give me a light.' This formula was not without explicit connotations: via the Paris agreements, Dulles wanted 'the magus' Mendès France to allow him to explode the hydrogen bomb.[82] Overcome by the personality of the French President of the Council,

in front of the TV cameras, in front of the most beautiful girls in the world, in front of a frenzied crowd, Mendès France was anointed Superman by M. Dulles. . . . Traders begged him to sign magnificent contracts which would authorize them to use his name on brands of toothpaste, brassières and bathing trunks . . . All the records set by Marilyn Monroe and Jane Russell were broken.[83]

These varied formulas recall all the classic images of anti-Semitism. In addition, an amazing sketch written by J.-F. Francis and Roger Vailland showed Pierre Mendès France 'in a Superman outfit, being pulled along by Madame Mendès France in mink and a diamond necklace'. The couple presented themselves at 'the House of Great International Capital' where sat 'people in black wolf-masks', singing the following chorus, in company with Churchill and Eisenhower:

> We have worked well for you,
> Robbing and swindling,
> Reward us as is our due.
> The old year is dwindling.
> Dear lords, we hope.[84]

Everything is jumbled up in the various texts: symbols of money, the endless refrain of prophecy and images of the magus or of conspiracy, Jewish-sounding names.... But, like the statements printed above which are devoid of all nuance, anti-Semitism never showed itself openly and systematically. This point must be emphasized. Apart from a few explicit, violent outbursts, everything is contained in impalpable insinuations, and the reading of the scattered passages calls for caution. None the less, a sinister atmosphere, frequently associated with the reign of maleficent powers, emerges. It is shown, for example, by this song supposed to be sung by Pierre Mendès France:

> M. Krupp, thanks to me,
> Has it lucky, clear to see,
> Little Bidault could not do
> So fine a trick and see it through.
> [*He takes up the stance of a conjuror*]
> You will see, ghili, ghili
> Inside my hat I put a dove,
> I take a bomb from out my glove,
> I make Germany arm again,
> I am Superman, it's plain.
> You will see, ghili, ghili,
> The Moroccans are in prison
> For the Algerians, the Legion.
> [*He obtains the help of Big Capital*][85]

These allusions, these nods and winks, must be taken seriously in the context of the period when violent anti-Semitism emerged, similar to that of the 1930s which had been believed gone for ever; more especially as it can be tempting to compare their significance with the cruelly explicit declarations examined earlier. Many other convincing indications would seem to confirm this: from Aragon's little-known remarks in 1954, in which he preferred Barrès's nationalism – despite his frenzied anti-Semitism – to Léon Blum's policy, and up to the astonishing outcry by communist deputies, which some witnesses interpreted as a warning to Mendès France that, if he pursued his policy, he would risk experiencing anew the tragedies of the gas-chambers.[86]

ANTI-SEMITIC RUMBLINGS IN THE SFIO

The hypothesis that an anti-Semitic trend existed within the SFIO seems at first glance even more surprising. The party of Jaurès and Léon Blum, the source of contemporary democratic socialism, seemed radically allergic to all forms of ostracism, implying the negation of the personality of any individual. In addition, from the Congress of Tours till Blum's death, the SFIO identified itself with its leader, who constantly exercised a sort of authoritative moral power. Witness the socialist organization's consistent solidarity behind the leader of the Popular Front in every test he faced. At the local level too, at

Narbonne, Léon Blum was both loved and respected by the militants and the local socialist leaders. For example, at the time of the attempt made on him, Montel, his faithful ally who led the socialist branch at Narbonne, sent him a telegram telling him of the effect on the feelings of his comrades 'shattered and ready for anything'.[87] Similarly, a meeting against anti-Semitism was organized by the *Union des socialistes juifs* on 28 March 1936. Maurice Delepine, of the *Commission administrative permanente* (CAP) of the SFIO brought 'the support of his party, at the head of which he and his friends are proud to have a Jew, M. Léon Blum'.[88] All the signs point to the absence of any form of anti-Semitism in the socialist organization which constantly identified itself with its leader.

And yet, here too illusions must be rapidly dispelled, because we find so much evidence to the contrary. Examples of unambiguous anti-Semitism very soon appeared on the part of the neo-socialists, fascinated by authoritarianism and challenging Blum's anti-fascist foreign policy. At the party congress in July 1933 specific threats of expulsion hovered over Déat, Marquet and their friends, which took effect the following November. In the interim, Déat replied to an attack by Blum: 'It is you and your subtle Byzantinism which are taking us towards fascism. I know you well, I know all about your thoroughly oriental passivity. Action is the exact opposite of what you are and what you want to represent.'[89] In December 1934 Déat still stuck to his ideological choices, which later led him to collaborate. This time he denounced Léon Blum's 'unconscious urge towards inverted racism'.[90] At the same period, in *L'Étincelle socialiste*, Maurice Martin, who belonged to the internal faction of *L'Action socialiste*, did not reject the idea of discussions with Hitler but took no account of the problem posed by the persecution of the Jews in Germany: 'We must say it loud and clear', he declared, 'and not fear that all the Blums, Lévys, Grumbachs will accuse us of being in the pay of German propaganda.'[91]

The situation undoubtedly worsened after 1938. Following a meeting when he was violently confronted by Salomon Grumbach and Jules Moch, the socialist deputy Chouffet lost his cool: 'I've had enough of the Jewish dictatorship of the party', he said. 'Socialism is not a ghetto. I for one am not going to march for a Jewish war.' Marquet also denounced 'the war for the USSR and Jewry', in this new menacing historical context.[92] Finally, at the Nantes Congress in May 1939 anti-Semitic remarks seemed fated to become common currency, particularly in the pacifist group under the influence of Paul Faure, another who later joined the Vichy régime. According to *La Lumière*, T. Bretin, a member of the CAP, thought that 'there are only Jews around Blum now, the Blumels, Grumbachs, Blochs, Mochs'.[93] Paul Zorretti, the inspiration behind the *Redressement* faction, declared in *Le Pays normand*, organ of the SFIO federation in Calvados: 'Yes, Blum, if war breaks out, it will be your responsibility ... the people of France do not follow you. They do not understand. In their hearts they do not want to have millions of men killed, a civilization destroyed in order to make life easier for the 100,000 Jews in the Sudetenland.'[94]

From now on, anti-Semitic jokes were increasingly common at the Cité Malesherbes, the party headquarters.[95] 'Blum would have us all killed for his Jews', Paul Faure, a fierce supporter of a policy of peace with the Axis powers, is said to have exclaimed.[96] The widely read popular press echoed these anti-Semitic rumblings inside the SFIO. Witness the following text published by the satirical paper *Le Rire*:

Here we have the Blum ministry virtually formed. All he needs now are names to put under the chapter headings. Now comes the implacable, orthographic problem: will we see more Aryan than non-Aryan names? They talk about a miserable 25 per cent. That makes a quarter. M. Paul Faure adds a quarter without the seraglio! Because the führer of the three other quarters gives no quarter. In any case, the new ministry will be very impressive to watch in the twilight, when long noses cast the longest shadows. Silhouettes? As at Jaffa. . . . [97]

These internal dissensions visibly delighted the extreme right-wing press. It devoted whole columns to them, only too happy to see the appearance of anti-Semitism in the very heart of the SFIO. As early as 1933 numerous commentators stressed the hostility tinged with anti-Semitism that Marquet displayed towards Blum: 'What the deputy for the Gironde cannot forgive the leader of the SFIO is being Jewish. M. Marquet's anti-Semitism has gained ground in the parliamentary group and in the party. One day, after a meeting when M. Marquet had been unusually hard on M. Léon Blum, M. Lafaye, another Girondist deputy was asked: "When are you going to found the French anti-Semitic branch of the workers' international?" '[98]

And it was left to *Charivari* to note 'that there are relatively fewer Jews in M. Marquet's house than in M. Blum's'.[99] It also set out to demonstrate that 'anti-Semitism is on show at the congress of the SFIO since Renaudel denounces the "apocalyptic faces" and Déat attacks "Judaic ideology" '.[100] *L'Action française* jubilantly appointed itself the permanent echo of the worsening socialist anti-Semitism. It also recalled Émile Buré's declarations in *L'Ordre*, that 'the sons or grandsons of peasants and artisans are no longer concealing their hostility to the nomad of the *Populaire*'.[101] It is obviously necessary to consider these assorted writings with a certain amount of caution. They were very much a reflection of the satisfaction the various right-wing groups felt at seeing their socialist opponents tearing themselves apart. According to *Gringoire*, as early as 1934 Déat's unhesitating reply to the question: 'Will neo-socialism be anti-Semitic?' was: 'We are not anti-Semitic but we have observed the detrimental effects of Jewish solidarity on the nation and even on the party, in unified socialism. M. Léon Blum's whole escort is composed of Jews. In an avant-garde party, this is still a danger.'[102]

The radical right was delighted to drive the nail in further, the better to disunite its socialist opponents. It called on the socialists it considered Frenchmen to remove their Jewish comrades, foreign to the national traditions. For *Le Nouveau Cri*, 'the war that Paul Faure and the "Frenchmen" in the party are waging on the Jewish clan, Léon Blum, Jules Moch and others'[103] seemed welcome news because it foreshadowed new alliances amongst nationalists. This is a recurrent theme in the writings of the star performers of anti-Semitism. On 16 May 1920 Léon Daudet sent an anguished letter to Marcel Sembat:

> I am not of the same blood as that oriental Blum. Your Blum with the mask of a semitic Adonis, not likely! But I am of the same blood as you, Sembat, and we know our great-grandparents, small artisans or farmers who bequeathed us their commonsense, love of family and the land, with the combined themes of tradition and revolt.[104]

Thus the outlines of a strategy of national union, excluding only Jews, existed well before Hitler's advent to power, the Popular Front and Vichy. It had already appeared explicitly in Maurice Barrès's populist campaign. This time it was to enjoy a few years' success in the not-so-distant future. Let French socialists at last become aware of their integration in the nation! Let them decisively reject the cosmopolitan chimeras of the internationalist Jews! Let them regain their commonsense! *Je suis partout* even launched into a history lesson:

> In August at the Vélodrome d'Hiver, the prophet Léon Blum is to pronounce the funeral oration on Jaurès. He is the Popular Front's Benign Bossuet. The Vélodrome d'Hiver is Saint-Denis! And the mob: they are Louis XIV. The Jeremiah of the Île Saint-Louis and the Hôtel Matignon will swing his arms full of Apocalypses and Lamentations. He will burn incense before the catafalque of the Mirabeau of Carmeaux. Between ourselves, if Jaurès, academic and lyricist, a member of the cassoule-eating race, if he had chosen a preacher, would he have sought one in the pool of Siloam? There's foreskin and there's also goose conserve.[105]

For the radical Right, badly in need of unanimity, the Frenchness of Jean Jaurès and Marcel Sembat should therefore inevitably set them apart from Léon Blum and the other socialist Jews. In the same vein, *Aspects de la France*, always faithful to this viewpoint, emphasized shortly afterwards that, unlike Léon Blum, 'Guy Mollet and Lacoste have French blood flowing in their veins'.[106] True, the extreme Right often ventured to hold out a hand . . . to the communists who, even if they were revolutionaries, were at least of sound French origin. From age to age, the radical Right extolled the virility which belonged only to Frenchmen of ancient stock, backs bent over their land. It was an appeal for the re-creation of a genuine organic community which would embrace both communists and such socialists as Paul Faure 'who still carries the soil of his native Périgord on his shoes and, in company with his friends, good Bretons, good Provençals, Picards or Languedociens, is drafting a motion opposing Blum's foreign policy conceived solely to save certain oriental tribes'.[107] That was why, as early as 1920 at the time of the historic schism in the French Left, Léon Daudet recognized the communist Vaillant-Couturier as his brother-in-arms in his battle against their common enemy, Léon Blum. In his eyes, 'a little ape-like Yid like Blum is completely indifferent and even hostile to French interests. To Blum, the Frenchman is a goy, he is the enemy. This is not the case with a young hot-headed idiot like Vaillant-Couturier. That depraved and hairy kid at least has a bit of us in him.'[108]

According to *Gringoire*, a Frenchman, 'even a communist', had a place in that society, restored to fraternity, founded on the land and the dead, and from which Léon Blum could only be excluded. This society on the other hand, opened its arms to Vaillant-Couturier and to stray communist militants such as Jaurès, Marcel Sembat, Paul Faure and, *a fortiori*, Marquet and Déat, as to all socialist and national militants.[109] Beyond even the most revolutionary ideologies, the radical Right observed the rifts forming within the socialist and communist Left, the internal dissensions sometimes due to rampant anti-Semitism, and appealed with all its might for national revolution. With Vichy, its wishes were largely fulfilled and a number of socialist leaders, as it had so much hoped, at last openly joined it.

WHAT WERE THE RADICALS THINKING?

It is instructive to read *L'Ère nouvelle*. While the large left-wing parties were negotiating conditions for a possible electoral alliance with high and low, the Radical Party seems to have taken umbrage at its exclusion from these discussions. *L'Ère nouvelle* strongly criticized 'the little Talmud teacher's contempt for the radicals'. The journal did not spare Léon Blum, describing his 'nervous, feverish hands...his sagging lip' and expressing surprise that '*Le Populaire* was to Blum and his tribe like the land of Canaan to the Lord'.[110] Unflaggingly storming at Blum, the Talmudist, the new Moses imposing his Law on Sinai,[111] *L'Ère nouvelle*, like the radical Right and some communist and socialist leaders, finally came to juxtapose the radicals, good Frenchmen all, attached to their land, and Blum, the rootless cosmopolitan Jew.

Blum had to make the best of a bad job: the radicals made no secret of the fact that they were 'very down-to-earth and matter-of-fact'.[112] And to sound the charge: 'Never did Waldeck, Rouvier, Combes, Ribot, Peletan, Jaurès, Sembat make any sacrifices to snobbery when they poked fun at the parliamentarians. It is true that they did not have M. Blum's very French intelligence at their command.'[113] Radical and socialist Frenchman on one side; Blum on the other, so scornful of the virtues of deepest France, incapable of understanding attachment to the land, indifferent to the pleasures of good food and wine: such was the contrast the radical journal, like many others, drew. 'The Grand Lama [i.e., Blum] despises us because we are the common herd, little country doctors still using a gig and Blanchette the mare to trot along the country roads; or lawyers in the county town owning a few acres on the hillside and never in our lives drinking Vichy water, etc.'[114]

There is no doubt about it, one could be reading Daudet or Béraud. This surprising passage might even more credibly have been taken from Maurice Bedel's frenetic *Bengali* where he described the countryside's revolt against Léon Blum in apocalyptic terms. If this passage is to be believed, the little French radicals, solidly rooted in their land, loving good food and local wine, certainly had nothing in common with the leader of the Socialist Party. They, for their part had 'republican blood in their veins' and therefore had no use for 'the oriental doctrine which is not from our part of the world', championed by this new Messiah.[115]

Here, curiously united, was the panoply of classic anti-Semitism – its existence unsuspected by most historians. The unity was more marked in that it was not just an isolated case within the very scattered radical organization. *L'Écho de la Nièvre*, a paper with radical–socialist sympathies, reported that 'MM. Léon Blum, Zyromski, Grumbach, Jules Moch, Louis Lévy, etc. have patronyms which smack of our soil for ten leagues round.'[116] *Le Rappel*, which also belonged to this group, strengthened even further this propensity to anti-Semitism within the radical world. Almost every issue denounced Léon Blum, the 'socialist Satan' with polymorphous and maleficent sexuality, the neurotic and 'miraculous rabbi', 'the most disturbing flower of evil of the SFIO' who constantly used the whip to force himself on the radical party.[117]

Pierre Dominique, who signed a large number of these articles in *Le Rappel*, remained true to his convictions: though now outside the radical group, his byline is also found beneath passages relentlessly stigmatizing Pierre Mendès France. For this heir of radicalism, who had moved over to another camp but who was still nostalgic, 'Mendès's strange character prompted the old radicals to distance themselves... Mendès the heretic wanted to transform the rue de Valois into the bastion of a personal "Irgun"'.[118] None the less, although only very inadequate and flimsy information is available, it would seem that anti-Semitism had not entirely disappeared, even within the radical organization. The following declaration which an important leader of the young radicals made before witnesses in October 1954 gives some indication of this: 'We are led by Jews. Since Mendès is in power I have discovered the sentiment of hatred in politics. I want Juin and the army to sweep them all away. In any case if there is a coup against Mendès, I will go down into the streets with the fascists if necessary... roll on the yellow star.'[119]

Of course, the historian's stance must become increasingly cautious as he nears the most recent period in contemporary French history. The archives are cruelly deficient and so is knowledge of internal debates, though the actors themselves sometimes described them later. Even though it had considerably diminished, left-wing anti-Semitism continued to exist in an indefinable way. It differed in that respect from the anti-Semitism manifested by its twin brother on the extreme Right, which was not slow to take due note of events on the Left, so strongly did they confirm its own vision of the world. This left-wing anti-Semitism can sometimes still be grasped in all its cruelty. The declaration

Bloated Capitalist and Little Revolutionary 219

by the radical leader quoted above is a good example of this type of outburst which speaks volumes.

A valuable addition to this discussion is the reasoning which expressed the model of racist cynicism. This is the comment Guy Mollet is said to have made loud and clear to his friends on the controlling committee of the SFIO in 1945: 'Monnerville, President of the French Republic?', he asked. 'Impossible, he is black! Mendès, President of the French Republic? Impossible, he is a Jew!'.[120] There is absolutely no proof that Guy Mollet actually made such a declaration; but it should be borne in mind that the right-wing press did not refrain from reporting other 'facts' which were just as difficult to verify and which seem to corroborate the hypothesis that pockets of anti-Semitism existed amongst some leaders of the left.[121] Even though they were incomparably less common in the thirties and, *a fortiori*, in the fifties than among the radical Right wing, these manifestations of ostracism – from which intellectuals of good faith were not always immune[122] – still leave a bitter taste.

NOTES

1 Pierre Birnbaum, *Le Peuple et les gros: Histoire d'un mythe* (Grasset, Paris, 1979); also, 'Anti-Semitism and anticapitalism in modern France', in F. Malino and B. Wasserstein (eds), *The Jews in Modern France* (Brandeis University Press, Hanover, N.H., 1985).
2 See Jean Bouvier (ed.), *La France en mouvement, 1934–1938* (Champ Vallon, Lyons, 1986).
3 *L'Action française*, 4 July 1920.
4 *L'Action française*, 18 April 1920.
5 Ibid., 29 June 1920.
6 *Le Charivari*, 6 Feb. 1936.
7 *Gringoire*, 8 April 1938.
8 *L'Action française*, 21 March 1938.
9 Hector Ghilini, *À la barre de Riom* (Jean Renard, Paris, 1942), pp. 114–15.
10 *Le Porc-Epic*, 3 Dec. 1938.
11 *Je suis partout*, 26 May 1934.
12 *Le Charivari*, 28 June 1925. In the same vein, *L'Action française* wrote: 'with Blum, a militant of the International of the workers and accessory to the International of gold, the interests of France are well protected' (5 June 1936). See also the issue of 24 Feb. 1937.
13 *Candide*, 8 Dec. 1927, quotes the famous exclamation 'I hate you!', which right-wing radicals claim Léon Blum hurled at Parliament on 13 Nov. 1924. There is no foundation for this imaginary assertion (J. Lacouture, *Léon Blum* (Le Seuil, Paris, 1977), p. 214). See also the issues of 20 April 1933 and 25 Feb. 1937. In the same vein, see *Paris-Soir*, 3 Aug. 1932.
14 *La Vie nationale*, 3 Aug. 1940.
15 Henry Coston, *Les Financiers qui mènent le monde* (La Librairie française, Paris, 1955), p. 147.
16 *Fonds Pierre Mendès France. Évreux*, 11 J 15. This document was pointed out to me by Françoise Chapron.
17 *Rivarol*, 12 Jan. 1956.
18 *Jeune Nation*, 5 July 1958.
19 Georges Virebeau. Lampoon published by the Office national de propagande directed by Henry Coston: *Bulletin du Centre de documentation et de vigilance*, no. 50.

20 Pierre Boutang, *La République de Joinovici* (Amiot-Dumont, Paris, 1949), pp. 39, 55 and 113.
21 *Fraternité française*, 7 April 1956.
22 Leaflet reprinted in *Le Droit de vivre*, Jan. 1955. In its issue of April 1956 this journal pointed out that the inscription 'Jews go home' was appearing on walls in Paris.
23 *Figaro-Magazine*, 15 Sept. 1984.
24 *Rivarol*, 26 Oct. 1984.
25 *Minute*, 21–27 July 1984.
26 *Le Matin*, 18 July 1984. Note that this association between Jews and silver dishes, which broke out so strongly in Blum's time, appeared as early as the turn of the century. See C. de la Badine, *Sac à Juifs* (Librairie A. Pierret, Paris, 1932), p. 53.
27 *Minute*, 11 Aug. 1984.
28 In 1886 Jacques de Biez already considered that 'Crémieux will have been the Moses of this procession of Jews on the land of France' (*La question juive: La France ne peut être leur terre promise* (Flammarion, Paris, 1886), p. 311).
29 *L'Émancipation nationale*, 13 March 1936.
30 Coston, *Les Financiers qui mènent le monde*, ch. 22.
31 *Écrits de Paris*, May 1985.
32 Reported by the *Bulletin du Centre de documentation et de vigilance*.
33 *Paris-Social*, 11 Jan. 1936, special issue on 'Les Juifs'. Again in 1943, *Le Franciste* was still drawing inspiration from this parable and showing that 'the return of a patched-up Léon Blum and a patriotic Mandel in the flying fortresses of Roosevelt's airmen, was commended to the blessings of Yahweh' (*Le Franciste*, 1 May 1943). Léon Blum was sometimes depicted in caricatures both as the Jewish Messiah and a freemason. See Dominique Rossignol, *Anti-France: Maçonnerie, Anti-sociétés secrètes*, IIIrd cycle thesis (EHESS, Paris, 1980), p. 545; reprinted under the title *Vichy et les francs-maçons: La liquidation des sociétés secrètes, 1940–1944* (Lattès, Paris, 1981).
34 Léon Guerden, *Je les ai tous connus* (Brentano's, New York, 1942), p. 33.
35 G. de La Fouchardière, *Histoire d'un petit Juif* (Éditions Montaigne, Paris, 1938), p. 183; Centre de documentation juive contemporaine.
36 Jacob Nathan Hourwitz, *Lettre au 'Cher Blum'* (Éditions du Siècle, Paris, 1925), p. 183; Centre de documentation juive contemporaine.
37 Ibid., pp. 116–19.
38 The author is using anything to serve his purpose; witness the following passage: 'Abd el-Krim irresistibly makes me think of our great Jewish heroes: the Judas Maccabaeuses and the Bar-Cochbas' (Hourwitz, *Lettre au 'Cher Blum'*, p. 86).
39 Léon Blum was very often compared with Kerensky; like him, he was said to have facilitated the coming of Bolshevism. See, for example, *Le Charivari*, 13 Dec. 1925 and 13 June 1936.
40 See, for example, *Le Charivari*, 13 June 1936, or the publication of the Institut d'étude des questions juives, created by Vichy, entitled *Non, les Juifs ne sont pas des gens comme nous!*, Bibliothèque du Centre de documentation juive contemporaine; and, more recently, Xavier Vallat, *Le Nez de Cléopâtre* (Les Quatre Fils Aymon, Paris, 1947), p. 239. Similarly, Henry Coston (ed.), 'Partis, journaux et hommes politiques', *Lectures françaises*, Dec. 1960.
41 That expression, 'the International of blood', which recalls the theme already discussed of the blood which anti-Semitic theorists claimed the Jews drank via wars and strikes, was utilized very frequently and always implicated Léon Blum. See, for example, Léon de Poncins, *La Mystérieuse Internationale juive* (Beauchesne, Paris, 1936), p. 4. For de Poncins, 'the International of blood and the International of gold are the two faces of the Jewish International' (p. 204). See also, *Le Charivari*, 27 June 1936.

42 See *L'Action française*, 27 March 1937, and *Je suis partout*, 20 March 1937.
43 *Gringoire*, 21 Feb. 1936. On 12 June 1936, *Gringoire* described Léon Blum as 'Lord of the proletariat'. For *Candide* on 18 July 1935, Léon Blum, 'the oriental intellectual, cannot gain the hearts of the popular masses'.
44 *Candide*, 19 April 1928. See also ibid., 20 Feb. 1936. In the same spirit, see *L'Action française*, 15 May 1928, where Léon Daudet maintained that the masses 'boo Léon Blum who is no longer good for anything but drawing water from Jacob's wells, weeping over the ramparts of Zion'.
45 *Le Franciste*, 23 April 1943.
46 *Le Charivari*, 20 Feb. 1937.
47 Henry Robert Petit, *L'Invasion juive* (Centre de documentation et de propagande, Paris, n.d.), p. 8.
48 Jules Blacas, *Sous l'étreinte juive* (Centre de documentation et de propagande, Paris, 1941), p. 81. In the same vein, see Georges Virebeau: 'Comrades', he wrote, 'you are being betrayed by the leaders of the Popular Front.... If you were real revolutionaries, you would not let yourselves be towed along by Jewish High Capitalism which is enslaving us and ruining us. Down with the Jews!' (*Le Front populaire instrument des Juifs*: this pamphlet can be found at the Centre de documentation juive contemporaine, B11239).
49 Discussing the policy pursued by Laurent Fabius, *Jeune Nation-Solidarité* wanted 'the rehabilitation of the blood and the soil' and added: 'What is taking place is really and truly the struggle between the forces of the blood and the soil on the one hand, and the forces of the financial messianism of other people, on the other, with the fate of the countries of Europe as the stake' (*Jeune Nation-Solidarité*, 'Troisième Voie', July, 1985, p. 6).
50 Z. Sternhell, 'Roots of Popular anti-Semitism in the Third Republic', in Malino and Wasserstein, *The Jews in Modern France*, p. 121. For a general view, see the article by M. Winock, 'La gauche et les Juifs', *L'Histoire*, May 1981, pp. 13–25.
51 Quoted by Annie Kriegel, *Le Pain et les roses* (Plon, Paris, 1973), p. 394; and by Jean Touchard, *La Gauche en France depuis 1900* (Le Seuil, Paris, 1977), p. 173. See 'Textes inédits de Maurice Thorez', edited by Stéphane Courtois, *Communisme*, 1 (1982).
52 Quoted, for example, by Philippe Robrieux, *Maurice Thorez* (Fayard, Paris, 1975), p. 254.
53 Quoted by *Preuves*, Nov. 1951.
54 See above, ch. 4.
55 *L'Humanité*, 11 and 12 Feb. 1925; 26 July 1925; 7 Feb. 1928; 26 July 1933.
56 *L'Humanité*, 8 Dec. 1928.
57 *L'Humanité*, 14 April 1928. On 11 May 1928 Pierre Sémard attacked 'the refined Blum, corrupted by gold, etc.'. See also the issue of 17 June 1928, which attacked the 'demagogue millionaire Blum'. There are too many examples to cite them all.
58 *L'Action française*, 27 Aug. 1936. In the same vein, see *Charivari*, 12 Sept. 1936.
59 *L'Action française*, 23 April 1936.
60 *L'Humanité*, 29 March 1931.
61 *L'Humanité*, 2 April 1931.
62 *L'Humanité*, 29 March 1931.
63 *L'Humanité*, 7 Feb. 1928. See also the issue of 22 May 1928.
64 See Kriegel, *Le Pain et les roses*, p. 392.
65 *L'Humanité*, 5 Feb. 1940. This formula is found word for word in the provincial communist press; for example, *L'Enchaîné du Nord et du Pas-de-Calais*. See Pierre Bloch, *Jusqu'au dernier jour* (Laffont, Paris, 1985), p. 131.
66 *L'Humanité*, 23 May 1929.

67 Quoted by Gideon Haganov, 'Les communistes et les juifs', *Spartacus*, Aug. 1951, p. 29.
68 *L'Humanité*, 6 Feb. 1934. See *Archives de la préfecture de police*, B.A. 1853 and B.A. 1855.
69 See, for example, B.-H. Lévy, *L'Idéologie française* (Grasset, Paris, 1981), pp. 86 and 180. In the same spirit, Louis Guitard unfairly maintains that 'the insults and offensive remarks by *L'Humanité* and Thorez [in respect of Blum] far surpassed those of *L'Action française*': *Mon Léon Blum ou les défauts de la statue* (Regirex-France, Paris, 1983).
70 See William Cohen and Irwin Wall, 'French communism and the Jews', in Malino and Wasserstein (eds), *The Jews in Modern France*, p. 96.
71 Various sources confirm this public declaration, uttered in the corridors of the Assembly. See *Le Figaro*, 23 June 1954; *Le Monde*, 29 Oct. 1982; *Libération*, 27 Oct. 1982; Roger Stéphane, Interview, IHTP; Simon Nora, Interview, IHTP, 204.
72 *Les Nouvelles littéraires*, 21 Oct. 1982.
73 Jean Recanati, *Un gentil stalinien* (Mazarine, Paris, 1980), p. 11.
74 See the remarks by Robert Antraygues, *France Observateur*, 8 July 1954. In the same spirit, André Blumel, 'Y a-t-il un antisémitisme de gauche?', *Agence de presse juive*, 15 July 1954. See also the comments by Jean Lacouture, Interview, IHTP, 518.
75 *L'Humanité*, 7 Feb. 1955.
76 *L'Humanité*, 28 Jan. 1954.
77 *L'Humanité*, 18 Nov. 1954.
78 *La Nouvelle Critique*, Jan. 1955.
79 See the articles by Annie Besse, *La Nouvelle Critique*, Feb. 1954, and by Maurice Kriegel-Valrimont, *La Nouvelle Critique*, Nov. 1954. Irwin Wall describes the suspicion which gripped the Communist Party in 1952 in respect of the international conspiracy of Jewish bankers linked, according to him, to Zionism (*French Communism in the Era of Stalin* (Greenwood Press, Westport, Conn., 1984), p. 154). See also Annie Kriegel, *Réflexions sur les questions juives* (Pluriel, Paris, 1984).
80 *L'Humanité*, 8 Dec. 1954.
81 Ibid., 1 Jan. 1955.
82 *L'Humanité-Dimanche*, 21 Nov. 1954.
83 Ibid., 5 Dec. 1954.
84 Ibid., 2 Jan. 1955.
85 Ibid., 2 Jan. 1955.
86 'I regret to have to say', Aragon declared, 'that however narrow it is, Barrès's nationalism is closer to what I feel and probably to what the working-class avant-garde in our country feels today... because, like Barrès, the men of our nation are not disposed to sacrifice what is national, to a Europe fabricated by M. Blum and Churchill and financed by M. Marshall' (*La Lumière de Stendhal* (Denoël, Paris, 1954), p. 265). Moreover, according to the *Bulletin de nos communautés* (the journal which preceded *Tribune juive*), certain communist members shouted out during the debate on German rearmament at the National Assembly: 'You'll get to know the crematoria again', which for that journal, could be regarded as an allusion to M. Mendès France's Jewish origin (*Bulletin de nos communautés*, 14 Jan. 1955).
87 *Archives nationales*, F 7 13964.
88 *Archives nationales*, F 7 12965.
89 *Le Populaire*, 16–17 July 1933. On this point, see Joël Colton, *Léon Blum* (Fayard, Paris, 1967), pp. 98–100.
90 Quoted by Philippe Burin, *La Dérive fasciste: Doriot, Déat, Bergery, 1933–1945* (Le Seuil, Paris, 1986), p. 149.

91 Quoted in Michel Bilis, *Socialistes et pacifistes, 1933–1939: L'intenable dilemme des socialistes français* (Syros, Paris, 1979), p. 142.
92 These statements are cited in Jacques Debû-Bridel, *L'Agonie de la IIIe République, 1929–1939* (Le Bateau ivre, Paris, 1948), pp. 422 and 483.
93 *La Lumière*, 9 June 1939. quoted by Marc Sadoun, *Les Socialistes sous l'occupation: Résistance et collaboration* (Presses de la Fondation nationale des sciences politiques, Paris, 1982), p. 49. See also Pascal Ory, *Les Collaborateurs* (Le Seuil, Paris, 1976), p. 32.
94 Quoted by Bilis, *Socialistes et pacifistes*, p. 332. In the same spirit, see Ludovic Zoretti, *France, forge ton destin* (René Debresse, Paris, 1941).
95 See Bilis, *Socialistes et pacifistes*, p. 332. Similarly, Louis Gros, SFIO and anti-Munich senator, maintained that: 'Blum has made mistakes; he has not always been happy in his choice of colleagues. He also made the mistake, say rather the weakness, of allowing too many Jews into the ministries' (quoted by Sadoun, *Les socialistes sous l'occupation*, p. 289).
96 See Ghilini, *À la barre de Riom*, p. 125.
97 *Le Rire*, 23 May 1936.
98 *Je suis partout*, 18 Feb. 1933.
99 *Le Charivari*, 26 May 1934.
100 Ibid., 22 July 1933. *L'Action française* also referred to the anti-Semitism of Renaudel in respect of Blum; for example, 8 March 1936.
101 *L'Action française*, 26 Oct. 1932, stated that there were already striking manifestations of it in certain writings by Longuet in 1920. See *L'Action française*, 9 Oct. 1920.
102 *Gringoire*, 1 June 1934. According to *L'Action française* of 18 July 1933, Déat declared from the platform of the SFIO congress: 'Marxism for us is not a collection of passwords that are recited like a certain type of Jewish tradition, to acknowledge that one is or is not a socialist.'
103 *Le Nouveau Cri*, 24 Dec. 1938.
104 *L'Action française*, 16 May 1920.
105 *Je suis partout*, 6 Aug. 1936.
106 *Aspects de la France*, 28 Dec. 1956.
107 *L'Émancipation nationale*, 23 Dec. 1938.
108 *L'Action française*, 18 Dec. 1920.
109 *Gringoire*, 19 April 1929.
110 *L'Ère Nouvelle*, 2 Jan. 1927; 9, 11, 17 Feb. 1927.
111 Ibid., 4 March 1927.
112 Ibid., 16 June 1927.
113 Ibid., 17 Aug. 1927.
114 Ibid., 2 March 1927.
115 Ibid., 25 Feb. 1927.
116 Quoted by Serge Berstein, 'Le Parti radical–socialiste, arbitre du jeu politique français', in René Rémond and Janine Bourdin (eds), *La France et les français, 1938–1939* (Presses de la Fondation nationale des sciences politiques, Paris, 1978), p. 301.
117 See *Rappel*, 8 Feb. 1924; 13 March 1924; 12 Aug. 1926; 5 Feb., 3 March, 21 May, 25 July, 1 Aug. and 27 Aug. 1927.
118 *Rivarol*, 21 Feb. 1957.
119 *Archives de l'Institut Pierre Mendès France*, C/Parti radical. Note from the house of the President of the Council.
120 Quoted by Michel Launay, 'La renaissance de l'antisémitisme sous Mendès France', unpublished article, p. 23.

121 According to *Aux écoutes du monde*, Guy Mollet had a check made on the naturalization decree of Léon Hovnanian, a radical deputy very closely associated with Pierre Mendès France, in order to demolish Mendès through M. Hovnanian (*Aux écoutes du monde*, 10 May 1957). According to Raymond Barillon, Guy Mollet and Pierre Mendès France were none the less still on good terms in 1966–7 (see Raymond Barillon, *La Gauche française en mouvement* (Plon, Paris, 1967), p. 140). As before, the extreme right-wing press clearly indicated where its preferences lay; for example, during the 1969 presidential election campaign, *Aspects de la France* commented apropos the Defferre–Mendès team: 'Mendès with his sideways step of a carpet dealer, his dogmatic tone, worries me. Next to him, the old Marseillais politician has a frank and sympathetic air' (*Aspects de la France*, 29 May 1969).

122 The book by Colette Audry, *Léon Blum ou la politique du juste* (Julliard, Paris, 1955), is typical from this point of view: its author has so few qualms about borrowing language and images, familiar to the radical Right of the 1930s to criticize that 'fine soul' (p. 135) who wanted 'France to love him' (p. 191), more than anything else. According to her, Léon Blum had 'a delicate and velvety appearance . . . half-open lips' which indicated 'a proffered and almost instantaneous tenderness' (p. 16); at the time of the schism in 1920, which, according to her, Léon Blum wanted, 'the Socialist Party in relation to the Communist Party looked a bit like Judaism in relation to Christianity, on one hand refusing to admit that the experiment taking place in Russia was entirely valid, on the other, maintaining the messianic character of the Revolution; it is we who are the real supporters of the doctrine, the legitimate heirs, the Messiah is still to come, the Revolution has still to be made' (p. 56). The author also describes Léon Blum's propensity for sacrifice, his own as well as that of his closest allies: 'The vaster the holocaust, the more sublime the sacrificed sacrificer' (p. 132). That 'persecuted righteousness' (p. 181) would finally fail: 'The miracle has not been brought about. . . . It has been prepared for a later time' (p. 200). The comments, which contain no anti-Semitism in themselves, are none the less expressed in a language more commonly employed by the extreme Right wing or amongst supporters of a healthy type of socialism in the French style.

Part III
Political Anti-Semitism: 'The Jewish Republic'

Introduction
Out of the State! Anti-Semitism and Anti-Protestantism

Drumont's legacy – Jewish gold, perversion and nomadism – still largely shapes the anti-Semitic thinking emerging in contemporary France. His influence has not miraculously faded away, even though sociologists and historians point to the first signs of a consensus suggesting that ideological confrontations will be less violent.[1] Despite profound social change, wider access to education, constantly accelerating de-Christianization, corollary perhaps to the entry of secularism into morals, almost unanimous agreement on the rules of the political game within a legitimate republican framework, the many features of Drumont's legacy remain potentially present in the innate consciousness of certain political and intellectual elites. They are, of course, more frequently manifested by the conservative and radical right-wing parties, especially at times of crisis and war or threat of war.

In the France of Léon Blum, Pierre Mendès France and, since 1981, of the new socialist experiment and the rise of the National Front, the paradigm established during the Dreyfus Affair, under the watchful eyes of Drumont and Barrès, remains almost unchanged. None the less, current 'national-populism'[2] affects far more than just the radical Right, and emerges in the most unexpected sectors of society. As has just been stated, the vision of the world which some authors unhesitatingly describe as 'national-socialism',[3] remains intact, with its diagnosis of decadence, its unbridled xenophobia, its fears of otherness, its denunciation of big cosmopolitan money, its wish for rootedness in the land, its metaphors of defilement, its obscene vocabulary, its sexual obsessions.

However, this traditional genre is not the only sort of anti-Semitism. It has a counterpart, which is in itself an unusual characteristic. This is political anti-Semitism proper, which was born under the Third Republic and gradually extended into the public arena itself, like the prevailing xenophobic discourse. It is in fact radically different from traditional anti-Semitism, virtually immutable through all changes of time and place. Careful reading of the references soon reveals that its clientele is also different, even if there is a certain amount of overlap. Political anti-Semitism emerges as a denunciation of the strong state which imposes both universalism and the equal status of every citizen and was propitious to the early emancipation of the Jews. This specific form of anti-Semitism came to the fore when the state, at the end of the nineteenth century, adopted a republican political regime which almost completed the slow establishment of egalitarian public space, a task to which the state order in France had long been dedicated.

In this sense, political anti-Semitism appears simply as one of the most radical manifestations of the rejection of a state which aspires to escape from the burden of its soil and its ancestral customs, from values anchored in the specific history of French society, in order the more conveniently to impose its own logic on everyone. In many ways, political anti-Semitism is just as much a French invention as the state itself. It measures its strength against a state aspiring to dominate society by complete political centralization and the administrative levelling of all regional, religious and cultural particularisms, while diminishing the influence of intermediary bodies. The state also makes no secret of its wish to secure for itself a complete hold over the education of its citizens and, more generally, over the values they profess. But the specific nature of political anti-Semitism, as compared with the more traditional forms it can assume in a number of countries and at every period, has rarely been perceived by historians who have scarcely taken cognizance of the crucial factor constituted by the type of state.

That political anti-Semitism shares in a more general rejection of a republican state is easily verified by examining its twin brother, political anti-Protestantism. Maurice Barrès's book, *Scènes et doctrines du nationalisme*, showed that he was aware of this. 'Anti-Protestantism, anti-Semitism are protests against the accession of foreigners to the offices of State', he wrote.[4] As he saw it, the cohesiveness of French society was based on the Catholicism which formed its very soul. In this perspective the state could not violate cultural traditions by imposing from outside universalist values which Jewish or Protestant civil servants, recruited on meritocratic principles, would set in motion. Barrès's master, Édouard Drumont, identified Protestants with Jews. For him, Waddington was 'Jewish or in the pay of Jews',[5] and 'as early as the beginning of the Republic, French Protestantism allied with Jewry'[6] to persecute a society attached to Catholicism, by dominating it from outside using their control of the state. A few years after the publication of *La France juive*, Ernest Renauld published *Le Péril protestant* (1898), then *La Conquête protestante* (1900), a veritable fire-ball of political anti-Protestantism.[7] In these lampoons he amplified Drumont's thesis and alerted Catholics to the dangers of the conquering policy of the 'Protestant Party'. With Jules Ferry, he said, it would succeed in bestowing the essential offices of politico-administrative power on its own members. Like the Jews, the Protestants would be the major beneficiaries of the advent of the republic. Many of them would sit in Parliament. They would dominate cabinets formed by Waddington or Charles de Freycinet. And, from L. Say to E. Le Royer, they would exert considerable influence on the policy followed by various governments, particularly in the educational field and the expansion of secular schools, as a result of prompt action by Ferdinand Buisson and Félix Pécaut.[8] In short, anti-Protestantism was a protest against Jules Ferry's Republic, a denunciation of the close bonds he had allegedly formed with the Protestant Party by encouraging its introduction into the various administrations.[9]

It also protested at the deliberate and systematic policy of secularizing public power which aimed to strengthen a still tenuous secularism while also enlarging the teaching role of the state. All thèse measures were intolerable to supporters of the maintenance of the pre-eminence of a Catholic France.[10] The rejection of secularism by political anti-Protestantism is crucial because it underlines the refusal to see the state make itself independent of a society which remained fundamentally Catholic. The emancipation of public education from all Church control, undertaken by Jules Ferry[11] – a man who moved away from his Catholic origins and integrated into a Protestant milieu after his marriage – aroused the wrath of all those who now confused the Republic with the power of the Jews or the Protestant party.[12]

From that time, political anti-Protestantism and anti-Semitism appear as a rejection of the institutionalization of the state which, contrary to their wishes, Jews and Protestants were calling for. Both Jews and Protestants favoured the centralization of the administration governed by the rules of public law in order to establish strict equality among all citizens. The Protestants, like the Jews, relied on the republican state to protect them against potential threats from a society where Catholic values predominated. Quite logically, both benefited from the various purges carried out amongst a politico-administrative personnel often hostile to the Republic.[13] In return, their entry into the state provoked phenomena specific to French society: purely political anti-Protestantism and anti-Semitism. The violence of this reaction was in proportion to the strength of the state within whose structures these minorities secured choice positions, often on a meritocratic basis.

Furthermore, this political rejection of the Protestant was accompanied by accusations similar to those disseminated by traditional anti-Semitism. Here again, caricature, if not frenzy, rears its head. It was now the turn of the Protestants to face accusations of serving big capital on the one hand, of being the best propagators of socialism on the other, and of debasing morality by their criticism of family traditions. Better still, they were said to set little store by the virginity of young girls, a criticism which it will be recalled was later applied to Léon Blum himself. In the eyes of their enemies, Protestants were indistinguishable from Jews, whose most loyal allies they were said to have been during the Dreyfus Affair. They were even frequently accused of trying to hide their Jewish origin, despite their 'hooked noses'.[14] There was, it was claimed, a 'Protestant society', just as there was a 'Jewish society'. At the end of the nineteenth century, Protestants and Jews appeared to be perfect scapegoats for anyone fighting the secular republican State. Nevertheless, these two movements of rejection emanating from certain sectors of Catholic France took different forms: only political anti-Semitism brought about intensive collective mobilization aimed at expelling the Jews from French society. 'Foreigners, out of the state!', L'Action française untiringly demanded.[15] Considered as an abstract entity,[16] only the Jews became the devil incarnate – sometimes even in the eyes of Protestants, since French Protestantism was not immune to anti-Semitism. Finally, there were other differences between these movements of rejection, parallel though they were in many ways. Left-wing anti-Protestantism scarcely existed, whereas left-wing anti-Semitism was visible up to recent times. Note too that if political anti-Protestantism was no longer active in contemporary France after the inter-war period, this was certainly not the case with political anti-Semitism.

NOTES

1 On this point, see, for example, Stanley Hoffmann, *Sur la France* (Le Seuil, Paris, 1976).
2 Pierre-André Taguieff, 'La rhétorique du national-populisme', *Cahiers Bernard Lazare*, June–July 1984.
3 Eugen Weber, 'Nationalism, socialism and national-socialism in France', *French Historical Studies*, Spring 1962.
4 Maurice Barrès, *Scènes et doctrines du nationalisme*, p. 113.
5 É. Drumont, *La France juive* (Marpon & Flammarion, Paris, 1886), vol. 1, p. 455.
6 Ibid., vol. 2, p. 360.
7 Jean Bauberot uses the term 'political anti-Protestantism' to give a remarkable description of the campaign against the Protestants at the end of the nineteenth century. See his two articles which appeared under the general title 'L'antiprotestantisme à la fin du XIXe siècle: Les débuts de l'antiprotestantisme et la question de Madagascar', *Revue d'histoire et de philosophie religieuse*, no. 4 (1972); and 'Les principaux thèmes antiprotestants et la réplique protestante', ibid. (no. 2) 1973.
8 André Encrevé, 'Les protestants et le début de la IIIe République', *L'Histoire*, no. 20 (March 1980).
9 Douglas Johnson, 'Jules Ferry et les protestants', in *Jules Ferry, fondateur de la République* (Éditions de l'EHESS, Paris, 1985).
10 Jean-Marie Mayeur, 'Jules Ferry et la laïcité', in ibid.
11 Pierre Baral, *Jules Ferry: Une volonté pour la République* (Presses universitaires de Nancy, Nancy, 1985), pp. 96ff.
12 At the turn of the century, A. Leroy-Beaulieu associated and condemned the anti-Protestantism and anti-Semitism through which the Catholics manifested their fears of being ousted from power (*Les Doctrines de haine: L'antisémitisme, l'antiprotestantisme, l'anticléricalisme* (Paris, 1902).
13 Christophe Charle, *Les Hauts Fonctionnaires en France au XIXe siècle* (Gallimard, Paris, 1980); Vincent Wright, 'L'épuration du Conseil d'Etat en juillet 1879', *Revue d'histoire moderne et contemporaine*, Oct.–Dec. 1972; Paul Gerbod et al., *Les Épurations administratives (XIXe–XXe siècles)* (Droz, Geneva, 1977); Jeanne Siweck-Pouydesseau, 'Sociologie du corps préfectoral', in

Les préfets en France, 1800–1940 (Droz, Geneva, 1978); Guy Thuillier, *Bureaucratie et bureaucrates en France au XIXe siècle* (Droz, Geneva, 1980); Jean-Marie Mayeur, *La Vie politique sous la Troisième République* (Le Seuil, Paris, 1984), pp. 110ff.

14 Bauberot, 'L'antiprotestantisme à la fin du XIXe siècle', II, 'Les principaux thèmes antiprotestants et la réplique protestante', p. 199.
15 *L'Action française*, 26 July 1940.
16 Pierre Sorlin emphasizes this difference in relation to anti-Protestantism in *'La Croix' et les Juifs*, p. 131. See also J. S. McClelland, *The French Right: From De Maistre to Maurras* (Jonathan Cape, London, 1970), pp. 30–1.

10
A State within the State?

From a populist viewpoint, similar to that held by certain socialists, Drumont regarded 'the administrative and parliamentary Republic [as] the milch cow of the bourgeoisie'.[1] He never tired of repeating that 'the '89 Centenary is the Centenary of the Jew' who, through his money, had caused that decisive break in the history of France with the birth in 1789 of the 'Jewish Republic'.[2] The dominant thread in the thought of Toussenel, Drumont and Barrès was crystal clear: for them, the Jews bought their place in the republican state with the gold at their disposal. There was general agreement on this point, and even men like Jacques de Biez, who opposed the return of the monarchy, agreed: there was no question of 'leaving the Republic to the Jew. The Republic with the Jew is death to France. The Republic will not be Jewish or it will not be.'[3] The economic justification certainly did not disappear from this type of anti-republican anti-Semitism. In 1922 René Gros, a Jewish writer and member of *L'Action française*, maintained that 'the state has sold out to gold . . . only the monarchy is free of Jewish gold because it is of French blood'.[4] This idea later recurred in the writings of Maurras and of many authors sympathetic to collaboration.[5]

However, the birth of another purely political anti-Semitic trend can be distinguished as early as this period. It was already concerned about the implications of the successful model of the republican meritocracy, which gave competence priority over mere possession of wealth. In this spirit, the advent of the Republic proved favourable to the Protestants, as it did to the Jews. This was not because they possessed economic power. It was actually because their respect for the written word and their orientation towards acquiring knowledge now gave them the advantage in the frantic race to the highest levels of the politico-administrative bureaucracies. Political anti-Semitism thus introduced a new form of frenzy, its intensity geared down by the irrefutable empirical fact that a considerable number of Jews and Protestants were admitted to major schools, such as the *Polytechnique* or the *École normale supérieure*. From there, as a result of the republicans' purge of the great corps, they embarked, as we have said, on brilliant administrative and political careers, which sometimes took them to the most senior positions in the state.[6]

A State within the State? 233

The circumstances allowing political anti-Semitism to blossom, which often co-existed with traditional economic anti-Semitism, were now in place. Some people were aware of this as early as Drumont's time. In 1899, for example, L. Vial, drew up the programme that would be adopted by every champion of political anti-Semitism up to the present day:

No more Jews in the administration. No more Jews in the ministries, no more Jews in the magistrature, no more Jews in Public Education, in War, in Fine Arts, in Bridges and Highways! No more Jews at the Polytechnique or Saint-Cyr! No more Jews on the Council of State! . . . No more Jews in the Councils of the Nation! From the least council of the least commune up to the Palais-Bourbon and the Palais de Luxembourg.[7]

In France it was the state, much more than society, which must be *Judenrein* (de-Judaized, to adopt Nazi vocabulary). Jews who supported the monarchy agreed with this themselves. The famous Arthur Meyer, for example, maintained that

anti-Semitism is a poisonous flower born on the republican dunghill. Anti-Semitism is truly the work of the republicans. In order to attack Catholics, to de-Christianize France, Jules Ferry naturally had to rely on the three forces hostile to Catholics: Jews, free-thinkers and above all, freemasons. And the Jews, the free-thinkers and the freemasons have made themselves at home in the Republic. This is a fatal repercussion.[8]

Political anti-Semitism thus derived from a premise which is valid in itself. True to the old revolutionary pact set up by Franco-Judaism, the Jews strove to become worthy members of the public service. This empirically verifiable fact generated the worst nightmares amongst the theorists of political anti-Semitism. Fear of invasion multiplied the supposed number of Jews in the state to infinity. In their eyes, it was no longer a few Jews – or a few Protestants – who, after meeting the stringent requirements of the competitive examination, were finally appointed to the higher positions in the public service. It was the entire republican state which had become Jewish (or Protestant). This was the source of incredible stories, which grew and grew and ended up by being accepted as historical truths. Even specialist historians of the period still echo them. Unscrupulous or simply carried away by their frenzy, the champions of the new political anti-Semitism used any means available. For them, there was no doubt: Marat, like Jules Ferry, Jules Simon, Waddington, Léon Say and Gambetta in a later period, were all Jews![9] It was untruths like these that strengthened their denunciation of the reign of the Jewish Republic.[10] They never stopped. In the inter-war period, the supporters of political anti-Semitism unflinchingly maintained and continued to repeat endlessly and erroneously that the presence of Zyromski, Rosenfeld and Jean Zay heightened the Jewish character of Léon Blum's entourage![11]

STATE ANTI-SEMITISM AND THE END OF THE REPUBLIC

The man who alone was responsible for ensuring the transition from the old legacy of Drumont to the more recent and genuinely political anti-Semitism was indisputably Charles Maurras. But mention must also be made of the writings of Urbain Gohier, Drumont's loyal collaborator who took on the work of the master up to Vichy. In 1914, under the pseudonym of Isaac Blumchen, he published the imaginary history of this character, born in Cracow in 1887. Blumchen came to Paris in 1904, got himself naturalized, and succeeded brilliantly at competitive examinations, while Durkheim, Lévy-Bruhl and Joseph Reinach, all state Jews, were manoeuvring in the background. After finally securing election to the Chamber of Deputies, he bluntly stated: 'We can say "*l'État, c'est moi*".'[12] In this essay, which was reprinted several times, Gohier not only showed the fertility of his imagination, but he was also warning his fellow citizens of the seizure of state power which would take place under the Third Republic.

However, only Maurras proved capable of formulating what was almost a theory of political anti-Semitism. Although his writings abound in remarks worthy of Drumont or Barrès, he must none the less be recognized as the pope of political anti-Semitism. To demonstrate this, it is enough to examine the amazing text which, stripped of its anti-Semitic dimension, might have been written by Tocqueville or some other sociologist of the state. Maurras denounces

the sickening spectacle of the tribe of Blums settled at the summit of the French state. In a country as state-controlled as ours, in a country where the state network has so tightened its hold, in a country where state action and state influence constantly extend to the very heart of the nation . . . the presence of Blum at the head of our innumerable administrations represents . . . nice cushy little jobs for the tribe of the electorate and the subscribers to the SFIO.[13]

From his point of view as a convinced monarchist, Maurras describes the centralization of the state, its growing hold on the totality of society on which it sought to impress its own values. But he adds to this unchallengeable comment the idea – central in our eyes – that the Jews benefited most from this strong state-control of society. From a simple sociological comment, he moves into utter delirium. The idea of state anti-Semitism is easier to understand.[14] Maurras invented it, in order radically to transform the state from a centralized, abstract and universalist entity, aiding the Jews' upward mobility, into an instrument which was a state in name only, finally placed in the service of a political anti-Semitism born of a society hoping thereby to defend its traditional values. Paradoxically, but none the less logically, once its nature had been changed, the hitherto reviled state might well serve to put into operation the political anti-Semitism its adversaries desired.

It is inaccurate to talk about state anti-Semitism as Maurras did. It was more a form of anti-Semitism put into operation by a non-state, a power which had reverted to particularism, acting as the representative of the most traditional values of society. Reversing the hierarchy, Maurras considered that 'the state is only a necessary and primordial organ of society. The state, whatsoever it may be, is society's civil servant.'[15] The formula is particularly striking if it is compared with the concept of the state defended by Durkheim, a Jewish sociologist, who supported a strict Franco-Judaism and whose ideas on education were propagated on a massive scale by the écoles normales and by teachers at the secular schools that Maurras hated. For Durkheim, the state should not 'follow in the wake' of its citizens; its function is to 'think': it was, in short, 'a group of civil servants *sui generis*'.[16] More antithetical concepts of the state it is impossible to imagine.

As early as the turn of the century, Maurras was formulating the theory that rationalized this new form of specifically political rejection. In 1889 he already considered that for 'Europe to become Catholic again', it would have to 'subject the Israelites to special treatment when it clearly understands that the Israelites are in no way individuals like others but that, citizens and families, they form within the state another state, which hopes to dominate the first'.[17] He never abandoned this theme, and in 1941 he was still protesting at 'the existence of a state within the state, the Jewish state in the French state',[18] to justify the restrictions on entry into public office. In actual fact, for *L'Action française* and its numerous emulators, whose dream was finally realized under Vichy, the real enemy was the universalist state. In their opinion, it had to be replaced by a French and Catholic state wedded to the dominant norms of society, that is to say, by a narrowly particularist power which rejected meritocratic republicanism. Generally speaking, Maurras totally rejected the idea of competition as a means of access to the state. He turned his back on state tradition strengthened by the republican model and considered that 'the state must not recruit its agents from "exam swots" but from men of character, whose particular aptitudes for predetermined tasks have been ascertained'.[19] As *Je suis partout* very explicitly worded it in respect of Blum and his team, 'the Jews, with their connections and their precocity are exam swots: they occupy the principal channels of the Republic'.[20] Whence the claim for the expulsion of the Jews, which Vichy finally granted. Maurras proclaimed his overflowing gratitude for the law of 2 June 1941 which redefined the status of the Jews by strengthening the Aryanization of public office. For him, 'that law goes straight to the root of the matter, to the community'.[21] The result of state anti-Semitism was therefore to end the secular, universalist and centralized state. Under Vichy, Maurras was also consistent in passionately desiring a return to the regions and provinces of former times. Traditional organic thought, so hostile to the French Revolution, thus hoped to find its revenge in Marshal Pétain's regime through a return to the past community. And the Jews would obviously be excluded from this community, after having benefited so much from the advent of the republican state.

For the theorist of *L'Action française*, 'four confederated foreign states have hold of the electorate. They constitute it. They secure the personnel in public office. This creates a government.'[22] This was Maurras's global denunciation of the Protestants, the Jews, the freemasons and the foreigners who, in his view, had pitilessly oppressed French society since the Revolution.[23] He raised the banner of political anti-Semitism which, more than any other myth, was to have the most tragic consequences.[24]

Its first victim was Abraham Schrameck, today regrettably almost unknown. At the time, every aspect of political anti-Semitism was deployed. Abraham Schrameck exemplified the archetype of the Israelite follower of an assimilationist Franco-Judaism. As such, his career profile was typical: head of the office of the prefect of the Loire as early as 1892, he became prefect of Tarn-et-Garonne in 1900, prefect of the Aisne in 1906, acting prefect of Bouches-du-Rhône in 1911, senator of Bouches-du-Rhône in 1920 and finally, Minister of the Interior in the last two Painlevé governments. In 1940, like many Jewish senior civil servants, he wrote a remarkable letter to 'Monsieur le Maréchal, head of the French State', to claim membership, not of the Jewish race, but rather of a Jewish past and traditions which had also given France – from his family as from many others – so many dedicated servants of the state, both in peace and in war.[25] Like Georges Mandel and Jules Moch, Abraham Schrameck occupied the politico-administrative office most crucial for ensuring the continuity of republican state order, that of Minister of the Interior. This was decisive proof, in the eyes of Daudet, Maurras and many other declared opponents of the Republic, of the Jews' essential role within a state which, they claimed, had deviated from the Catholic values of the real France. Firm defender of secularism, strict in his defence of the republican order, Schrameck aroused the implacable hatred of *La Libre Parole* and *L'Action française*. In Tarn-et-Garonne and in Marseilles anti-Semitic attacks by the local press were legion. As far as the theme of this chapter is concerned, the most decisive moment came when he moved to the Ministry of the Interior. Shots were fired in rue Damrémont and AF militants were killed. The incident was elevated to the status of a myth in the annals of the extreme Right which thereby acquired its first martyrs.[26]

The 'Open Letter from Charles Maurras to Abraham Schrameck' deserves a place in the pantheon of political anti-Semitism, along with a few of his other texts and some writings of the same kidney by Léon Daudet and Pierre Gaxotte. In this unprecedentedly violent letter, which was peddled in leaflet form all over France, the theorist of *L'Action française* declared: 'For us, you symbolize rather too visibly the foreigner who has seized the government unawares and is making it serve anti-governmental and anti-national ends. You, Abraham Schrameck, have become the absolute and precise image of the tyrant. . . . As such, you belong to us. You are our man to the letter. . . . It is without hatred, and without fear, that I will order your dog's blood to be shed if it should happen that you abuse public office to open the sluice-gates of French blood.'[27]

After Maurras's condemnation the press was unleashed, using the metaphors that it normally reserved for Léon Blum, for example. For *Charivari*, 'come from Judaea to be Minister. . . . Abraham has hollow eyes, a dried-up body and a thin face and, although he is shrewd enough, he looks like a fool'. Several provincial papers also declared war on the 'Minister of the Interior in France'.[28] Whereas Schrameck, as a state Jew attached to his office, justified his actions in keeping order during the feast day of Joan of Arc by simply saying: 'I do not have to account for acts of the government',[29] anonymous letters piled up and death threats became more specific. 'I am the one, not Maurras', wrote the author of one of them, 'who will burst your belly.'[30]

Such friendly sentiments expressed towards Léon Blum were commonplace. His name too was sometimes explicitly associated with Schrameck's.[31] Maurras repeatedly warned that 'he will be the first to be killed. I would prefer to tell him so. Out of pure humanity.'[32] 'He must not be missed',[33] he said again, adding: 'Now, there is a man to be shot . . . in the back'.[34] Charles Maurras was literally obsessed with the idea of Léon Blum's murder: 'It is in his capacity as a Jew that one must see, conceive, hear, fight and kill Blum [who] aspires to impose a super-state on our Homeland.'[35] In the same tone, remember the sadly famous:

> If these cannibals persist
> In making us heroes, who enlist,
> Our first bullets must surely go
> To Mandel, Blum and Paul Reynaud.[36]

Similarly, at Jacques Bainville's funeral on 13 February 1936, members of *L'Action française* recognized Blum in his carriage in the procession, and insulted him, with shouts of 'Kill him!', 'Death to the Jew!'.[37] The repetitive nature of these threats, which irresistibly recall Louis Aragon's famous 'Fire! Fire! Shoot Léon Blum', was a true measure of the real significance of political anti-Semitism. It was as if physical and verbal violence was the only response to the power of a state open to Jews on purely meritocratic criteria. And this violence was even stronger than that evoked by traditional anti-Semitism.

Many examples can be found in the street and at the various political meetings held during these years of crisis. There were recurrent anti-Semitic demonstrations in the streets of Paris, violence reigned, causing deaths amongst both demonstrators and representatives of the forces of order.[38] On 2 April 1942 *L'Appel* wrote to Blum as follows: 'I address you intimately as "*tu*" because it embarrasses me to use the more polite "*vous*" towards you. One does not say "*vous*" to one's dog, to one's Jew, to one's republican head of state. You are this country's stinking beast.'[39]

Charles Maurras embarked on an outright war against Blum. He held up his favourite target to public obloquy:

We have described the curriculum vitae of the little Carpathic, Balkan or Rhenish Jew a hundred times in the past 40 years. He arrived in the quartier Saint-Antoine in a squalid dressing-gown, dealing in old clothes. Then, he dabbled on the stock market. Finally, he emerged shaved, washed, togged up, even a little bit bilingual now, having added a limited amount of French to his natural Yiddish. He sends his son to the *lycée*, makes him study law, then, with the support of all the Jewish groups in the Palais, pushes him into the administration and into politics. This offers various openings, leading to the Chamber, the Senate, the ministry, the Presidency of the Council . . . such is the story of Léon Blum.[40]

Many people shared this collective nightmare and maintained that Léon Blum's advent to power meant that the state itself had become Jewish. Maurras and the whole radical Right, as well as Mounier and Mauriac on the other side, were agreed on this point. In André Tardieu's words, L. Blum's government 'was a three-branched candlestick'.[41] It is understandable, then, that Léon Daudet thought that 'because of Blum, the Talmud will be the law of the new Assembly'.[42]

The general body of 'national' deputies now lived in fear of a purge of the administration, like the one that marked the beginnings of the Third Republic.[43] Innumerable lists of supposedly Jewish people appointed to sit alongside Blum or to public office were published everywhere; the number of these lists is so staggering that it is not easy for a historian to record them. Long series of names, accompanied by first names and professions practised within the state apparatus as well as in the various areas of society (law, medicine, press, and so on), appeared daily in countless papers, and were echoed by a vast profusion of leaflets across the whole country. They were all inspired by Drumont's earlier statistics and each and every one constituted an appeal for exposure and expulsion.[44] At this point the historian becomes unable to explain the effect on him of being faced with such a Who's Who of political anti-Semitism inspired by endless frenzy, in which every republican statesman appears as a Jew, whether his name sounds foreign or not. For all those who engaged in this police logic in terms of plot or manipulation, the sweet names redolent of the French provinces always concealed shame-faced Jews, natives of Eastern climes, improperly metamorphosed into native Frenchman by a too-easy process of naturalization granted by an administration, itself controlled by Jews.

For Laurent Viguier, 'the evil is the Jew, the Jew in public affairs. Thanks to Léon Blum, a Jew, we have realized this.'[45] In a book which enjoyed immense success, Henri Béraud described at length the conquest of the state by the Jews under Léon Blum's guidance:

We have seen M. Blum co-opt M. Mendès France and M. Boris-Goldberg to the Treasury. What remains of our savings is in good hands . . . Léon Blum's cousins-once-removed will be found as . . . prefects, treasurers, governors, directors, etc. Next year in Parisalem, the pupils in our great schools will be able to prepare themselves for the belt trade. . . . And everyone will console themselves by reading the official, complete list of winners in the lottery of 6 May by the light of the seven-branched candlestick.[46]

In 1938 the names of Pierre Mendès France, Jean Zay, Georges Boris, Jules Moch ran like a leitmotif through articles in the press, vengeful speeches, satiric poetry. *Gringoire* published their portraits under the general heading of 'France, these are your masters', mocking 'little Mendès called France'.[47] *Choc* confirmed that 'the cabinet is breaking a record: it is the ministry of the Third Republic with the most Jews: M. Léon Blum, Jules Moch, Pierre Mendès France, etc.'[48] 'Blum holds the state', shouted *L'Action française*, pointing a finger at Pierre Mendès France, Jules Moch and Jean Zay, through whom 'Israel makes the law'.[49] Again and again Drieu La Rochelle attacked Blum, Mendès France and Georges Boris, maintaining that 'we cannot allow so many Jews to be at the controls of administration and policy'.[50] For Henry Coston and Jean-Louis Vannier, editors of *Cahiers de la France nouvelle*, 'Triumphant Jewry blowing the shofar sounded the knell. The rush for the spoils has begun: "We want all the places!" clamoured the Zays, Mochs, Abrahams and Brunswigs, bursting with greed',[51] in the wake of 'Léon Blum, deputy for Israel'.[52]

On 12 November 1936 *Der Stürmer*, a Nazi paper, also warned the French by publishing an enormous headline: 'A nation which takes a Jew as leader is heading for ruin.'[53] Street demonstrations and meetings against 'the Republic with Léon Blum's profile' followed relentlessly one after another, in both Paris and the provinces.[54] 'The edict of Nantes had to be reintroduced in the Christians' favour'[55] to combat this Republic and restore 'a proper state'.[56] The access to power of state Jews, such as Léon Blum, Jules Moch and the rest, was deliberately presented as the victory of the reviled Republic. For Maurras, 'M. Blum is right. The "French" Revolution has liberated him. The "French" Revolution has put him in a position to reign supreme in a country which is not his.'[57] *Je suis partout* went one better: 'We now know what the Ark of the Covenant of the Republic is: it is Blum.'[58] In these circumstances, many of the radical Right turned to Hitler from whom they expected an end both to Blum's power and to that of the republican regime, at one and the same time.[59] Others who remained republican none the less suggested equally radical solutions. *Progrès de Seine-et-Oise*, for example, launched a heartfelt plea: 'Repatriate Karfunkelstein. The corpse of the Popular Front must be buried and Marianne allowed to offer M. Karfunkelstein Blum, the treacherous great man of the Popular Front, a free ticket to Tel-Aviv (Palestine).'[60]

Céline's unhesitating answer to 'the Blum occupation'[61] was simple: 'For my part', he said, 'I would really like to make an alliance with Hitler.'[62] Marcel Jouhandeau shared his views. He rejected with horror 'M. Blum and his whole gang of Israelites in power. Léon Blum is the true successor of Louis XVI. That is what the Revolution has done for Israel.' He did not shrink from acknowledging – as we have said – that the head of the socialist government 'inspired [him] with far deeper repugnance' than he felt for Hitler.[63] Such were the extremes to which radical political anti-Semitism led, with its hostility to the Republic and its sympathy for Nazism which had been able to settle an analogous situation far more quickly and systematically. Vichy would set things to rights by imposing at last the expulsion of the Jews from the republican state, a temporary step towards their total rejection from society itself.

Denials changed nothing. An unbridgeable gulf had been created between the reality – the simple fact that certain Jews had entered the state structure on the basis of universalist criteria – and a nightmarish interpretation born of the over-active imaginations of the adherents of political anti-Semitism who saw a Jewish invader behind every senior civil servant. L'Univers Israélite conducted its own investigation and found a total of 20 Jews among the 237 people attached to the various ministerial offices of the first Blum government.[64] There were only three Jews in the Popular Front government (Blum, Cécile Léon-Brunschwicg and Jules Moch),[65] the same number as in the second Blum government in 1938 which contained Pierre Mendès France and Jules Moch as well, of course, as Léon Blum.[66]

Even the strongest denials were unable to put an end to the veritable frenzy which gripped the many anti-Semitic authors. Léon Blum's presence at the head of the government brought their imagination to boiling point. Their many lampoons, caricatures, satirical songs and poems gave substance to a new ideology, shared by everyone who professed a pure and steadfast political anti-Semitism.

The following two songs, the first dating from 1936, the second from 1941, clearly mark the stages in the preparation of a drama which was finally and inexorably brought to completion:

The Water-Closet Cabinet
Tune: 'Dupont–Durand'
by Maurice Chevalier

In each and every Ministry
The offices are full to burst,
It is the Popular Front, you see,
That's placed its pals from last to first.
They're overflowing everywhere,
The flood-gates are open, the sluices set,
Look at the horde foregathered there
Of those attached to the cabinet.

There is a whole, an entire stock
Of Abramovitz and of Bloch,
Ten Lévys, maybe even more,
Two dozen Dreyfuses, three score,
Each one, they tell us, is a Breton
Of the tribe of Solomon!
It's teeming with Isaacs

With Cohens and Brisacs,
With Brombergs and Duch'noks,
With Goldbergs and Staviskofs!

At the Ministers' Council
When Léon Blum's heard,
The interpreters will
Turn to Yiddish his word.
When these demagogues
On the newsreels are seen
It's so many synagogues
We find on the screen!

There are nothing but Levys,
Kahns and Isaiahs,
Moseses, Baers,
I give up and . . . the Mayers!
Are they relations – nobody knows –
These out and out Jew-boys?
This hysterical cabinet defies any prose.
There are no Duponts, nor yet a Durand,
Only Iscariots . . .
A cabinet? . . . No, more like sh-- ----[67]

Letter to Léon Blum
Words by Luc-Cyl
Tune: 'Ce qu'une femme n'oublie pas'

Although your fine-made shoes trail sand
Which they have brought from farthest Palestine,
Marianne, one night of crisis in our land,
Made you the Chief, the Premier, first in line!
Saying – she should have blushed by rights –
'The cabinet's best for him, no other way.'
That sort of chap comes from Orontes' heights,
He wears the colours of Monsieur Jean Zay.

You found good jobs for all your fellow Jews,
With armchairs and sunlight, for every man-jack,
Although with all the extra staff you use
There's a shortage of clerks to prop up their back!
One vexing result for your image, I'm told:
You, who led Cabinet one-o-one,
You gave Vincent Auriol the cash box to hold
And the state's budget therefore had none.

> The deserving poor then came to complain
> You jumped down its throat and showed it the door.
> When tiny tot, Petit Franc, joined the refrain,
> You circumcised him, as all of us saw.
> Chief Rabbi Blum then had a bright thought:
> A Leisure Department is just what we need,
> Minister-Leisures, they're of the same sort,
> Great Courteline might have managed indeed.
>
> And mother Brunscwick? Dear brother, confess:
> You called her a sister, we give that short shift.
> She caught her hooked nose in the folds of her dress
> Each time she wanted to enter the lift!
> She was screamingly funny, the poor damosel:
> When stretching her limbs going walking,
> She noticed the conk on one Georges Mandel...
> And lowered her eyes, crying: 'Shocking!'
>
> Surrounded by Jews and by men made of hay,
> Speculators, nobodies all in a row,
> You were preparing for battle one day...
> But your watchmen all came forth from the ghetto!
> When you were succeeded by the bull of Vaucluse:
> He looked through the Yid, seeing nothing but fire,
> Between two Picons and a Gentian Suze,
> His vision was always quite dire.
>
> With the plausible skill which has always been yours
> In the black design not to cop it,
> You thought you could plead not guilty with cause
> And say: the rabbi has already lopped it!
> But the wishes of France were there to be met
> And our Marshal has duly condemned you,
> You have not sniffed the just sentence as yet
> Which shows lack of nose – for a Jew![68]

FROM XAVIER VALLAT TO DARQUIER DE PELLEPOIX: POLITICAL ANTI-SEMITISM ENTERS THE REPUBLIC

Until the time when everything fell apart, when, with Vichy, the ideology of political anti-Semitism was translated into the installation of a non-state that abolished the meritocratic republican state, tension reached its climax in verbal confrontation. As has already been noted, anti-Semitic outbursts regularly punctuated the history of the Chamber of Deputies under the Third Republic. In this solemn setting, where national sovereignty found its expression, they

A State within the State? 243

were a challenge to the republican consensus, already under attack from all sides during a period of exceptionally violent ideological and social conflict. What erupted in these precincts when Léon Blum came to power was the most radical anti-Semitism. Xavier Vallat's speech on that occasion marked a crucial moment in the history of the Republic. Now it was not only newspaper articles, songs, caricatures and street demonstrations which spread anti-Semitism throughout society. For the first time, the *Journal officiel* of the Republic was, as it were, tainted, in front of all the assembled deputies in the very heart of the state.

The gravity of the moment can be felt even today by reading the report of the debates in the Chamber of Deputies on Saturday, 6 June 1936 in the *Journal officiel* of 7 June. We need to recall the violent incident which broke out during the debate following the ministerial declaration read by Léon Blum from the tribune:

M. XAVIER VALLAT: Your arrival, Monsieur le Président, is indisputably a historic date. For the first time, this ancient Gallo-Roman country will be governed...
MONSIEUR LE PRÉSIDENT: Be careful, Monsieur Vallat.
M. XAVIER VALLAT: ... By a Jew. (*Strong objections from the Left and the extreme Left. Deputies on the Left and extreme Left rise and applaud the President of the Council*)
MONSIEUR LE PRÉSIDENT: Monsieur Xavier Vallat, I regret to have to tell you that you have just uttered words which are not admissible from a French tribune.
M. XAVIER VALLAT: I did not think that was an insult. (*Interruption from the extreme Left*)
MONSIEUR LE PRÉSIDENT: Gentlemen, only your silence can give my comments some authority. Monsieur Vallat, I am convinced that even amongst your friends, you would not perhaps find complete approval for your words which, let me tell you, contrast somewhat strangely with the very lofty tone of the declarations by M. Le Cour Grandmaison that we heard a minute ago.
M. JEAN LE COUR GRANDMAISON: I do not accept that they contrast, Monsieur le Président. (*Applause from the Right*)
M. XAVIER VALLAT: Gentlemen, I do not really understand all this emotion because, after all, amongst his co-religionists, M. le Président du Conseil is one of those who has always – and I find this quite natural – been proud to acknowledge their race and their religion with pride.
MONSIEUR LE PRÉSIDENT: That is true.
M. XAVIER VALLAT: Then I note that, for the first time, France will have its Disraeli. (*Interruptions from the extreme Left*)
M. ANDRÉ TROQUER: That would make a change from the Jesuits!
M. XAVIER VALLAT: I shall add that, contrary to the hopes of M. Jéroboam Rothschild, he will not be called Georges Mandel... I do not intend to forget the friendship that binds me to my Israelite comrades in arms. I do not intend to deny members of the Jewish race who come amongst us the right to become acclimatized like so many others who have just been naturalized. I say... that, to govern a peasant nation such as France, it is better to have someone whose origins, however modest, are deep in our soil, than to have a subtle Talmudist. (*Protests from the Left and extreme Left*)
MONSIEUR LE PRÉSIDENT: Monsieur Vallat, as President of this Assembly, in this country, I for one know neither Jews, as you say, nor Protestants, nor Catholics. I know only Frenchmen. (*Loud applause from the Left, the extreme Left, and from various Centre benches*)[69]

244 Political Anti-Semitism

It was a crucial moment for the Republic. As the *Journal officiel* noted in its usual dry fashion, the political anti-Semitism which Xavier Vallat, future commissioner for Jewish affairs under Vichy, had openly shown, provoked protests only from the extreme Left and only once from a few Centre benches. This demonstrates to what extent the explicit political anti-Semitism which emerges from Xavier Vallat's blunt declarations was generally accepted by the great majority of the nation's representatives, who did not protest. One of them, who is named, even denied that any distinction whatsoever could be made between his remarks and those of Xavier Vallat (who had polled 150 votes against Édouard Herriot in the election for the Presidency of the Chamber). Thus in this key period in the history of French society when, well before Vichy and independent of any Hitlerian influence, political anti-Semitism had become visible, all the representatives of the right-wing parties and most of those from the Centre were implicitly accepting them, by failing to protest at such remarks made in what was by definition a most solemn place. There were already grounds for predicting that some of their number would be future Vichy supporters – like so many other socialist deputies, though for the moment they unanimously defended Léon Blum. What must really be emphasized, over and above Xavier Vallat's remarks which instantly became famous because they proved the extent of the changes taking place in French society, is the very broad, still implicit, support of a number of politicians.

Tribune juive waxed indignant that the 'principles proclaimed by the great revolution have been violated by the statement by M. Vallat, supporter of racist theory'.[70] *L'Action française*, on the contrary and predictably so, unreservedly supported him. Charles Maurras and Léon Daudet, in two successive articles, approved of his intervention in unusually vulgar terms.[71] *Le Charivari* considered that Xavier Vallat had simply drawn his inspiration from the viewpoints already published in this satirical journal, and consequently claimed the paternity of his remarks.[72] But what was more surprising was the point of view expressed by the very serious paper, *Le Temps*, only a few days before Xavier Vallat provoked the incident. This important paper, more the mouthpiece of the moderate Centre than in any way affiliated to the radical Right, stated:

For the first time in the history of our ancient land, a leader invested with political power has spoken to the French nation without claiming to be the representative of the entire nation. For the first time, the bearer of republican authority has announced his intention of governing exclusively in the interests of a group of parties, and no longer of governing in the interests of all.[73]

Unlike Xavier Vallat's declaration, there was nothing anti-Semitic about this. To start with, it dramatized Léon Blum's legal and legitimate advent to power, accusing him of the worst designs; then it began with that well-worn formula, 'for the first time in the history of our ancient land'. A large number of observers certainly considered that France was living through the most crucial moment since Léon Blum had led the Popular Front to power.

A State within the State? 245

This feeling of living through unprecedented events 'for the first time' not only reflected the fear that could be expected to surround the Popular Front's victory and, through it, the first victory of the working class or the 'people' generally, as their opponents imagined and feared them. In actual fact, over and beyond the triumph of the Popular Front, what 'for the first time' really meant was rather the advent of a Jew to political power, and this aroused a feeling of stupefaction. Many and varied were the images and metaphors that were brought into play to take account of this exceptional event. Pierre Villette wrote in *Je suis partout*: 'I respect the France of Bayard, not that of Léon Blum.'[74] Xavier Dubois-Chatel took the same line when, speaking on behalf of the *Comité antijuif de France*, he declared on 11 May 1937, before a thousand people gathered in the Salle Wagram: 'Forty kings have made France. Will we allow a single Jew to ruin it for ever?' The meeting then passionately shouted 'Long live Hitler!'[75]

For many people, what Léon Blum's advent to power shattered was really the royal mythology of the Most Christian Kings.[76] *Le Charivari* raged at the idea that he might in this way follow Cardinal Richelieu,[77] while the Toulouse paper *Franchise* did not understand that he 'could sit where Richelieu sat' and threatened 'to use its fists'.[78] The Lille *La Dépêche*, for its part, preferred to go further back in time and invoke its 'Celtic and Latin heredity' to justify its revolt against this 'Semitic intellect, educated in Talmudism'.[79] Robert Brasillach stressed the sharp contrast between Blum and the music played by the Guards – '*Fiers Gaulois à têtes rondes*'.[80]

The second incident was just as dramatic and makes it possible to assess the radicalism of political anti-Semitism. It occurred in the General Council of the Seine at almost the same time. Less well-known than the first, it was provoked this time by Darquier de Pellepoix, who later followed none other than Xavier Vallat as head of Vichy's Commissariat for Jewish Questions. It showed to what extent France in 1936 was already living in the atmosphere of the Vichy regime. On 4 June 1936 Darquier de Pellepoix tabled a motion which proposed to abolish Franco-Judaism at a stroke:

'On the grounds that it is time to put an end to the liquidation of France.
'On the grounds that the acquisition of French nationality up to the present day has not been subjected to any real guarantee.
'On the grounds that there is reason to be particularly watchful of the Jews, a wandering nation from among whom the international agents of political anarchy and vagrant financial power are recruited . . .
'On the grounds that national education, religious policy, the integrity of our colonial empire, even the stability of the French family have been and are still strongly influenced by the interference of Jews (politicians, writers, senior civil servants, etc.) with the object of bringing about the enslavement and the degradation of the French . . .
Declares his wish to obtain from the public authorities
1. The complete annulment of all naturalizations effected since the armistice of 11 November 1918.
2. The promulgation of a specific statute regulating the Jews' right to vote and their eligibility and accession to public office.[81]

An extremely violent debate took place in the General Council of the Seine. The report published by the *Bulletin municipal* of 23 June 1936 conveys the atmosphere of civil war that prevailed.[82] It is punctuated by a large number of 'protests from the Right' when speakers tried to prevent Darquier de Pellepoix defending his motion, and 'interruptions from the extreme Left' when he succeeded in resuming his speech, supported by several members who intervened publicly in his favour. This report no longer leaves any doubt about the extent of the upheavals to come. Xavier Vallat and Darquier de Pellepoix were far from isolated on the political scene. Apart from the support of the radical Right, they had the explicit approval of a large proportion of the representatives of the nation, as well as of the city of Paris. The preliminary question drafted by Jean Longuet, Firmin Aury, Allemane, Paul Rivet, Armand Leroux, and others, which aimed at averting this discussion, was worded as follows:

Referring to a proposal by M. Darquier de Pellepoix tending to challenge the principles of the equality of all French citizens before the law proclaimed by the Declaration of the Rights of Man and to recreate the intolerable antagonisms of race and of religion which the Revolution definitively condemned and abolished. . . . Decision to oppose the preliminary question.

A long speech by Darquier de Pellepoix ended with the statement: 'When I see Jews who are seeking to attack my homeland whose soil clings to my shoes, as M. Caillaux said to M. Blum yesterday with reference to Jaurès, I feel anger.' The oldest member, Paul Fleurot, after declaring that in 30 years he had never attended such a 'painful' session, solemnly evoked the memory of Abbé Grégoire who had played a crucial role at the time of the emancipation of the Jews and their integration into the nation on an egalitarian basis. Outside the general council, Charles Maurras rushed to help his disciples and enthusiastically supported both Xavier Vallat and Darquier de Pellepoix.[83] It shows how clear the issues were. For the first time, political anti-Semitism, hostile both to the Republic and to the emancipation of the Jews, had erupted forcefully in the very heart of the institutions of the Republic. Of course, it was a few years before it became legal and emerged under Vichy in the paradoxical form of state anti-Semitism. None the less, in 1936, confronted by Léon Blum, it had many allies and the Republic itself was already under threat.

Thereafter, political anti-Semitism remained constantly in the public eye. Long after Vichy, it was the main trigger in contemporary France of a more or less constant mobilization directed against the republican state. In one sense, the aim of 'France for the French', cherished by some people from the 1930s till today, inevitably implies the end of the state, its dedifferentiation, in favour of a return to the values of society itself.[84] In this nightmare vision, the republican state, seen as Jewish, must disappear to allow the final triumph of the essential values emanating from a society which remained Catholic. That is why the radical Right, but also its many and most unexpected allies, endlessly

A State within the State? 247

hammered out the same slogans: a vehement protest against the Jews' 'invasion' of a state which must therefore be returned to society.

The Popular Front government was the first victim of this new form of anti-state mobilization which found its perfect form of rationalization in political anti-Semitism. There are countless declarations of this type, often followed by street demonstrations launched against the Blum government.[85] The same arguments were also repeatedly, although less frequently, employed against Georges Mandel.[86]

FROM PIERRE BOUTANG TO PIERRE POUJADE

Once the post-war calm had passed, state anti-Semitism was reborn and blossomed just as vigorously during the Mendès France experiment. The ever present Xavier Vallat had to be more cautious now, as he himself acknowledged, because of the Marchandeau decree which strictly repressed manifestations of anti-Semitism (one of Vichy's first measures was to abolish it). But Vallat had renounced nothing, and began right away to refer to his outburst about Léon Blum. The statement he made in 1936 was now, he said, regarded as 'commonplace'. He then apologized, explaining that fear of the thunderbolts of the law prevented him from openly repeating it in 1955, when Pierre Mendès France came to power.[87] Others seemed less faint-hearted. Jean Pleyber, for example, stated in *Écrits de Paris*: 'I am not an anti-Semite. I do not believe in races, but I believe in civilizations. And I do not think that M. Mendès France is sufficiently steeped in our Romano-Christian tradition to understand the soul of our country.... What is known of his career and of his entourage does not seem to me to be reassuring.'[88]

State anti-Semitism could then run free. Pierre Boutang invoked it in article after article in *Aspects de la France* and various other equally radical publications, emphasizing that he himself, like other 'Frenchmen by birth', found it 'hard to contain within reasonable bounds the anger of a people betrayed'.[89] For Pierre Boutang, 'the Jew has not answered our legitimate question about the separation required by the old Gallo-Roman country between the Cairo bazaars and the Republic'.[90] The bearers of state anti-Semitism resolutely upheld this contrast which was thought to emphasize the specific character of Catholic France as compared with a state ruled by Blum or Mendès France.

Just as at the time of the Popular Front, Pierre Mendès France's entourage became the target and Pierre Boutang again led the attack. 'Frenchmen', he wrote, 'watch out for the Jewish dictatorship' with which Mendès France and 'his Jewish entourage' threaten us. It would be infinitely more formidable than the part-dictatorship set up by Léon Blum. He was only 'an aristocrat and man of letters', while the new radical President of the Council 'is in a great hurry, has few prejudices, no principles. He has made himself the absolute other, the stranger', and he also had no scruples about imposing his will through reliance on his 'tribe'.[91] Pierre Boutang could then conclude: 'So long as the Jewish problem is not solved, nor the mystery of the Jew unveiled, the explanation of his [Mendès France's] actions, his policy, his choice of colleagues, by virtue of his membership of the world Jewish community remains a probability.'[92]

Le Charivari, which had lost none of its verve, gave a very detailed description of the entourage of the 'curious Capetian' who had succeeded Léon Blum at the head of the government of the Republic.[93] 'People have started shouting again' against 'Mendès the First'[94] and his vassals. 'They are shouting "Down with the Jews" more and more, because the deputy for the Eure has had neither the decency nor the caution of Georges Mandel.'[95] Alfred Fabre-Luce agreed with André Siegfried in denouncing the 'brains-trust Jew' who was now governing French society, guided by Georges Boris, faithful friend of the inter-war period.[96] And, remaining true to the theory formulated by Maurras, Écrits de Paris concluded: 'Under a monarchy, the Jews could have been the faithful servants of the king. In a Republic, they can only help to ferment dissolution, so true is it that the Republic, by its very nature, is a primary cause of discord.'[97]

Charles Maurras had laid the foundations of political anti-Semitism at the turn of the century. Almost half a century later, those who drew their inspiration from it were coming to the same conclusions which were hostile to the very existence of the Republic. And, as in the days of Daudet and Maurras, death threats were made which also aimed to bring down the republican regime as rapidly as possible. By 'knocking off Mendès France'[98] people were again hoping to free the nation from the unnatural yoke laid upon it by the republican state. As at the end of the nineteenth century, in the days of the Popular Front, and during Vichy, state anti-Semitism was thus grafted on to the radical contradiction which its supporters claimed existed between the French nation and the republican political regime. And on each occasion, the Jews were accused of preferring the Republic and of being indifferent to the fate – tragic at times – of the nation. 'For M. Mendès who is a Jew combined with a Frenchman and with a republican Frenchman, the choice between France and the Republic is obvious.'[99]

Léon Blum, as has been seen, came to power in a period of grave international confrontation. At that juncture, a violent anti-Semitic mobilization took place when the radical right-wing parties were trying to build themselves up in order to overthrow the republican regime and expel the Jews from the French nation. For the first time since then, precisely when Pierre Mendès France became President of the Council, the Poujadist movement suddenly erupted on to the political scene. Here again, the enthusiastic mobilization it aroused was largely accomplished by opposing the presence of a Jew, Pierre Mendès France, at the head of public affairs. Pierre Poujade waged war against the head of the government, employing the same rhetoric as that used by the leaders of the radical Right in the Vichy period and even at the time of the

Dreyfus Affair. He raged against 'foreigners and elements of decay'[100] and, in the tradition of Maurras and the supporters of political anti-Semitism, he depicted himself as the expression of the 'true France', 'son of an ancient land', while Mendès France was said to lack a single 'drop of Gallic blood in his veins'.[101] And one of his lieutenants added: 'Go and ask those people called Isaac Mendès, Servan Schreiber or Ben Said to have French guts.'[102]

History at this period seemed to be repeating itself in the revival of the impassioned climate of the Dreyfus Affair or the Popular Front when conflicts over decolonization were stirring up hatred and creating an atmosphere of civil war, reminiscent in many respects of 'the earlier Dreyfus Affairs'.[103] Captain Dreyfus, an archetypal State Jew, Léon Blum, Jules Moch and Georges Mandel had all in their day been victims of anti-Semitic attacks. Now, it was Pierre Mendès France, already a frequent target during the inter-war period, who appeared as the new target for the energies of the supporters of state anti-Semitism.

On 21 December 1955 several hundred people attended a public meeting at the 'Bal Lafon', called by Pierre Poujade and Jean-Marie Le Pen. It should first be noted that *Nouveaux Jours*,[104] a paper belonging to the radical right-wing grouping, greeted Le Pen's election in January 1956 with a heartfelt: 'A Breton at last.' At this meeting, Pierre Poujade exclaimed: 'We are governed by a gang of stateless men and pederasts.'[105] This opinion irresistibly recalls a later speech by Jean-Marie Le Pen when he attacked the equally 'pederast' Jews in the Fabius government.

It is, in fact, impossible to count the anti-Semitic statements by the leader of the Poujadist movement. I merely mention this retort: 'M. Mendès France calls me racist. I have proved that I could not be racist because I do not have a pre-determined race, but he himself has one.'[106] In the course of time, 'Poujadolf', as his opponents nicknamed him, succeeded in bringing about the sudden resurgence of the days of the leagues. On hearing of the meeting organized by the Poujadist movement in the Vel' d'Hiv in January 1956, an observer might easily be tempted to believe in a cyclical conception of history, so unchanged did the phantoms of the past appear. Before a baying crowd of tens of thousands, Pierre Poujade gave a thunderous speech against the Jews and the Republic, to the great joy of those who mourned the inter-war period and the Vichy regime.[107] A few years after the end of the Second World War it was in places like this that the best manifestation of the 'Vichy syndrome',[108] recurrent in the history of contemporary France, was to be found. The Poujadist wave which suddenly swept more than 50 members of that party into Parliament, appeared so irresistible that everything pointed to French society being prepared to relive a major crisis. *Fraternité française* and other less well-known and aggressive papers, such as *Chevrotine*, relentlessly proclaimed the Poujadist demands.[109] The movement could also rely on the nationalist press which spared no effort in its support of Pierre Poujade. *Rivarol*, *Aspects de la France*, *La Nation Française* and many other radical right-wing papers identified with the battle being waged by the Poujadist leader. Xavier Vallat himself, staunchly at his post, even thought he could establish a clear affiliation between Poujade and General Boulanger, Colonel de La Rocque, Doriot, and ... de Gaulle.[110] Apart from General de Gaulle (sworn enemy of Vichy), this was really the legacy of the radical right-wing and populist parties which were now re-emerging and forming ranks against Pierre Mendès France, as they had once done against the Republic and Léon Blum. And even if at first Poujade, unlike Maurras, simply wanted to 'clean up' and not overthrow the Republic, none the less everything contributed to plunge the Poujadist movement into the grouping of the anti-parliamentary right-wing parties. In addition, together with the National Front, it was a breeding ground producing a constant supply of new members for these parties.

LOUVIERS AND GRENOBLE

During the Pierre Mendès France experiment, Poujadism and its diverse allies, almost all of which were associated with the group of radical right-wing parties, multiplied anti-Semitic attacks aimed at accelerating mobilization against the political regime. 'Death to the Jews!'[111] was a cry heard again and again at public meetings in Paris and the provinces. This latent or explicit political anti-Semitism punctuated the latter stages of Pierre Mendès France's political life.

The legislative elections of 1958 marked a turning point. Pierre Mendès France stood again in his fiefdom of Louviers, to which he had always been deeply attached. The Eure had formerly voted massively in favour of adopting the new constitution in the referendum organized by General de Gaulle. In November 1958 Rémy Montagne stood against Pierre Mendès France and defeated him, taking advantage of the Gaullist tidal wave. It was a cruel defeat, but above all it took place in a climate from which anti-Semitism was not absent. Mendès France himself stressed that his opponent 'has not been able to ignore the anti-Semitic arguments of the dirty little rags, anonymous pamphlets and a certain amount of trash which has been in circulation'.[112] Witness this anonymous pamphlet:

> A vote for Mendès France
> is a vote against de Gaulle
> is a vote against France.
> So vote French
> Vote UNR[113]

UNR's response was immediate: it strongly denounced the distribution of this pamphlet, but in ambiguous terms:

A State within the State? 251

Usurping UNR's name, some miserable champions of the old system with their backs to the wall have thought it smart to fall back on an ignoble manoeuvre: they have just circulated pamphlets and leaflets against the Jews.

The people will not allow themselves to be misled by such ignominies. They will say NO, with us, to those who have fought against General de Gaulle. But our YES of 23 November confirming that of the referendum, will not be tarnished by the duplicity of his enemies.[114]

This incident is irrefutable proof that political anti-Semitism survived in latter-day France. Moreover, the denial itself seems a little strange in view of the fact that the UNR's principal opponent was none other than... Pierre Mendès France himself. Things did not stop there. After the defeat at Louviers, political anti-Semitism, like an anachronism that nothing could banish, again surfaced in Grenoble. In this town, the symbol *par excellence* of progress and modernity, Pierre Mendès France faced the outgoing deputy Jean Vanier in the electoral campaign of February–March 1967. The campaign was hard and tense and there were a number of incidents, particularly when political anti-Semitism, which almost always kept a low and anonymous profile, broke out again in public during a debate in the Grenoble skating rink between Pierre Mendès France and Georges Pompidou, who had come along to support Jean Vanier, the Gaullist deputy. According to the paper, *Volonté socialiste*,

One of the last manoeuvres by the Grenoble UNR brains-trust consists of more or less disguised anti-Semitic propaganda activity. A certain number of people from the outgoing deputy's entourage moved around the town, making anti-Semitic remarks about the candidate Pierre Mendès France to their generally dumbfounded interlocutors. 'After all, we're not going to elect a Yid; there are quite enough of all these Yids in commanding positions', etc.[115]

There is much evidence to confirm the extent of these manifestations of political anti-Semitism, noisily expressed during the skating-rink debate. People shouted 'To Jerusalem',[116] and anti-Semitic outbursts were heard on all sides.[117] They never stopped.

During the new electoral campaign following General de Gaulle's dissolution of the Assembly on 30 May 1968, Pierre Mendès France this time stood against Jean-Marcel Jeanneney at Grenoble. In the tense atmosphere of the electoral campaign and also at Charléty, outbreaks of anti-Semitism occurred again. An incredible caricature of the former radical President of the Council even appeared in the campaign journal through which Jean-Marcel Jeanneney addressed the electors. The front page of the *Grenoble Avenir* carried the picture of the Gaullist candidate under a portrait of General de Gaulle, but on the next page, it is curious to find an anti-Semitic caricature of Pierre Mendès France which would have delighted *Je suis partout* or *Gringoire*.[118] Obviously the Gaullist candidate's own views were in no way involved. But this caricature, characteristic of an era which one might have thought to be gone for ever, still appeared in this news-sheet which the majority party in Grenoble, city of democratic liberties and self-rule, was distributing to the public.[119]

252 Political Anti-Semitism

Political anti-Semitism has never disappeared from the contemporary public scene. It may be expressed with infinite caution, since the 1972 law has proved so harsh towards those who show that they still support it. None the less it still comes to the surface, intact and true to its logic of exclusion and its challenge to republican emancipation. The same expressions recur in the writings of journalists in the right-wing nationalist press. *Rivarol*, for example, gave a detailed description of 'the Fabius Tribe' which had moved into power, and asked whether François Mitterand intended to provoke 'an unprecedented wave of anti-Semitism'.[120] By 'propelling it to the summit of the socialist state', President Mitterand had created a 'climate conducive to pogroms'.[121] And, after wishing electoral success to the ranks of Jean-Marie Le Pen, who, it will be recalled, was already participating in the anti-Mendès France battle, it actually invoked 'the shades of Doriot'!

Is this history repeating itself again: from Dreyfus to Blum, Mendès France and finally Laurent Fabius? The answer might well be 'Yes', judging by this question in *Présent*: 'What do Laurent Fabius and Léon Blum have in common? Blum was the first head of a French government and Fabius is the most recent to use Matignon as an official residence.'[122] How discreetly they worded these comments![123] Similarly, *Écrits de Paris*, which had shown such virulence towards Pierre Mendès France, now associated Laurent Fabius with Léon Blum 'on ethnic grounds'.[124] *Minute* began by reproaching Laurent Fabius for 'lying on the Day of Atonement' before comparing him this time with Georges Mandel.[125]

In order to make the comparisons clear for all time, François Brigneau, also in *Minute*, argued that 'the madness which seizes *Le Monde* and *Libération*, the frenzy which grips them when they imagine Jean-Marie Le Pen making a return to the Chamber where only Mendès's and Blum's disciples should have the right to sit, throw light on the real state we live in'.[126] This makes the conclusion seem irrefutable: from Maurras up to the present day, the presence of Jews at the head of the state brings to light strong political anti-Semitism. Depending on the period concerned, this anti-Semitism has been grafted on to movements of varying degrees of strength for the purpose of mobilization against the state. Abraham Schrameck, Léon Blum, Georges Mandel, Pierre Mendès France and Laurent Fabius (whose family, by the way, is far removed from Judaism), were all bearers of a Franco-Judaism which was particularly well-suited to the meritocratic functioning of the republican state. On each occasion, because of their presence at the summit of the state, they became the target of a political anti-Semitism specific to the history of modern France. This testifies to resistance to the state by certain sectors of French society which remained hostile to the laws of a Republic oriented towards universalism.

NOTES

1 É. Drumont, *La Fin d'un monde* (A. Savine, Paris, 1889), p. 47.
2 É. Drumont, *La Dernière Bataille* (E. Dentu, Paris, 1890), pp. 8 and 96. In the same spirit, see *La France juive* (Marpon & Flammarion, Paris, 1886), pp. 16 and 292.
3 Jacques de Biez, *La Question juive: La France ne doit pas être leur terre promise* (Flammarion, Paris, 1886), p. 16.
4 René Gros, *Enquête sur le problème juif* (Nouvelle librairie nationale, Paris, 1922), pp. 30–1.
5 See *Le Parlement, agent d'exécution de la judéo-maçonnerie* (Institut d'études des questions juives, Éditions nouvelles, Paris, 1941); and, in the same spirit, *L'Émancipation des Juifs en France* (Institut d'études des questions juives, Éditions nouvelles, Paris, 1941).
6 See Perrine Simon, *Contribution a l'étude de la bourgeoisie intellectuelle juive à Paris entre 1870 et 1914* (DEA, Institut d'études politiques, Paris, 1982), pp. 61, 92–7. See also Elwyn Elms, 'The Conseil d'État under the Third Republic, 1879–1914', doctoral thesis, Macquarie University, 1986, pp. 61–3.
7 L. Vial, *Le Juif Roi: Comment le détrôner* (P. Lethielleux, Paris, 1899), p. 87.
8 Arthur Meyer, *Ce que mes yeux ont vu* (Plon, Paris, 1912), pp. 128–9. *La Vieille Grille* also wanted to expel Jewish senior civil servants from the ministries. See, for example, the issue of 12 Jan. 1922.
9 Freakish estimates of this type were put forward by an infinite number of anti-Semitic pamphlets and books. For the recent period, see *Charivari*, no.1, Oct.–Dec. 1967, p. 15.
10 None of them was Jewish. Nor was Gambetta, contrary to what certain authors carelessly maintain. On the family origins of Gambetta, who was educated at Catholic institutions, see J. P. Bury, *Gambetta and the Making of the Third Republic* (Longman, London, 1973), pp. 1 and 2.
11 Pierre Bloch, *Jusqu'au dernier jour*, p. 88.
12 Isaac Blumchen, *Le Droit de la race supérieure* (Isidor Nathan Goldlust, Cracow, 1914).
13 *L'Action française*, 2 April 1937.
14 *L'Action française*, 3 July 1941. 'In favour of a state organized anti-semitism, we are not anti-Semites of skin', declared Charles Maurras. In practice, things would be far less clearcut.
15 Charles Maurras, *Mes idées politiques* (Fayard, Paris, 1937), pp. 121–2.
16 See Pierre Birnbaum, *Dimensions du pouvoir* (PUF, Paris, 1984), pp. 42–5.
17 Quoted by Victor Nguyen, 'Note sur le problème de l'antisémitisme maurrassien', in *L'idée de race dans la pensée politique française contemporaine* (CNRS, Paris, 1977), p. 146.
18 Charles Maurras, *La Seule France* (H. Lardanchet, Paris, 1941), pp. 182 and 196.
19 *L'Action française*, 21 July 1942.
20 *Je suis partout*, 14 Dec. 1935.
21 *L'Action française*, 17 June 1941. On Maurras's state anti-Semitism, see Frédéric Ogé, 'Le Journal *L'Action française*', thesis, University of Toulouse–Le Mirail, 1984, pp. 352–72.
22 *L'Action française*, 12 June 1914. After stating that the Blum government was solely composed of Jews, Mgr Jouin added: 'The state is the Jew.... The Jews are not a state within the state but the state itself' ('Le péril judéo-maçonnique', *Revue internationale des sociétés secrètes* (1926), pp. 1, 7, 21).
23 See Colette Capitan-Peter, *Charles Maurras et l'idéologie d'Action française* (Le Seuil, Paris, 1972), pp. 54ff. In the same spirit, James McCearney, *Maurras et son temps* (A. Michel, Paris, 1977), p. 223.

24 In this sense, one can only challenge Malcolm Anderson's assessment. After describing the anti-republican programmes of Maurras, Bucard and Déat, he considers that 'left-wing propaganda had identical corrosive effects. From the point of view of national unity and respect for established institutions, the myth of the two hundred families has been just as damaging as the myth of the foreigners' (*Conservative Politics in France* (George Allen & Unwin, London, 1974), p. 65).

25 See Claire Darmon, *Abraham Schrameck, administrateur et homme politique sous la IIIe République*, DEA of the Institut d'études politiques de Paris, 1978.

26 Ibid., ch. 8. See also *Archives de la préfecture de police*, BA 1851.

27 *L'Action française*, 9 June 1925.

28 *Archives nationales*, F7 13197. This rich file does not ever seem to have been exploited. Very much later, on 31 Jan. 1941, *Au Pilori* again launched a violent attack on A. Schrameck.

29 *Ibid.*

30 *Archives Nationales*, F7 13964.

31 See, for example, the scurrilous text in *L'Action française*, 26 Sept. 1925.

32 *L'Action française*, 14 May 1936.

33 *L'Action française*, 16 May 1936.

34 *L'Action française*, 9 April 1935. On the numerous death threats that Blum received, see the unpublished letters held by André Blumel and quoted by J. Colton, *Léon Blum* (Fayard, Paris, 1967), p. 340. See also *Archives nationales*, F7 13196.

35 *L'Action française*, 15 May 1936.

36 *L'Action française*, 29 Sept. 1938. The passage by Léon Pujo is also illuminating: 'Léon Blum, attacked in the street. . . . Ah! Bravo! / At last! At last something new / And that Blum should be given a pasting! / Come along, Croix-de-Feu!' (quoted by *Le Droit de vivre*, 22 Feb. 1936).

37 *Archives de la préfecture de police*, BA 1648. On the reaction by the forces of the Left, which organized an immense protest march from the place du Panthéon to the place de la Nation on 16 Feb., see BA 1862. See also, *Archives nationales*, F7 14683.

38 For the precise figures, see the *Archives de la préfecture de police*, BA 1852, BA 1853, BA 1854, BA 1865. During a meeting the Francist movement held in the Salle Wagram on 6 May 1936, praise of Mussolini preceded the following statement: 'The Palais Bourbon must be cleared of its excrement, Blum killed.' At another political meeting organized by the Francist party on 26 May 1936, in the rue Blomet, the speaker declared: 'We will not tolerate Blum at the head of this country and there are means of suppressing a man. For example: disguise oneself as a pastry cook, get through the security service, go up to M. Blum with all the necessary in one's basket: grenades, revolver and other weapons. The blow struck, one can leave without being challenged' (*Archives Vanikoff*, Archives nationales, 72 AJ 602).

39 *L'Appel*, 2 April 1942. See also Jean Roland, *Auteurs de notre défaite* (Caen, n.d.). It was probably in 1940–1 that Roland wrote: 'We have come back into the light, let us take advantage of it to kill the traitor Blum' (University of Jerusalem Library).

40 *L'Action française*, 23 April 1937.

41 *Gringoire*, 11 Sept. 1936. See also an article by the same author, in ibid., 19 Feb. 1937.

42 *L'Action française*, 1 June 1936. Daudet incessantly denounced that 'oriental cabinet'. See, for example, *L'Action française*, 31 July 1936.

43 *Archives nationales*, F7 13983. For Pierre Gaxotte, 'M. Blum has promised his loyal supporters places in the high administration' (*Candide*, 14 May 1936).

44 For example, the Centre de documentation et de vigilance estimated that the Centre antisémitique de documentation et de propagande alone distributed 1,800,000 pamphlets, 95,000 books and brochures, and 425,000 anti-Semitic leaflets in 1936 (Centre de documen-

A State within the State? 255

tation et de vigilance, Bulletin 15, no. 3).

45 Laurent Viguier, *Les Juifs à travers Léon Blum: Leur incapacité historique á diriger un état*, (Éditions Baudinière, Paris, 1940), p. 8.

46 Henri Béraud, *Popu-roi* (Éditions de France, 1938), pp. 146–7. See also, Louis Bodin and Jean Touchard, *Front populaire, 1936* (A. Colin, Paris, 1961), pp. 204–7. The following text is contained in the catalogue of the exhibition, 'The Jew in France', organized by Vichy in the Palais Berlitz in September 1941 and visited by tens of thousands of people, including vast numbers of school groups: 'The Jews Blum, Mendès France, Jules Moch, Jean Zay, Georges Mandel... were masters of the democracy' (see *Exposition 'Le Juif de France' au palais Berlitz*, Institut d'études des questions juives, Bibliothèque nationale, 8oLd 183d64). See also the inaugural address by Captain Sezillie honouring Drumont's foresight, Information service of the Institut d'étude des questions juives. See also *Enquête sur le judaïsme en France* (Institut d'études des questions juive, Éditions nouvelles, Paris, 1940), p. 58; and *Leurs noms: Petite philosophie des patronymes juifs* (Institut d'étude des questions juives, Éditions nouvelles, Paris, 1942), p. 18; *Français, il faut redevenir*, published by the same Institut; Gabriel Malglaive, *Juifs ou Français?* (Éditions du CRRN, Paris); Henry-Robert Petit, *Les Juifs au pouvoir* (Centre de documentation et de propagande, Paris, 1943); AJSM de la Cambre-Mielet, *Français, vous êtes trahis* (OPN, Paris, 1938); Georges Ollivier, *L'Accession des juifs au pouvoir* (Ligue franco-catholique, n.d.). These texts can be consulted at the BAIU or at the Centre de documentation juive contemporaine. Note that texts of the same ilk were still to be found in 1946: see, for example, Arouet, *Voyage en Absurdie*, lampoon, 1946, p. 175, CDJC.

47 *Gringoire*, 18 March, 1 and 8 April 1938. This paper never stopped publishing this sort of list, very often containing the names of P. Mendès France, G. Boris, J. Moch. For the same phenomenon under Vichy: see, for example, the issues of 12 Feb., 17 April, 24 April 1941. *Candide* also frequently associated the names of P. Mendès France, J. Zay, G. Boris with L. Blum. See, for example, 14 April 1938. On 31 May 1938 *Candide* mentioned the 'Blum, Weil, Goldberg, Mendès and Co.' cabinet. In the same spirit, see *Je suis partout*, 15, 16 and 29 April 1938. On 29 April 1938, the journal considered that Blum, Mendès France, Zay, etc., 'dominate the state'. See also *L'Émancipation nationale* which considered that 'Blum, Moch, etc., do not think French' (23 Dec. 1938). Likewise René Gontier, *Vers un racisme français* (Denoël, Paris, 1939); Louis Thomas, *Les Raisons de l'antijudaïsme* (Les Documents contemporains, Paris, 1942); André Chaumet and H. Bellanger, *Les Juifs et nous* (Jean Renard, Paris, 1941); Paul Lombard, *Front populaire* (Éditions de France, Paris, 1936). See also anti-Semitic leaflets consisting of long lists of names (Bibliothèque nationale, *Tracts antisémites*, 4oLd 18346). For other anti-Semitic leaflets opposed to Léon Blum's presence in the government, see *Archives nationales*, F7 14781, F7 14818 and F7 14782, the file, for example, containing the following tract: 'Down with the Jewish, called Popular, Front'. Similarly, a leaflet was distributed at Nîmes in 1936, denouncing the degradation of France: 'Its schools, its traditions, its state are a prey to invading Jews who hold the levers of control' (*Archives nationales*, F7 13034). The Centre de documentation juive contemporaine also owns other leaflets of the same type (12441). For the opinion of a contemporary who was opposed to anti-Semitism, see Jean Bazin, *Vichy-les-Bains, ou une station de l'histoire de France* (Chanteclerc, Rio de Janeiro, 1942, Bibliothèque nationale). Note also that the Comte de Paris very harshly condemned radical right-wing anti-Semitism in respect of Blum and his government ('L'antisémitisme jugé par le comte de Paris', *Courrier royal*, 1 Jan. 1939, BAIU).

48 *Choc*, 17 March 1938. In the same spirit, G. Verdeveine, *Israël, nation sans territoire contre la nation française*, brochure, University of Jerusalem Library, 1937.

49 *L'Action française*, 14, 15, 17, 21, 28 and 30 March 1938.

50 *L'Émancipation nationale*, 26 March, 1 April and 29 July 1938.
51 'Les Juifs en France', *Cahiers de la France nouvelle*, no. 1, p. 16. See also Paul Lombard, *Quatorze mois de démence* (Éditions de France, Paris, 1937). In the same spirit, Lucien Pemjean, *La Presse et les Juifs* (Nouvelles Éditions françaises, Paris, 1941), p. 106; 'L'invasion continue', *Les nouvelles économiques et financières*, 22 Nov. 1938. On this theme, see Philippe Ganier-Raymond, *Une certaine France: L'antisémitisme* (Belfond, Paris, 1975).
52 Léon Daudet, 'Léon Blum, deputé d'Israel', *L'Action française*, 27 Aug. 1927.
53 Centre de documentation et de vigilance, 12 Oct. 1936.
54 See the remarkable file gathered by the Centre de documentation et de vigilance, 'L'Antisémitisme en France', Jan. 1939. See also Samuel Osgood, 'The Front Populaire views from the right', *International Review of Social History*, 9 (1964) and Martine Kriskris, 'L'antisémitisme de droite en France à l'époque de la nuit de cristal', master's dissertation, University of Paris I, 1972.
55 *Archives nationales*, F7 13238. On 7 June 1937 the Centre de propagande des républicains sociaux organized a large meeting in the Salle Wagram; amidst applause, the speaker declaimed: 'And one day, thank God, the reign of the foreigners will be angrily swept away by the recovery of French reason' (Centre de documentation et de vigilance, 10 June 1937). At a meeting of the Club du Faubourg on 17 June 1937, Jacques Ditte denounced 'the advent of 54 Jews to power' (Centre de documentation et de vigilance, 1 July 1937, no. 39). This freakish figure of 50 or more frequently recurs; for example, *La France réelle*, 2 June 1937, warns the country against 'the Jew Blum and the 50 Jews of the Ministry'. See also the file in the *Archives nationales*, F7 13986; on 20 May 1936, at an important meeting in the Salle des Centraux, the president of the Ligue France catholique declared: 'We are on the eve of having a Judeo-socialist government in the person of Léon Blum.' Quite a few meetings of the same type are described in this series. See also the *Archives Vanikoff* in the *Archives nationales*, 72AJ 602 and 72AJ 5982, which catalogue some provincial demonstrations. *La France réelle* denounced 'parliamentarianism, the expression of political liberalism, which has resulted in Blum' (1 July 1937). *La France enchaînée* also attacked 'the Jewish Republic of France' (15 Oct. 1938). *Contre-Révolution*, which claimed Catholic affiliations, considered that Blum was 'appointed as President of the French Council in the interests of the Jewish nation' (July 1938, p. 126. Centre de documentation juive contemporaine).
56 *Cahier jaune*, Nov. 1942. In the same spirit, Robert Launay, *Figures juives* (Nouvelle Librairie nationale, Paris, 1921), pp. 7–8.
57 *L'Action française*, 16 May 1936. In the same spirit, Urbain Gohier, Drumont's old loyal supporter, considered that Jews were now everywhere in the Republic ('L'Union contre le seul ennemi', *Centre de documentation et de vigilance*, no. 50).
58 *Je suis partout*, 15 Feb. 1936. For Léon Daudet, the Jews grouped round Léon Blum served as an 'administrative sub-structure to the republican state' (*Au temps de Judas* (Grasset, Paris, 1933), p. 131). In the same spirit, see Fayolle-Lefort, *Le Juif, cet inconnu* (Éditions de France, Paris, 1941), p. 115.
59 For George Batault, the 'Jews of finance and the Jews of the Revolution have conquered the state.... The emergence of a man, very solitary, without support, without money, but strong in his mission, strong in his destiny has been enough to arouse a wave of irresistible depth which has swept everything away: Hitler' (*Israël contre les nations* (Gabriel Beauchesne, Paris, 1939), p. 68). See also *La France réelle*, 1 April 1939.
60 *Progrès de Seine-et-Oise*, 28 May 1938. Quoted in Centre de documentation et de vigilance, no. 67, 2 June 1938. This bulletin also lists a very large number of anti-Semitic articles against Blum in the provinces, in *Le Cri de Lyon*, *La Province* (Rennes), *Le Progrès Agricole* (Amiens), *La*

A State within the State? 257

Nantronnaise, etc. See nos 50 and 53, 13 Jan. 1938. In addition, *Le Phare de Royan*; see, for example, 16 April 1938.

61 L. F. Céline, *Bagatelles pour un massacre* (Denoël, Paris, 1937), p. 97.
62 Ibid., p. 317. See Paul Kingston, *Antisemitism in France during the 1930s: Organization, personalities and propaganda* (University of Hull Press, Hull, 1983), p. 118.
63 Marcel Jouhandeau, *Le Péril juif* (Fernand Sorlot, Paris, 1936), pp. 10 and 12.
64 *L'Univers israélite*, 29 Jan. 1937.
65 Jean Zay was often wrongly regarded as Jewish. See Antoine Prost's introduction to Jean Zay's book, *Souvenir et solitude* (Éditions Talus d'Approche, Paris, 1987), p. 14. In fact, Jean Zay's mother was Protestant and only his father was a Jew.
66 See Colton, *Léon Blum*, pp. 153–4. In our day, Stephen Schuker almost adopts the theses of the supporters of political anti-Semitism when he surprisingly considers that historians underplay the strong presence of Jews in the Popular Front government; he himself regards it as far too high and understands how it was able to provoke anti-Semitic reactions ('Origins of the "Jewish Problem" in the Third Republic', in F. Malino and B. Wasserstein (eds), *The Jews in Modern France* (Brandeis University Press, Hanover, N.H., 1985), pp. 158ff.
67 *Le Charivari*, 20 June 1936. See also the issues of 30 May, 11 and 25 July, and 14 November 1936. The issue of 11 July 1936 is particularly scurrilous. It contains the following comment: 'Soon, it will not be possible to get into the presidency without having been duly "frisked" by Léon Blum's myrmidons and without having given proof, member in hand, that one is really of the tribe that governs France' . . .; or again, this: 'We live at the moment under the sign of M. Léon Blum, under the sign of the secateurs.' On 11 July this journal declared: 'the 32 ministers of the Jewish cabinet are sacred, consecrated, circumcised'. See also *Le Rire*, 20 June 1936.
68 *Cahier jaune*, no. 1, Nov. 1941.
69 *Journal officiel*, 7 June 1936, p. 1327.
70 *Tribune juive*, 19 June 1936.
71 Charles Maurras, 'Le Ministère du juif Blum fait son entrée', *L'Action française*, 9 June 1936.
72 *Le Charivari*, 13 June 1936.
73 *Le Temps*, 2 June 1936.
74 *Je suis partout*, 7 Jan. 1938. See Pierre-Marie Dioudonnat, *Je suis partout, 1930–1944: Les maurrassiens devant la tentation fasciste* (La Table ronde, Paris, 1973).
75 *Comité de vigilance*, no. 49.
76 See, for example, *La Libre Parole et Le Porc Epic*, 1 June 1936; and Jean-Charles Legrand, *Paroles vivantes* (Éditions Baudinière, Paris, 1941), p. 186.
77 *Le Charivari*, 6 June 1936.
78 *Franchise*, 10 June 1936; quoted by the *Comité de vigilance*, no. 50.
79 *La Dépêche*, 31 March 1937; quoted by the *Comité de vigilance*, 15 April 1937.
80 Robert Brasillach, *Notre avant-guerre* (Plon, Paris, 1941), p. 186. For *Choc*, 'an old-French heritage is rising up before the provoking Asianism of Blum' (24 Dec. 1936).
81 Quoted by *Le Droit de vivre*, 10 June 1936.
82 *Bulletin municipal*, 23 June 1936. See Jean Laloum, *La France antisémite de Darquier de Pellepoix* (Syros, Paris, 1979).
83 *L'Action française*, 5 June 1936.
84 On this point, Pierre Birnbaum, 'La fin de l'État?', *Revue française de science politique*, Dec. 1985.
85 In addition, see *L'Assaut*, 8 Dec. 1936; *La Tempête*, 8 Jan. 1938; *La Province*, 10 Sept. 1938; *La Flèche*, 11 Nov. 1938, an issue in which Gaston Bergery notes 'the multiplication of Jews under

the Blum ministry' and adds: 'I am convinced that Léon Blum did not desire this and was unwillingly led into it by his friends, his relations, his affinities and above all by his thought according to which the Jewish question cannot be posed.'

86 See, for example, Marcel Jouhandeau, 'Vous prendrez possession du pays', *Je suis partout*, 30 July 1937; *Le Franciste*, 25 April 1937. On this point, see Alain Deniel, *Bucard et le francisme* (Jean Picollec, Paris, 1979); *Pas difficile*, no. 1, Feb. 1939, which declares: 'the Jew Mandel places members of his race before Frenchmen. He follows the example of his leader, Léon Blum who has infested all the ministries, the whole administration with Yids'; A. de Puységur, *Qu'était le Juif avant la guerre? Tout. Que doit-il être? Rien* (Éditions Baudinière, Paris, 1942), p. 105. John Sherwood, on the contrary, curiously thinks that 'in contrast to Léon Blum, Mandel was usually careful not to surround himself with colleagues of Jewish origin' (*Georges Mandel and the Third Republic* (Stanford University Press, Stanford, Conn., 1970), p. 3.

87 *Aspects de la France*, 7 Jan. 1955.

88 *Écrits de Paris*, July–Aug. 1955. See also Pierre-Antoine Cousteau, another ghost from the 1930s, *Après le déluge* (La Librairie française, Paris, 1956), p. 51.

89 See, for example, *Aspects de la France*, 9 July 1937. In *La République de Joinovici*, Pierre Boutang compares Blum with Mendès France and claims kinship with State anti-Semitism (Amiot-Dumont, Paris, 1949, p. 36).

90 *Aspects de la France*, 13 Aug. 1954.

91 *Aspects de la France*, 24 Sept. 1954 and 25 June 1954. See also the issue of 13 Aug. 1954. On Sept. 24 1954 the front page of this weekly, stated: 'The Jew Mendès has won his bet against France.' In the face of such attacks, the Attorney General wanted to prosecute Pierre Boutang and *Aspects de la France* for defamation. Pierre Mendès France first refused, then agreed. On 18 Jan. 1955 the county court of the Seine condemned Pierre Boutang, finding him 'guilty of public abuse and defamation'. The latter appealed on 3 May 1955 and the chamber of the Court of Appeal confirmed the decision and increased the fine. This affair caused disagreement at *L'Action française* and Pierre Boutang left the journal shortly afterwards. On the whole file, see 'Affaire "Aspects de la France" ', *Archives privées Marie-Claire Mendès France*. This file contains the whole of the judgments, letters from Pierre Mendès France to the Minister of Justice and his lawyers, a police report on the journal *Aspects de la France* of 27 Sept. 1954, etc. These same *Archives privées* also contain two files of prosecutions for anti-Semitic remarks against *Rivarol* and *Nouveaux Jours*, with letters from the Minister of Justice to Pierre Mendès France asking him to pursue the prosecutions; a report from the Minister of the Interior on the internal operation of *Rivarol*, as well as on its contributors, such as Alfred Fabre-Luce; the sentence on *Nouveaux Jours* by the 17th county court of the Seine, 22 Feb. 1956, etc.

92 *Aspects de la France*, 29 Oct. 1954.

93 *Le Charivari*, Oct.–Dec. 1967, no. 1, p. 21.

94 *Aspects de la France*, 30 July 1954.

95 *Carrefour*, 19 March 1958.

96 Sapiens (Fabre-Luce), *Mendès ou Pinay* (Grasset, Paris, 1953), p. 40; André Siegfried, *De la IIIe à la IVe République* (Grasset, Paris, 1956), p. 172. See also *Minute*, 23 Oct. 1982.

97 *Les Écrits de Paris*, Oct. 1954.

98 *Aspects de la France*, 5 June 1953.

99 *Les Écrits de Paris*, Oct. 1954.

100 *Fraternité française*, 31 Dec. 1955.

101 Pierre Poujade, *J'ai choisi le combat* (Société générale des Éditions et des Publications, St Céré, 1955), p. 116.

A State within the State? 259

102 *Fraternité française*, 7 Jan. 1956.
103 Michel Winock, 'Les affaires Dreyfus', *Vingtième Siècle*, no. 5 (Jan.–March 1985), pp. 32ff.
104 Quoted by Stanley Hoffmann, *Le mouvement Poujade* (Cahiers de la Fondation nationale des sciences politiques, Paris, 1958), p. 354.
105 Ibid., p. 181. The similarities with the period of Léon Blum are devastating.
106 This declaration was made during a press conference which Pierre Poujade gave to the foreign press at Claridges on 18 Jan. 1956; quoted by the *Bulletin d'information interne du CRIF*, 12 Feb. 1956.
107 See the report of this demonstration in *Franc-Tireur*, 19 Jan. 1956.
108 See Henry Rousso, *Le Syndrome de Vichy, 1944–198*... (Le Seuil, Paris, 1987).
109 See, for example, *Chevrotine*, 15 April, 1957. On the Poujadist movement and anti-Semitism, see Pierre Birnbaum, *Le peuple et les gros* (Grasset, Paris, 1979), pp. 70–8.
110 See Hoffmann, *Le mouvement Poujade*, p. 354.
111 For example, *Jeune nation*, allied to the *Rassemblement national* organized a meeting in the Salle Wagram on 24 November 1954 where such calls were heard, while a leaflet was distributed saying: 'Israel is colonizing France' (see *Droit et Liberté*, Nov. 1954). The same journal pointed out that at Bézier and also at Montpellier and other provincial towns, one could hear shouts of 'Dirty Jew' and 'Mendès the Yid': (Feb. 1956). On Monday, 16 Dec. 1955, a leaflet was also distributed at Nîmes in the following terms: 'No, to Mendès the Anti-France' *(Archives privées Simone Gros)*.
112 Quoted by Jean Lacouture, *Pierre Mendès France* (Le Seuil, Paris, 1981), p. 447. Jean Lacouture quotes, for example, an extract from the paper *L'Éclair*, edited by Rémy Montagne, which stressed that 'in November 1954 the old radical party felt more and more uncomfortable.... Certain members of the party left it at that time or were expelled. New recruits with names like Servan-Schreiber, Hovnanian, Lipkowski replaced them....'
113 *Archives privées Simone Gros.*
114 Ibid. See also *Le Droit de vivre* which echoes these anti-Semitic attacks in the name of the UNR, and the immediate denial by this party (12 Dec. 1956).
115 *Volonté socialiste*, no. 38 (15 Feb. 1967); quoted by José Alain Fralon, 'Les élections législatives de mars 1967', dissertation of the 3rd cycle of the LEP of Grenoble, Grenoble, 1967. The author also quotes leaflets which refer to Pierre Mendès France's family origins and emphasize that 'his family took care not to make any non-Mosaic alliances'.
116 *Minute*, 2 March 1967. At the same period, Pierre Mendès France was still receiving anti-Semitic letters at his private home (see *Archives privées Simone Gros*).
117 See Françoise Gaspard's evidence (lecture 'Sur l'antiracisme de Pierre Mendès France', at the Institut Pierre Mendès France, 13 Jan. 1987).
118 M. François Lanzenberg kindly showed me this document.
119 Pierre Mendès France had not come to the end of his difficulties; even as late as 1978 he was still receiving anti-Semitic letters addressed to him personally (see *Archives de l'Institut Pierre Mendès France*).
120 *Rivarol*, 24 Aug. 1984, and 31 Jan. 1985.
121 Ibid., 7 Feb. 1985.
122 *Présent*, 9 July 1984. This paper added that 'L. Fabius met the revolution in the features of Georges Dayan, a former Jewish lawyer from Oran, head of M. Mitterrand's cabinet'.
123 *Le Monde*, 21 July 1984, picked out this comparison and considered that *Présent* 'is renewing the anti-Semitic tradition of the thirties. [It is] taking precautions with its style since a law has existed since 1972 curbing racist activities and remarks.' Making fun of *Le Monde*'s comments, *Rivarol* considered that the parallel that *Présent* attempted to draw between Blum and Fabius

'commands attention' (27 July 1984). See also the extremely cautious comments in *Lectures françaises*, Sept. and Nov. 1984.
124 *Écrits de Paris*, Oct. 1984.
125 *Minute*, 26 Oct. and 2 Nov. 1985.
126 Ibid., 26 Oct. 1985.

11
Society Betrayed

The supporters of political anti-Semitism saw the Jews as the lords of the republican state, enjoying their victory and not hesitating to increase to the maximum the hold it gave them over society. For their plan to succeed, they shamelessly utilized the enormous power of the absolutist state built up by the monarchy and which the French Revolution, the Empires and the Republic had continued to reinforce. In fact, their privilege was unique since the state that they allegedly dominated was indubitably one of the strongest in the Western world. By leaving the ghetto, becoming emancipated citizens, espousing the religion of state, and finally, by acceding to politico-administrative power, they could now carry through their plan. This plan was to pervert society, abolish its traditional beliefs by remoulding as they pleased the soul of those who had fashioned it and still continued to give it life.

SECULARISM OR QUASI-CIVIL WAR

To build a rational and universalist state first required the reduction of the Catholic sphere of influence, which entirely structured the collective consciousness of French society. The construction of state space disrupted the unity of the social body. Its homogeneity had always been derived from the values spread primarily through the educational system by the Catholic Church, so fine was the network that the hierarchical structure of the Church cast over the country. In this sense, the ultimate point of the struggle for secularism expressed the state's desire to challenge this control of minds. This being the case, the head-on collision could only be brutal and decisive. It was here that the future of the republican state was really played out, since it too claimed to fashion the values of its citizens.

From Gambetta to Jules Ferry, Waldeck-Rousseau and Clemenceau, republicans thought that the cult of Reason provided the new code to ensure the legitimacy of a state which intended to take autonomization to its logical conclusion by withdrawing itself from the grip of Catholic values. To sweep away metaphysical beliefs and impose its own identity they embarked, in the name of the Enlightenment and science, on a merciless struggle with the Catholic Church, destroying the moral order, conservative and hostile to the Republic, which the Church had often encouraged. At the end of the nineteenth century, republican ideology proclaimed the ineluctable character of secular existence, capable by itself of defining the new frontiers of the state. This seemed the inescapable price for the definitive emancipation of the state.[1]

On 10 February 1879 Jules Ferry appointed Ferdinand Buisson, 'Combes's *éminence grise*', to direct primary education. Buisson personified this battle for what he called 'integral secularism'. From this time, Republic and secularism in France merged into one. Buisson was conscious of this peculiarity arising from the history of the state. 'Yes', he said, 'we are the only people in the world to be pursuing in our own logical way an ideal which seems almost a chimera to all other peoples.'[2] 'The secular invasion', to use a metaphor invented by Louis Capéran, the campaign for free-thinking it provoked, the creation of the Fédération de la jeunesse laïque and so many other secular organizations, the decisive role that teachers played, caused a serious eruption of deep-seated anti-clericalism which led at the turn of the century to the final separation of Church and state. Barrès, bard of anti-Semitism, saw the confrontations that took place in the Chamber as the expression of 'the struggle between Catholicism and irreligion'. To the Dreyfusard, Charles Péguy, they symbolized 'the state metaphysics' which it was now planned to impose throughout society by excluding the priests from the schools and by overturning the educational apparatus from top to bottom.[3] 'The reawakening of anti-clericalism' (Georges Weil) roused angry emotions.[4]

Paradoxically, anti-clericalism assumed features identical with those of anti-Semitism and anti-Protestantism, as though in France every myth obeyed the same logic. People who supported secularism and the separation of Church from state thought that the Church actually formed 'a state within the state' in the service of the Catholic international, betraying France to the Germans. The servants of the Church did not fulfil their military obligations, they claimed; on the contrary, they deliberately set out to emasculate adolescents.[5] The outpourings of anti-clericalism followed a path identical to those other 'doctrines of hate', in Anatole Leroy-Beaulieu's famous phrase, which anti-Semitism and anti-Protestantism were.[6] Here, therefore, was the surprising establishment of a sort of political anti-clericalism, the parallel to political anti-Semitism.

In this spirit, Gambetta was basically the Maurras of anti-clericalism, stubbornly pursuing with his obloquy every symptom revealing the presence of the Church in the heart of the republican state. 'I intend', he said in Lille in 1876, 'that the Church remains the Church, that it never comes down into the public arena, that it never enters Parliament nor the councils of state.' And in a speech at Lyons he added, 'A sort of league, a sort of association was formed in the heart of France. . . . It did not stop there. The administration gave it the utmost co-operation, and showed the greatest favour to the unusual development of religious corporations.'[7]

At the same time, there was a curious mythological 'general post' between Jews and Catholics. Whereas champions of anti-clericalism were denouncing the Church's influence in the state and devoting all their energies to its final expulsion, supporters of political anti-Semitism thought that it was rather the Jews who were gradually making themselves masters of the state. Secularism, in their view, was only an ideology to mask the total domination that the Jews would exercise when the Republic subsequently became 'absolute'. Drumont had already advanced this nightmarish theory at the turn of the century before the great explosion which marked the separation of Church from state. He never ceased to attribute the 'decadence of the French soul'[8] to the activities of the Jews who had made themselves dominant in schools and universities, spreading teachings hostile to the Catholic Church. Likewise, as has already been noted, most of the heroes of the Republic, such as Gambetta, Jules Ferry and Jules Simon, as well as Waddington, Millerand and Clemenceau, were really Jews disguised as disinterested supporters of rationalism and science.[9] Obviously none of them was a Jew, any more than Briand, Combes, Jaurès or Waldeck-Rousseau.

In the same spirit, Urbain Gohier thought that 'the Jews who are secularizing France do not secularize their own nation. It is a religious war they are waging against the Church of Rome.' Combes and Jaurès were only 'puppets whose strings are pulled by the synagogue'.[10] The author of *La France juive* endlessly associated Jews with freemasons, whose ideal of free-thinking fitted in very well with a secular Republic. In fact, freemasons had long been linked with Jews in the minds of anti-Semitic authors, in the sense that both were thought to share the same maleficent power.[11] They were seen as equally obscure and cosmopolitan forces which allied themselves with the Jews to consolidate this secular Republic which was proving so favourable. To the Comte de Colleville, for example, 'the Jews and the freemason are the two cankers gnawing at France', and were responsible for the 1903 and 1905 separation laws.[12]

This alleged association of Jews with freemasons proved utterly explosive. In fact, contrary to the legends eagerly spread, there was not one Jew among the founders of the Republic (though Paul Grunebaum-Ballin, member of the Council of State and friend of Combes, was responsible for formulating the report on the Separation).[13] But historians do not contest the very active presence of freemasons, emphasizing their crucial role in implementing secularism.[14] Yet the idea of a 'Jewish conspiracy',[15] linked to the equally satanic activity of the freemasons and fomented under cover of the republican ideal, became commonplace at a time when an atmosphere of masked civil war was incubating. The struggle against secularism now formed an integral part of the arsenal of the champions of political anti-Semitism.

In the inter-war period, however, its cutting edge was considerably blunted, so much had secularism become part of an idea accepted by almost everybody.

264 Political Anti-Semitism

Other than for a few nostalgic folk, secularism had at last become part of everyday life, like the separation of Church and state which had provoked so much sound and fury. Anti-clericalism likewise no longer drew the crowds. As early as 1925, for example, in a debate on the embassy to the Holy See, Léon Blum showed much tolerance and understanding towards the religious realities.[16] Anti-clericalism did, of course, break out from time to time. For example, during the 1924 legislative elections it was vigorously claimed that

> the left-wing coalition stands for secularism. It stands for freedom of the secular school, mother of democracy, it stands for freedom of conscience for everyone, but it stands for absolute respect for the law of separation, the immediate withdrawal of the embassy from the Vatican, the struggle against the Congregation, the Republic's eternal enemy.[17]

Anti-clericalism was still forcibly expressed in this way in many professions of electoral faith by the candidates of the Cartel of the Left. Despite everything, the religious war was no longer a reality and consensus on these various questions was no less real. All this changed considerably, however, with the Popular Front and the violent crisis of anti-Semitism it provoked. Léon Blum and his various political allies took constant care to 'extend a hand' to the Catholics. But the social and ideological quasi-civil war which suddenly broke out is reminiscent of the schisms at the turn of the century because of the gravity of the stakes involved, which inevitably had repercussions in the religious domain. The Spanish war, in which the religious question played a crucial part, further complicated matters in France and pushed numerous Catholics into the moderate or nationalist camp – almost entirely won over to anti-Semitism. French Catholics rejected the Spanish *'frente crapular'* with horror and moved further and further away from the Popular Front led, to cap it all, by a Jew.

It was basically in this context that the strong resurgence of the old question of secularism, which had formerly divided Frenchmen so sharply, took place. Before 1936, attacks on Blum on the grounds of the rejection of secularism were rare. None the less, in 1919 *La Vieille France* attacked 'Lévy-Bruhl, Durkheim, Sée, Basch, Blum who rule over public education in France'.[18] And in 1920 *L'Action française* accused Léon Blum of 'preparing the way for the reconstruction of the secular coalition' by attacking Catholicism.[19] Another voice raised in the same cause was that of Mgr Jouin, editor of the *Revue internationale des sociétés secrètes*, which also did much to spread the most virulent anti-Semitism up to Vichy and is famous for one of the very first complete editions of the *Protocols of the Elders of Zion*.[20] He declared war on 'the anti-clericalism which is the crux of Judeo-masonic activity', and denounced 'the law of separation with Grunebaum-Ballin, the secular policy with the Blums, Lévy-Ulmans, etc.'.

But all this was only a foretaste of the ever more exaggerated accusations which broke out after the formation and victory of the Popular Front. As usual,

Charles Maurras led the assault. 'Blum', he said, 'is a messianist who believes in the secularized mission of Israel.'[21] *Le Franciste* concluded that 'the Jews have become a majority in the state', and accused Léon Blum, Jean Zay and Jules Moch of seizing the banner of secularism in order to initiate a new anti-clerical campaign. The conclusions drawn from this by *Le Franciste*, journal of the best-structured radical right-wing organizations, were clear and simple. 'Towards pogroms', it predicted; proof, if proof were required, that the current debate on the reality of fascism in France does not cover the question of anti-Semitism as such.

Both in discussion and in everyday practice, its undeniable presence now constituted the most serious threat to the Jews. The anger of the radical right-wing parties knew no bounds when they learned with amazement that Jean Zay had been appointed head of the Ministry of National Education. Faced with such infamous conduct, Léon Daudet put the point plainly: 'The cabinet of the Talmud has entrusted the portfolio of National Education to an unknown Jew called Jean Zay.... Here, the order of the synagogue meets up with that of the synagogue-lodge, which is the masonic lodge.'[22] A wave of a magic wand and one is transported back to the heroic times at the end of the nineteenth century and to the battle between Catholic Frenchmen, faithful heirs to ancestral tradition on the one hand, and the Jews and freemasons on the other, instruments of satanic internationals, who ended up merged into one.

So complete was this identification in the minds of his unbridled opponents that Léon Blum was presented as a fanatical freemason, activated by the desire to extend the de-Christianization undertaken by the Republic through the complete secularization of the educational system. The pressure was so intense that even the journal *La Croix*, which gave him a very favourable reception – comparing him, it will be recalled, with Poincaré – still went so far as to express the fear of seeing a resumption of Combes's strategy, thereby making a fresh attack on the influence of Catholicism in the schools.[23] *La Croix* reserved its thunderbolts for the teachers, veritable 'conquerors' imposing, through the single state-controlled school, a 'totalitarian régime that the Catholic world, under threat of complete secularization, will suffer in all its harshness'.[24] There was nothing more to add, since even *La Croix* now felt the same. The violently anti-Semitic incidents in Alsace-Lorraine, which have already been mentioned, showed how Catholics ardently rejected any sign of a resumption of a secularizing policy for schools. Under the Vichy regime, this accusation would be at the centre of the case built up against Léon Blum. It was frequently emphasized that the 'Jewish clericalist' saw it as his mission to pursue the demolition work begun by Gambetta. This 'Judeo-masonic clericalism has become the master of our public affairs', to the detriment of Catholic values which were shared by the vast majority of Frenchmen.[25] For a number of Vichy supporters, Léon Blum, as a result of his control of the SNI and the Ligue de l'enseignement, and in agreement with the freemasons, was the person really responsible for the disintegration of France which resulted from the imposition of the secular school.[26] He never managed to dispel this myth.[27]

Many leaflets and pamphlets depicted Léon Blum as a Jewish freemason. In that role he extended the secularization of French society, as the republicans always had. It is known for certain, however, that Léon Blum never belonged to a masonic lodge.[28] Even so, like the men who founded the Third Republic, he appeared as a formidable freemason. Here again, compared with the myths, the facts really carried very little weight. It was true that a large number of those present at the birth of the Third Republic, such as Félix Faure, Aristide Briand, Gambetta, Jules Ferry, Jules Simon and Camille Chautemps and Gaston Salengro, were freemasons. None of them was of Jewish origin.[29] On the contrary, Pierre Mendès France was the only one of the state Jews who had access to the heights of freemasonry. He had joined the Pacy-sur-Eure masonic lodge in the thirties, but subsequently left it.[30] Neither Léon Blum nor Georges Mandel ever belonged.[31] In other words, although the founders of the Republic were often freemasons, they were never Jews. On the other hand, even the state Jews who came to power long afterwards rarely included freemasons.

The zealous propagandists of the theory of political anti-Semitism had little interest in these distinctions. They enveloped republicans, Jews and freemasons in the same accusation without paying any attention whatsoever to the fact that these three groups of actors only rarely overlapped. Léon Blum was still the incarnation of the perfect freemason in the iconography of professional political anti-Semitism. As early as 1920 *La Vieille France*, ever true to Drumont's inspiration, made fun of 'B ∴ Blum and B ∴ Téry who received the Chief Rabbi's blessing'.[32] After its reappearance, *La Libre Parole* outdid them all in heaping insults on B ∴ Blum.[33] In the same spirit, for *L'Action anti-maçonnique*, 'The B ∴ has delivered France over to the Jews and B ∴ L. Blum is president of the Council. With him triumphs the clique of greedy foreigners.'[34] Innumerable caricatures depicted Léon Blum as a freemason,[35] and he was the favourite target of the *Revue internationale des sociétés secrètes* which saw him as the most formidable Jew of the masonic order.[36] At a lecture in the Salle des Centraux on 27 February 1936 a speaker from the *Ligue franc-catholique* forcefully declared 'the patriots will not for ever permit B ∴ Léon Blum and B ∴ Jean Zay to raise the workers against us'.[37]

Denials could not stop the rumours spreading, nor finally put an end to these fantastic assertions. Historians of freemasonry confirm the inaccuracy of the accusations by the champions of political anti-Semitism who ceaselessly associated state Jews with the mysterious and supposedly maleficent forces of freemasonry. Today it is known that Léon Blum never maintained any links with freemasonry, any more than Georges Mandel, Jules Moch or any of the state Jews who held politico-administrative office in contemporary France.[38] It is known that only Pierre Mendès France was initiated into the Paris lodge, Paris Orient, in 1928 and belonged to the Honour and Probity lodge, Pacy-sur-Eure Orient. After 1945 he withdrew from all masonic activity.[39] Jean Zay too was certainly initiated into the Orléans Orient in January 1926 and his name figures on lists of freemasons published by the *Journal Officiel* under the Vichy government.[40] He was Minister for Education from the formation of the Popular Front government and retained this post until September 1939. At first glance, therefore, he seems to fit the image that the enemies of the Republic drew of the freemason and republican Jew, anxious to strengthen secularization, following on from many Ministers of Public Education, from Jules Simon to Jules Ferry, Paul Bert and Léon Bourgeois, who were all in fact freemasons. What ruins this nightmare vision is that Jean Zay was no more a Jew than his predecessors and claimed no kinship with Judaism – which Léon Blum and Pierre Mendès France could openly do. Like many of the ministers for Public Education, so feared by the radical right-wing militants, he was really closer to the Protestantism he had inherited on his maternal side, even though his background through his paternal grandparents – Alsatian Jews who had opted for France in 1871 – was to an extent identical to that of Léon Blum.

Eager to give their theories undisputed lustre but economical with the facts, the champions of political anti-Semitism held up the freemason Jews, Blum, Mendès France, Mandel and Jean Zay to public obloquy. As early as 1936 their names were associated – particularly those of Léon Blum and Pierre Mendès France – in anti-Semitic lampoons which denounced them as freemasons.[41] In particular Henry Coston's many articles from 1935 till today have striven to unmask these two Jewish heads of government in order to unveil their common allegiance to freemasonry.[42] From this point of view, Coston became part of the untiring struggle against the radical President of the Council waged by Pierre Boutang who, in *Aspects de la France*, denounced 'the supra-nationality of Mendès's masonic and Jewish training.'[43]

FRANCE FACES WAR: JEWISH WAR-MONGERING

The Jews, it was said, were colluding with the freemasons to damage the fundamental values of a French society that was still Christian, using secularism as a pretext to conceal their enterprise. Supporters of the nationalist right-wing parties saw this internal quasi-civil war as a symbol of the inevitable betrayal the Jewish freemasons were striving for. To the inveterate defenders of the tradition exemplified in the Barrèsian concept of 'the land and the dead', France faced another and even more terrible menace: the menace that resulted from Jewish war-mongering. The internal war therefore ran parallel to an external war, becoming increasingly more probable every day and deliberately provoked by the Jews, who would in this way satisfy their own passions.

What was common to all, from Charles Maurras to Paul Rassinier, father of revisionist theories, was a refusal to assume the consequences of the 'Jewish war' which both Léon Blum and Georges Mandel wanted to unleash to forward their own interests. From 1936 to 1967, the same interpretation of Jewish war-mongering prevailed in the ranks of the radical right-wing parties. Maurras issued several warnings against the deadly plans of the 'Camel, Blum-the-

War'.⁴⁴ Much later, Paul Rassinier still sought to maintain that 'for Léon Blum, it was no longer a question of seeking justice between nations but of overthrowing Hitler because of his racial policy'.⁴⁵ Hostile at first to Hitlerian Germany, the extreme Right declared that it favoured a policy of appeasement and entente. It was soon joined by new supporters of out-and-out pacifism, recruited from the moderates as well as from the ranks of the socialists, grouped around Paul Faure whose anti-Semitic remarks have already been examined. Their hatred of the Popular Front and Léon Blum now caused them to take a different view of Hitlerian society.⁴⁶ The old atavism of the nationalist Right, which had always proclaimed its fierce hostility to Germany, suddenly disappeared.

At a time when a general conflagration threatened the European nations, 'Blum-the-War is really leading the dance. Will France fight for Israel and be the instrument of Jehovah's vengeance on the nations?', asked the *Revue hebdomadaire*.⁴⁷ Henri Béraud thought the answer was clear. On the eve of Munich, the last chance for a rapprochement with Germany, Blum-the-War, leader of the 'Hebrews living on our land', 'racial brother of Lecache' and the militant Jews of the LICA, was openly sabotaging this hope of peace to go to the help of the German Jews.⁴⁸ These dark, macchiavellian plans must be thwarted before it was too late: 'Frenchmen, stand up against the Jews! Peace, Peace, Peace!' screamed *La Lorraine déchaînée*, which proudly proclaimed its loyalty to Drumont's memory.⁴⁹ *La Libre Parole*, which also prided itself on expressing the thoughts of the author of *La Faune juive*, earnestly posed the following question. 'Frenchmen reading this, are you ready to die and sacrifice your children for the Jew Blum's crusade against the ungodly anti-Semite Hitler?'⁵⁰ The reply was obvious; even Roger Martin du Gard supported it when he solemnly stated: 'All Hitler rather than war'.⁵¹

Pierre Gaxotte had no doubts. Blum-the-War 'will be very content'⁵² when he succeeds in his aims: 'To offer, as Charles Maurras bluntly said, our skins to his blood brothers'.⁵³ To the theorist of *L'Action française* there was an obvious 'remedy for war': 'Repeat daily: Down with the Jews. The Jew Blum wants your skin. You are not going to give it to him! But we advise him to look out for his own if it so happens that he makes us part of a universal massacre.'⁵⁴

His colleague Léon Daudet said the same, but in his own inimitable style. He too refused to participate in the 'crusade for Israel' and issued a warning

Frenchmen, young and old, from every background, from every class, from every province, from every profession, are you prepared to go off to avenge Israel for the persecutions inflicted on it by Hitler and the swastika? Are you enrolling in the new crusade, this one starting from Jerusalem, which the ethnic hybrid and hermaphrodite Léon Blum is inviting us to join?⁵⁵

We shall cite a few final examples of this logic, which so many of Blum's contemporaries seemed to share and which drove them straight into Hitler's arms. According to *Candide*, 'France has a million reasons for thinking that M.

Blum's quarrel with Monsieur Hitler is primarily personal. He has no right to speak in the name of France.... While Germany seems to be meeting our wishes, Blum and Moch are imposing a dangerous war-like psychosis on us.'[56] Céline made the same comment more harshly: 'I say what I think quite frankly. I would prefer a dozen Hitlers to an omnipotent Blum.'[57] What followed is history. When Hitler's armies had conquered the French Republic, Vichy avenged the Popular Front by offering up the state Jews Léon Blum, Pierre Mendès France, Georges Mandel (but also Jean Zay) as expiatory victims. They were made into real scapegoats, responsible for the defeat of France. But their activities, considered so dire, had finally made possible the end of the republican state, 'that heavenly surprise', in the eyes of the radical right-wing parties.[58]

So many people at that time regarded the Jews as possible traitors that allegations about which power they were serving to safeguard their own interests varied considerably. For some, paradoxically and contrary to all appearances, it was Germany itself. Others saw Blum and Mendès France as highly efficient agents either of the Anglo-Saxon countries or ... of the Soviet Union. As early as 1923, at the time of the occupation of the Ruhr, *L'Action française* denounced Léon Blum's 'pro-German pleading'.[59] In the face of all opposition, the journal of the monarchist Right backed this theory, strange as it may seem at first glance. In 1932 Maurras regarded Blum as 'the leader of the pro-German party in France'.[60] Unconcerned about the improbability of his comments, Pierre Gaxotte also saw Léon Blum as 'a secret agent of the Gestapo, a Hitlerian'[61] who did everything he could to prevent Hitler attacking the Soviet Union, then in a weak position, and strove to persuade him to turn against France instead. His accession to the Presidency was itself a deliberate encouragement to Hitler, since it considerably weakened France. No doubt, proclaimed *L'Action française*, 'that in the case of France being wiped out by German arms, we will find the large gang of Jewish deserters whom our state Jews have so warmly welcomed to France in the front rank of the informers–profiteers'![62]

Blum's 'heart was always in Berlin', and his secret wish was to obliterate all 'traces of the victory of 1918'.[63] This seemed to be the innermost conviction of the radical right-wing parties who, for the time being, proclaimed their Germanophobia. According to *Je suis partout*, 'M. Blum is really hoping to take advantage of the situation to serve the only country – we mean Germany – to which he could declare, like Chimène to Rodrigue: "So! I don't hate you at all" ... M. Blum is working to disarm France with all the sophisticated weapons of a subtle, oriental mind, fashioned by the discipline of the Talmud.'[64]

Je suis partout stuck to its guns. Léon Blum, it wrote, 'is working furiously for the Germany of Barons von Papen and Hindenburg'.[65] The most fantastic explanations of this paradox, which was surprising to say the least, circulated in the ranks of the nationalist Right. The most common consisted quite simply of maintaining that the leader of the French socialist movement was really of German nationality. Suddenly, 'Blum is not a traitor since one can only be betrayed by one's own and M. Blum is a German Jew'.[66] As always, political anti-Semitism reached the depths of abomination in song[67] and verse:

> Léon Blum's a German good,
> In heart and soul if not in race.
> At this time, he really should
> Take a walk at gentle pace
> Down Wilhelmstrasse, if he could.
>
> He will not go! It may sound lame
> But Germany has changed its style.
> Berlin and Paris meant the same,
> But Berlin's value falls the while
> Since the time that Hitler came.
>
> Israel's copping it, they say,
> And if our Blum to Prussia went,
> They'd ask him there without delay
> What his foreskin really meant –
> Awkward to explain away.[68]

That state Jews could pursue a pro-German foreign policy prejudicial to France was what really marked a peak in the intrigues dreamt up to feed the delirious ravings of the imaginative champions of political anti-Semitism. And yet this same nightmare reappeared, and was just as seriously reported in our own day, when Pierre Mendès France was accused of being none other than 'a Jewish politician restoring German militarism'.[69]

The radical and conservative right-wing parties were not bothered by these contradictions. Even in the 1920s they maintained that Léon Blum 'trembles like a flower at every wind from the steppes. He shivers at every breath from Moscow. M. Blum is towed along by Bolshevism.'[70] This accusation was clearly and irrefutably made only a few years after the great breach at the Congress of Tours when Léon Blum used every effort to stop the French socialist movement rejoining the Third International, thus provoking the great schism in the French workers' movement. For Léon Daudet, 'the French nation is warned by the Jew Léon Blum of the compelling need to allow itself to be massacred for the Moscovite executioners'.[71] When the SFIO leader said that he favoured a Franco-Soviet alliance, he was therefore effectively serving the Bolshevik interests which he so vigorously opposed on the political scene. And when he incessantly attacked Hitlerite Germany, it was solely for the better protection of the Soviet Union threatened by Nazism. Léon Blum, so the claims went, was really an agent of the Third International hiding under the banner of socialism, 'delegated by Moscow, together with Moch, to lead the Popular

Front in order to provoke war ... putting France at the service of Bolshevism'.[72] 'Admit', demanded *Candide*, 'that it is the flag of the USSR that you want to hoist over our buildings and the Red Army star that you want to make us wear on our helmets.'[73]

In the same way as they unanimously denounced Léon Blum as a Germanophile, Charles Maurras and Pierre Gaxotte now claimed with equal conviction that the President of the Council was humbly subjected to Soviet power.[74] For *Je suis partout*, 'if Léon Blum is a messiah, Thorez and Duclos are nothing more than miserable gang leaders. He will overcome them with the full force of his intelligence. Poor things!'[75] This was a different interpretation of the breach between the leaders of the workers' movement which took place in 1920. Now Léon Blum was depicted as an infinitely more cunning ally of the Soviet Union than Thorez or Duclos, in so far as he always concealed his progress. The 'Marxist experiment' supposedly being conducted in France under the control of the new Moses, Léon Blum, had innumerable opponents.[76] Even the serious *Journal des débats* was convinced that 'the Popular Front and the Blum cabinet are indispensable to Moscow as agents of the destruction of the state and as protectors of Soviet enterprises'.[77] The newest fantasy of the champions of political anti-Semitism was therefore that state Jews really masked dangerous Bolshevik agitators. It was not easily forgotten; in 1954 Pierre Mendès France was depicted as 'a Jacobin Jew who began his career with a pilgrimage to Moscow'. Thereafter he always proved 'a zealous agent of the USSR', and that included the policy of decolonization in Indo-China, which will be dealt with later.[78]

It would be too simple to leave things there. After the betrayal of France in the name of Germany or the USSR came the scenario of equally evil activity by the Anglo-Saxon world, which found valuable allies in the state Jews. Pierre Gaxotte, a skilful dialectician, revealed the key to all these dark intrigues which the uninitiated might find slightly contradictory. 'Because he is Marxist and circumcised', he wrote, 'Blum wants to polish Hitler off; because he is an anglophile and a freemason, he wants Mussolini's hide'.[79] Everyone could interpret it as they wished.

One might, as a last resort, attempt to understand the fluctuating tactics of the propagandists of political anti-Semitism through the medium of international events. In this sense, the defeat of France and the shift in alliances in favour of Germany under Vichy would explain the new accusation of Anglo-Saxon sympathies that was made against the state Jews. Alas, this solution is scarcely productive since as early as 1931, at a time when Blum was considered both an agent of the Gestapo and a fierce defender of the Soviet Union, he was also being criticized for acting as the City bankers' odd-job man![80] They are so inconsistent, our state Jews! 'London Jewry provided Blum's anti-French policy with all the support he needed' to pursue his policy of devaluing the franc which benefited them, maintained *L'Action française*.[81] *Je suis partout* unambiguously argued that the fall in the franc which Léon Blum aimed for was negligible to

Anglo-Jewish financiers. 'The first circumcision was not thought sufficient. The Shylocks of speculative capitalism require an additional pound of French flesh.'[82]

The propagandists of political anti-Semitism displayed unrestrained imaginative power in a final effort to disclose the motives behind Léon Blum's foreign policy. An anonymous lampoon published in 1937 surpassed even Pierre Gaxotte's very subtle argument and easily took the palm for anti-Semitic dialectic. 'How can one fail to admit', it ran, 'that Blum only took power to unleash a financial crisis, revolution and foreign war under the patronage of Big American Banking? Blum is in the process of surrendering France into the hands of American Jews with the aim of dragging us into war against Germany for the Soviets.'[83]

These jewels of the imagination no longer had a place in the German France that was set up in 1940. Things became simpler: a hue and cry over greedy Albion manoeuvred by the nation of Israel and freemasonry to humiliate France even further![84] The hereditary enemy was suddenly transformed into a maleficent power, in concert with the United States, obeying the orders of the Jewish international which had only one desire: to take revenge on the triumphant national Revolution. And, as Jacques Doriot warned on 19 September 1941, if Great Britain perchance succeeded in its aims and invaded French territory, 'MM. Mandel, Blum, Reynaud would once again become the masters of France. Jewish finance would stifle us with its corruption.'[85]

At the Riom and Claremont-Ferrand trials and in the months which followed, Léon Blum as well as Pierre Mendès France and Georges Mandel were violently attacked as agents of the hostile Anglo-Saxon powers which were under the thumb of Jewish financiers.[86] Pierre Antoine Cousteau, editor of *Je suis partout*, considered that 'it was just as shocking to see M. Blum at the head of an old Gallo-Roman country like ours, as it is normal for the Jews of New York to choose to be administered by one of their own'.[87] All the same, he added, 'when the Americans really understand, there will be quite a jolly pogrom in the shadow of the skyscrapers'. The threat of pogroms was always explicit, as it had been previously in the inter-war period.

Hatred of Jewish America and its vassal, Great Britain, now definitively marked the French radical Right wing's vision of the world. It re-emerged intact when Pierre Mendès France came to power. For Pierre Boutang, 'the Jewish press in the United States has welcomed him with open arms'.[88] Likewise, in 1956, Pierre Antoine Cousteau published *Après le Déluge*, a book fiercely critical of Pierre Mendès France, which challenged both 'his ethnic origins' and the 'Americanization of France'. In 1942, as has been seen, Cousteau had already brought out *L'Amérique juive*, attacking Léon Blum.[89] In the minds of radical right-wing militants, America was gradually becoming the hydra symbolizing the power of the Jews who were now operating on a world scale.

This seemed to be the last incarnation of political anti-Semitism: to project outside France the condemnation of the state Jews, to extend to the Western world a model which was utterly foreign to it. To maintain that 'Roosevelt thinks and acts as if he were 100 per cent Jewish . . . if his name were Disraeli or Blum, his intentions would automatically be suspect and there would be a risk of his actions being much less effective', is to reinforce the idea that Jews had penetrated into the leadership of the Western powers who were fighting against Vichy France.[90] It was as if the Jews, either in person or through people they had installed, would always succeed in forcing their way to the top, irrespective of the type of state in place in any of the countries involved. This vision was a total figment of delirium since it will be recalled that, in Western countries with weak states, there were practically no Jews in leading positions. Once again, facts did not matter. The French model was so significant that the champions of political anti-Semitism, completely perverting the principles of Franco-Judaism, set out to reveal the control that other state Jews exercised over politico-administrative power, particularly in the Anglo-Saxon countries.

In this way, it is no surprise to find that political anti-Semitism came by a natural process of development to adopt the theories propagated by the famous *Protocols of the Elders of Zion*.[91] The historical forgery found its application in a most unexpected manner, for it presupposed the idea of world control organized from the outside by a mysterious Kahal meticulously programming its grip on every society. In the final resort, political anti-Semitism completely reversed the historic significance of Franco-Judaism. Within the framework of Franco-Judaism the emancipated Jews became citizens identical with the rest, and as such had legitimate access to the various public offices, while respecting the rules of state service and limiting the expression of their particularism solely to the private domain. Now the meaning of entry into the state radically changed: it served to establish from within the seizure of world power loudly proclaimed in the famous *Protocols*. In short, that was why, according to this crazy perspective, the policy Léon Blum pursued was far from being seen as serving the state. Instead, it was depicted as a simple link in the implacable strategy of the formidable and mysterious world-wide Jewish struggle, which organized the outbreak of wars so as to ensure the total victory of Zionism by the conquest and domination of all nations. This, then, was the true significance of 'Jewish war-mongering', so often denounced by the champions of political anti-Semitism who sought an alliance with Hitlerite Germany: it solely served 'the sinister task of Léon Blum exercised in accordance with the plan precisely set out in the *Protocols of the Elders of Zion*'.[92]

NOTES

1 Claude Nicolet, *L'idée républicaine en France* (Gallimard, Paris, 1982), ch. 6.
2 Quoted by Louis Capéran, *L'Invasion laïque* (Desclée de Brouwer, Paris, 1935), p. 138. See

Pierre Nora, 'Le Dictionnaire de Pédagogie de Ferdinand Buisson', in *Les Lieux de mémoire*, ed. Pierre Nora, vol. 1: *La République* (Gallimard, Paris, 1986).
3 These quotations are taken from Capéran, *L'Invasion laïque*, pp. 393 and 443. See also Jean-Marie Mayeur, *La Séparation de l'Église et de l'État* (Gallimard-Julliard, 'Archives', Paris, 1966). Similarly, Jean-Marie Mayeur, 'La France bourgeoise devient républicaine et laïque, 1875–1914', in L. H. Parias (ed.), *Histoire du peuple français* (Nouvelle Librairie de France, Paris, 1966).
4 See Georges Weil, *Histoire de l'idée laïque en France au XIXe siècle* (F. Alcan, Paris, 1925), ch. 13.
5 See the indispensable book by René Rémond, *L'anticléricalisme en France: De 1815 à nos jours* (Complexe, Brussels, 1985).
6 See Anatole Leroy-Beaulieu, *Les Doctrines de haine: L'antisémitisme, l'antiprotestantisme, l'anticléricalisme* (Paris, 1902).
7 Quoted by Rémond, *L'anticléricalisme en France*, pp. 178 and 182.
8 Édouard Drumont, *Le Testament d'un antisémite* (E. Dentu, Paris, 1891), p. 220.
9 Édouard Drumont, *La France juive* (Marpon & Flammarion, Paris, 1886), vol. 2, pp. 442ff.
10 Urbain Gohier, *La Terreur juive* (L'Édition, Paris, 1909), pp. 37 and 43.
11 On this point, see, for example, Jacob Katz, *Jews and Freemasons in Europe, 1723–1939* (Harvard University Press, Cambridge, Mass., 1970).
12 Comte de Colleville, *Les Dessous de la séparation* (Librairie antisémite, Paris, 1906), pp. 31 and 46; University of Jerusalem Library.
13 See Maurice Larkin, *Church and State after the Dreyfus Affair* (Macmillan, London, 1974), p. 141.
14 See, for example, Weil, *Histoire de l'idée laïque en France au XIXe siècle*, p. 355.
15 Pierre Nora, '1898: Le thème du complot et la définition de l'identité juive', in Maurice Olender (ed.), *Le Racisme et la science* (Complexe, Brussels, 1981).
16 Jean-Marie Mayeur, *La Vie politique sous la Troisième République* (Le Seuil, Paris, 1984), p. 315.
17 Quoted by Rémond, *L'anticléricalisme en France*, p. 251.
18 *La Vieille France*, 31 Dec. 1919.
19 *L'Action française*, 16 July 1920.
20 Mgr Jouin, 'Le péril judéo–maçonnique', *Revue internationale des sociétés secrètes*, 5 (1925).
21 *L'Action française*, 25 May 1936.
22 Ibid., 30 June 1936. See also the issue of 6 July 1936.
23 *La Croix*, 26 May 1936.
24 Ibid., 3 July and 11 Aug. 1936.
25 *Le Pays libre*, 8 Feb. 1941.
26 See, for example, Jean Bertrand and Claude Wecogne, *La Fausse Éducation nationale: L'emprise judéo-maçonnique sur l'école française*, Paris (Centre d'action et de documentation, 1941; University of Jerusalem Library). In the 1930s René Benjamin gave lectures opposed to secularism and to teachers in several provincial towns, most often in the company of Léon Daudet. Numerous incidents broke out (*Archives nationales*, F7 13 196).
27 See *L'Émancipation nationale* which attacked the 'Judéo-normalien fanatic Léon Blum', comparing his activities with those pursued by Durkheim at the *écoles normales* (22 April 1938). In the same spirit, Henri Labrove, 'L'histoire du judaïsme en Sorbonne', *La France européenne*, 20 Dec. 1942, BAIU: *Présent, Hebdomadaire de la France nouvelle*, 15 April 1942, which maintained that 'Blum did not like Catholics, the law of the separation of church and state saving him from having to inaugurate churches'; Henri Faugeras, *Les Juifs, peuple de proie* (Documents contemporains, Paris, 1943), p. 61; Joseph Santo, *Niaise et impie laïcisation des manuels scolaires*, Centre de documentation juive contemporaine; *Je suis Juif et j'en suis fier,*

anonymous lampoon, Centre de documentation juive contemporaine.
28 Pierre Chevallier, *Histoire de la franc-maçonnerie française, 1877–1944* (Fayard, Paris, 1975), p. 34.
29 In *Itinéraires*, a Catholic integralist revue, François Brigneau again recalls this period, describing the activities of Naquet, a Jewish freemason, showing how 'the crime of the Dreyfus Affair has benefited the Jews ... and freemasonry', and reviving the connections between Gambetta, Waldeck-Rousseau, the freemasons, in their struggle for secularism (July 1984; Jan. 1985; June 1985).
30 See Françoise Chapron, *Pierre Mendès France dans l'Eure: Trente années de vie politique (1932–1962)*, doctorate of the 3rd cycle, University of Rouen, 1984, p. 49.
31 Chevallier, *Histoire de la franc-maçonnerie, 1877–1944*.
32 *La Vieille France*, 13 May 1920.
33 See, for example, *La Libre Parole and Le Porc-Epic*, 1 March 1936.
34 *L'Action anti-maçonnique*, no. 25, June 1936; Centre de documentation juive contemporaine.
35 See Dominique Rossignol, *Anti-France Maçonnerie, Anti-Sociétés secrètes*, thesis for the 3rd cycle, EHESS, Paris, 1980, p. 545.
36 *Revue internationale des sociétés secrètes*, 15 Dec. 1936; 1 Oct. 1937, 15 Aug. 1938.
37 See the improbable book by Jean Rateau describing in frenzied terms the regime instituted in Russia by Jewish freemasons, similar to those who governed France under the leadership of Léon Blum (*Les franco-métèques* (Librairie d'Action française, Paris, 1936). See also *L'Accession des Juifs au pouvoir: Ligue franco-catholique*, Centre de documentation juive contemporaine. See 'La Franc-Maçonnerie au Parlement', *Les Cahiers de l'Ordre*, 1928, special issue; *Le Porc-Epic*, 17 Jan. 1934; Albert Vigneau, *Franc-Maçonnerie et Front populaire* (Éditions Baudinière, Paris, 1936); Bibliothèque Nationale, Manuscrit Baylot. Imp. 552; Henry Robert Petit, *L'Émancipation des Juifs en France* (Institut d'études des questions juives, Éditions nouvelle, Paris, 1940), p. 41; René Louis Jolivet, *Sociétés secrètes; Maçonnerie et Judaïsme* (Paris, 1940); Centre de documentation juive contemporaine). Henry Coston considered that 'Freemasonry said: the State is me' and particularly attacked Georges Mandel in his book, *Dans les coulisses de la République* (CAD, Paris, 1944; Centre de documentation juive contemporaine). Paul Ganem, *L'Étreinte mortelle et la judéo-maçonnerie* (Éditions 'Anticipation', Paris, 1940), pp. 21, 45, 65. Léon Brasat, *Synthèse de la question juive* (Fernand Sorlot, Paris, 1943), p. 132. On this subject, see more generally Doctor Ansonneau, *Les Puissances occultes contre la France: La dictature judéo-maçonnique: Juifs, Francs-Maçons et Libres Penseurs*, Bibliothèque nationale, Manuscrit Baylot. Imp. 967.
38 Chevallier, *Histoire de la franc-maçonnerie*, pp. 21–8. See also Daniel Ligou, *Dictionnaire de la franc-maçonnerie* (PUF, Paris, 1987).
39 Ligou, *Dictionnaire de la franc-maçonnerie*, p. 788.
40 Ibid., p. 1268.
41 See, for example, *La Judéo-Maçonnerie en Parlement, Législature 1936–1940*, Centre de documentation et de propagande, Bibliothèque nationale, 4o Le8839. See also *La Bataille et l'Action Antimaçonnique*, April 1939, Centre de documentation juive contemporaine.
42 Henry Coston, *Juifs et Francs-Maçons démasqués* (La Propagande nationale, Bar-le-Due, 1935; Centre de documentation juive contemporaine). See the long document entitled 'Le F. ∴ Juife Mendès France' published by *Documents Maçonniques*, no. 3, Dec. 1943, which appeared under the signature of Georges Ollivier, although Henry Coston was none the less involved in the publication of these documents. See also *Lectures françaises*, a revue published by Henry Coston, 'La Franc-Maçonnerie gouverne', Oct.1958, pp. 38, 46, 53; and H. Coston, *Dictionnaire de la politique française* (La Librairie française, Paris, 1967), in which the author considers that 'the

discreet but effective support that the Great Orient of France will give him in the election at Grenoble can be decisive' (p. 692).
43 *Aspects de la France*, 15 Oct. 1954.
44 See, for example, *L'Action française*, 8 June 1936.
45 Paul Rassinier, *Les Responsables de la Seconde Guerre mondiale* (Nouvelles Éditions latine, Paris, 1967), p. 112.
46 Charles Micaud, *The French Right and Nazi Germany, 1933–1939* (Duke University Press, Durham, N.C., 1943).
47 *Revue hebdomadaire*, 23 Nov. 1935. During the 1870 war numerous caricatures could already be found representing Jews as traitors and German spies. See Ouriel Reshef, *Guerre, mythes et caricatures* (Presses de la FNSP, Paris, 1984), pp. 115–25.
48 Henri Béraud, *Sans haine et sans crainte*, pp. 231–41.
49 *La Lorraine déchaînée*, 9 April 1939.
50 *La Libre Parole* and *Le Porc-Epic*, 1 June 1936.
51 Roger Martin du Gard, 'Lettre à un ami', 9 Sept. 1936, in *Nouvelle Revue française*, Dec. 1958, p. 1150.
52 'Blum-la-Guerre', *Je suis partout*, 14 Sept. 1935.
53 *L'Action française*, 22 May 1936. In the same spirit, see his article in *L'Action française*, published as early as 4 May 1921.
54 *L'Action française*, 19 May 1936. In the same spirit, see the issue of 1 Aug. 1936.
55 *L'Action française*, 2 Sept. 1933.
56 *Candide*, 4 Jan. 1939. In the same spirit, see *Le Grand Occident* which attacked Léon Blum, 'the circumcised frenetic', who only dreamed of war (15 Sept. 1936). See also *Le Charivari*, 19 Sept. 1936; *La Libre Parole* and *Le Porc-Epic*, 1 April 1936.
57 Quoted by Kaminsky, *Céline en chemise brune* (Nouvelles Éditions Excelsior, Paris, 1938, BAIU; re-publ. Plasma, Paris, 1977), p. 53.
58 Apart from the press file already analysed when we discussed the trials of Riom and Clermont-Ferrand, see Paul Allard, *La Guerre du mensonge* (Éditions de France, Paris, 1940); Pierre Dignac, *Les Malfaiteurs publics* (Arthaud, Paris, 1941); Jean Fabry, *De la place de la Concorde au cours de l'Intendance* (Éditions de France, Paris, 1942); Raymond Recouly, *Les Causes de notre effondrement* (Éditions de France, Paris, 1941). Henry Michel also described this use of Léon Blum as a scapegoat (*Vichy-Année 40* (Laffont, Paris, 1966), p. 141).
59 *L'Action française*, 15 Dec. 1923.
60 Ibid., 9 July 1932.
61 *Candide*, 3 Sept. 1936.
62 *L'Action française*, 29 Dec. 1936. See also the issue of 4 May 1933.
63 *L'Action française*, 17 Jan. 1937.
64 *Je suis partout*, 11 June 1932. See also the issues of 24 Feb. 1934, 23 March 1935 and 4 Jan. 1936.
65 Ibid., 29 Oct. 1932. In the same spirit, see *L'Ami du peuple*, 17 May 1932.
66 *Le Charivari*, 8 Nov. 1930. In the same spirit, see *L'Action française*, 16 April 1932, and *Le Rire*, 21 Sept. 1935.
67 On 21 March 1934, at the Théâtre des Dix Heures, Max Régnier performed a song depicting Blum praising the virtues of German culture (*Archives nationales*, F7 12965).
68 *Le Charivari*, 25 March 1933.
69 Pierre Boutang, 'La vie politique', *Aspects de la France*, 29 Oct. 1954.
70 *L'Ère nouvelle*, 2 April 1927.
71 *L'Action française*, 8 May 1935.

72 *Candide*, 30 July 1936.
73 *Candide*, 4 March 1937. See also *Candide*, 10 Oct. 1935, 20 July 1936.
74 See the articles by Charles Maurras in *L'Action française*, 17 May 1936; and by Pierre Gaxotte in *Je suis partout*, 19 June 1937. In the same spirit, see the article by Pierre Gaxotte in *Candide*, 17 Sept. 1936.
75 *Je suis partout*, 10 April 1937. See also the issue of 19 June 1937.
76 François Herbette, *L'Expérience marxiste en France, 1936–1938* (Éditions Genin, Paris, 1959), p. 133.
77 *Le Journal des débats*, 18 Oct. 1936. See also the issues of 22 May and 15 Sept. 1936.
78 *Écrits de Paris*, Oct. 1954, p. 102. In the same spirit, see *Contacts littéraires et sociaux*, supplement to no. 15, 15 Oct. 1954.
79 *Gringoire*, 10 Jan. 1936. Similarly, according to Georges Suarez, Blum lived under two foreign protectors: the guardianship of Moscow which he could not dispense with at home; and the guardianship of England whereby he protected himself against encroachments of Russian policy abroad (*Nos Seigneurs et nos maîtres* (Éditions de France, Paris, 1937), p. 35). On this subject, but more generally, see Roger Lambelin, *Le Règne d'Israël chez les anglo-saxons* (Grasset, Paris, 1921).
80 See, for example, *Gringoire*, 21 July 1931.
81 *L'Action française*, 6 March 1937. See also *Candide*, 15 Oct. 1936.
82 *Je suis partout*, 13 March 1937. See also *Gringoire*, 11 March 1938.
83 Anon., *Face au front populaire* (Éditions des Oeuvres latines, Paris, 1937).
84 See, for example, Jean Jacoby, *Mille neuf cent quarante* (Les Libertés françaises, Paris, 1941). There was a positive flood of works directed against England during the Occupation. See Gérard Loiseaux, *La Littérature de la défaite et de la collaboration* (Publications de la Sorbonne, Paris, 1984), ch. 4.
85 *L'Émancipation nationale*, 14 Sept. 1941.
86 Apart from the press file cited in the chapter in this book describing these trials, see, for example, Paul Allard, *Les Provocateurs de la guerre* (Éditions de France, Paris, 1942).
87 Pierre Antoine Cousteau, *L'Amérique juive* (Éditions de France, Paris, 1942), pp. 51 and 120.
88 *Aspects de la France*, 20 Aug. 1954.
89 Pierre Antoine Cousteau, *Après le déluge* (La Librairie française, Paris, 1956), pp. 175 and 222.
90 Cousteau, *L'Amérique juive*, p. 58.
91 See Norman Cohn, *Histoire d'un mythe: La 'conspiration' juive et les Protocoles des Sages de Zion* (Gallimard, Paris, 1967). In France they were spread by Mgr Jouin, who, as has been seen, very frequently attacked Léon Blum and Georges Mandel (Mgr Jouin, 'Le péril judéo-maçonnique: Les Protocoles de Sages de Sion', *Revue internationale des sociétés secrètes*, 1920).
92 *Français! Il faut redevenir*, Institut d'études des questions juives (Éditions nouvelles, Paris, 1942), p. 10. In the same spirit, see L. Fry, 'Le Juif, notre maître', *Revue internationale des sociétés secrètes*, 1931; Georges Saint Bonnet, *Le Juif ou l'internationale du parasitisme* (Éditions Vita, Paris, 1932), which contains a very long chapter describing Léon Blum's work in the service of 'Jewish imperialism' (p. 200); Jacques Ploncard, 'Pourquoi je suis anti-juif', *La lutte nationaliste*, no. 2; Jean de la Herse, *Judaïsme et Bolchevisme* (Éditions La Porte latine, Vichy, 1942; Bibliothèque de l'AIU); Pierre Miles, *Voici la cause de nos maux: la Juiverie* (Sorlot, Paris, n.d.); A. Pokrovsky, *B'nai B'rith et ses esclaves: Wilson, Roosevelt, Churchill, Blum, Staline et Cie* (Petite Bibliothèque, no. 1, Paris, 1941; Centre de documentation juive contemporaine).

12
The Empire Abandoned

Supporters of political anti-Semitism added one final element to their indictment of the presence of Jewish citizens at the summit of the state. In their view, state Jews, after perverting the soul of French society through the policy of secularization, after drawing France into fatal wars which were not its concern, were unquestionably completing their work of destruction by attacking the Empire. Now, using every possible means to pursue their criminal strategy of weakening the French nation, the Jews were unscrupulously liquidating the Empire itself in order to expunge for ever every sign of its greatness. To this end, they were encouraging the introduction of foreign interests, Soviet or Anglo-Saxon, with whom they had earlier devised their war-plans. Political anti-Semitism was constantly and openly manifest from the 1930s until the implementation of decolonization – a crucial issue that confronted French society from the 1950s until Algerian independence. Its impact was all the greater because political anti-Semitism served to arouse such sharp Franco-French passions that they ended up by putting the fate of the Republic itself at risk. By a strange coincidence, both Léon Blum and Pierre Mendès France played an important role in this drama which, as at the time of the Dreyfus Affair, almost tipped France into civil war.

FROM THE CRÉMIEUX DECREE TO THE BLUM–VIOLETTE PLAN

The drama basically came to a head in connection with the decolonization of North Africa, where the French presence was particularly strong. First Léon Blum, then Pierre Mendès France were drawn along in the wake of the action. Both strove to implement a cautious decolonization policy favourable to the emancipation of the Arab populations of North Africa. The model of Franco-Judaism was applied in Algeria early on, first in the framework of a green paper of July 1865, then as a decree of 24 October 1870. Known as the Crémieux decree and also signed by Gambetta, it proclaimed that 'the Israelites, natives of the departments of Algeria, are declared French citizens'. The Moslems were also offered this emancipation at the same time but not as a right, though several bills throughout the period of the Third Republic sought to make the Crémieux decree generally applicable. As early as 1860, measures had been in force naturalizing Algerian Jews and bringing them within French jurisdiction in a variety of ways. In 1864 Napoleon III himself, while visiting Oran, declared: 'I hope that the Israelites will soon be Frenchmen.'[1] It so happened that the Crémieux decree which established this long-desired emancipation was the work of one of the most famous state Jews. He was for a long time a deputy and a minister, and, before Blum, Mandel and Mendès France, personified the access of some Jewish citizens to the heights of the state. Political anti-Semitism soon found favourable soil here for the most lunatic ravings.

Drumont, as usual, was in the forefront of the struggle, denouncing Crémieux's policy and espousing, as was so often the case, the defence of the Arab populations. According to him, Crémieux 'was thus purely and simply betraying France to serve the interests of his race. In 1871 this measure had a particularly odious character. The Arabs did their duty heroically during the war.'[2] In Algeria also, acquisition of citizenship and entry into local politico-administrative office provoked an anti-Semitic mobilization even more violent than in metropolitan France. Its logical outcome was the abrogation of the Crémieux decree by an independent and voluntary decision of the Vichy government on 7 October 1940. This measure marked at a stroke of the pen 'the end of a seventy-year scandal', to quote Charles Maurras. It exacerbated the consequences of the Jews' Statute passed on 3 October 1940, which expressly forbade them to hold elective office or to exercise political and administrative functions, and expelled them entirely from the state structure.[3]

To reach this point, it is first necessary to retrace the events which marked the development of anti-Semitism in North Africa, especially in Algeria, from Drumont's election in Algiers in 1898 to the Blum–Violette plan. There was an immediate reaction to the Crémieux decree, particularly because the local administration gave it an extremely cautious reception, and the senior civil servants of Algeria made no secret of their absolute hostility.[4] In 1892 Max Régis, the local anti-Semitic leader, created the Ligue antijuive and published a daily paper, *L'Antijuif algérien*, with a circulation of some 20,000, which was infinitely more violent than *La Croix* or even *La Libre Parole* of that time.[5] The anti-Semitic mobilization drew its followers most particularly from new Spanish and Italian colonists as well as from working-class and Catholic circles. Anti-Semitic agitation reached its peak between 1898 and 1900 when riots broke out in nearly 50 towns and turned into veritable pogroms.[6]

Withdrawal of the Crémieux decree was demanded loudly on all sides and on 4 February 1898 Charpentier, deputy-mayor of Algeria, put forward a plan to this effect. The various facets of traditional anti-Semitism (economic, racial and sexual) came to the surface in these pogroms which set Algeria alight. But purely political anti-Semitism still appeared to be the driving force behind the mobilization, being essentially directed at the consequences of the emancipation of the Jews which now allowed them to be appointed to public posts in Algeria, as was the case in metropolitan France. This theme emerged explicitly in the lampoons, newspaper articles, leaflets and poems which circulated on a massive scale. Here is one example widely distributed in Algeria in 1898:

> There is more than one Jew
> At the Palais Bourbon.
> The nose is the clue,
> You can always tell one.
> Give the whole gang the sack,
> Clear the place of the stench.
> What we have to get back
> Is France for the French.[7]

Le Réveil algérien, *Le Petit Africain* and *La Cravache d'Oran* demanded in every tone of voice the revision of the electoral rolls so as to exclude Jews. As Geneviève Dermenjian noted, 'the originality of Algerian anti-Semitism lay in the fact that its detonator was political. This was because the Jews intervened in local political life and ceased to be agreeable to native Frenchmen whose plans they disturbed.'[8] In short, political anti-Semitism started life in Algeria at almost the same time as in France. It was spread, even more than in France, by means of a multitude of particularly close social networks; for example, the social groupings which held countless 'anti-Semitic banquets' where people drank 'anti-Jewish anisette' together, as they did in cafés.

Although it died down in the years before the First World War, political anti-Semitism re-emerged worse than ever, culminating in a veritable pogrom which erupted in August 1934 at Constantine. It resulted in the savage murder of 23 Jews in a lynch-mob atmosphere. It was a pogrom unique in the contemporary Western world and the influence of its extreme violence can be seen as heralding the future massacres perpetrated by Hitler's armies – systematically carried out in their case.[9] What laid Constantine open to political anti-Semitism was the relatively strong presence of Jews in the various public posts in the department to which they, like all citizens, had access on a meritocratic basis.[10]

In Constantine, and in Algeria generally, where every confrontation was exacerbated by the colonial context, political anti-Semitism clearly appeared, perhaps even more strikingly than in mainland France, as a movement rejecting the republican egalitarianism which had emancipated the Jews and put them in politico-administrative positions. The anti-Semitic journal, *Le Tam-Tam* called for the end 'of Jewish domination of public posts'.[11] *Action française* seemed to revel in that 'spectacle' which it claimed was provoked by the consequences of the Crémieux decree.[12] In the same year Léon Blum was already being taken to task by Charles Hagel in a book overflowing with anti-Semitism that was published in Algiers. It accused 'the haughty and Talmudic Blum' of serving, in succession to André Gide(!), Lévy-Bruhl, Durkheim and Bergson, as 'public poisoner and propagator of degeneracy'.[13]

In 1934 shouts of 'Down with the Jews!', 'France for the French!', 'Down with Blum!', 'Death to the Jews!' resounded in the streets of Algerian towns.[14] Up to the end of the Algerian war, during the time of the Pierre Mendès France government and its local extensions, they never ceased.

The victory of the Popular Front under Léon Blum's leadership brought things to a head. Abbé Lambert, mayor of Oran, decreed 'general mobilization against the Jews and the Popular Front, against these people who have no French soil on the soles of their shoes'.[15] When, in addition, the Blum–Violette plan, also signed by Marx Dormoy, Paul Faure and Camille Chautemps, was introduced and presented to the Chamber of Deputies in December 1936, anti-Semitic mobilization knew no bounds. In fact, this plan had the courage to state that, as 'native Algerians were Frenchmen' they should be progressively admitted to the exercise of political rights. The plan then specified what categories of 'French native Algerians' would enjoy political rights at once (some 20,000) and provided for a gradual extension every year. The hostility of the Europeans in Algeria was immediate and absolute. Relentlessly, they set out to sabotage the plan because it challenged their predominance in the medium term. Three hundred mayors proclaimed their total opposition. At their head, Abbé Lambert clamoured: 'All the anti-French are in favour of the Blum–Violette plan.'[16] On the other hand, a Moslem delegation went to Paris to discuss with Léon Blum the new possibilities for emancipation that the plan offered. The President of the Council greeted them with these words: 'I am pleased about this visit by French Moslems to a French Jew, by democrats to a democrat.'[17]

Before it was transmitted to the local level, political anti-Semitism began by opposing this reform on the political scene in the home country. True to form, *L'Action française* opened immediate hostilities, accusing Léon Blum of being 'towed along by the communists'. Were this reform applied, it said, 'together with Algeria, it would make us lose our possessions in North Africa'. And *L'Action française* generously added that the President of the Council's strategy was so limited that it did not even take into consideration 'the hatreds and passions of the Jews' themselves, a large number of whom were afraid of the possible implementation of such a plan.[18] For this journal, 'Blum's Algerian decree is a simple pogrom-deterrent. A juicy little scrap of French sovereignty is thrown to 20,000 Algerian 'non-Jews' so that they will tell their anti-Jewish brethren: "No! Look! It's a Jew who's offering us this lovely manna. We must make an exception in the case of this Jew." '[19]

So the accusation never changed. Blum's policy was conducted solely in the Jews' interests and not on the basis of the national interest. In France, this disapproval was very widely shared.[20] On the extreme Right, Doriot also seized on this argument which also allowed him to fight the Popular Front. He had no scruples about going to Algeria to carry the good word and to add his efforts to those who were contesting the Blum–Violette plan with every means at their disposal.[21] True to form, he demanded at the same time the abrogation of the Crémieux decree. Barely two years later, under the Vichy regime, his wish was granted. As part of the same process, the stars of mainland anti-Semitism, Xavier Vallat, Philippe Henriot and Pierre Pucheu, went to Algeria in their turn to visit their troops.[22]

The condemnation also had more general implications. Many people thought that Léon Blum's presence at the head of the government could only undermine France's position in North Africa because of the hostility it would inevitably arouse amongst the Moslem population. *L'Époque*, for example, declared its firm belief that the natives 'cannot understand that a Yid can become great chief' of the French nation.[23] Similarly, *L'Émancipation nationale* wrote: 'that France should be led by an Israelite is harming us down there . . . for the men of the Atlas mountains Blum will really always be a Yid: one of those characters in black skull caps, with frizzy hair, in dirty dressing-gowns, usurious and miserable, whom they see vegetating in the stench of the red-light districts'.[24]

One PPF leader declared at the party congress: 'When Blum leads us, 25,000,000 Moslems despise us.'[25] For *Le Nouveau Cri*, 'the Blum–Violette plan aims at imposing Jewish supremacy on our fundamentally anti-Semitic North Africa.'[26] More cautiously, Raymond Cartier stated in *L'Écho de Paris* that 'the fact that France has a Jewish sultan confuses and dumbfounds the Moslems. A formidable wave of hatred is flooding the mellahs [Jewish quarters in Morocco] and is about to break.'[27] In general, there was no hesitation in once again utilizing all the resources of the old traditional anti-Semitism by maintaining that 'Léon Blum, like his protégé M. de Coppé, governor-general of the AOF, passive in his erotic habits and powerless in respect of the natives, will make us lose the AOF.'[28] As can be seen, political anti-Semitism had no trouble at all in rediscovering the vocabulary of the most obscene traditional anti-Semitism in order to pass judgement on the colonial policy of the socialist President of the Council.

On the ground, in Algeria, it was easy to believe that the era of Max Régis and Drumont had returned overnight. As early as 5 June 1936, *Le Petit Oranais* wrote: 'Here are the *Protocols of the Elders of Zion* turned into reality in France: Blum I, Great Judge or King of the French – dating from 1 June 1936 of the Christian era.'[29] A little later the same journal adopted for its own purposes the vicious statements made by Xavier Vallat and Darquier de Pellepoix in the Chamber of Deputies and in the Municipal Council of Paris.[30] *Tricolore*, an Algiers weekly, urged nationals to take 'the Bastille of Judeo–masonic feudalism' set up by Léon Blum.[31] *Le Républicaine sud-oranais* declared its conviction that 'the seizure of power by the tribe' led by Léon Blum 'proves conclusively that the Jews have decided to form themselves into a state on our soil'.[32] Indignant at 'Nero–Blum's' presence at the head of the government which was meticulously supervising the 'enactment of the *Protocols*', anti-Semitic mobilization took off under the leadership of the mayor of Oran, Abbé Lambert.[33] Its vocabulary, as we have seen, was copied from the metropolitan heirs of Drumont and Charles Maurras combined. On the one hand, there were denunciations of the Jews' economic power, of their hostility to Catholicism, their sexual perversions, the conspiratorial tactics they employed, under the leadership of 'B ∴ Léon Blum',[34] in accordance with the *Protocols*. But on the other hand, there were also vehement attacks on the Jews 'who govern us'.[35] All shades of anti-Semitism were represented. They mingled, blended and emerged stronger than ever. Algerian political anti-Semitism rivalled its home-country counterpart in imagination. The Constantine *Tam-Tam*, for example, offered the following sketch:

Revue Scene
M. Léon Blum's office at the Presidency of the Council
M. Léon Blum – M. Jules Moch

BLUM: Yes, France will soon die beneath our blows!

MOCH: And who is going to get rich on its spoils?

BLUM: Us. We're already in command, but then
We're only plotters who drive other men:
Demagogues, masons, deputies, politicos...
Compassionately watched by conniving police,
We lead the ballet from the coulisses.
The triumphal moment will come, the time
When France will be officially mine.
As this country is the finest in the world
We must have it...

MOCH: And quickly!

BLUM: In order that we can beget
A Jewish nation... Then we'll forget
Twenty centuries of scorn, slavery and shame.
Our state will be free and strong,
We'll un-baptize every public monument and hall,
River, bridge, boulevard, street, square and mall,
Which does not have a biblical name
Their Faubourg Saint-Germain
Will the Faubourg of the Promised Land become...
The Arc de Triomphe will be Moses's Arch for some...
And since everything with us must change its name,
France will no longer be called 'France'.[36]

Local representatives of the radical right-wing parties used metaphors which were already fashionable on the mainland to draw up their own detailed lists of people they thought were state Jews illegitimately dominating the French nation.[37] For example, *L'Éclair*, a journal published in Algiers which called itself the 'official organ of French national–socialism', enumerated the allegedly Jewish ministers in the government of Léon Blum, whose 'tribe' had just seized control of the state without a blow being struck.[38] The French Popular Party, led by Jacques Doriot, was very active. Its publications covered all Algerian territory and it embarked on a systematic mobilization against the Blum government and its reform plans aimed at encouraging access to citizenship by the Moslems of Algeria. Every day during the first PPF Algerian congress *Oran-Matin* described the bitter hostility to the Blum–Violette plan which emerged in every debate, and also at the meetings held in Algiers at the time, all of which were attended by several thousand people.[39] In the same vein, *L'Oranie populaire*, the PPF's official federal weekly, attacked the intentions of 'Citizen Blum Léon, first of the name, President of the Council of Ministers of France by the will of Stalin'.[40] It also threatened 'the governmental tribe which is too un-French to understand how we value our ancestral heritage. The firm Blum, Moch, Dormoy, Brunschwig, Zay and Co.', it said, 'shall not throttle France.'[41] From 1936 to 1937, therefore, open political anti-Semitism was frequent in the PPF, both at national[42] and local level – to such an extent that it embarked on a lively controversy with Colonel de La Rocque, accusing him of not being sufficiently 'anti-Jewish', whereas the PPF openly declared itself 'anti-Judaist'.[43]

The anti-Semitic mobilization continued to spread, supported by a press which enjoyed a fairly large circulation: *Oran-Matin*, for example, printed an estimated 10,000 copies and *Petit Oranais*, 2,000.[44] Collective action took place in the streets. Thousands of people attended a meeting in Oran chaired by Abbé Lambert.[45] Over 10,000 more went to another meeting organized by the *Rassemblement national d'action sociale* on 9 August 1936 at the Algiers municipal stadium, in the presence of the mayor of Algiers, M. Rozis. There were continuous shouts of 'France for the French', 'Down with Léon Blum', 'Down with the Jews!'[46] The many meetings at which political anti-Semitism was given free rein showed the extent of this anti-Semitic mobilization. At a large mass meeting held under the auspices of the *Parti social français* (PSF) at Mostaganem on 13 December 1936, for example, the president of the local section of the PSF criticized Léon Blum's 'Judeo-Marxist' government.[47] Similarly, 'the rule of Jewry, of Blum, Zay, Moch, Mendès-Palestine, Boris, etc.' was violently challenged at a meeting organized at Oran by the *Amitiés latines*, an extreme right-wing group, and attended by several hundred people.[48] Noteworthy too was a meeting organized by *La Libre Parole* at Oran on 13 December 1936 under the auspices of Henry Coston who called on 'citizens to refuse to be taxed and made liable to forced labour at the pleasure of Seigneur Léon Blum's Jewish Republic'.[49] The police commissioner's report noted that on 14 May

1937 at another demonstration organized by *La Libre Parole*, the audience applauded the speakers and shouted: 'Down with the Jews!', 'Down with Blum!'. The peroration by the main speaker, René Barthélemy, was again punctuated by shouts of 'Down with Blum!' and the public immediately began to chant in chorus:

> Down with the Jews!
> Down with the Jews!
> We have to take them by the conk.[50]

Leaflets of rare virulence were circulated in almost all the large towns of Algeria; for example, a lampoon was pushed through letter-boxes in Algiers attacking the 'warmongering by Roosevelt, Blum and freemasonry' and ending with the following phrase: 'A single solution to the problem: sterilization. The final and entire sterilization of both sexes, the measure must extend to ½ and ¼ Jews.'[51] Hitler's influence was undoubted, German propaganda blending with the specific traditions of the radical right-wing parties. Witness, for example, a leaflet distributed to 'Latin workers and employees' which denounced the role of Léon Blum, Rothschild and Dreyfus and which had two swastikas at the bottom.[52] This leaflet was stuck up on the walls of Sidi-bel-Abbès and distributed in the streets of Oran in August 1937. It was a fresh symptom of the radical character which political anti-Semitism now assumed in Algeria, inspired by Hitler's Germany. Café windows in Sidi-bel-Abbès and Oran also sported anti-Semitic handbills proclaiming 'Léon Blum, German Jew; Victor Basch, Hungarian Jew; France is under the rule of the foreigner.'[53] Other leaflets were distributed in Algiers in December 1936, hostile to the 'Jew Léon who is calling on a million Jews to invade France'.[54] Another handbill stuck systematically on the walls of the Cité Lalloum at Constantine makes *Stürmer* look pale by comparison:

> Whoever says he is a Jew, is saying he's a bastard.
> Whoever says he is a Red is saying he's a cuckold.
> Whoever says 'Long Live Blum' is lowering his trousers.
>
> Morality
>
> Under the conspiratorial signs of the three
> arrows, the Soviet star and the masonic triangle,
> if you want to keep up with the times, lend your wife, unless
> you prefer to join it yourself.[55]

La Libre Parole nord-africaine opened a fund to help fight 'the yoke' that it claimed Jewish power was imposing on the French. It received large sums of money accompanied by comments which at once recall those attached to the donations liberally made for the construction of the Henry Memorial at the turn of the century, at the time of the Dreyfus Affair.[56] Forty years later, the same insults, the same anti-Semitic gibes appeared, this time from the pens of these hundreds of new subscribers. They were simply set within the context of the new possibilities offered by Hitler's advent to power: This is 'to cut Léon Blum's throat', wrote one donor; 'Down with Blum and all the circumcised'; 'For Blum's nose'; 'To put the Jews under the swastika'; 'Long Live Hitler'; 'Long Live Franco'; 'Down with Blum'; 'To put Blum in prison'; from 'An anti-Jew and his children'; 'Down with the B ∴ and the Jews'; 'Down with the Crémieux decree'; 'My small savings against the Jewish peril'.[57]

Historians have shown an interest in the list of emotions that subscribers to the Henry Memorial did not hesitate to express, but this later list, published in 1936, is almost totally unknown. Yet it says much about the hatred which continued to exist and poured shamelessly over Léon Blum. It increased constantly. So strong was the pressure exercised by the countless supporters of political anti-Semitism in Algeria that as soon as the Vichy government was formed, it succeeded in securing the annulment of the measure emancipating the Algerian Jews, the Crémieux decree. The local representatives of Vichy immediately applied the anti-Jew laws specific to Vichy in all their harshness to Algeria. Furthermore, in November 1942, long after American troops had landed in Algeria, Murphy, like Eisenhower, was alive to the arguments of Darlan and Giraud and did nothing about the racial laws. The Crémieux decree was not restored until October 1943.[58] Anti-Semitic mobilization none the less continued, unaffected by legal measures. In November 1943, for example, the walls of Oran were covered with slogans attacking the Jews, including the obsessive and eternal 'Frenchmen, the Jew is your enemy. Blum to the scaffold'.[59]

FROM PEACE IN INDO-CHINA TO WAR IN ALGERIA

Pierre Mendès France became President of the Council at a time when France was passing through a dramatic period caused by the setback suffered by the French army in Indo-China. He embarked on a race against time to surmount every obstacle and bring about a quick peace acceptable to all parties within the framework of the Geneva conference. From the start, his activities took place in a setting of internal confrontation provoked by the most serious crisis the Fourth Republic was to experience, that of decolonization. The pressure of nationalist movements seeking independence was making itself felt ever more strongly throughout the empire, as in the whole of the Third World. After harsh confrontations in Sétif and Madagascar, violence broke out in French Indo-China, only just failing to provoke a world war with the siege of Diên Biên Phu.

When Pierre Mendès France came to power, Roger Stéphane, one of his close associates, enthusiastically rushed to tell him: 'You are going to make peace in Indo-China. You are going to begin the decolonization of North

Africa. What an extraordinary role!' Looking anything but pleased, Mendès France replied: 'Yes, they will say that I am the Jew who sold off Indo-China, the Jew who sold off Tunisia and Morocco.'[60] This gloomy prediction was to prove truer than he imagined. G. Bourdat, a close colleague of Mendès France during his Presidency of the Council, stressed, 'the old anti-Semitism acted in the same way as it did with Blum: the Jew is selling off the empire on the cheap'.[61]

As early as June 1954, one of his bitterest enemies, Pierre Boutang, raged against the plot Mendès was weaving with his accomplices, the 'Jews of *L'Express*', and denounced 'the Disraeli of an emasculated France, not the founder but the destroyer of the Empire'.[62] The headlines on the front page of *Aspects de la France* on 23 July 1954 read: 'The Jew Mendès has brought off his first coup: he has won his bet against France.'[63] Pierre Boutang's offensive continued without respite. According to him 'when the Jew took the helm in July 1954 ... Mendès showed himself a defeated figure in the mosaic of lies, a loser with nothing to show for it; and at Geneva he touched it up and recast it for the worse.'[64] And the President of the Council was violently accused of opting for peace in Indo-China, the better to preserve his wife's economic interests. Her Cicurel family, it was claimed, had retained a few commercial properties in Egypt and had dictated his policy in both Indo-China and North Africa. 'I dreamt that a French deputy had been bold enough to bring a legitimate case against him on grounds of opinion. Barrès perhaps? Drumont, probably?'[65]

As can be seen, the history of anti-Semitism in contemporary France repeated itself again and again, cheerfully mixing traditional anti-Semitism and political anti-Semitism. The actors in the drama remained amazingly constant, from Drumont and Barrès to Maurras, Henry Coston and even Pierre-Antoine Cousteau. Cousteau was an anti-Semitic author, whose prose has been mentioned frequently and who was still in fine form in 1956 when he published *Après le déluge*. In this book he accused Pierre Mendès France of capitulating to Hô Chi Minh before betraying the army in Algeria. True to the vocabulary of the inter-war period, he then asked: 'But who took the trouble to rub M. Mendès's nose into his gross filth?'[66]

This reputation as a 'cheap-jack salesman of the French empire' reappeared in 1968–9 in *Carrefour*.[67] It ceaselessly pursued Pierre Mendès France throughout his career. Using any means to serve their end, many people tried to explain the President of the Council's Indo-China policy by his alleged connections with banks interested in developing the south of the country. At the same time, this reasoning argued, he abandoned the defence of the north where other bankers, just as Jewish but represented by René Mayer, had competing interests which must therefore be rapidly eliminated. This typifies the fundamentally economic anti-Semitism, product of extreme mental confusion, that came to the surface in connection with Indo-China. Its trail can be followed through a large body of writings and, for example, in *Fraternité française*, Pierre

Poujade's journal.[68] He bobbed up again later, still the same, in connection with North Africa.

The fate of the Fourth Republic, and the beginning of the Fifth, was entirely dominated by the drama of the decolonization of North Africa. A vast population originating in metropolitan France lived there and rejected, with an energy born of despair, any challenge to the politico-administrative status which ensured its leading role. Systematically blocking any evolution, this total focusing on acquired rights was probably partly responsible for the trial of strength unleashed in Tunisia as early as 1952. It extended to Morocco in the same year, followed not long afterwards by the Algerian war which broke out suddenly and unexpectedly on 1 November 1954. Pierre Mendès France at first devoted all his efforts to extinguishing the blaze in Indo-China, but he was soon confronted by the serious situation prevailing in North Africa. On 31 July at the palace of Carthage, before the bey, he recognized Tunisia's internal autonomy and envisaged the transference of internal sovereignty to Tunisian institutions. In August he set in motion a series of reforms in Morocco[69] and in the same month received a delegation of Algerian representatives, led by Ferhat Abbas, who came to present its claims. Reforms were immediately worked out but, faced with the revolt of the Kabyles and the Aurès, the Mendès France government sent military reinforcements without delay. The President of the Council thought that 'no secession of Algeria from France is possible.... We are able to create in Algeria the good life that France must ensure for all its citizens and all its children, by the exercise of democratic rights, with the generous co-operation of the home country.'[70] François Mitterrand, Minister of the Interior, declared: 'Algeria is France. From Flanders to the Congo, there is the law, a single nation, a single Parliament. It is the Constitution and it is what we wish.'[71] In January 1955 Pierre Mendès France appointed Jacques Soustelle, a liberal, as governor-general of Algeria, and seemed about to embark on important reforms. It was at the end of the debate on the policy pursued in North Africa that the Mendès France government fell in an atmosphere of open hatred. It was a striking indication of the importance of the drama of decolonization in the brief Mendès France experiment.

In this inflammatory context, the political anti-Semitism which the Blum–Violette plan had aroused again found fertile soil. It was exacerbated by the fact that the image of Pierre Mendès France had been pervading anti-Semitic hallucinations for a long time, as has already been seen. This political anti-Semitism was not confined to the radical right-wing parties. It also emerged when unexpected lapses during speeches or heated exchanges revealed the deep hostility felt towards Jews. It must however, be emphasized that in some cases this gut rejection was not expressed right away. Certain journals, and not the least-important, began by showing a great deal of good will towards Pierre Mendès France. The break came later, in some cases long after his government had fallen. It is noteworthy that anti-Semitic statements did not reach their peak until 1957–8. For example, in 1954 *Aux écoutes du monde* began by praising 'the intellectual loyalty' of the new President of the Council. It stressed that 'he is a young man who wants the good of his country'. And when the government fell, it always maintained that Pierre Mendès France 'had spoken the truth'.[72]

But these assessments radically altered when the problem of the fate of Algeria itself took a disturbing turn. Pierre Mendès France was now depicted as a man in favour of 'the murderers of the FLN', whose strategy was motivated solely by his personal interests in the Cairo bazaars, as at the time of the peace in Indo-China.[73] Likewise, on 22 June 1954 Roger Priouret wrote in the *Journal du Parlement* that Pierre Mendès France 'is a patriot in the noble meaning of the word'[74] and until July no attack of a personal nature appeared. From 3 August, however, the President of the Council was reproached for his Tunisian policy and described as 'Mendès the capitulator',[75] and a rapid metamorphosis occurred in the vocabulary employed. The radical President, lampooned in decapitated form as 'Mendès-rance', was now subjected to unbridled criticism, though the *Journal du Parlement* still considered anti-Semitism 'inadmissible', even condemning the 'vulgar anti-Semitic royalist (Camelot)', which was how this journal regarded Pierre Poujade.[76] The policy pursued in North Africa was already being questioned. 'For whom does the bell toll?', the *Journal* asked. 'For M. Mendès or for France?'[77] Things became worse in April 1955. For the *Journal du Parlement*, 'M. Mendès France, native of Normandy, met M. François Mauriac, native of the Bordelais, and M. J.-J. Servan-Schreiber, a native of Guinea, not only to denounce the French "atrocities" but to demand wider diffusion of the Fellaghist doctrine.'[78] Anti-Semitism was now clearly evident everywhere. The former President of the Council was described as a 'eunuch' of 'Judaic origins'. His 'messianic conception' was criticized, and Frenchmen were warned of the work of the 'goat Mendès, the evil genie' whose politics were dictated by 'the Eygptian lobby'.[79]

Similar vacillations appeared in journals such as *Nouveaux Jours*. In July 1954 it was already asking the question, so frequently asked by authors inspired by the vision peculiar to political anti-Semitism: 'Mendès or France?' But *Nouveaux Jours* unexpectedly added: 'Will you at last be the man whom the White World, beyond France, needs if it is not to disappear?'[80] On 15 August it had decided on its line and the journal clamoured 'Drive him out', although it specified that it was acting 'outside any ideological or religious consideration'.[81] In the face of Pierre Mendès France's 'capitulation' in Indo-China and North Africa, René-Lignac returned to a distinction commonly found in the anti-Semitic speeches of the 1930s. 'There is Mendès', he said, 'and France. Saying this and repeating it in no way implies that one is anti-Semitic. And I appeal to my many French friends of the Israelite faith who fortunately think as I do and have really wanted to tell me so.'[82] As in the days of Léon Blum, Edmond Bloch immediately published a long article in the same issue of the journal. He maintained that Mendès France 'committed no one but himself ... his co-religionists do not ask to share with him either glory or opprobium'. Like other journals, *Nouveaux Jours* was still resolutely engaged in harsh anti-Semitic criticism of 'Mendès the capitulator', of 'Mendès's bazaar', and finally concluded on 15 February 1955: 'Pierre Mendès France has gone. He makes way for France.'[83]

While certain organs of the press displayed many fluctuations in their assessment of Pierre Mendès France's North Africa policy, the mood of others, such as *Fraternité française*, the organ of the Poujadist movement, did not vary in this respect. According to this journal, Mendès France was surrounded only by Jews who 'smelt so finely of France', and was preparing to 'surrender Algeria'.[84] It published enormous photographs of massacres committed by the FLN, and accused Pierre Mendès France of turning a blind eye and not feeling involved. 'Go and ask the people called Isaac Mendès, Servan-Schreiber or Ben Said to show French guts.... Go, Mendès, go, Schreiber, go, Ben Said. France has been too generous in having you at its hearth. When will you cease to howl and grimace at death like the jackals of your ancestral deserts?'[85]

Fraternité française repeatedly attacked 'Isaac Pierre Mendès France and other carpet dealers' who 'are selling off Algeria dirt cheap' in the same way as they abandoned Indo-China. They were concerned 'only to fly to the help of the state of Israel, their one and only homeland'.[86] In this impassioned context, Pierre Mendès France soon appeared as a perfect scapegoat and 'muffled indignant protests' were heard against him even in the ranks of the army.[87] For those inspired by profound anti-Semitism, a policy which irrevocably led to the independence of a French territory could only be grounded in solid economic considerations. The radical President of the Council's actions in both Indo-China and North Africa were said to be dictated by the defence of the Rothschild bank. And the author of his fall, 'René Mayer, like him a Jew... who tried to look like an authentic Frenchman', was only seeking to put an end to it in order to defend other banking interests just as Jewish.[88] Economic anti-Semitism reappeared here as the ultimate explanation of a decolonization that seemed like an intolerable and otherwise inexplicable nightmare.

This sort of interpretation was taken up by *Le Charivari*, which had been repeating the same chant since the thirties.[89] It was used also by Paul Rassinier, the spiritual father of M. Faurisson and of supporters of theories which deny the reality of the genocide of the Jews. To Rassinier, Pierre Mendès France, 'the Messiah', was nothing more than the servile agent of Jewish cosmopolitan capitalism which was carefully dismembering the French empire.[90] The continuity with the thirties becomes even more apparent in the light of the same sort of statements about the radical leader made by Pierre Clementi, already very active during the period of absolute anti-Semitism. He depicted Mendès France 'with a face like a gorilla, a traitor although not really French, or even a European, who is gladly abandoning a territory with western allegiance'.[91]

The habit had not been lost. Once again anti-Semitic leaflets and lampoons, hostile to Pierre Mendès France, accusing him of 'depravity' and 'cowardice' circulated in France and North Africa.[92] The mobilization organized to defend French Algeria by every means was used to this type of vocabulary. The *Salut public d'Algérie française* wrote: 'No people could be more guilty of arousing accursed passions than these Jewish politicians, writers and journalists who engage in subversive activity, propagate hatred in a Christian country. . . . What evil men such as Mendès, Servan Schreiber, André Wurmser can do!'[93]

Similarly, Joseph Ortiz, leader of the OAS, the clandestine organization which aimed to defend French Algeria by any means at its disposal, declared on the barricades of Algiers:

We will defend French Algeria, weapons in hand. We were robbed on 13 May. Treachery is in power. De Gaulle is no better than the Jew Mendès. We will clean France of these traitors. We will not stop at anything. We will carry out justice ourselves. We need men ready to die. From Algiers, we will take the Revolution to Paris.[94]

As early as the 1950s, anti-Semitism again broke out in Algeria against 'the Jew Mendès' or 'Mendès the Judas',[95] though it did not reach the peaks of the 1930s or arouse real collective mobilization in the streets. None the less, a very large number of leaflets circulated aimed at 'Monsieur Ossona, called Mendès France (we dispute the France), who has liquidated Tunisia after Indo-China in exchange for a diamond watch'.[96] The radical President of the Council received a post-bag of anti-Semitic mail, rarely equalled in obscenity. A letter was sent to him from Oran on 6 May 1955: 'You don't give a damn for Algeria because you are a long way away, f--- Jews that you are, sell your dirty clothes now and f--- off in top gear to your own country and look after your f--- ignoble life, if the cap fits, wear it . . . you are all dirty Jews, you and your whole filthy underworld, all Jews are the accursed of god.'[97]

Another was the postcard signed by 'Frenchmen of pure blood' which he received at his home in February 1958: 'Mendès who has the cheek to call himself "France"!! What a nerve! He was born Cerf-Hirsch. Dirty Jew. Rogue, you abandoned Indo-China and then Tunisia. You sold them, you dirty swindler, and got nothing in return, you dirty scum. You are the source of all the misfortunes of France. A curse on you. Down with Cerf. Death.'[98]

This postcard was soon followed by another bearing the same signature: 'How dare you even mount the tribune of the National Assembly? You filthy fellow with your nose and your cauliflower ears. Scum. Deputy Le Pen has put you down, you bloody scum. Le Pen told you: "You symbolize for France many a patriotic revulsion." To this country, which needs pride like the bread it eats, you mean defeat in Indo-China and the abandonment of Tunisia. Yes, Bourguiba and Mendès France, two rogues hand in hand. Death to the traitors.'[99]

Lampoons and anti-Semitic leaflets galore circulated in Morocco too.[100] Perhaps the worst thing was that nothing could stop the spread of this anti-Semitic clamour which, far from North Africa, insidiously entered Normandy, the region to which Mendès France had been affectionately attached for so long. Anti-Semitic letters attacking his Algerian policy not only reached Évreux in 1955;[101] in addition, as in the 1930s, a section of the regional press, such as *L'Impartial*, a journal published in the Andelys and at Vernon, the very heart of this department to which he was attached by many emotional ties, lent a more-than-sympathetic ear to the anti-Semitic allegations of the President of the Council's opponents, which hurt him deeply.[102] It was as if all the many facets of anti-Semitism were only waiting for some pretext in order to manifest themselves anew, always in the same forms but in a very different context. The dramas of decolonization, as has been noted, gave renewed vigour to the well-worn themes.

In contemporary France this source of anti-Semitism has dried up with the almost complete disappearance of the Empire. And yet, lurking in the shadows, hatred springs out from time to time, however infrequently the status of French overseas territories is called into question. Witness the headline in *Aspects de la France* in connection with Laurent Fabius's New Caledonia policy: 'Treason in power. France? Fabius knows nothing about it.'[103] And *Minute* added, as if explicitly closing the circle: 'The shadow of Mendès is on the move.'[104]

NOTES

1 Geneviève Dermenjian, *Juifs et Européens d'Algérie: L'antisémitisme oranais, 1892–1905* (Ben Zvi Institute, Jerusalem, 1983), p. 53. See also, E. Sivan, 'Stéréotypes antijuifs dans la mentalité Pied-Noir', in *Relations entre Juifs et Musulmans en Afrique du Nord, 19e–20e siècle* (Éditions du CNRS, Paris, 1980); and Paul Siblat, 'Cagayous Antijuifs', *Mots*, Oct. 1987.
2 É. Drumont, *La France juive* (Marpon & Flammarion, Paris, 1886), vol. 2, p. 12. In the same spirit, see Henri Desportes, *Tué par les Juifs: Histoire d'un meutre rituel* (A. Savine, Paris, 1890), Preface by E. Drumont, pp. 11 and 57.
3 See Michel Abitbol, *Les Juifs d'Afrique du Nord sous Vichy* (Maisonneuve & Larose, Paris, 1983), pp. 63ff.
4 Michel Ansky, *Les Juifs d'Algérie, du décret Crémieux à la Libération* (Éditions du Centre de documentation juive contemporaine, Paris, 1950), p. 42.
5 P. Sorlin, '*La Croix' et les Juifs* (Grasset, Paris, 1967), p. 115.
6 See Stephen Wilson, *Ideology and Experience: Antisemitism in France at the time of the Dreyfus Affair* (Associated University Press, London, 1982), ch. 9. On the connections between emancipation and anti-Semitism in Algeria at that period, see Yves Deloye, 'Citoyenneté et sens civique dans l'Algérie coloniale: l'émancipation politique de la minorité juive au 19e siècle', DEA de sociologie politique, University of Paris I, 1987.
7 This poem accompanies a letter from the Attorney-General of Algiers, Dubuc, to the Minister of Justice. It is dated 15 Feb. 1898 (*Archives Nationales*, BB 18263).
8 Dermenjian, *Juifs et Européens d'Algérie*, p. 33.

The Empire Abandoned   293

9 Charles-Robert Ageron, 'Une émeute antijuive, Constantine (Aug. 1934)', *Revue de l'Occident musulman et de la Méditerranée*, 1973.
10 Ibid. In the same article, n. 41, Charles-Robert Ageron shows that at Constantine there were 36 Jews amongst the 114 policemen, and 37 Jews amongst the 61 agents of the PTT. The 214 ministerial officials in the District of Constantine included 49 Jews.
11 *Le Tam-Tam*, 15 Sept. 1934.
12 *L'Action française*, 8 Aug. 1934.
13 Charles Hagel, *Le Péril juif* (Éditions nouvelles africaines, Algiers, 1934), p. 72.
14 Ansky, *Les Juifs d'Algérie, du décret Crémieux à la Libération*, p. 71. See also Charles-Robert Ageron, *Histoire de l'Algérie contemporaine* (PUF, Paris, 1979), vol. 2, p. 370.
15 Quoted by Ageron, *Histoire de l'Algérie contemporaine*, vol. 2, p. 369.
16 Charles-André Julien, *L'Afrique du Nord en marche* (Julliard, Paris, 1972), p. 114.
17 Ageron, *Histoire de l'Algérie contemporaine*, vol. 2, p. 440.
18 *L'Action française*, 2, 7 and 8 Jan. 1937. See also the issue of 4 April 1938.
19 *L'Action française*, 9 Jan. 1937.
20 See, for example, the anonymous lampoon entitled *La Rocque et les Juifs*, Centre de documentation juive contemporaine.
21 See Marc Knobel, *Doriot, le PPF et les Juifs*, DEA in history, University of Paris I, 1983, p. 7.
22 Ansky, *Les juifs d'Algérie du décret Crémieux à la Libération*.
23 *L'Époque*, 14 Nov. 1937. On 2 Dec. 1937 this journal added that this was 'a serious offence against Islam which will not forgive us for it'. The Italian journals in Tunisia, such as *Africano* and *Cacodé* were equally hostile to the 'Jew Blum' (Centre de documentation et de vigilance, 21 Oct 1937).
24 *L'Émancipation nationale*, 17 Oct. 1936.
25 Ibid., 19 March 1938.
26 *Le Nouveau Cri*, 7 March 1938.
27 *L'Écho de Paris*, 16 Oct. 1936.
28 *Le Nouveau Cri*, 15 Oct. 1938.
29 *Le Petit Oranais*, 5 June 1936; *Archives de la France d'Outre-Mer*, Oran 3327. As early as 19 July 1929, *Le Petit Oranais* stated that Léon Blum and his co-religionists still had blisters on the soles of their feet from the stakes of the Inquisition.
30 Ibid., 15 April 1937.
31 *Tricolore*, organ of the Union nationaliste et sociale, 14 July 1936.
32 *Le Républicain sud-oranais*, 20 May 1938; *Archives de la France d'Outre-Mer*, Oran 3327.
33 *Le Petit Oranais*, 19 June 1936.
34 Ibid., 25 June 1936.
35 *Archives de la France d'Outre-Mer*, file: Department of Algiers, 1 K 38.
36 *Le Tam-Tam*, 24 April 1937.
37 See, for example, *L'Éclair*, 12 Oct. 1937; *Le Tam-Tam*, 10 Oct. 1936.
38 *L'Éclair*, 10 Nov. 1938. In the same spirit, see *La Presse libre*, an Algerian daily, according to which Léon Blum 'has a horror of the Homeland, and France, in the grip of fanaticism, offered herself to him and followed him without seeing him as the High Priest. He will sacrifice France to his God' (26 May 1936). See also the issue of 11 May 1936.
39 *Oran-Matin*, 3, 4, 6 and 10 Jan. 1937. Signed *Contre-Révolution, Organe de la défense de la prépondérance française*, a notice was posted up in Algiers which demanded 'the rejection of the Blum–Violette plan as attacking national sovereignty' and 'the abrogation of the Crémieux decree as securing for the Jews a political superiority damaging to the Algerian natives' (Centre de documentation juive contemporaine).

40 *L'Oranie populaire*, 15 May 1937.
41 Ibid., 29 May 1937.
42 See Philippe Burin, *La dérive fasciste: Doriot, Déat, Bergery, 1933–1945* (Le Seuil, Paris, 1986), p. 296. Jean-Paul Brunet thinks that 'up to May 1941, Doriot remained moderate in his anti-Semitism'. Then, 'it would be an understatement to say that in the question of anti-Semitism, Doriot howled with the pack, he was its leader' (*Jacques Doriot* (Balland, Paris, 1986), pp. 341 and 349). It appears that his anti-Semitism became more developed, particularly in Algeria, from 1936 to 1937.
43 *L'Oranie populaire*, 7 May 1938.
44 *Archives de la France d'Outre-Mer*, Préfecture of Oran, file Oran 3121. *L'Oranie populaire* printed only about 500 copies.
45 *Le Petit Oranais*, 10 June 1936.
46 *Archives de la France d'Outre-Mer*, report of the departmental Sûreté, Department of Algiers, no. 1 K 26.
47 Ibid., report of the police inspector, file Oran 70.
48 *Le Petit Oranais*, 5 April 1938.
49 *Archives de la France d'Outre-Mer*, file Oran 3121.
50 Ibid., departmental Sûreté of Oran, file Oran 3121.
51 Ibid., Office of the Prefect, Department of Algiers, File 1 K 38.
52 Ibid., file Oran 3121.
53 Ibid., departmental Sûreté, file Oran 3227 and 3121.
54 Ibid., department of Algiers, 1 K 38.
55 Ibid., department of Constantine, BI 253.
56 See Pierre Pierrard, *Juifs et catholiques français* (Fayard, Paris, 1970), pp. 55ff; and Wilson, *Ideology and Experience*, ch. 4.
57 *La Libre Parole nord-africaine*, 3 Dec. 1936.
58 See Abitbol, *Les Juifs d'Afrique du Nord sous Vichy*, ch. 9.
59 *Archives de la France d'Outre-Mer*, State police of Oran, file Oran 3327.
60 Claude Bourdet, 'La faute de PMF', *Témoignage chrétien*, 25 Oct. 1982.
61 Interview IHTP, 1983.
62 *Aspects de la France*, 4 and 18 June 1954.
63 *Aspects de la France*, 23 July 1954. See also the issue of 30 July 1954.
64 *Aspects de la France*, 20 Aug. 1954. As early as 1953 this journal wrote: 'M. Edgar Faure, who is not Jewish but who has very powerful Jewish connections, is, like Mendès (France), a supporter of the abandonment of Indo-China by France' (19 June 1953). On 23 July 1954, moreover, it described *L'Express* as 'Mendès's Israelo-cosmopolitan monitor'.
65 *Aspects de la France*, 13 Aug. 1954.
66 Cousteau, *Après le déluge*, p. 12.
67 *Carrefour*, 12 June 1968 and 21 May 1969; see also 16 Jan. 1957.
68 *Fraternité française*, 3 March 1956; see also the issues of 17 and 31 Dec. 1955.
69 See Pierre Guillen, 'Le gouvernement Pierre Mendès France face aux problèmes tunisiens et marocains', in *Pierre Mendès France et le mendésisme*.
70 See Charles-Robert Ageron, 'Le gouvernement Pierre Mendès France et l'insurrection algérienne', in François Bédarida and Jean-Pierre Rioux (eds), *Pierre Mendès France et le mendésisme* (Le Seuil, Paris, 1986), p. 333.
71 Quoted by Jean-Pierre Rioux, *La France de la Quatrième République* (Le Seuil, Paris, 1983), vol. 2, p. 67.
72 *Aux écoutes du monde*, 18 June and 16 July 1954, and 11 Feb. 1955.
73 Ibid., 7 June 1957, and 14 Feb. 1958.

74 *Journal du Parlement*, 22 June 1954.
75 Ibid., 3 Aug. 1954.
76 Ibid., 8 Oct. and 4 Nov. 1954. See also the issue of 27 Jan. 1955.
77 Ibid., 27 Jan. 1955.
78 Ibid., 24 April 1955.
79 Ibid., 24 April, 4 Oct., 13 Nov. and 20 Dec. 1956.
80 *Nouveaux Jours*, 1 July and 1 Aug. 1954.
81 Ibid., 15 Sept. 1954.
82 Ibid., 1 Oct. 1954.
83 Ibid., 15 Feb. 1955.
84 *Fraternité française*, 31 Dec. 1955.
85 Ibid., 7 Jan. 1956.
86 Ibid., 19 Nov. 1955.
87 Jules Roy, 'Un religieux de la politique', *Le Monde*, 23 Nov. 1984.
88 *Écrits de Paris*, March 1955.
89 *Le Charivari*, May–June 1958.
90 *Contre-courant*, Summer 1954, Feb., March and Oct. 1955.
91 *L'Action européene*, 15 March 1972.
92 *Qui a intérêt à brader l'Algérie française?*, Front national des combattants, Bibliothèque nationale, Tracts politiques, 4o LB 60465. See also Roger Duchet, *Pour le salut public* (Plon, Paris, 1958). The latter declared that 'Mendès is always there when the homeland is humiliated', and it thought that it was more important to worry 'about the defence of the Morice line than that of the bazaars of Cairo and the service of the Orient' (pp. 135 and 154). See again *Minute*, 23 Nov. 1977. On 19 June 1954 a leaflet was distributed in Paris in the name of a '*Comité pour l'Empire juif mondial*'. It said that 'behind our Mendès and his team of authentically circumcised colleagues' who are delivering Indo-China to Hô-Chi-Minh and Tunis to Bourguiba, 'the messianic times are close at hand' (*Archives privées Marie-Claire Mendès France*).
93 *Salut public de l'Algérie française*, Algiers, 7 Jan. 1960. See also the issues of 24 Dec. 1959 and 3 June 1960, Centre de documentation juive contemporaine.
94 *Archives Pierre Mendès France*, BT 2157.
95 Albert Bensoussan, 'Regards sur l'antisémitisme verbal en Algérie', *Informations juives*, June 1980.
96 *Archives Pierre Mendès France*, Tunisia II.
97 Ministry of the Interior, *Archives Pierre Mendès France*, unclassified.
98 *Archives privées Simone Gros*.
99 *Archives privées Simone Gros*.
100 See the file concerning the anti-Semitic statements made by the journal *Zadig*, comprising an exchange of correspondence from the end of 1954 to 1955 between Pierre Mendès France, the Minister for Moroccan and Tunisian affairs, etc. (*Archives Pierre Mendès France*, unclassified).
101 *Archives Pierre Mendès France*, Algeria, VII.
102 On this file, see the *Archives privées Bourdat*. *Aux écoutes du monde* also describes with satisfaction an electoral meeting in 1958 at Pont-de-l'Arche, during which Pierre Mendès France had to face violent anti-Semitic gibes from one part of the audience (*Aux écoutes du monde*, 14 Feb. 1958).
103 *Aspects de la France*, 13 Dec. 1984.
104 *Minute*, 12 Jan. 1985.

Conclusion

Drumont's legacy is still alive today on the fringes of the extreme Right, which sometimes also openly professes explicit political anti-Semitism. The phobia in respect of immigrants, most frequently of North African origin, is, in addition, accompanied by denunciations (more restrained now, of course) of the misdeeds attributed to the Jewish Republic. However, collective anti-Semitic action is most often absent from the public scene, replaced as it sometimes is by mobilization against immigrants. Moreover, in the usual means of expression, neither contemporary traditional anti-Semitism nor political anti-Semitism are in any way comparable to those which prevailed at the turn of the century, in the inter-war period or during the Mendès France experiment and the years preceding Algerian independence.

It must be said that the law has become much more repressive and now, particularly since 1972, most effectively prevents public expression of all forms of anti-Semitism. Also, the remarkable decline in the number and diversity of the organs of the press since the turn of the century and of the Popular Front, as well as the seeming disappearance of lampoons, scurrilous satires, almanacs, and so on, considerably limits the open expression of the anti-Semitism which found them a useful vehicle to disseminate it throughout the land.[1] The great radical nationalist press with its considerable circulation has quite simply disappeared. Since the Second World War and particularly in the contemporary period, anti-Semitism in all its forms has consequently lost much of its visibility. The historian no longer has such plentiful or varied sources available to evaluate its real extent, especially as the archives on these most recent periods are at present closed to him. This makes any comparison very difficult and, apart from the great similarity of the themes which has been emphasized here, any calculation proves risky because of the absence of reliable material.

None the less, Captain Dreyfus or Léon Blum[2] and Pierre Mendès France are still attacked today. The memory of the radical and populist right-wing parties remains active, and there is still total loyalty to the commitments of yesteryear. Witness, for example, the many incidents which have dogged the search for public sites on which to erect statues in honour of these famous state Jews. Rigid in their convictions, people affiliated to the nationalist trend preserve a gut-hatred for them, to such an extent that it still seems sacrilegious to erect such statues. Sites have had to be found for them which only painstaking walkers can manage to ferret out, away from symbolic or very crowded places.[3]

The call of 'France for the French' still resounds, as it did at the end of the nineteenth century and in the 1930s. And *Itinéraire*, which frequently exalts Drumont's memory, proclaimed: 'Thank you, Jean-Marie Le Pen!', congratulating the latter for so brilliantly prolonging the movement which brought fame to Léon Daudet, Xavier Vallat, Phillipe Henriot and Jean-Louis Tixier-Vignancour, and emphasizing that 'in the twentieth century this trend has never before had a parliamentary group of 35 members at its call'.[4] As has already been noted, in the most recent period, Captain Dreyfus, Léon Blum, Georges Mandel and Pierre Mendès France have been joined by Laurent Fabius (who, like Jean Zay in the past, is too taken aback to protest) and particularly by Robert Badinter, on the list of state Jews against whom the present representatives of the radical Right voice their anger without restraint.

None the less, times have changed, French society is no longer experiencing either the ravages caused by the painful consolidation of the Republic or those provoked by the severe ideological confrontations in the international context, heavy with military threat, of the 1930s and 1950s. The enemy is no longer openly prowling the frontiers, and the theme of betrayal and of the fifth column is now – or temporarily – out of vogue. Likewise, the dramas of decolonization, which fuelled ever-increasing passions, have rapidly faded into the past. And the town, modernity and capitalism no longer give rise to beautiful flights of lyricism in favour of a return to the joys and virtues of the traditional rural society from which foreigners, the bearers of degeneracy, were formerly excluded.

The market has itself become legitimate as has the large-scale acquisition of shares by small investors, who too are anxious to enrich themselves from the spoils of the state brought about by denationalizations. Each has an eye for the Stock Exchange, and money is no longer accursed in a France where de-Christianization is slowly and inexorably increasing. It is no longer hidden; it is paraded. Cosmopolitanism is no longer a fault and no Maurice Barrès, Léon Daudet, Charles Maurras, Jacques Chardonne, Louis Ferdinand Céline, Paul Morand or Drieu La Rochelle arises now to denounce it in flashing and devastating books that glorify the blessings of rootedness in a protective soil. The great nationalist writers who were seldom above adding a strong pinch of anti-Semitism to their extremist or simply reactionary potions have become a rare breed. Of course, France has not entered a period which will see the end of ideologies: the numerous factors of consensus should not mask the continued existence of divergencies brought about by totally contrary visions of the world – the recent controversies about the French Revolution are a reminder of this. If the political struggles have died down and if there is no longer anything comparable to the confrontations that occurred when unrestrained anti-Semitism, which also blurred the issues, had free rein, the collective antagonistic memories still live.

For all that, the Republic has acquired a legitimacy that few still dare dispute and the extremist trends themselves, cautiously, almost always refrain from any challenge. This means that the Republic can no longer be denounced as simply Jewish and, in this spirit, foreign to the national traditions. Now almost the entire nation recognizes itelf in the republican framework. In these circumstances, what can be the fate of political anti-Semitism which only recently confounded rejection of the Republic with rejection of the universalist emancipation of the Jews as citizens?

Let us suggest a hypothesis here, however flimsy it may be. If almost everyone sees the Republic as the definitive political regime, a recognition that at the same time dries up the basic source of political anti-Semitism, the state with which it was so long confused is, on the contrary, seeing itself challenged, at least at the level of discussion and of prevailing value-systems, in its strength and its aspiration to dominate the entire social order. The state is already being put in doubt because of the relative failure of its own institutions and particularly because of a certain decline in its educational system that is increasingly incapable of ensuring the political socialization which its strong army of totally devoted teachers had guaranteed since the time of the Third Republic. It must in addition face up to the new challenges issued by society itself. Plans to reduce its pre-eminence are now emerging on all sides. Some of them produce an up-dated version of the traditionalist paradigm of the 'land and the dead' and aspire, for example, to link in future the acquisition of nationality with a *jus sanguinis* which would detach it from a citizenship conferred solely on criteria formulated by the state itself – notably the *jus solis*, which grants citizenship to everyone born on French soil. Others, concerned to ensure the pre-eminence of the market out of respect for liberal economic theories, work unceasingly to obtain the reduction of state ascendancy.

A two-fold backward movement thus emerges: on the one hand, back to a nation regaining its purity, unsullied by foreign inputs; on the other, back to a market whose logic would no longer be thwarted by the omnipotent intervention of a state conceived as alien. If these tendencies, which emerge only vaguely and which come up against the solid institutionalization of the state, were to triumph, then we would perhaps witness a resurgence of traditional anti-Semitism which, far from disappearing, had none the less receded to some extent in the face of the rapid blossoming of a specifically political anti-Semitism. What would then happen, as some premonitory signs seem to indicate, is that an anti-Semitism of Catholic origin or constructed by way of biological metaphors, would know a second youth, while economic anti-Semitism would again have freer rein.[5] The worst is certainly never sure. Escaping from its demons, confident in its emancipating values, will French society one day be able to create the indispensable balance between the expression of the many social and cultural particularisms and the sovereign authority of a universalist state, forestalling at the same time the ever threatening resurgence of xenophobic mobilizations?

NOTES

1 At the time of the Dreyfus Affair, on the other hand, the press experienced a positive explosion which correspondingly increased the gravity of the confrontation. See Norman Kleeblatt (ed.), *The Dreyfus Affair: Art, truth and justice* (University of California Press, Berkeley, Cal., 1987). Under the Third Republic this trend in the press gathered strength. After the Second World War the position was no longer as before and the political press increasingly declined.
2 See the astonishing interview when Jean-Marie Le Pen took up a well-worn accusation of the 1930s slightly changing it to maintain that, at the time of his marriage at Buchenwald, Léon Blum gave 'a dinner for 60' (*Globe*, Sept. 1987).
3 See, for example, *Présent*, 7 Sept. and 14 Oct. 1985. On this point, see Pierre Birnbaum, 'La valse des statues', *L'Arche*, Nov. 1985.
4 *Itinéraires*, April 1986. See also the issues of April 1984 and Jan. 1985.
5 Thus, at a meeting held by integralist Catholic circles supported by the National Front at the Mutualité, the omnipotence of 'Judeo-anarcho-Protestantism' and the power of the Rothschilds were denounced at one and the same time before 500 people (*Le Monde*, 18 Oct. 1987). In the same spirit, the Abbé de Saint-Nicolas du Chardonnet attacked the dictatorship which, according to him, 'great Jewish banking' had exercised over France for '45 years'(?) (*Libération*, 18 Sept. 1987). By way of denial, the Abbé added: 'I have simply said that the Jews ceaselessly brandish the questions of racism, and this works. As soon as they start up anything, all the media seize on it. This power can only be explained by their domination over banking, particularly for financing electoral campaigns' (*Agence France Presse*, 18 Sept. 1987). More generally, see Pierre-André Taguieff, 'L'identité nationale saisie par les logiques de racisation: Aspects, figures et problèmes du racisme différentialiste', *Mots*, March 1986.

Postscript

Apart from an exceptional surge during the period of decolonization and the Pierre Mendès France experiment, the radical right-wing trend lost some of its influence under the Fourth Republic, particularly in view of its great compromise with Vichy. This time the Catholic world seems definitely to be throwing in its lot with the Republic. Today, *a fortiori*, even regularly practising Catholics consider the separation of church and state legitimate.[1] In 1989, according to *La Croix*, 'the Republic no longer has to be built. It exists. The republican regime is barely seriously challenged.' This journal emphasized 'the irreversible fact of secularism', which not so long ago still provoked so many conflicts. 'The war is over', it announced again.[2]

The integration of Catholicism into the French Republic and its definitive acceptance of a universalist citizenship now considerably limit the influence of the integralist movement. This is all the more so because France seems to be moving away from the 'Franco-French wars' and, in certain respects, is entering the era of a relative consensus not favourable to extremist ideologies. This is so marked that certain observers already consider that a 'banalization of French politics' is in progress. According to François Furet, France is closing down 'the political theatre of the exceptional and returning to the standard path of the democracies'.[3]

Thus the Fifth Republic marks the moment, in the French fashion, of 'the end of ideologies', bringing the various extremist doctrines to a conclusion and making the French Republic definitively legitimate. The heirs of Drumont, as well as the loyal followers of Barrès and Maurras, benefit no less today from a situation which is exceptionally favourable to their extreme theses. Once again, the National Front trend relies on the integralist movement in order to make the rejections of yore reappear. Moreover, its activities are set in a more general context where the French elector, far from becoming more 'rational', always seems to make his choice essentially on the basis of a religious variable, with the result that the majority of practising Catholics, and even Catholics who only occasionally practise their religion, vote for the Right.[4] Generally speaking, it is still noticeable today that 'the more the level of integration into Catholicism is important, the more one feels oneself close to Catholics attached to tradition'.[5] Further, 'if intolerance is independent of faith and religious practice, authoritarianism regularly increases with the degree of integration into the Catholic community and its values'.[6] The breakthrough of the National Front bears witness to this blossoming of the ethnocentric values which have long fed French-style nationalism and again today provoke its re-emergence on the widening margins of society. And if National Front sympathizers themselves attend Mass less frequently than supporters of the classical Right and seem to have less confidence in the Church than the latter, if a number of them claim to be non-believers,[7] if certain of its intellectuals turn rather towards paganism,[8] this movement as a whole is still ideologically integrated into a nebula carrying into the present day the movement of intransigent Catholicism.

Its ideologists are very often the same people who breathe life into integralist journals in which they spread the values of a nationalism similar to that of Drumont or Maurras. For example, Jean Madiran, one of the Front's intellectuals, belongs to that integralist trend in which nationalism à la française, product of the turn of the century, is today concentrated. He became famous through his denunciation of the 'four or five confederate states' which realized and justified Maurras's formula according to which the Jews and the Protestants, in company with the freemasons, formed a 'state within the state'. He attacks Jews, freemasons, Protestants, foreigners and communists with extreme violence, metamorphosing the foreigners into 'a show-biz of cosmopolitan intellectuals'. According to him, it is a fact that 'Jewish power exists, it is not a myth, it is sovereign': whence there comes a 'colonization of Christian France'. As Jean Madiran argues, 'heirs in danger of being the last survivors of the nation of the cathedral and the crusade, of chivalry and mission, we are being colonized'.[9]

Little emphasis has been placed on this close correlation between a mystique claiming kinship with pure, hard Catholicism, and the reappearance of a virulent anti-Semitism in contemporary France, widely prevailing over the other 'doctrines of hate' which are accompanied more by violent hostility towards the Moslems. In those of his writings which relate to religious problems, Jean Madiran declares war on secularism, a true 'Christian heresy',[10] takes alarm at the Protestantization of the Catholic Church, maintaining that it dates from the condemnation of *Action française* which dealt a fatal blow to the true French Catholic tradition. He rages against the 'persecution' of traditionalist Catholics, further increased in 1944–5 by the '10,000 summary executions, for the most part of Catholics of the Syllabus, who had naturally adhered to Marshal Pétain's national revolution. . . . And more than a million various condemnations, imprisonments, dismissals, removals. Putting the nation in the dock.' For Madiran, even today, the temporal power, distinct from the spiritual power, is not solely the state, its ministers and its prefects. They, such as they are today, are foreigners to Christianity. The Christian suffers them because he can do no other ... the civic life of a nation like France requires the Roman catechism and the traditional Mass. Is it necessary for French Catholics that the agnostic Maurras reappear to teach them this once again?[11]

This anti-state, anti-republican nationalist trend, claiming kinship with an intransigent Catholicism, is evincing great vitality today. Several books by André Figueras, figurehead of the Saint-Nicolas-du-Chardonnet movement, sing the praises of Maurras and Barrès, the virtues of the France of the monasteries betrayed by the bishops of the Church,[12] all the more easily because 'enemy infiltrations into the Church', essentially by Jews, are dealing an increasingly severe blow to traditionalist Catholics.[13] References to Drumont's redemptive books proliferate, while his own writings are being republished, as are those of his heirs. Henry Coston, his customary and still very active spokesman, ceaselessly strives to make his theses a reality and apply them to contemporary France. H. Le Caron states that what is taking place is 'the decomposition of Christian society in which Jewish politicians and the Jewish media are playing an important part', and he denounces the role of Cardinal Lustiger in the 'Judaization' of French society.[14] Like many others, he calls for a vigorous reaction against this subversion carried on to the greater advantage of the Devil. In this perspective, France must rediscover the tradition of de Maistre and Maurras and return to Christ by fighting the Protestants as well as the Jews and by putting an end to democracy.[15]

A 'national-Catholicism', true to Maurras, is gradually being reconstructed today with a large part of the nationalist extreme Right, often close to the Le-Penist movement, regrouping around Abbé Georges of Nantes and Mgr Lefebvre. From Pierre Sidos to François Brigneau and Jean Madiran, the whole crowd of those nostalgic for the Catholic tradition and for royalist or extreme right-wing France sing the praises of the 'crusaders', those 'conquistadores' – the troops of Saint Nicholas de Chardonnet who do not hesitate to move into action based on the model of the Christian Solidarity movement.[16]

This 'national-Catholicism' also corresponds to a 'traditio-nationalism' which links Maurrassian nationalism to integral Catholicism.[17] Mgr Lefebvre is beyond any doubt the true hero of these new crusaders. He is indisputably their charismatic figure.[18] Propagated by many organs of the press, ranging from the *National-Hebdo* to *Minute, Itinéraires, Présent, Révision, Lecture et Tradition* or again *L'Anti-89*, this extremist nationalist ideology is certainly heterogeneous and its champions sometimes clash vigorously on the points of doctrine which divide them (republicans and monarchists, conservatives and fascists, Catholic integralists and atheists, and so on). But stimulated by the bicentenary of the French Revolution, which it still regards as the beginning of the regime of 'Judeo-anarcho-Protestantism',[19] it seems to be rising again intact, ready to encourage new movements in favour of the electoral acceptance of the National

Front. The National Front has shown itself able to win over these multiple traditions of the extreme Right, collecting them in an attempt to build a new, genuinely 'French', Republic.[20] The Catholic identity of this Republic would justify the exclusion of a number of Frenchmen from citizenship. They would henceforth be regarded as 'cosmopolitans' and the nation would have to protect itself from them in order to preserve its own culture.

The National Front seems to be continually enlarging its electoral base, threatening to gain power rapidly in the big towns, and at the beginning of the 1990s, has often even come to the fore as the second party at many local elections. Similarly, in May 1990, 35 per cent of the French thought it acceptable to express anti-Semitic sentiments in a democracy,[21] and a number of incidents occurred to reawaken an anti-Semitism which is always in the wings. The drama of Carpentras thus resurrected those hatreds which it was thought had been extinguished, especially as the impalement of the body of a Jew reawoke the most desperate sexual anti-Semitism. All over France crowds marched to protest against this violation, denouncing this revival in company with the highest authorities of the state. The President of the Republic himself, M. François Mitterand, joined the march together with the leaders of all the political groupings who were all united in an effort to exorcise the old demons who periodically re-emerge. The National Front's interpretation of the defilement of Carpentras in terms of manipulation, which was taken up by commentators in the serious journals,[22] does nothing to remove doubt on that score: in reality, is this not pure fabrication, as in Rumania at Timisoara, but in this case serving the martyrology of the Jews and enabling them finally to impose their own legitimacy?[23] Jean-Marie Le Pen did not hesitate to make use of this incident in order to identify it with traditional political anti-Semitism. Attacking Laurent Fabius, he declared: 'he is not afraid to bring his descriptive endorsement to the impalement of the corpse by the anus: the word, in Fabius's mouth, sounds in some way like a rhyme'.[24]

This political anti-Semitism, which has been discussed so often in this book, came again to the fore during a televised debate, on 5 December 1989, when Jean-Marie Le Pen asked Lionel Stoleru, Minister of the Rocard government, if he had dual nationality, French and Israeli, implying in the eyes of all television viewers that a state Jew was really only a concealed Israeli. And François Brigneau exclaimed, 'that a man like Le Pen from western Brittany should think he has the right to ask someone of the status of M. Stoleru, son of Elijah and of madame, née Blum, and married to Francine Wolff, "do you have dual nationality" – that goes beyond the bounds permitted by Judeo–Christian society'.[25] And Romain Marie, another champion of this radical right-wing trend, did not hesitate to attack Simone Veil in terms which again evoke some of the debates examined in this book. For him, 'if it is possible to imagine that Holophernes had the athletic build of Le Pen, it's a long time since Dame Simone could claim to be as fatal as Judith. She certainly would not be able to stab Le Pen in his sleep.'[26]

Rejection of the presence of Jews is constantly expressed, from the attack on the synagogue of rue Copernic – when the Prime Minister of the day, Raymond Barre, thought it a good idea to separate the 'innocent' non-Jewish victims from the rest – to the anti-Semitic incidents at Aix-les-Bains, not to mention a number of local acts of violence against people and property. This rejection was reinforced by incessant attacks from Jean-Marie Le Pen and the film director Autant-Lara who accused the Jews of profiting from the 'dividends' of Auschwitz. This comment was picked up by several of the most unexpected commentators, such as Jean-Marie Domenach himself, the former editor of the progressivist-inspired Catholic journal, *Esprit*. The myths of former times are long-lived.[27] The Jews were accused of utilizing the fact of genocide, which a number of widely read French revisionist lampoonists regard as pure fabrication, in order to manipulate opinion and impose their own power. Their 'plot' is untiringly exposed, to such a point that several extreme right-wing journals had no hesitation in re-issuing the *Protocols of the Elders of Zion* in 1990,[28] stating that they demonstrated the ever-present reality of the Jewish plot perverting the Republic. The Gulf war recently gave new impetus to such accusations, stabbing to the heart of political nightmares, since it was denounced in the streets of Paris as 'the Jews' war', encouraging once and for all their installation in total power over French society.[29] Contrary to all expectations, the period seems to be increasingly suited to the emergence of new 'Franco-French wars', this time involving the Moslems in place of the Protestants. The upshot of such wars seems all the more uncertain in that they are taking place at a time when both the frontiers of public space and the legitimacy of secularism or militant citizenship and the republican ideal are to some extent receding.

NOTES

1 SOFRES–La Croix poll, 11 April 1989, *La Documentation catholique*, 18 June 1989.
2 *La Croix*, 30 April and 11 July 1989.
3 François Furet, 'La France unie', in F. Furet, J. Julliard and P. Rosanvallon, *La République du centre* (Calmann-Lévy, Paris, 1988), p. 54.
4 See *L'Électeur français en question* (Presses de la FNSP, Paris, 1990), p. 206.
5 Guy Michelat, 'L'identité catholique des Français: Les dimensions de la religiosité', *Revue française de sociologie*, July–Sept. 1990, p. 380. J.-M. Donegani and G. Lescanne think that what one is seeing is the 'progressive abandonment of Catholicism as a system of values unifying all one's life' (J.-M. Donegani and G. Lescanne, *Catholicismes de France* (Desclée Bayard-presse, Paris, 1986), p. 274. With personal identification becoming more diverse, political behaviour would lose almost all its specificity in relation to one party or another. See also Henri Madelin, 'Catholiques dans la vie politique française', *Études*, March 1988.
6 Nonna Mayer, 'Ethnocentrisme, racisme et intolérance', in *L'Électeur français en question*, p. 40. On the links between nationalism and Catholicism, see the classic book by Guy Michelat and Jean-Pierre Thomas, *Dimensions du nationalisme* (Armand Colin, Paris, 1962), p. 37.

7 Jean Ranger, 'Le cercle des sympathisants', in Nonna Mayer and Pascal Perrineau, *Le Front national à découvert* (Presses de la Fondation National des sciences politiques, Paris, 1989), p. 139. See also Birgitta Orfali, *L'Adhésion au Front national* (Éditions Kimé, Paris, 1990).
8 Ariane Chebel d'Appollonia, *L'Extrême-droite en France: De Maurras à Le Pen* (Complexe, Brussels, 1988).
9 Jean Madiran, 'Les quatre ou cinq États confédérés', *Itinéraires*, special issue, Oct.–Nov. 1979.
10 Jean Madiran, *L'Hérésie du XXe siècle* (Nouvelles Éditions Latines, Paris, 1968), p. 85.
11 Jean Madiran, *Réclamation au Saint-Père* (Nouvelles Éditions Latines, Paris, 1974), pp. 54, 65–6, 71, 123–4.
12 See, for example, André Figueras, *Traité du balayage: Liberté, égalité, fraternité du balai!* (Publications André Figueras, Paris, 1985).
13 See Edith Delamare *et al.*, *Infiltrations ennemis dans l'Église*, Documents et témoignages, Paris, 1970. See also Jean Ousset, *Pour qu'il règne* (Dominique Morin, Angers, 1986), which vigorously attacks the Protestants, the freemasons and the Jews in the name of the defence of Catholicism (pp. 238ff).
14 H. Le Caron, *Dieu est-il antisémite?* (Éditions Fidelitrer, Escurolles, 1987).
15 See Jacques d'Arrioux, *L'Heure des héros* (Résiac, Montsurs, 1980); Dom Gérard, *Demain la chrétienté* (Dismas, Dion-Valmont, 1986).
16 See Franck Lafage, *Du refus au schisme: Le traditionalisme catholique* (Le Seuil, Paris, 1989), pp. 99ff. See also Jacques Maitre, 'Catholicisme d'extrême-droite et croisade anti-subversive', *Revue française de sociologis*, 2 (1961); Jean-Yves Camus, 'Intégrisme catholique et extrême droite en France: Le parti de la contre-révolution (1945–1988)', *Lignes*, Oct. 1988.
17 Pierre-André Taguieff, 'Nationalisme et réactions fondamentalistes en France', *Vingtième siècle*, Jan. 1990.
18 See the apologetic books by Denis Marchal, *Mgr. Lefebvre: 20 ans de combat pour le sacerdoce et la Foi* (Nouvelles Éditions Latines, Paris,1988); Roland Gaucher, *Mgr. Lefebvre: Combat pour l'Église* (Éditions Albatros, Paris, 1976); Paul Sérant, *Les Grands Déchirements des catholiques français, 1870–1988* (Perrin, Paris, 1989).
19 *Le Monde*, 18 Oct. 1987.
20 Pierre-André Taguieff, 'Un programme révolutionnaire?', in Mayer and Perrineau (eds), *Le Front National à découvert*.
21 CSA poll, *Le Parisien–France Inter*, 14 May 1990.
22 Paul Yonnet, 'La machine Carpentras: Histoire et sociologie d'un syndrome d'épuration', *Le Débat*, Sept.–Oct. 1990.
23 See the astonishing discussion on the reality of the impalement in the anus of M. Félix Germon and on the accusations of a manipulative plot in *Libération*, 9 and 27 Nov. 1990; *Le Monde*, 31 Oct. 1990; and *Le Point*, 5 Nov. 1990.
24 *Libération*, 2 July 1990.
25 *National-Hebdo*, 14 Dec. 1989. See Pierre-André Taguieff, 'Antisémitisme politique et national-populisme en France dans les années 1980', in Pierre Birnbaum (ed.), *Histoire politique des Juifs de France* (Presse de la Fondation nationale des sciences politiques, Paris, 1990).
26 *Chrétien-Solidarité*, Oct. 1983.
27 Henry Weinberg, *The Myth of the Jew in France, 1967–1982* (Mosaic Press, Oakville, Ontario, 1987).
28 *Lectures françaises*, Dec. 1990; *Révision*, May 1990.
29 *Minute*, Oct. 1990.

Index

Abbas, Ferhat, 288
Abitbol, Michel, 292, 294
Abraham, Pierre, 45
Adler, Alfred, 170
Ageron, Charles-Robert, 292, 293, 294
Agulhon, Maurice, 144, 169
Albert, Phyllis Cohen, 33, 79
Albouy, Robert, 139
Allard, Paul, 127, 173, 276, 277
Allemane, Jean, 246
Allen, Louis, 197
Anderson, Malcolm, 254
Anderson, Thomas, 96
Andreu, Pierre, 144, 172
Angress, Werner T., 23
Ansky, Michel, 292, 293
Ansonneau, Dr, 275
Anspach, 166
Antraygues, Robert, 222
Appel, John, 22
Aragon, Louis, 153, 213, 222, 237
Arbellot, Simon, 177
Arendt, Hannah, 5, 6–7, 18, 22, 25, 29, 32, 49
Aron, Jean-Paul, 174
Aron, Raymond, 37
Arouet, 255
Ascheim, Steven, 24
Astier de la Vigerie, General Emmanuel de, 74, 81, 122
Aubery, P., 79
Audry, Colette, 224
Auriol, Vincent, 241
Aury, Firmin, 246
Austin, Roger, 196, 197
Autant-Lara, 304

Badie, Bertrand, 22, 24, 33
Badine, C. de la, 220
Badinter, Robert, 18, 297
Bainville, Jacques, 117, 237
Balzac, Honoré de, 151
Bannister, Joseph, 9
Baral, Pierre, 230
Barbey d'Aurevilly, 153
Bardèche, Maurice, 87
Barillon, Raymond, 223, 224
Barre, Raymond, 304
Barrès, Maurice, 49, 92, 93, 94, 95, 98, 109, 110, 116, 117, 124, 125, 129, 141, 150, 154, 155, 160, 200, 206, 213, 216, 222, 227, 228, 230, 232, 234, 262, 287, 297, 300, 302
Barrière, Bertrand, 175
Barrows, Susannah, 169
Barthélemy, René, 285
Barthes, Roland, 133, 135, 144
Basch, Victor, 53, 264, 285
Bastaire, Jean, 96
Batault, Georges, 256
Bauberot, Jean, 230, 231
Bazin, Jean, 255
Beau de Lomenie, E., 87, 96, 107
Beaune, Colette, 25
Becker, Raphael, 150
Bédarida, François, 40, 41, 107, 146, 294
Bedel, Maurice, 100, 106, 131, 143, 218

Index 307

Beerbohm, Max, 154
Beilis, 111
Bein, Alex, 171
Bellanger, H. 255
Bellessort, André, 172
Benda, Julien, 101
Ben Gurion, David, 47
Benjamin, René, 274
Ben Said, 249, 290
Bensoussan, Albert, 295
Bérard, Léon, 190
Béraud, Henri, 2, 101, 102, 105, 107, 121, 130, 144, 156, 159, 172, 173, 218, 238, 255, 268, 276
Bergery, Gaston, 21, 127, 184, 195, 222, 257, 293
Bergson, Henri, 281
Berl, Emmanuel, 72
Bernanos, Georges, 178, 179, 181, 186, 194, 200
Bernard, Tristan, 47
Bernhardt, Sarah, 151, 152
Bernier, mayor, 90
Bernos, Marcel, 169
Bernstein, Henry, 79, 166
Berstein, Serge, 21, 223
Bert, Paul, 267
Bertrand, Jean, 274
Besse, Annie, 222
Béteille, Pierre, 127
Bidault, Georges, 181, 190, 192, 196, 213
Bietrix, 204
Biez, Jacques de, 97, 99, 106, 220, 232, 253
Bilis, Michel, 222, 223
Billacois, François, 177
Billig, Joseph, 96
Bismarck, prince Otto von, 29, 30, 33
Blacas, Jules, 99, 106, 206, 221
Blackbourn, David, 23
Bleichröder, 29, 33
Bloch, Abraham, 116
Bloch, Edmond, 69–75, 76, 80, 112, 116, 189, 289
Bloch, F., 165
Bloch, Marc, 32
Bloch, Pierre, 60, 85, 177, 221, 253
Bloch-Lainé, François, 36, 40, 41, 212
Bloy, Léon, 178, 200
Blum, Madame Abraham, 46

Blum, Jules, 65
Blumchen, Isaac, see Gohier, Urbain
Blumel, André, 58, 59, 61, 77, 78, 188, 189, 214, 222, 254
Blumenkranz, Bernard, 25, 33
Bodin, Louis, 255
Boissel, Jean, 122
Bokanowski, 117
Bonhomme, Jacques, 65
Bonsirven, Father, 179
Bonte, Florimont, 151, 209
Bordeaux, Henry, 110, 181
Boris, Georges, 74, 81, 101, 119, 124, 127, 153, 172, 194, 202, 239, 248, 255
Borne, Dominique, 144
Borne, Étienne, 195
Bossuet, Jacques, 178, 216
Bothorel, Jean, 58, 59
Boulanger, General, 250
Bourdat, G., 287
Bourdet, Claude, 294
Bourdin, Jeannine, 223
Bouret, Henri, 193
Bourgeois, Léon, 267
Bourgin, Hubert, 104, 108, 139, 146, 155
Bourguiba, Habib, 193, 291, 295
Bournand, François, 97
Boutang, Pierre, 76, 100, 106, 193, 203, 220, 247–50, 258, 267, 272, 276, 287
Bouvier, Jean, 97, 219
Brasat, Léon, 275
Brasillach, Robert, 86, 121, 148, 172, 245, 257
Braudel, Fernand, 25
Bretin, T., 214
Briand, Aristide, 190, 263, 266
Brigneau, François, 275, 302, 303
Brinin, M. de, 87
Britt, S., 22
Brown, Michael, 22
Brummel, Georges Bryan (called Beau Brummel), 154
Brunet, Jean-Paul, 293
Brunschvicg, Léon, 79
Brunschwicg, Cécile Léon, 188, 240
Brunswick, Duke of, 44
Bucard, Marcel, 86, 148, 169, 254
Buisson, Ferdinand, 229, 262, 273
Bulawko, Henry, 77

308 Index

Buré, Émile, 215
Burin, Philippe, 21, 127, 195, 222, 293
Burns, Michael, 21
Buron, Robert, 197
Bury, J.-P., 253
Busi, Frederick, 21, 95
Byrnes, Robert, 7, 21, 22, 96, 97

Cachin, Marcel, 80, 209, 210
Cahen, 140
Cahn, Joseph, 134, 144
Caillaux, Joseph, 130, 143, 246
Caillavet, Henri, 59, 158, 174
Cambre-Mielet, A. J. S. M. de la, 255
Camus, Jean-Yves, 305
Camy-Darmon, Judith, 170, 176
Canac, Yves, 41
Capéran, Louis, 262, 273
Capitant-Peter, Colette, 170, 253
Carlebach, Julius, 169
Cartier, Jacques, 114
Cartier, Raymond, 282
Casanova, Laurent, 211
Cassin, René, 79
Castellani, Charles, 162, 175
Castelnau, General de, 117, 180
Céline, Louis-Ferdinand, 87, 96, 134, 151, 160, 161, 183, 239, 257, 276, 297
Chabauty, abbé A., 89, 93, 98
Chanel, Mlle., 144
Chapman, Guy, 21
Chapple, Gérard, 169
Chapron, Françoise, 143, 144, 145, 219, 275
Charcot, Jean-Martin, 150, 151, 153, 171
Chardonne, Jacques, 154, 297
Charle, Christophe, 24, 230
Charles V, 19
Charles VII, 147
Charpentier, 279
Chaumet, André, 255
Chautemps, Camille, 266, 281
Chevalier, Yves, 25
Chevallier, Pierre, 274
Chiappe, Jean, 80
Chirac, Auguste, 92, 94, 95, 98
Chiron, Yves, 98
Chollet, Mgr, 180
Chouffet, 214

Christophe, Paul, 194, 196
Churchill, Winston, 47, 119, 212, 222, 277
Cicurel, Lily, 46, 146, 287
Citti, Pierre, 175
Clark, Priscilla, 144
Clary, Norman James, 96
Clemenceau, Georges, 37, 41, 48, 117, 119, 143, 152, 165, 261, 263
Clémenti, Pierre, 290
Clermont-Tonnerre, comte de, 30
Clovis, 19, 139, 181
Cohen, Carl, 23
Cohen, J., Chief Rabbi, 44
Cohen, Naomi, 60
Cohen, Stuart, 60
Cohen, William, 222
Cohn, Norman, 277
Colleville, comte de, 263, 274
Colton, Joel, 58, 222, 254, 257
Combes, Émile, 197, 217, 262, 263, 265
Comte de Paris, 255
Conte, Arthur, 145
Coppe, M. de, 282
Costa Pinto, Antonio, 21
Coston, Henry, 2, 86, 87, 96, 202, 204, 219, 220, 239, 267, 275, 284, 287, 302
Coty, François, 153
Coty, René, 60, 103
Courtois, Stéphane, 221
Cousteau, Pierre-Antoine, 258, 272, 277, 287, 294
Coutrot, Aline, 194, 196
Crémieux, Adolphe, 29, 126, 174, 204, 220, 278, 279, 280, 282, 286, 293
Crémieux-Foa, Captain, 166, 177

Dairnwaell, Georges (known as Satan), 97
Daladier, Edouard, 118, 119, 121
Dalby, Louise Elliot, 58, 59, 172, 174, 175
Dalio, 104
Da Ponte, 159
Darlan, François, 286
Darmesteter, James, 32
Darmon, Claire, 254
Darquier de Pellepoix, 87, 135, 171, 181, 183, 242, 245–7, 282

Index 309

D'Arrioux, Jacques, 305
Darwin, Charles, 151
Daudet, Alphonse, 151
Daudet, Léon, 2, 68, 72, 79, 86, 112, 117, 125, 135, 139, 145, 150, 151, 152, 154, 155, 156, 160, 163, 164, 166, 167, 170, 171, 173, 176, 181, 193, 201, 216, 218, 221, 236, 238, 244, 248, 254, 256, 265, 268, 270, 274, 297
David, Pierre, 116
Davidson, Jean, 41
Dayan, Georges, 259
Déat, Marcel, 21, 127, 195, 204, 214, 215, 217, 222, 223, 254, 293
De Bonald, 130, 178
Debré, Michel, 37, 41, 59, 106
Debû-Bridel, Jacques, 223
Defferre, Gaston, 224
De Gaspéri, Alcide, 190, 191, 197
De Gaulle, Charles, 36, 37, 40, 73, 123, 124, 137, 168, 171, 198, 250, 251, 291
Delamare, Edith, 305
Delbos, Yvon, 118, 119
Delbourg-Delphis, Marylène, 172
Delepine, Maurice, 214
Delmaire, Danielle, 97
Deloye, Yves, 292
Delpech, François, 33
Delumeau, Jean, 169
Deniel, Alain, 258
Dermenjian, Geneviève, 280, 292
Deroulède, Paul, 166
Desportes, Henri, 125, 292
Deutscher, Isaac, 40
Dignac, Pierre, 276
Dindes, Alan, 23
Dioudonnat, Pierre-Marie, 257
Disraeli, Benjamin, 10–11, 12, 13, 23, 48, 59, 63, 76, 78, 154, 243, 273, 287
Ditte, Jacques, 256
Doblowski, Michael, 22
Domenach, Jean-Marie, 191, 197, 304
Domhoff, G. William, 22
Dominique, Pierre, 87, 147, 153, 163, 170, 171, 172, 173, 176, 218
Donegani, J.-M., 304
Donnay, Maurice, 54
Dorgères, Roland, 136, 138, 140
Doriot, Jacques, 21, 72, 121, 126, 127, 153, 195, 222, 250, 252, 272, 281, 284, 293, 294
Dormoy, Marx, 113, 114, 115, 121, 281, 284
Dorsay, 113
Doumergue, Gaston, 41
Drault, Jean, 85, 86, 95, 165, 177
Dreyfus Affair, 1, 2, 3, 4, 5, 7, 16, 19, 21, 22, 32, 33, 49, 50, 51, 53, 54, 60, 66, 78, 85, 88, 91, 96, 116, 123, 142, 165, 167, 168, 175, 191, 227, 229, 248, 249, 259, 275, 278, 285, 296, 297, 299
Dreyfus, Camille, 165, 166
Dreyfus, Louis, 140
Dreyfus, François, 194
Dreyfus, Maxime, 165
Drieu La Rochelle, Pierre, 151, 153, 154, 164, 172, 176, 239, 297
Drumont, Édouard, 2, 7, 9, 11, 19, 21, 29, 50, 53, 83–226, 227, 228, 230, 232, 233, 234, 238, 253, 255, 256, 263, 266, 268, 274, 279, 282, 283, 287, 292, 297, 300, 301, 302
Dubois-Chatel, Xavier, 245
Dubuc, 292
Duchet, Roger, 295
Duclos, Jacques, 77, 78, 112, 211, 271
Duguay-Trouin, René, 114
Duguesclin, 114
Duhamel, Olivier, 41
Dujonchay, Captain, 167
Dulles, John Foster, 212
Dundes, Alan, 106
Dupont, Léon, 171
Duquesne, Jacques, 197
Durkheim, Émile, 32, 51, 103, 110, 234, 235, 264, 274, 281
Duroselle, Jean-Baptiste, 97
Duval, Alexandre, 133, 141, 142

Eichmann, Adolf, 205
Eisenhower, Dwight David, 212, 286
Eldan, Israel, 58
Eley, Geoff, 23
Elms, Elwyn, 253
Encrevé, André, 230
Endelman, Todd, 24
Epstein, Simon, 19
Evans, Peter, 22

310 Index

Fabius, Laurent, 86, 88, 101, 105, 106, 134, 135, 151, 152, 155, 158, 162, 174, 194, 203, 204, 206, 221, 249, 252, 259, 292, 297, 303
Fabre-Luce, Alfred, 81, 101, 107, 155, 173, 248, 258
Fabry, Jean, 276
Faguet, Émile, 110, 125
Faugeras, Henri, 174, 274
Faure, Edgar, 294
Faure, Félix, 266
Faure, Paul, 214, 215, 216, 217, 268, 281
Faurisson, 290
Fayolle-Lefort, 108, 172, 256
Ferdonnet, Paul, 171
Férenzy, Oscar de, 179, 182, 189
Ferro, Marc, 128, 144
Ferry, Jules, 16, 228, 229, 230, 233, 261, 262, 263, 266, 267
Feuerwerker, David, 33
Fichte, 31
Field, Geoffrey, 23
Figuéras, André, 125, 170, 171, 302, 305
Finaly, bank, 176, 210, 211
Finkelstein, 111
Fleg, Edmond, 53
Fleurot, Paul, 246
Fleury, Alain, 197
Fliess, 149
Foch, Marshall, 117
Ford, Henry, 9
Fouchardière, G. de la, 204, 220
Foucher, Paul, 166
Fould, family, 29
Fourier, Charles, 98, 159, 200, 206
Fralon, José Alain, 259
Francis, J. F., 212
François, General, 167
Franco, 286
Frank, Léo, 8
Frank, Robert, 127
Frankel, Jonathan, 60, 108
Fraser, Geoffrey, 58, 172, 174
Freud, Sigmund, 149, 150, 153, 171
Freycinet, Charles de, 228
Friedländer, Saul, 176
Frossard, L. O., 131
Fry, L., 277
Fumet, Stanislas, 182, 186, 187, 189

Furet, François, 300, 304

Gabel, Émile, 198
Gambetta, Léon, 16, 37, 39, 41, 106, 233, 253, 261, 263, 265, 266, 275, 278
Ganem, Paul, 275
Ganier-Raymond, Philippe, 256
Garçon, François, 171
Gaspard, Françoise, 259
Gay, Peter, 14, 24, 171
Gaxotte, Pierre, 2, 48, 100, 101, 102, 103, 105, 117, 156, 159, 173, 202, 236, 254, 268, 269, 271, 272, 277
Georges, abbé of Nantes, 302
Gérard, 174
Gerber, David, 22
Gerbod, Paul, 230
Gerlier, Cardinal, 190
Germon, Félix, 305
Ghilini, Hector, 121, 127, 161, 175, 202, 219, 223
Gide, André, 154, 161, 162, 175, 187, 196, 281
Gide, Charles, 55
Gilam, Abraham, 23
Gilman, Sander, 24, 170
Girard, Patrick, 33
Girard, René, 22
Girardet, Raoul, 98
Giroud, Françoise, 88
Glanz, Rudolf, 22
Glock, Charles, 22
Goebbels, Joseph Paul, 160, 175
Goguel, François, 41
Gohier, Urbain, 85, 104, 117, 234, 253, 256, 263, 274
Goldberg, Harvey, 60
Goldenbach, M. de, 174
Goldmann, Nahum, 57, 68
Goldscheider, Calvin, 33
Goléa, Antoine, 191
Gombault, Georges, 194, 197
Gontier, René, 255
Gougenot des Mousseaux, 89, 92, 95, 97, 111, 125, 178
Gouraud, Henri, 117
Gourdon, Alain, 58, 59
Graeber, I., 22
Green, Nancy L., 59, 107
Grégoire, abbé, 246

Index   311

Groddeck, Georg, 149, 169
Gros, Louis, 223
Gros, René, 232, 253
Grouer, Frédéric, 172
Grüber, Helmut, 58
Grumbach, Salomon, 188, 214, 218
Grunebaum-Ballin, Paul, 263, 264
Grunewald, J., rabbi, 63
Guerden, Léon, 204, 220
Guesde, Jules, 35, 54, 97
Guillen, Pierre, 294
Guitard, Louis, 143, 176, 222

Habermas, Jürgen, 18, 25
Haganov, Gideon, 222
Hagel, Charles, 280, 293
Halévy, Daniel, 154
Halévy, Leon, 32
Halls, Bill, 197
Hamburger, Ernest, 23
Hamon, Léo, 41
Hasan-Rokem, Galit, 23, 106
Hassine, Juliette, 170, 176
Hegel, Georg, Wilhelm Friedrich, 11
Helbronner, Édouard, 72, 73
Heller, Peter, 169
Hellman, John, 195
Henriot, Philippe, 136, 137, 187, 190, 282, 297
Henry, memorial, 285, 286
Herbette, François, 277
Hermet, Guy, 24
Herr, Lucien, 50, 54, 59
Herriot, Édouard, 113, 118, 119, 158, 163, 164, 176, 192, 244
Herse, Jean de la, 277
Hertz, Henri, 55
Herzberg, Arthur, 33
Herzl, Theodore, 53, 54
Herzog, William, 96
Higham, John, 8, 22, 23
Hincky, Canon, 187
Hindenburg, Paul von, 269
Hirschman, Alfred, 60
Hirshfeld, Claire, 23
Hitler, Adolf, 47, 74, 75, 86, 87, 95, 101, 149, 150, 164, 175, 196, 214, 216, 239, 245, 268, 269, 270, 271, 280, 285, 286
Hô Chi Minh, 287, 295
Hoffmann, Paul, 173

Hoffmann, Stanley, 146, 230, 259
Holmes, Colin, 9, 23
Hourdin, Georges, 195
Hourwitz, Jacob Nathan, 204–5, 220
Hovnanian, Léon, 223, 259
Huppert, Elizabeth, 158
Hyman, Paula, 24, 58, 60, 61, 80
Hyndman, Henry, 10

Ihuel, 113, 114
Isaac, Ferdinand, 90
Isaac, Jules, 194
Isnards, Charles, 182

Jackson, A. B., 59
Jacob, François, 88
Jacobs, Gabriel, 127
Jacoby, Jean, 171, 277
Jarblum, Marc, 54, 60, 61
Jaurès, Jean, 35, 36, 41, 50, 54, 60, 101, 130, 139, 213, 216, 217, 246, 263
Jeanneney, Jean-Marcel, 119, 251
Jeanneney, Jean-Noël, 96
Joan of Arc, 122, 139, 147–8, 169, 170, 171, 174, 237
Johnson, Douglas, 230
Joinovici, 203
Jolivet, René Louis, 275
Joll, James, 58
Jospin, Lionel, 162
Jouhandeau, Marcel, 101, 104, 107, 181, 239, 257, 258
Jouhaux, Leon, 164
Jouin, Mgr, 117, 126, 180, 253, 264, 274, 277
Jouvenel, Bertrand de, 105
Julien, Charles-André, 293
Julliard, Jacques, 21, 304
Juvigny, P., 41

Kadhafi, Colonel, 57
Kahn, Zadoc, Chief Rabbi, 53, 66
Kaminsky, 276
Kaminsky, Alice, 172
Kaplan, Jacob, Rabbi, 67, 69, 79, 80
Katz, Jacob, 5, 22, 31, 33, 92, 274
Kaufmann, 140
Kautsky, Karl, 12
Kedward, Roderick, 196, 197
Kerensky, Alexander Feodorovitch, 220
Kérilis, Henri de, 71, 119, 180

312 Index

Kingston, Paul, 21, 24, 257
Klarsfeld, Serge, 128
Kleeblatt, Norman, 299
Klutznick, Philip, 57, 68
Knibiehler, Yvonne, 169, 173
Knobel, Marc, 96, 293
Kramer, William, 22
Krauss, Karl, 13
Kriegel, Annie, 221
Kriegel-Valrimont, Maurice, 222
Kriskris, Martine, 256
Krupp, family, 213
Kun, Bela, 205

Labrove, Henri, 274
Lacoste, Robert, 216
Lacouture, Jean, 40, 58, 60, 127, 144, 219, 222, 259
Lacroix, Maurice, 140, 180
Lafage, Franck, 305
Lafaye, M., 215
Lafon de Savines, 125
Lagrenée, marquis de, 167
Laloum, Jean, 257
Lamase, M. de, 166
Lamberlin, Roger, 277
Lambert, abbé, 281, 283, 284
Lambert, Raymond-Raoul, 62, 70, 78, 79
Lamberti, Marjorie, 60
Landau, Lazare, 80, 96, 175, 194
Landeau, Philippe, 79, 126, 144
Lanzenberg, François, 259
Lapeyre, Paul, 151
Lapie, Pierre-Olivier, 171, 198
Larkin, Maurice, 274
Las, Nelly, 58, 61
Lasierra, R., 21
Lassalle, Ferdinand, 49
Lasteyrie, 164
Launay, Louis de, 106
Launay, Michel, 197, 223
Launay, Robert, 174, 256
Laur, Francis, 90
Lautman, 125
Laval, Pierre, 164
Lazare, Bernard, 49, 50, 54, 60, 165
Le Bon, Gustave, 169
Lebzelter, Gisela, 23
Leca, Jean, 24

Lecache, Bernard, 47, 70, 73, 75–81, 268
Lecaron, H., 302, 305
Lecoc, Louis Charles, 119, 126, 173
Lecoo, Anne-Marie, 25
Le Cour Grandmaison, Jean, 243
Lefebvre, Mgr, 302
Lefort, Charles, 22
Le Goff, Jacques, 169
Legouez, Modeste, 133, 136, 138, 140, 141, 142, 146
Legrand, Jean-Charles, 115, 126, 160, 175, 181, 257
Lémann, abbé, 170
Lemonnier, judgment, 39
Le Pen, Jean-Marie, 144, 152, 249, 252, 291, 297, 299, 303, 304
Le Rider, Jacques, 169, 173
Lerner, Henri, 145
Leroux, Armand, 246
Leroux, Pierre, 29, 89, 98, 146, 200
Leroy, Géraldi, 127, 176
Leroy-Beaulieu, Anatole, 274
Leroy-Beaulieu, Henry, 230
Leroy-Beaulieu, Paul, 139, 262
Le Royer, E., 229
Le Ruel, Maurice, 59
Lescanne, G., 304
Le Troquer, André, 118
Levaillant, I., 97
Levigne, Catherine, 60, 61
Levillain, Philippe, 194
Lévy, Bernard-Henri, 21, 222
Lévy, Julien, 41
Lévy, Louis, 218
Lévy, Louis Germain, rabbi, 47, 69, 80
Lévy, Marc, 171
Lévy, Paul, 72
Lévy-Bruhl, Lucien, 79, 234, 264, 281
Lévy-Coeur, Lucien, 175
Lewinter, Roger, 169
Liber, Chief Rabbi, 116
Liebknecht, Karl, 12
Liénard, Cardinal, 187
Ligneau, Jean de, 97
Ligou, Daniel, 275
Limagne, Pierre, 191
Lindenberg, Daniel, 59
Lipkowski, De, 259
Lipset, Seymour Martin, 22
Litvinoff, Barnet, 74, 81

Loewenstein, Rudolph, 170, 194
Logue, William, 58, 174
Loiseux, Gérard, 277
Lombard, Paul, 255
Longuet, Jean, 246
Lorrain, Jean, 167
Loubet del Bayle, J. L., 24
Louis XIV, 94
Louÿs, Pierre, 154
Lovsky, F., 194
Luc-Cyl, 241
Luca, Charles, 112
Lustiger, Cardinal, 302
Luther, Martin, 11
Luxembourg, Rosa, 205
Luzzatti, Luigi, 25

Machefer, Philippe, 21
Madelin, Henri, 304
Madiran, Jean, 301, 302, 305
Maistre, Joseph de, 111, 231, 302
Maitre, Jacques, 305
Malglaive, Gabriel, 255
Malhotra, Ruth, 170
Malino, Francis, 21, 96, 97, 219, 221, 222, 257
Mallarmé, 154
Malon, Benoît, 206
Mandel, Georges, 18, 47, 59, 71, 85, 94, 104, 106, 107, 117, 118, 119, 121, 126, 127, 132, 150, 151, 152, 155, 156, 157, 158, 162, 171, 173, 175, 190, 197, 220, 236, 237, 242, 243, 246, 248, 249, 252, 255, 258, 266, 267, 269, 272, 275, 277, 279, 297
Mandelbaum, Jacques, 81
Mangin, Charles, 117
Marat, Jean-Paul, 233
Marchal, Denis, 305
Marchandeau, decree, 247
Marie, Romain, 303
Marin, Louis, 139, 164
Maritain, 196
Marquet, Adrien, 38, 204, 214, 215, 217
Marr, William, 11, 23
Marrus, Michael, 21, 24, 32, 33, 58, 60, 128
Marshall, 222
Martin, Maurice, 214
Martin du Gard, Roger, 121, 268, 276
Martinet, Gilles, 40, 80

Martinez, Dr, 125
Marty, André, 208
Marx, Karl, 7, 11, 12, 34–6, 49, 59, 89, 144, 145, 195, 201, 205, 207, 208
Massa, Anna-Lise, 145
Massis, Henri, 155, 172, 175, 181
Maupassant, Guy de, 151
Mauriac, Claude, 184, 195
Mauriac, François, 162, 182–7, 189, 192, 238, 289
Maurras, Charles, 2, 20, 48, 49, 72, 79, 88, 101, 103, 104, 110, 116, 120, 126, 130, 138, 139, 140, 142, 145, 150, 152, 156, 159, 162, 168, 171, 181, 183, 204, 208, 209, 231, 232, 234, 235, 236, 237, 238, 239, 244, 246, 248, 249, 252, 253, 254, 257, 262, 265, 267, 268, 269, 271, 277, 279, 283, 287, 297, 300, 301, 302
Maxence, Jean-Pierre, 113, 156, 173
Mayer, Daniel, 77, 151, 171
Mayer, Germain, 165
Mayer, Hans, 24, 169
Mayer, Léon, 85
Mayer, Nonna, 304, 305
Mayer, P. A., 59
Mayer, René, 18, 48, 59, 74, 106, 123, 191, 210, 287, 290
Mayeur, Françoise, 195
Mayeur, Jean-Marie, 194, 196, 230, 231, 273, 274
McCearney, James, 253
McClelland, J. S., 231
Mehlman, Jeffrey, 175
Memmi, Albert, 42, 58
Mendès, Catulle, 153, 166
Mendès-Flohr, Paul, 23, 24, 108
Mendès France, Jean Mardochée, 45
Mendès France, Marie-Claire, 47, 168, 177
Merklen, abbé, 179
Metzger, André, 194
Meyer, Armand, 165–6
Meyer, Arthur, 165, 166, 176, 177, 233, 253
Meyer, Jean, 125
Micaud, Charles, 276
Michel, Henry, 127, 276
Michelet, Edmond, 198
Miles, Pierre, 277
Millerand, Étienne Alexandre, 252, 263

Milza, Pierre, 21
Mitterrand, François, 162, 259, 288, 303
Moch, Jules, 18, 71, 77, 79, 80, 94, 101, 102, 114, 131, 132, 134, 152, 153, 156, 171, 188, 210, 214, 216, 218, 236, 239, 240, 249, 255, 265, 266, 269, 270, 283, 284
Mollet, Guy, 216, 219, 223
Monnier, Pierre, 173
Monnerville, Gaston, 219
Monniot, Albert, 85, 111, 125, 166, 176
Monroe, Marilyn, 157, 212
Montagne, Rémy, 250, 259
Montandon, Jacques, 87
Montel, 214
Montuclard, Maurice, 194
Morand, Paul, 154, 297
Morès, marquis de, 97, 166
Mosse, George, 3, 12, 21, 23, 24, 170, 175, 176
Mosse, Werner, 23
Mounier, Emmanuel, 181, 182–7, 189, 192, 195, 196, 238
Murphy, 286
Mussolini, Benito, 254, 271

Nantet, Jacques, 58
Napoleon I, 30, 33, 94, 181
Napoleon III, 279
Naquet, Alfred, 159, 174, 275
Natanson, Thadée, 58, 172, 174
Nguyen, Victor, 253
Nicault, Catherine, 60
Nicolet, Claude, 15, 24, 41, 58, 59, 61, 273
Niewyk, Donald, 24
Nizan, Paul, 67
Noguères, Henri, 180, 194
Nora, Pierre, 21, 25, 169, 273, 274
Nora, Simon, 40, 41, 194, 222
Nordau, Max, 13, 165

Ogé, Frédéric, 253
Ollivier, Georges, 255, 275
Orfali, Birgitta, 305
Ortiz, Joseph, 291
Ory, Pascal, 223
Osgood, Samuel, 256
Ousset, Jean, 305
Oustric, Albert, 155, 208, 210
Ozouf, Jacques, 24

Painlevé, Paul, 163, 236
Panouille, Jean-Pierre, 144
Papen, Franz von, 269
Paraz, Albert, 146
Parias, L. H., 274
Parkes, James, 5, 22
Pascal, Georges de, 97
Paul, René, 192
Paul-Boncour, Joseph, 72
Paxton, Robert, 21, 128
Pécaut, Félix, 229
Péguy, Charles, 262
Peletan, Camille, 217
Pellet, Alain, 41
Pellisson, 107, 125
Pemjean, Lucien, 85, 256
Pereire, brothers, 29
Perrineau, Pascal, 305
Perrot, Guy, 43
Peschanski, Denis, 128
Pétain, Marshal, 5, 47, 88, 117, 118, 120, 121, 128, 137, 144, 148, 235, 301
Petit, Henry-Robert, 86, 95, 125, 206, 221, 255, 275
Philip the Fair, 19
Philippe, Beatrice, 33
Pierrard, Pierre, 21, 96, 97, 170, 194, 197, 294
Pleyber, Jean, 74, 247
Ploncard D'Assac, Jacques, 86, 87, 95, 107, 277
Pluymène, J., 21
Poincaré, Raymond, 180, 265
Pokrovsky, A., 277
Poliakov, Léon, 22, 194
Pomme, Dr, 156
Pompidou, Georges, 251
Poncins, Léon de, 220
Porto-Riche, 47
Poujade, Pierre, 1, 2, 8, 66, 73, 81, 129, 133, 142, 144, 146, 171, 198, 247–50, 258, 259, 287, 289
Poulantzas, Nicos, 98
Poulat, Émile, 194
Prague, H., 32
Prenant, Marcel, 211
Priouret, Roger, 289
Prost, Antoine, 237
Proudhon, Pierre-Joseph, 89, 98, 156, 200, 206

Proust, Marcel, 47, 149, 150, 154, 155, 167, 172, 177
Pucheu, Pierre, 282
Pujo, Léon, 79, 254
Pulzer, P. G., 23, 176
Puységur, comte A. de, 157, 173, 258

Quinley, Harold, 22

Rabi, W., 59, 78, 175
Rachel, Elizabeth, 151
Rajsfus, Maurice, 79
Ramette, Arthur, 210
Ranger, Jean, 305
Raphael, Freddy, 194
Rassinier, Paul, 267, 268, 276, 290
Rateau, Jean, 275
Rathenau, Walter, 12, 13–14, 24, 162
Ravoux-Rallo, Elisabeth, 169
Rebatet, Lucien, 86, 121, 127
Recanati, Jean, 177, 211, 222
Recouly, Raymond, 175, 276
Régis, Max, 279, 282
Régnier, Max, 276
Reinharz, Jehuda, 24, 60
Reinach, Joseph, 32, 166, 170, 234
Rémond, René, 21, 40, 41, 79, 194, 196, 197, 223, 274
Renaud, Jean, 143, 153, 172
Renaudel, Pierre, 215, 223
Renauld, Ernest, 228
René-Lignac, M., 81, 289
Renoir, Jean, 104
Renouvin, Pierre, 40, 41, 79, 197
Reshef, Ouriel, 276
Reynaud, Léonce, 176
Reynaud, Paul, 118, 121, 164, 237, 272
Rhillon, 176
Ribot, Théodule, 217
Richard, Eliane, 169
Richelieu, Cardinal de, 94, 181, 245
Rimbaud, Christiane, 126, 127
Rioux, Jean-Pierre, 40, 41, 107, 294
Rivet, Paul, 246
Rivollet, Georges, 116
Robrieux, Philippe, 221
Roche, Anne, 127, 176
Rochefort, Henri, 166
Rocque, Colonel de la, 67, 68, 69, 102, 115, 121, 138, 145, 250, 284

Rohling, Auguste, 97, 151
Rokkan, Stein, 14, 24
Roland, Jean, 254
Rolland, Maurice, 60
Rolland, Romain, 161, 163, 175
Rollat, Alain, 144, 171
Roosevelt, Franklin Delano, 220, 273, 277, 285
Rosambert, A., 125
Rosanvallon, P., 304
Rose, Peter, 22
Rosenberg, Alfred, 175
Rosenfeld, 233
Rossignol, Dominique, 220, 275
Rothkrug, Lionel, 170
Rothschild, family, 9, 22, 29, 74, 89, 90, 96, 97, 104, 107, 117, 121, 140, 166, 170, 194, 211, 285, 299
Rothschild, Robert, baron de, 67
Rouault, Jean-Marie, 87
Rousseau, Jean-Baptiste, 130
Rousso, Henry, 259
Rouvier, 217
Roy, Jules, 295
Rozis, 284
Ruch, Mgr, 188, 189
Rudelle, Odile, 24, 41
Rueschemeyer, Dietrich, 22
Rürup, Reinhard, 23
Russell, Jane, 157, 212

Sabatier, Émile, 135, 139
Sadoun, Marc, 223
Saint-Bonnet, Georges, 145, 227
Saint Louis, 19, 101, 181
Saint-Paulien, see Sicard, Maaurice Yvan
Saint-Serge, René, 106
Saive, René, 174, 175
Salbstein, M. C., 23
Salem, Daniel, 40, 41
Salengro, Gaston, 266
Salengro, Roger, 121
Saliège, Jules-Géraud, 190
Samuel, Lord, 119
Sand, Shlomo, 21
Sangnier, Marc, 180
Santos, Joseph, 274
Sapiens, see Fabre-Luce
Say, Léon, 223, 228
Schacht, Dr, 4
Schatzberg, Walter, 24, 60

Index 315

Scherr, Lilly, 108
Schnapper, Dominique, 58
Schor, Ralph, 107
Schrameck, Abraham, 18, 236, 237, 252, 254
Schuker, Stephen, 257
Schulte, Hans, 169
Schuman, Robert, 190, 192
Schuster, Zachariah, 58, 79
Schwartz, Chief Rabbi, 189
Schwob, Marcel, 47, 165
Sée, Camille, 264
Seiden, Morton, 170
Seigel, Jerrold, 172
Sembard, Pierre, 221
Sembat, Marcel, 54, 117, 164, 216, 217
Sérant, Paul, 305
Serman, William, 177
Servan-Schreiber, Jean-Jacques, 194, 249, 259, 289, 290, 291
Sezillie, Captain, 255
Sherwood, John, 59, 126, 127, 175, 197, 258
Shylock, 9, 91, 119, 209, 272
Siblat, Paul, 292
Sicard, Maurice Yvan, 119, 126
Sidgwick, A., 194
Sidos, Pierre, 302
Siegfried, André, 187, 196, 248, 258
Silberner, Edmund, 98
Simon, Jules, 233, 263, 266, 267
Simon, Pierre-Henri, 48, 59, 180
Simon, Perrine, 59, 253
Singerman, Robert, 23
Sirinelli, J.-F., 174
Sivan, E., 292
Siweck-Pouydesseau, Jeanne, 230
Skocpol, Theda, 22
Smilévitch, Éric, 33
Soboul, Albert, 33
Sombart, Werner, 107
Sorlin, Pierre, 97, 194, 231, 292
Soucy, Robert, 176
Souday, Paul, 16
Soupault, Ralph, 114, 202
Soustelle, Jacques, 288
Spatz, Erwin, 175, 176
Spinoza, Baruch, 153
Spire, André, 53, 55, 149, 166, 169, 175
Stalin, Joseph, 161, 207, 284

Stam, 140
Stavisky, Serge Alexandre, 155, 174
Stember, Charles, 22
Stéphane, Roger, 40, 222, 286
Stern, Fritz, 23, 33
Stern, Norton, 22
Sternhell, Zeev, 4, 8, 21, 24, 60, 88, 89, 96, 97, 98, 124, 184, 195, 221
Stockes, Richard, 58
Stoecker, 11
Stoleru, Lionel, 303
Stonequist, Everett, 22
Streicher, Julius, 175
Suarez, Georges, 102, 152, 171, 181, 277
Sue, Eugene, 153
Suhard, Cardinal, 190
Surcouf, Robert, 114
Sweets, John, 128
Szajkowski, Zosa, 58, 98

Taguieff, Pierre-André, 239, 299, 305
Taine, Hippolyte, 49, 110, 169
Taittinger, Pierre, 113, 136, 143
Tannenbaum, Edward, 96
Tarde, Gabriel, 169
Tardieu, André, 41, 238
Taxil, Léo, 151
Teitgen, Pierre-Henri, 192, 197
Téry, Gustave, 155, 172, 266
Tessan, François de, 189
Tharaud, brothers, 154
Théas, Bishop Pierre-Marie, 190
Thiébaut, Marcel, 172
Thomas, Jean-Pierre, 304
Thomas, Louis, 255
Thorez, Maurice, 77, 121, 162, 180, 208, 209, 210, 211, 221, 222, 271
Thuillier, Guy, 231
Tilly, Charles, 22
Tixier-Vignancour, Jean-Louis, 297
Tocqueville, Charles Alexis de, 16, 24, 89, 234
Toda, Michel, 172
Toinet, Marie-France, 81, 127, 172
Tönnies, Ferdinand, 130
Touchard, Jean, 24, 221, 255
Toussenel, A., 2, 29, 89, 92, 94, 95, 98, 200, 206, 232
Trachtenberg, Joshua, 22, 171

Index 317

Treitschke, 11
Trigano, Shmuel, 33
Trochu, Charles, 71, 112
Troquier, André, 243
Trotsky, Leon, 40, 205
Turner, Bryan, 169

Vailland, Roger, 212
Vaillant-Couturier, Paul, 173, 209, 216, 217
Vallat, Xavier, 66, 72, 87, 136, 181, 193, 220, 242–7, 249, 282, 297
Vanier, Jean, 251
Vannier, Jean-Louis, 239
Vanor, Georges, 166
Veber, Pierre, 167
Vermeersch, Jeannette, 211
Veil, Simone, 303
Verdès-Leroux, Jeanne, 21, 97, 98, 170
Verdeveine, G., 255
Vergennes, 193
Veuillot, Eugene, 178
Vial, L., 239, 253
Viau, Raphael, 106, 165, 166, 177
Vigneau, Albert, 275
Viguier, Laurent, 100, 106, 139, 145, 146, 172, 176, 238, 255
Villette, Pierre, 245
Violette, 281–2
Viollis, André, 67
Virebeau, Georges, 203, 219, 221
Vishniac, Albert, 275
Volkov, Shulamit, 23
Voltaire, 22, 31

Waddington, William Henry, 228, 233, 263
Wagner, Richard, 22, 105
Waldeck-Rochet, Émile, 211
Waldeck-Rousseau, Pierre, 41, 261, 263, 275
Wall, Irwin, 41, 222
Wasserstein, Bernard, 21, 96, 97, 219, 221, 222, 257
Weber, Eugene, 2, 5, 21, 24, 170, 175, 230

Weber, Max, 11, 94
Wecogne, Claude, 274
Weil, Julien, Chief Rabbi, 47
Weil, George, 188, 262, 274
Weil, Maurice, 81
Weil-Curiel, A., 127
Weinberg, David, 58
Weinberg, Henry, 305
Weininger, Otto, 13, 24, 149, 150
Weizmann, Chaim, 54, 56, 60
Welter, G., 171
Werth, Alexander, 58, 198
Wilde, Oscar, 154
Wilentz, Sean, 169
Willard, Claude, 60
Wilson, Nelly, 60
Wilson, Stephen, 21, 97, 98, 170, 194, 292, 294
Winock, Michel, 21, 22, 60, 88, 96, 169, 195, 221, 259
Winter, Jean-Pierre, 174
Wistrich, Robert, 23, 40
Wolff, Francine, 303
Worms, family, 29, 140
Wright, John, 195
Wright, Vincent, 230
Wrong, Denis, 9, 23
Wurmser, André, 79, 156, 291

Yonnet, Paul, 305
Young, Jean Nelson, 96

Zay, Jean, 85, 101, 104, 114, 117, 118, 119, 123, 126, 152, 162, 171, 174, 188, 233, 239, 241, 255, 257, 265, 266, 267, 269, 284, 297
Ziebura, Gilbert, 40
Zimmermann, Moshe, 23
Zola, Émile, 151
Zoretti, Ludovic, 223
Zoretti, Paul, 214
Zuckerman, Alan, 33
Zweigenhaft, Richard, 22
Zyromski, Jean, 210, 218, 233